THE WORLD'S BEST
WHISKIES

THE WORLD'S BEST WHISKIES

750 UNMISSABLE DRAMS FROM TAIN TO TOKYO

DOMINIC ROSKROW

jacqui small

This book is dedicated
to friends, family
and whisky drinkers
everywhere.

First published
in hardback in 2010
This edition published
in 2012 by

Jacqui Small Llp

an imprint of
Aurum Press Ltd,
7 Greenland Street,
London NW1 0ND

Text copyright ©
Dominic Roskrow 2010

Design and layout
copyright © Jacqui Small 2010

Publisher Jacqui Small

Editorial Direction Joanna Copestick

Managing Editor Kerenza Swift

Designer & Art Director Robin Rout

Picture Research Kika Sroka Miller

Production Peter Colley

British Library
Cataloguing-in-Publication Data
A catalogue record for this book
is available from the British Library.

ISBN 978-1-906417-89-5

Printed and bound in China.

Contents

INTRODUCTION

Adventures with whisky

When one whisky distiller heard about this project he said 'does the world really need another whisky book?'

The immediate response may well appear to be 'er... no, not really'. Or at least it doesn't need another book that rehashes the history of each distillery, regurgitates a mass of statistics about the number, size or capacity of its stills, or reproduces figures showing the volume of spirit it produces.

But I have never been big on history and right from a very young age I was up there painting the wagon with Lee Marvin, always looking forward to the next adventure.

It's why I became a journalist and, indeed, why I love whisky. And make no mistake – whisky is an adventure, an ever-changing map comprised of new roads to explore and new people to meet.

Whisky should not be about cold copper or sterile steel, nor about dull dates and horrible history. Important as provenance and heritage are, evolution and innovation interest me more. Whisky should be a living, dynamic thing. It is a dichotomy: a simple mix of grain, yeast and water, crafted and shaped into a complex drink that is constantly evolving and continues to perplex. Most of all though, whisky is a proud representation of the people who produce it, an integral part of the community from which it comes.

This book, then, is an attempt to capture some of the wonder of whisky and the magic of malt. It is more than a list of the world's best whiskies. Rather, it is a collection of some of the stories and anecdotes behind the drink, and an introduction to at least a handful of the characters who have played a key role in creating a craft in a glass.

Not just in the obvious territories either. Never has there been a more exciting time for whisky; new versions of the spirit are appearing in the unlikeliest places across the globe, from Austria to Australia and from Wyoming to Wales.

Whether you're a seasoned whisky expert or a novice just starting to dip your fingertips into the glass, this book is an attempt to lead you on a colourful tour through the world of whisky, to point you towards some new roads to explore, and to give you a glimpse of the passion that produced it and the limitless pleasure it can give. It's a wagon ride, if you like, into whisky's wildest new frontiers.

So when you're ready, Mr Marvin, let's move 'em on out...

Dominic

History

Pinpointing when whisky distilling began is like trying to spot shining pebbles in the murky depths of Scotland's Loch Lomond.

History points us to the Far East, Middle East and Northern Africa. The earliest stills were found in Taxila in Pakistan and in Cyprus, while there is some evidence that distillation was used in these regions for medicine and perfume. We know, too, that a heavy form of beer was fermented in Mesopotamia, in the region now covered by Iran and Iraq. Quite when grain-distilled drink was first consumed for pleasure is lost in time. I like to think, though, that an Irish priest stumbled upon it and, being Irish, didn't bother waiting to be ill to start to appreciate its redemptive qualities.

Clues to whisky's origins are all here, though. Much of the language of drink is derived from Arabic, for instance, including the word 'alcohol'. The link between distilled drink and distilled medicine is borne out by the large number of drinking toasts that refer to good health and happiness.

And, of course, the church has had a long and fruitful relationship with alcoholic beverages. It is highly likely that priests brought the techniques of brewing and distilling back first to Ireland and then to the west of Scotland. The monasteries became thriving centres for beer and spirits production. Monks and priests were among the few sectors of society able to flee from the ravages of the Black Death, taking their distilling skills with them further afield. When Henry VIII consigned many of them to the dole queue by decommissioning their places of worship, many of them changed careers and became brewers and distillers instead. So thanks Henry – not great on the women front, but on the plus side a big help for the British drinks trade.

The Irish make many claims when it comes to whisk(e)y, but claiming to have brought grain spirit to Scotland is probably among the more credible ones. Ireland can also boast the world's oldest licensed distillery in Bushmills, which was registered in 1608, and Irish whiskey, the choice tipple of the nobility, was established on the high table of gentry long before its Scottish counterpart. Scotch whisky, meanwhile, rapidly gained a foothold among the tenant farmers and landed masses of Scotland as both a libation and a currency, with communities trading it for clothes and shoes with travelling salesmen. That in turn attracted the attention of the authorities, who quickly saw a chance to make money through taxation, and so began a cat- and-mouse game of tax avoidance between the governments in Edinburgh and London and local Scottish communities who saw it as a patriotic duty to avoid paying the tax.

One of the driving forces behind the Jacobite uprisings of the seventeenth and eighteenth centuries was a campaign against malt tax. When those uprisings finally ended in defeat for the Jacobites and the brutal slaughter of Culloden in 1746 and in the ensuing Highland Clearances which drove crofters from their lands, many Scots took their distilling skills to the furthest corners of the world. In America, they were joined by Europeans such as Johannes 'Jacob' Beam, by Irishmen, and by Welshmen forced from their homeland by the Temperance movement. Among them were Kentucky's Evan Williams and the Scottish and Welsh grandparents of Jack Daniel of Tennessee whiskey fame.

Scotch whisky's journey to the drinks cabinets of first England, then the Empire and finally the world was to be defined by a remarkable 50-year period between 1825 and 1875. The foundations had already been laid in the decades beforehand, with the start of the Industrial Revolution and the technological advances that came with it. The Industrial Revolution brought railways to Scotland, and with them the means and fuels for greater and better quality production. Highland whiskies began to be smuggled to the pubs and drinking houses of Edinburgh and Glasgow, and their reputation rapidly spread well beyond these environs.

Three events would promote Scotland to the position of world leader in whisky. First, whisky makers in Scotland and the authorities called a truce in their battle over taxes, reaching a compromise. From 1823, distillers began to turn their trade in to a legal one, providing quality malt.

Secondly, Scotsman Robert Stein developed a completely new way of distilling grain in a continuous process. The

system would be improved upon by Irishman Aeneas Coffey, but the new column-still process was eschewed by the Irish while being gleefully seized upon by the Scots, who found that when coupled with their rough malts it made for a smoother, easier-to-drink style of whisky.

Finally, Scotland's whiskies were to benefit massively from a disaster that struck across Europe in 1860. A destructive aphid by the name of *Phylloxera vastatrix* began a 15-year feeding frenzy that was to wipe out the vineyards of France and beyond, destroying the wine and brandy industry in the process. Scotch was ready and willing to take brandy's place.

It has never looked back. Scotch whisky reinforced its new status in the twentieth century, finding its way to the Prohibition-era speakeasies of the United States and into the affections of American servicemen stationed in Great Britain during World War II. By contrast, Irish whiskey has undergone a century of decline, although it has pulled out of its tailspin in recent years.

Canadian whisky, a dominant player in the American market for many years, has been treading water of late, and Japanese whisky, established more than a century ago, has made massive advances in recent years and is arguably now the world's number-four whisky nation. But the competition from other countries is fierce; France, Belgium, Germany, Switzerland, Austria, Australia, England and Sweden have all scratched a significant mark on the whisky map. It's hard to keep up and, indeed, during the production of this book a new player arrived from nowhere – Taiwan.

Whisky already has a proud and glorious history to point to, but it's clear that the story has only just begun. The history of this great drink is being written by the day.

LEFT Scotland's history and whiskies are intrinsically linked to each other. This is the ruined castle at Balvenie near Dufftown.

ABOVE A snapshot of the past: workers at what is now the Buffalo Trace distillery in Franklin County, Kentucky.

Making whisky

Water, malted barley and yeast are the holy trinity of whisky – three ingredients that are bland individuals, yet their whole is very much greater than the sum of their parts. They are to the world of drinks what certain household items are to homemade explosives: innocuous until combined by an expert into a combustible mix. So what role do they play?

WATER

If you have visited a distillery pretty much anywhere in the world, you have undoubtedly sat through one of those cutesy documentaries where clichéd local folk music accompanies pictures of gurgling brooks and vast waterways, and a portentous über-voice melodramatically explains how centuries of evolution and geology have combined to provide the perfect water for producing the distillery's liquid gold.

These movies can be unintentionally hilarious. In one, made by a Scottish island distillery, the celebrity actor hired to narrate the distillery's story looked positively ill as he concluded his dramatic speech and sipped at his dram. It turned out that midway through filming he had suddenly discovered he had an allergy to malt whisky and was violently ill on set. Rather than dispense with his services, the film-makers carried on, replacing his dram with a glass of cold tea. It didn't stop him looking dreadful though.

But we digress. These movies, as well as occasionally being awful, may also be guilty of being economical with the truth. Much store is put on the importance of water. Distillery owners sometimes go to extreme lengths to protect their sources by buying up neighbouring land, and undoubtedly the bond between pure, clean water and the resulting malt spirit is an important one. The source of water has long been held in reverence and many claims have been made for it. And to some extent the facts support the romance. Soft water, with low mineral content, may help the malting process and make for better absorption of water by the grain and therefore result in higher-yielding barley. Undoubtedly the peaty journey experienced by water on Islay, in particular, influences the island's malt.

But the science works against the argument, too. Many would maintain that the nature of distillation is such that the influences of the water are all but removed. And, if they aren't, then how is it that some distillers – although they don't like to shout about it – have used treated and chlorinated water in their production process on occasion, and yet have continued to make great whisky?

Most of Scotland's water is soft, and the country's distillers understandably argue that this is a key factor in the excellence of Scottish single malt. But there is an argument, too, that nutrients and minerals feed yeast and therefore aid fermentation. Single malt whisky is successfully made in other countries, including Wales and England, where the water is hard. Also, when it comes to brewing, the best British source is considered to be around Burton-on-Trent, in Staffordshire, where the water is rich in minerals.

The waters of Kentucky in the United States are deemed essential to the bourbon-making process because they contain calcium – the same reason that the state produces strong-limbed thoroughbred racehorses. And while it is true that you can count on one hand the distilleries in Scotland that use hard water, on that shortlist are true heavyweights Highland Park and Glenmorangie. How does that work?

Moreover, water can be, and is, treated these days to be whatever it needs to be. Some argue that mashing, fermenting and finally distilling mean that the difference between soft and hard water in the end flavour is negligible.

That's not to say water is not important – of course, it is. Pure water – water free of micro-organisms – is crucial to ensuring that the rest of the process passes off correctly.

But today, in the twenty-first century, the most important factor governing water source isn't whether it is hard or soft, or whether it contains certain minerals or not, or even whether it passes through flavour-imparting peat beds. No, the most important factors governing water are that there is plenty of it and that it is of sufficiently cool temperature.

In recent years, climate change certainly seems to have made its mark on whisky production. In Scotland, for instance, there have been an alarming number of instances where water shortages have forced distilleries to stop production. The picture is far from predictable, however. After a series of mild winters in Scotland that saw water levels as low in April as they would usually be in September, the winters of 2007–2010 were all exceptional for their long and deep snowfalls.

A further problem stems from the generally warmer climate. If water isn't cool enough for condensing, it means either longer closed seasons for distilleries or an investment in expensive cooling equipment.

RIGHT Cereal thriller: whisky at its embryonic stage.

FAR RIGHT Barley being turned in a traditional floor maltings. Barley malted in this way, on a wooden floor, is said to provide better flavour for whisky.

BARLEY

Barley is nature's answer to Doctor Who's Tardis – a simple telephone box on the outside, a complex giant engine room within. It has been part of brewing and distilling history for centuries, a durable grain capable of growing on harsh, infertile terrain, seemingly the simplest of grains, loved and cherished by generations of folk living off the land since medieval times. But science has caught up with barley, and on a regular basis laboratories create a new strain that moves the goal posts when it comes to yield. Some argue that higher-yielding barley produces barley which results in a sacrifice of flavour and some distillers stay loyal to particular barley strains, but attempts to stem the tide of commercialism will ultimately prove fruitless. Macallan and Glengoyne, for instance, both extolled the qualities of Golden Promise and chose it despite its relatively low yields. In 2009, Golden Promise ceased to exist.

Some argue that, as long as barley meets certain production criteria, it does not matter where it comes from. Others contend fiercely that provenance of the barley is of crucial importance. Some take the default position that while Scottish barley is ideally best for making Scottish whisky, the practical realities are that there is not enough of it. Certainly a fair proportion of barley used in Scotch whisky production is imported, particularly from the east of England.

And nothing makes a distiller pale quicker than when a Scottish National Party politician calls for Scotch whisky to be made with only home-produced ingredients.

YEAST

Yeast is the great unknown in whisky, rarely talked or written about, or fully understood. A living micro-organism, yeast can lay for years in a dormant state, but in the right wet and warm conditions and with the right food – sugar – it will multiply rapidly, feed ravenously, and produce carbon dioxide and alcohol. This fermentation process can be an impressively aggressive and violent one, and can make a huge and sturdy washback rock with the force.

Thousands of yeasts occur naturally, which is why some fermentation can take place without any yeast being added, and when a successful strain is created artificially it must be stored carefully to avoid contamination. Exactly what effect yeast has on flavour is the subject of fierce debate and the degree of attention given to yeast production varies from one distiller to another. Most yeasts used in whisky production are a combination of brewers' yeasts and yeasts created in the lab, and in some cases – particularly in the United States – brewers and distillers fiercely guard details about the exact nature of their yeasts.

The role of peat and oak

Single-malt whisky may be made only with malted barley, yeast and water. Apart from supposedly flavourless caramel for colouring, nothing else may be added.

That said, though, there are two other major influences on the flavour of a single malt – peat and oak – and for a full appreciation of single malt it is essential to understand their role in the overall flavour of the finished whisky.

PEAT

Peat is made up of decaying vegetation and grasses that has formed over centuries in boggy and wet marshland areas. It has been used as a burning fuel in communities across the world for centuries. In Scotland, in particular, peat has played a central role in the drying of barley for Scotch whisky making. When the Industrial Revolution brought trains and they in turn carried coal across the country, many distilleries abandoned peat as a fuel, but it remained in use in the islands – and it is on the islands that it is still most widely used today.

Most of the big phenolic, smoky-flavoured whiskies derive their taste from this process, and not from the water that has travelled through peat bogs.

Peat in Scotland is graded into three categories. The deepest layer looks like dark chocolate fudge cake when it is wet, and dries in to a hard fuel that resembles coal and burns slowly. The top layer, made up of the least decayed or suppressed vegetation, crumbles in the hand when dry and burns rapidly, but produces high quantities of peat smoke.

The three layers are cut from the ground in spring and dried naturally during the summer, before being collected in the autumn. A distillery such as Highland Park on Orkney will cut just enough peat to see it through the ensuing year.

Peat differs from place to place because it is made up of vegetation. This is significant because the vegetation in a country such as Australia will be vastly different than that found in Scotland, so while the raw ingredients would seem to be the same they have different effects on the whisky. In Sweden, some of the peat was submerged under the Baltic Sea at one time, and is therefore very salty. Furthermore, the rules governing malt whisky production do not dictate what exactly barley should be dried over, so in Sweden Mackmyra has incorporated the traditional drying method of using juniper twigs in the drying of malted barley. This process makes a further distinction from the usual whiskies produced in Scotland.

OAK

If geographical differences affect the flavours that peat gives to malt, then oak from different parts of the world results in even greater variations. The differences between oak from Europe and its cousin in America is so pronounced that you can see it with the naked eye. Even within Europe there is variance, with Swedish and Spanish oak imparting different flavours to spirit.

It takes 100 years or more to grow an oak big enough to turn in to a cask and, while some environmentalists are critical of an industry that fells trees for whisky making, more oak is being planted in the second decade of the new millennium than at any time in the last 1000 years, and most distillers are keenly aware of their environmental responsibilities and the need for sustainability. Certainly few countries face the acute shortages of oak that resulted in the Middle Ages after the great warring nations had felled the trees for ships, fortifications and weapons in the desire to build empires.

Oak is in such demand because it is very strong but still malleable, as well as being waterproof yet porous and able to let oxygen (and indeed water and alcohol) molecules pass through it. Additionally, it is rich in flavour compounds that are easily accessible by charring or toasting the wood.

On its own in a brand new cask, the spirit contained within would be quickly dominated by the spiciness of the wood, the maturing process is therefore improved by using a cask that has been used previously for maturing a different liquid. Most malt spirit is matured in casks that have already been used for the production of sherry in Europe or bourbon in the United States. While all bourbon casks will be made of American wood (even though there is no law saying they have to be), it does not follow that all sherry produced in Spain is matured in European oak. Sherry styles such as oloroso are matured in American oak, so there are on the whole three main types of casks for whisky making: bourbon cask, European oak sherry, and American oak sherry.

SPECIAL FINISHES

The rules governing the production of single-malt whisky do not stipulate what the cask has to have contained before, and considerable experimentation has taken place in recent years. It is not unusual to find whiskies that have been matured in part in wine casks, port pipes or casks used for the production of madeira or rum. Although the rules forbid the addition of anything to a single-malt whisky, some do take on distinctly ruddy and pink hues from their contact with the spirit- or fortified wine-soaked wood, and such casks can have a major impact on flavour.

RIGHT Coopering skills are much in demand again now that barrels are such a valuable commodity. This one is at William Grant's own cooperage on the site of Glenfiddich and Balvenie in Scotland.

How to make single-malt whisky

The magic of single-malt whisky lies in the fact that it contains just three simple ingredients: malted barley, yeast and water. The process of making single malt and the equipment needed to make it are pretty much the same throughout the world. And yet such a simple and uniform production process produces a vast array of different flavours and aromas.

Whisky is like a collection of seemingly identical landscape paintings; each picture looks the same from a distance, but study them closely and there are countless differences between each one. The first step in whisky making is to turn barley into malted barley by tricking it into growing, which is done by soaking the barley in water. The grains will start to produce shoots, breaking down the grain husk, and this in turn gives access to the enzymes and starches contained within each barley kernel.

After a few days it is necessary to halt the growing process, and this is achieved by drying out the barley over a heat source. Traditionally barley was dried over fire fuelled by peat. This process imparts the smoke and peaty flavours that produce the phenolic medicinal styles of whisky for which Scotland's west coast is famous. Nowadays, though, most barley is malted in large commercial maltings and most malt is dried in modern electricity-fuelled ovens.

Once dry, the malted barley is ground into flour, known as grist, and mixed with hot water in a vessel known as a mash tun. The water removes the starches and enzymes which are needed to produce alcohol. The process is known as mashing and is exactly the same as the one used to make a pot of tea. The spent grains are removed from the process at this point, leaving a sweet brown non-alcoholic liquid known as wort.

The wort is moved to a large vessel called a washback and yeast is now added to the mix to start the process of fermentation. Yeast feeds on the wort, converting the starches to sugars and the sugars to alcohol and carbon dioxide. After a period of two to three days the wort is converted into a beer with an alcoholic strength of about 7 per cent to 9 per cent alcohol by volume (ABV). Unlike beer produced in breweries, which is made under sterilised conditions, distillery beer is sharp and sour – not unlike Belgian lambic beer. This is due to the presence of bacteria and is crucial to the success of the whisky-making process.

Distillation is the process of separating water from alcohol

through the use of heat. For malt whisky, this involves boiling the beer solution in large copper kettles known as pot stills. Alcohol evaporates at a lower temperature than water and, once in vapour form, will pass up the copper still. It is condensed back into liquid by passing through a condenser cooled by cold water, lowering its temperature so that it returns to a liquid state. The copper plays a pivotal role in the process, catching fats and oils as they pass over

ABOVE The size and shape of pot stills vary from distillery to distillery, and often affect the taste of the spirit made. You will find these ones at the Glendronach distillery in Speyside, Scotland.

it and reacting with the spirit to influence flavour and removing unwanted sulphur compounds from the vapour.

Malt distillation is usually – but not always – carried out twice. The first process is carried out in a wash still and produces a solution known as low wine with an alcoholic strength of a little over 20% ABV. This is mixed with the rejected residue from the previous distillation, raising its alcoholic strength to the high twenties, and this is distilled in the spirit still.

This is where the first major piece of magic takes place. The spirit collected in the second distillation is the spirit that will be put into casks to make whisky, so its composition needs to be considered carefully. Unlike the first distillation, where all the condensed liquid is retained, much of the second run will be rejected. As the liquid is heated, the first alcohols to evaporate are by definition the most volatile. They have the highest alcoholic content and tend to be at worst poisonous and at best, foul tasting. They are not desirable. So the first part of the run, known as heads or foreshots, is collected in a holding vessel and rejected.

Over time the strength of the alcohols in the vapour will fall and flavoursome spirit worthy of keeping will be produced. So this spirit is collected in a second vessel. This is known as the cut and is the part of the run that will be put into casks for maturation. Finally the condensed spirit will reach a point where the alcohols are weak and unpleasant to taste. This portion will also be rejected and is known as the tails or the feints.

The whole process was once vividly described to me as like cutting the head and tail off a fat fish and retaining the juicy, fleshy part in the middle. Where exactly that cut is made varies from distillery to distillery, and in some cases is little more than a sliver. At the end of the run, the middle cut forms the 'new make' spirit that will be stored to make whisky. The rejected parts of the cycle are recycled and used in the next distillation, and then the whole process begins again.

To make whisky the new spirit – which is clear, but has a distinctive and strong flavour – must be stored in oak casks and matured. In Europe, this process has to be for a minimum of three years. Malt spirit is not robust enough to fend off the dominant spicy flavours of new oak over this time, so it is matured in casks that have already been used for something else, most often bourbon or sherry.

Malt's greatest mystery is how it matures. No two casks will produce exactly the same whisky and, although recognisable distillery characteristics may be found in each one, there will be significant variations on the central theme. Casks of different sizes will be used, and they will have previously contained different liquids. But even two identical casks containing spirit from the same run and stored side by side in exactly the same conditions and for exactly the same period of time may well produce different whiskies.

So the bottle of 12-year-old single malt you eventually buy will contain a marriage of whiskies from an array of different casks, cleverly combined together by a whisky maker so that, whether you taste the distillery's malt in New York today or London next year, you will not notice any great variance in taste, even though the two bottles will have been produced from different batches. The word 'single' in single-malt whisky refers to the fact that the whisky is the product of just one distillery, rather than referring to it being from a single cask or batch.

How to make blended whisky

Blends are to whisky what fast food is to catering: immensely successful across the world, popular and enjoyed by the mainstream, but rarely truly loved or cherished; often unfairly dismissed as bland and unexciting; and only occasionally garnering the positive press bestowed elsewhere.

There are two principle reasons for this. Firstly, because while the world of single malts is all about variety and new expressions are constantly being added to the menu, fuelling the enthusiasm of aficionados, blended whiskies are all about consistency and reliability and new releases in the category are few and far between. As a result blends rarely create news. Secondly, while the rules governing the production of single malts are rigid and ensure an extremely high standard, the rules governing blends are more flexible. Poor quality blends can be made within the rules so a vast number of ordinary or poor blends have sullied the reputation of the category as a whole. This is a shame, because blended whiskies at their best can be stunning and require a level of craftsmanship that not even the very best malts can match.

Scotland actually produces four styles of whisky, but it is blended whisky which has given the country its status as the world's best and leading producer of whisky. Most single malt whisky is produced with the intention of forming part of a blend rather than for being consumed alone. Even with all the current focus on single malt whisky, blended whisky still accounts for nine out of 10 glasses of Scottish whisky consumed across the world.

Blended whisky not only constitutes an important export market for Scotland, but also for Great Britain. Not surprisingly, therefore, Scottish whisky makers take blends very seriously indeed. The biggest ones – Johnnie Walker, Chivas Regal, Bell's Famous Grouse, Teacher's – are made to exacting standards and are supported by huge marketing budgets. They might not be anywhere near as sexy as a premium single malt, but they are the industry's bread and butter and are quality products. Trouble is, there are plenty of inferior brands that cannot make the same claim.

FAR RIGHT Checking on the blending process at Glendronach.

RIGHT Glendronach (single malt), Johnnie Walker Black Label (blended whisky), Compass Box Spice Tree (blended malt) and The Snow Grouse (grain whisky) are the main types of Scottish whisky.

Blended whisky's inconsistent reputation stems from the inclusion of grain whisky. Grain plays an essential role in rounding off some of the more extreme flavours of single malt, making the drink more palatable to a greater cross-section of people. Grain has a less distinctive taste than single malt and much of the flavour it does have is given to it by the cask. The rules governing blends do not dictate what proportions of grain and single malts need to be in the blend, so often a higher proportion of less tasteful grain is used. Moreover, grain is often matured in old and much-used casks, where the wood has little to offer the spirit, further making for a bland and characterless whisky. Buy a cheap bottle of Clan Bagpipe McTavish and chances are you're going to get a low-quality grain-heavy blend coloured with caramel to make it more impressive than it actually is.

But it does not have to be that way, and the great names of blended whisky have obtained their status through generations of blending perfection and the employment of the finest malt and grain whiskies. A good blend is a lovingly constructed oil painting, balanced and in harmony, and bursting with colour and style. It may include more than 40 malts and grains, and the number might actually be considerably higher. The Scottish whisky industry has cleverly adopted an exchange system by which each whisky company swaps its malts with other producers, so that each one has the widest possible range of flavours to work with.

Master blenders understand the characteristics of different malts and know how to construct beautiful blends with them. A great blend is like an American football team; there are big-name heavy-hitting stars in the line-up but many of the most important jobs are done by lesser-known names. If they weren't there, the team would fall apart. When the whole team is firing, the result is a study in excellence. When they're not, it's one big unholy mess.

Although each brand of blended whisky is designed to be consistent time after time, different blends can be suited and tailored to satisfy the palates of different people in different countries. For this reason blends are often created for specific markets with specific tastes and are not sold elsewhere, making it a difficult, bordering on impossible, task to monitor them all.

How to make bourbon

Bourbon is whisky because it is made with grain, yeast and water. But these three ingredients vaguely connect it to single-malt whisky in the same way as a bat, ball and the participation of two teams links baseball to cricket. Beyond the basics the two have little in common, and where there is an opportunity to head off in a different direction, the Americans have tended to take it.

Although bourbon and single-malt whisky follow a template under which grain is converted to beer and the beer is distilled, the raw materials, the distillation process and the maturation of the spirit differ significantly.

Single malt is made using malted barley alone. Bourbon, meanwhile, is made up with more than one grain in the mix and must include at least 51 per cent corn, although in practice this percentage is much higher. While some malted barley will probably be included in the process because malted barley is a good catalyst for aiding the conversion of sugars to alcohol, it is also probable that there will be some wheat, rye and/or unmalted barley in the mix, which is known as the mashbill.

As with malt whisky, American whiskey makers at different distilleries will tweak the process so that each distillery has its own whiskey DNA, but in broad strokes the process is similar across them all.

As with malted barley, the aim of the US whiskey maker is to release the sugars and starches from the grains so that yeast can convert them to alcohol through fermentation and, as with malted barley, the process is known as mashing because hot water is used to flush out the sugars. The three grains are crushed into flour individually, before being added to boiling water in what is known as the three-step process. Each distillery will have its own view of what temperature the water should be when each grain is added, but generally corn, which is a tough grain with a hard outer shell, will be added at the highest temperatures, with wheat, unmalted barley and rye being added at slightly lower temperatures and malted barley, the most delicate of the grains, added last and when the water has cooled significantly. When mashing is complete, the whole solution, spent grains and all, goes forward to the fermentation stage.

THE SOUR MASH PROCESS

The sour mash process plays a key role in the production of American whiskey, and it is a further point of difference from Scotch whisky production. At the end of each bourbon distillation process there is stillage, a residue made up of the used grain from the process. This is known as backset, and is made up of the last of the solution left after distillation and the remnants of the grain with all its sugars removed. It has a sharp, sour taste – hence it is 'sour'. This stillage is added back to the mash before the yeast is added. Its purpose is to provide a chemical balance to the solution and control bacteria, creating a fermentation process that is conducive to distilling clean and characterful spirit.

When fermentation is complete, the beer – a thick viscous solution that is completely different to the wash that is produced in Scotland – is ready for distillation. Where distiller's beer in Scotland is thin, sour and fruity, in bourbon production it is rich, creamy and sickly, more akin to warm milk on soggy cornflakes.

THE CONTINUOUS STILL

Single-malt whisky is produced in batches, with a quantity of single malt converted into beer, and the beer distilled in two stills before the process starts again. Bourbon is produced in a continuous still, where the distillery beer is passed in at one end and comes out as a spirit at the other. The continuous still is just that, allowing an ongoing distillation, and it is capable of producing larger quantities of spirit in a more efficient and commercial manner. But far less copper is involved, the separation of spirit from water is done differently, and the resulting spirit has a higher alcoholic strength, but none of the depth and variety of flavour that single-malt distillation produces. Where single-malt whisky spirit is created by boiling the beer solution in a glorified copper kettle, the continuous still works by forcing the distiller's beer down pipes containing a series of sloping plates and into a wall of pressurised and very high temperature steam, which converts the alcohol into vapour and drives it out. It is recondensed and channelled out of the still at different points during its downward journey, is collected, and undergoes what is effectively a second distillation process by being passed through a simple pot still known as a doubler. The resulting spirit is clear and is known as white dog.

ABOVE Woodford Reserve's stills in Kentucky are unconventional because they're pot stills, like those used in Scotland. Bourbon is normally distilled in column stills.

LEFT Open top fermentation at Maker's Mark distillery in Kentucky.

MATURATION

Even the maturation process in the United States is different. Because the spirit that continuous distillation produces is less distinctive than new-make single malt, and hence maturation is particularly important to the overall process. While US law requires that an oak barrel be used, it also dictates that a new barrel is used for each production run. When you consider the size of Jack Daniel's, the world's biggest whiskey, and Jim Beam, the world's biggest bourbon, and the huge number of barrels that they are using which, by law, must become redundant each year, it explains why so much single malt is matured in ex-American whiskey casks.

The new barrels are charred or toasted to varying degrees on the inside before spirit is added, helping to release all the qualities in the wood that will impart flavour and character as the spirit matures. Once more, bourbon maturation is to single-malt whisky maturation what baseball is to cricket: an altogether more brash, aggressive and less time-consuming affair. Kentucky is, in every sense, a state of extremes, and the weather is no exception. It has long, extremely hot, and high-humidity summers and viciously cold, sharp winters. When the sun is at its hottest, temperatures at the top of the tower block warehouses can hit the 40 centigrade-plus mark. In winter fierce frozen winds from the Appalachians bring sub-zero temperatures.

The effect on the spirit is to provoke rapid and dramatic distillation. As with all chemical reactions, heat makes change happen faster. The extreme changes in temperature make the spirit expand and contract faster, and to move more rapidly in the cask, regularly bringing all the spirit into contact with wood and accelerating the transfer of flavour and colour from wood to spirit.

For these reasons, bourbon reaches maturity much faster than malt whisky does in Scotland.

There is one final difference between the ways in which the two whiskies reach their destinations. In Scotland, alcohol evaporates from the maturing spirit, escaping from the cask and providing the angels with their share. This gradually reduces the alcoholic strength of the spirit in the cask. Alcohol also evaporates from the cask in Kentucky, but in the vast majority of cases, not as fast as water does.

The humidity makes a crucial intervention and in most cases the alcoholic strength of the bourbon spirit gets higher during maturation, though this process is not uniform and in some Kentucky distilleries there are areas where spirit in the cask remains at about the same strength throughout the process, and in some cases actually declines as it does in Scotland. US law requires that 'straight' bourbon is matured for a minimum of two years. Unlike the case in Scotland, where colouring may be added to the finished product, nothing at all may be added to bourbon.

WHISKY BASICS

Key whisky questions answered

While the vast majority of people on the planet have heard of whisky and have an inkling as to what it is, there remains a huge level of ignorance on the subject and some great myths about it have grown up. It is not the purpose of this book to look in any great detail at the styles of whisky and the detailed aspects of their production, but nonetheless there are a few questions that arise time and time again. Here are some of them.

Why do Scottish single malts vary from region to region?

Scottish malt whisky is the result of a combination of culture, history, politics and economics. Scotland is effectively three countries in one – the Highlands, the Lowlands and the Islands – and the differences in the histories and cultures of each region is reflected in the whisky they produce, though it should be noted that there are exceptions to every rule, increasingly so nowadays as whisky makers strive to find new flavours by dispensing with as many barriers as possible. Each of the regions can be divided again, with the island of Islay on the west of Scotland demanding its own category within the Islands region, the area around the River Spey separate from the rest of the Highlands, and the Campbeltown region distinct to the Lowland region.

Regional variations explained

The Lowlands With the invention of the continuous still came the golden age of blended whisky and the need for a big supply of malt whisky. Big commercial malt stills were built in the Lowlands, close to the ports of Glasgow and Leith, and where there was a plentiful supply of barley because of the better farming climate. The bigger the still, the lighter and more floral the style of spirit produced, because the spirit vapour has to travel further over the copper, giving it more time to remove impurities and making the longer journey for the heavier and flavourful oils and congeners more difficult and less likely. Hence the Lowlands is known for light, floral, aperitif-style whiskies. Triple distillation was also commonplace in the Lowlands, further producing light and smooth malts.

The Highlands It is harder to grow barley in The Highlands so traditionally there was less of it to distil and so smaller stills were adequate. Much Highland malt was distilled illegally so it helped to have a still that was easy to conceal or which was portable. Small stills allow more heavy compounds and oils to pass over to be condensed, creating a heavier, richer and more flavourful malt spirit.

The Islands The Industrial Revolution brought trains to the whisky regions of mainland Scotland, and with them came coal. Most distilleries therefore abandoned the use of peat and replaced it with first coal and eventually oil and gas heating. This did not happen on the Islands so more traditional methods of whisky making continued there. Today the islands produce a wide range of whisky styles, with peat used prominently across all the islands but cleaner, lesser peated whiskies coming from the islands of Jura, Mull, Orkney and Arran, and in one or two cases, Islay.

Speyside About two-thirds of all Scotland's distilleries are based in the northeastern region between Aberdeen and Inverness, alongside the River Spey or one of its tributaries. They sprung up here to take advantage of the soft river water that is considered ideal for producing sweet, fruity malts ideal for blending.

Islay The island of Islay has eight distilleries and is world-famous for the big, peaty phenolic whiskies from distilleries such as Laphroaig, Lagavulin and Ardbeg. All eight distilleries produce a peated style of whisky though three also make considerable volumes of whisky where peat is not the dominant characteristic.

Campbeltown The peninsula to the west of Glasgow used to boast a large number of distilleries and was a principle base for export of whisky to America. Today whisky production there survives by a thread, made up of a distillery which produces intermittently, a new distillery, and the iconic three-for-the-price-of-one distillery Springbank, which houses the eponymous malt, the peated Longrow, and the triple-distilled Hazelburn. Hard to pinpoint a regional style, then, though the word 'rustic' comes to mind.

Is older whisky better than younger whisky?

No, not necessarily. The longer spirit is in the cask, the more flavour it will have. But there will come a point when the wood is not only no longer contributing to the flavour but will be impacting in a negative way, with the wood overwhelming the subtleties of the spirit. When this process happens varies from cask to cask and whisky style to whisky style. Meaty, oily Highland malts are likely to resist the wood for longer and continue to improve into their third, fourth and occasionally fifth decades. Lighter whiskies may not be able to hold off the effects of wood for more than 15 years.

Age is only a guide to quality, and younger whiskies can be zesty and zippy, refreshing, uncomplex and fruity. These are desirable traits. Moreover, a young peaty whisky will be rawer and spicier, but this may well be what the drinker wants. It is like cooking curry; the longer you leave it, the more integrated and balanced the flavours become in time. But if you are after a big, raw spicy hot hit, time is not necessarily your friend.

Can you tell the age of a whisky by its colour?

Not really. A sherry cask will turn whisky deep reddy brown very quickly, while a bourbon cask makes it a rich yellow. If it is the first time the cask has been used for making whisky after being used for something else, the effects of the cask will be more pronounced than when it is used for the second or third time. Some casks naturally work on spirit better than others. And at the end of the process some whisky makers add caramel to enrich colour, making the visual guide to age redundant. So colour is not necessarily a lot of help.

ABOVE At the foot of the Mannoch hills, beside the Rothes Burn in Speyside the Glenrothes distillery. makes use of water from two local springs for the distilling process.

What does cask strength mean?

Simply that the whisky has been put in to the bottle at the strength it came out of the cask.

What does the age on the label refer to?

If there is an age on the label, this refers to the youngest whisky in the mix. Most bottles of whisky will contain whiskies of various ages but just one drop of 12 year-old whisky in a bottle of 25-year-old malt makes that bottle 12 years old. No age statement doesn't necessarily indicate an inferior whisky. Some great blended whiskies (Johnnie Walker Blue Label, Dewar's Signature, Royal Salute 100 Cask Selection) use small amounts of young whisky to pep up the grand old malts that they are mainly made up with — and have no age statement because the small volume of young whisky that would have to be stated on the label would not do justice to the composition of the rest of the blend.

What does 'non-chill-filtered' mean?

Naturally produced whisky clouds when it is cold because the fats in the solution solidify at lower temperatures. To prevent this and ensure clear whisky, makers have tended to chill the whisky and filter out the solidified fats. But in recent years there has been a trend towards leaving these fats in because they also contain flavour.

So 'non-chill-filtered' is regarded as a statement of quality and reflects the fact that drinkers are becoming increasingly demanding and knowledgeable about their drinks.

Tasting whisky

Whisky suffers from an identity crisis, particularly when it comes to nosing and tasting it.

Whisky is a simple drink made of grain, yeast and water, and is effectively distilled beer. It is the drink of the tenant farmer and the common man. In its crudest form it is harsh firewater, and at its most sophisticated it is an ideal lubricant for socialising, celebrating, bonding, and peace-making. It should have no airs or graces and most of the time it doesn't.

But the world of whisky is split between those who accept whisky as the drink of the people and those who would prefer it to sit on an altogether higher table. They prefer to link it not with the grain but with the grape, and they dress it in the livery of wine and of wine language. There was even a magazine that brought the two together. It failed.

And it is from this that the identity crisis stems. For while many whisky books are broadly in agreement as to how whisky should be nosed, tasted and appreciated, scratch below the surface and there is little common agreement among writers and experts on the subject. Some believe that water should be added, others not. Professional 'nosers' or tasters add lots of water. Some say that you should spit

whisky, others that you cannot appreciate the full experience without swallowing it.

My view is that whisky is not wine and should not be treated as such. Whisky is three or four times as strong for a start, and the process of distillation takes spirit several steps away from the provenance of the ingredients from which it is made. While many flavours and aromas can be found in whisky, it does not command the same degree of nuance or subtlety as wine and therefore does not demand the same indulgences of language. Whisky is made all the more attractive because, on the whole, it is free of the pretentiousness that goes with wine tasting, and snobs and drinks bores would not be tolerated in the distilleries of Scotland, Kentucky, Ireland – or anywhere else for that matter. Whisky is all about independence and free spirit, and for this reason nobody should tell you how to taste it. That said, though, while how you travel down the whisky road is a matter entirely for you, but it doesn't hurt to have some signposts along the route. Here are a few pointers.

TASTING SEQUENCE
First look at the whisky, note the colour and whether it has 'legs'; approach at arm's length. Breathe in the aromas through both nostrils then one at a time. Finally, taste it.

VIEW

APPROACH I

WHAT GLASS TO USE
It is one of the great ironies of whisky writing that no matter how many book chapters are written explaining the best glass for whisky nosing, the publishers often feature a tumbler on the front cover. Tumblers are fine for blended whisky or bourbon, when mixers or ice might be added. They are useless for nosing single malt whisky. For the record, the whisky industry favours a tulip-shaped glass with a tapered neck, because this concentrates the aromas into the nose. You can buy them from most whisky shops at a modest cost. A champagne flute, sherry glass or small red wine glass are all better than tumblers for tasting.

BEWARE HIGH-VOLTAGE ALCOHOL
Approach a glass of neat whisky with caution. Whisky has a strong alcoholic content and should be respected. Nose a strong spirit too quickly and it will hurt your nostrils. Not only that, but your senses will batten down the hatches if they perceive that they are under threat, making further sensory perception redundant, at least in the short term. Approach a new glass of whisky in the same way that you would approach an unfamiliar animal; at arm's length at first, then with caution until you are both happy in each other's company. Taste a very small amount of the spirit neat before you do anything else to it.

RIGHT The Glencairn whisky glass shape is perfect for nosing whisky. Ignore anyone who says you should not add water – it is a personal choice. Drink water between whiskies to refresh the palate.

WATER OR NOT?

If any so-called expert says you should not add water to your whisky, tell them that the whisky industry started the practice. New spirit comes off the still with an alcoholic strength in the high 60s or early 70s. Until recently, when warehouse space and barrel shortages became an issue and casking smaller quantities of liquid at higher strength became fashionable, most distillers brought the strength at which the spirit entered into the cask down to about 63% ABV by adding water. After maturation the whisky has a strength of anywhere from 55% to 65% and again, water is added to bring the strength down to the bottling strength of normally 40%, 43% or 46%. In other words, more than a third of the whisky in your bottle is added water. Who's to tell you that you should not add a bit more? Blenders will take samples down to just 20% ABV and water is crucial for breaking down the whisky and releasing an array of aromas, thereby making appreciation of the drink easier.

But it's not for everyone. A few tasters dislike adding water and only do so when tasting strong whiskies.

SPIT OR SWALLOW?

Whisky is a strong spirit, which means that the palate will tire quite rapidly when swallowing, and after three or four samples further tasting is impossible. It therefore makes sense to spit if you intend to be judging or appraising whisky for more than just fun or personal reasons. But that doesn't happen very often does it?

There are two compelling arguments for swallowing and not spitting. One is the fact that whisky is a drink. There is a clue in the title. The other is that when describing whisky we talk about the finish. How can we do this if we do not finish it? It's like watching a film then leaving 15 minutes before the end. Surely the warming feeling as the spirit passes down the throat and the taste left in your mouth afterwards are crucial to the whisky-tasting experience. For this reason it is best to sip and savour any whisky you have not tasted before, in order to fully appreciate the sight, aroma, flavours and finish of the drink. This is the way to gather a complete profile of each whisky you taste.

APPROACH 2 NOSE SIP

Flavour categories

While whisky isn't wine, identifying flavours will enhance your enjoyment of it, not least because you will be able to identify the specific flavours that most appeal to you.

THE MAIN CATEGORIES

Perhaps the easiest way to improve your tasting and nosing skills is to start with the broadest and most general of categories. When you are happy with those, introduce sub-sectors, and then sub-sectors of those, and so on. I base my sub-categories around high street stores.

PEATY/SMOKY – OR NOT

This is the most fundamental split certainly in Scottish whisky. Drying barley over peat fires imparts smoky and peaty flavours that some people hate and some people would kill for. The characteristics are:

SWEET OR SAVOURY?

In whisky, these two are not mutually exclusive, but at the same time there are many where these are defining characteristics. Most American and Irish whiskey, many Speyside and Lowland whiskies and some Highland whiskies fall into the sweet category, a number of Highland and Island whiskies and a proportion of Japanese whiskies could be considered to be in the savoury spectrum.

PEATY
TCP/medicine
Tar, coal and engine oil
Iodine and salt
Seaweed
Chilli and pepper

SMOKY
Barbecue
Grilled meat
Bonfire
Charcoal
Tobacco

SWEET
Exotic tinned fruits in syrup
Maple syrup
Candy sticks
Banoffee pie
Vanilla ice cream
Sweet ginger barley
Christmas cake
Summer pudding

SAVOURY
Mushrooms
Meat
Earthiness
Olives
Nuts
Cheese
Stewed fruits
Forest walk, damp leaves
Autumn bonfires
Seaside and beach
Fish and seaweed

SUB-CATEGORIES

From these three broad categories I like to take a stroll down the high street:

THE FRUIT SHOP (FRUIT)
Green fruit
Apple, pear, gooseberries, grapes and unripe fruit such as banana and melon
Orange fruit
Marmalade, blood oranges, mandarins, tangerines
Sweet yellow fruit
Ripe melon, tinned pear, plum, banana, pineapple
Red and berry fruits
Summer fruits, raisins, currants, blackberries, strawberries, raspberries
Citrus and exotic fruits
Grapefruit, lime, lemon, kiwi, guava, lychee
Nuts

THE FLORISTS
Scented flowers
Heather
Lavender
Powdery and sherbety, zingy
Handbag, perfume, lipstick
Grass and hay
Christmas tree, firs, forest walk

THE SWEET SHOP (SWEET)
Candy sticks
Parma violets
Toffee
Banoffee pie
Vanilla ice cream
Maple syrup
Liquorice
Crystallised ginger

THE BAKERS
Dough
Yeastiness
Fresh bread
Toast and melted butter
Biscuits
Crème brûlée and cake

THE PET SHOP
Muskiness
Breakfast cereal
Porridge
Pencil shavings, wood chips, sap, sawdust

THE FURNITURE STORES
Furniture polish
New wood
Cleaning products
Pine

THE HIPPY JEWELLERS
Sandalwood and incense stick
Nutmeg, cinnamon and sweet spices
Spent matches
Leather

THE DIY STORE
Oil and lubricant
Rubber
Creosote
Charcoal

THE TOBACCONISTS
Tobacco and cigars
Cigar box
Leather saddle
Smoke

The art of drinking whisky

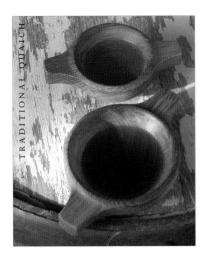

TRADITIONAL QUAICH

It may not be politically correct to say it these days, but alcohol has played a major and positive role in society for thousands of years. It has been used for medicinal purposes and as a tonic.

It was consumed before battle to give warriors courage, taken by defeated armies to drown their sorrows or by conquering armies to celebrate victory. Former enemies coming together to make peace have blessed their deals with alcohol.

In Scotland and Ireland clans have shared whisky at the end of conflict, passing around a shared cup – a quaich – in a communal ritual that is echoed in many Christian churches to this day. But whisky stands apart from many other drinks. It takes years to make, and centuries to make well, so it deserves respect, like wine.

A culture has grown up around whisky. Today there are different glasses for different occasions but in short, if you want to appreciate whisky by nosing it, you need a narrow, relatively short glass like those illustrated below. While a tumbler is fine if you are adding ice, it is not a glass that is particularly suited to nosing.

GLENCAIRN TASTING GLASS

MODERN TASTING GLASS

CLASSIC TUMBLER

TRADITIONAL SNIFTER

CLASSIC TULIP TASTING GLASS

CLASSIC TASTING GLASS

Whisky styles

All whisky is made with grain, yeast and water, but under that umbrella there are many variations. Here are the main ones.

Ardbeg Nasda SINGLE MALT

Compass Box Hedonism GRAIN WHISKY

Johnnie Walker Blue Label BLENDED WHISKY

Monkey Shoulder BLENDED MALT

Redbreast 12 year-old POT STILL WHISKEY

The Irishman IRISH BLENDED WHISKEY

SINGLE MALT WHISKY

Whisky made only of yeast, water and malted barley and the product of one distillery only. Scotland is the leading player in this sector but single malts are made across the world, in countries including America, Japan, Australia, South Africa and many European countries.

In Europe malt must be matured for a minimum of three years in oak casks, and must be of at least 40 per cent alcohol by volume (ABV).

GRAIN WHISKY

Whisky made with grain or grains other than malted barley only. Grains might include wheat, corn, unmalted barley and rye. In Europe the minimum maturation period of three years also applies. Great Scottish examples include Cameronbrig from Fife and Imperial from Morayshire, as well as Compass Box Hedonism, produced by a young London company that specialises in artisanal blends.

BLENDED WHISKY

A combination of single malts from different distilleries mixed together with grain whisky. Look out for Johnnie Walker, Chivas Regal, Grant's, Famous Grouse and Ballantine's for a taste of blended whisky which steers away from the bland and is rich in flavour.

BLENDED MALT WHISKY

Whisky made using malted whisky from a number of different distilleries. Monkey Shoulder – made from a blend of single malts from Glenfiddich, Balvenie and Kinivie – and Johnnie Walker Green Label from Scotland exemplify this particular style.

POT STILL WHISKEY

An Irish style of whiskey which in its purest form is made using malted barley and another grain, normally unmalted barley, mixed to form the grist before mashing and then fermentation. The term has been used to describe any whiskey made in a pot still but this does not do this unique style of whiskey justice.

IRISH BLENDED WHISKEY

Most commercial Irish whiskeys are blends, and are normally made up of pot still whiskey mixed with grain whiskey, though The Irishman 70 is made up of 70 per cent single malt and 30 per cent Midleton pot still whiskey, a unique north-meets-south whiskey which may be described as a blend but is in effect in a category of its own.

Buffalo Trace BOURBON

Jack Daniel's TENNESSEE WHISKEY

Sazerac Rye RYE

Bernheim Original WHEAT WHISKEY

Mellow Corn CORN WHISKEY

Glen Breton CANADIAN RYE WHISKEY

BOURBON

Whiskey made in the United States using grains including at least 51 per cent corn, although in practice the amount is normally considerably higher. Bourbon is produced under strict guidelines and must be matured in fresh oak barrels. The most celebrated US bourbons include Jim Beam, Maker's Mark, Buffalo Trace and Woodford Reserve. Straight bourbon must be matured for two years.

TENNESSEE WHISKEY

Whiskey made in the state of Tennessee in a similar style to bourbon, but which differs to bourbon because it has undergone the 'Lincoln County process' – where the spirit is passed through Maplewood charcoal before it is put into the cask. Jack Daniel's is the most famous example.

RYE WHISKEY (UNITED STATES)

Whiskey made in a similar way to bourbon, but with a minimum of 51 per cent rye in the grist. It must also be matured for more than two years. Look out for Rittenhouse Rye and Pappy Van Winkle's Family Reserve 13-year-old Rye, both produced in Louisville, as well as Sazerac Kentucky Straight Rye from Frankfort.

WHEAT WHISKEY

Whiskey made in a similar way to bourbon but including a minimum of 51 per cent wheat. One of the best-known wheat whiskeys is Bernheim Original, a relative newcomer from the Heaven Hill distillery in Louisville, Kentucky.

CORN WHISKEY

Whiskey made up of at least 80 per cent corn. There are no ageing requirements and, if corn whisky is aged, it is usually for no more than than six months. Heaven Hill's Mellow Corn and Georgia Moon are key examples of the style, as is Dixie Dew from the same distillery.

RYE WHISKY (CANADA)

Canadian Rye is a term used to describe any whisky which has the aroma, taste and character of Canadian whisky' whether it contains rye or not. There is an irony here because rye produces aggressive and spicy whiskies and Canadian whisky can be soft, rounded and quite characterless. In practice, Canadian whisky will probably have a number of different whiskies in it, with only a small proportion of rye among them. Canadian whisky also permits a small amount of a totally different liquid and this may include American bourbon and fruit juice. Look for Canadian Club, Glen Breton and Forty Creek.

Whisky and food matching

The idea that you can match whisky to food appalls some people. Traditionalists in particular have a problem with it. Their loss, and here's why.

It is all about perceptions. Mention the idea of cheese and wine and most of us accept the pairing as naturally as we do salt and pepper, or Laurel and Hardy. But for years beer and food as a match were not widely accepted at all, and this pairing is only now making headway through the dedication and hard work of people within the beer industry. And so it is with whisky. Yet talk to a food scientist, and they will tell you that the grain is a much better suitor to many foods than the grape. The fats in cheese, in particular, react more comfortably with beer and whisky than they do with wine or brandy. Seafood is the other natural partner for whisky.

In recent years, there have been commendable attempts to bring whisky to the dining table, and there have been some wonderful dinners featuring six food courses and six whiskies. What we learned from these is that whisky is generally most successful when served with one course or with one particular food type during a meal.

Here are a few tried-and-tested combinations.

ARDBEG WITH CROTTIN

LAGAVULIN WITH ROQUEFORT

FIVE WINNING COMBINATIONS

ARDBEG WITH CROTTIN Ardbeg is a big peaty Islay whisky and when combined with this pungent, slightly nutty goat's cheese, the result is wonderfully loud, rustic and spicy. Works best when the crottin is crumbling.

LAGAVULIN WITH ROQUEFORT Quite possibly the best whisky–cheese combination of them all. The Lagavulin brings out the saltiness of the cheese, the Roquefort batters down the sharp whisky taste and leaves smoke and fruit. Astounding.

RITTENHOUSE RYE WITH PARMESAN Don't skimp on the cheese here – fork out for one of the better-quality parmesans. The fully spicy rye and the more delicate hard cheese make for a stimulating pepper and salt mix.

GLEN ELGIN WITH CHEDDAR Be careful with the cheddar – nothing too strong. This combination works with most fruity Speysiders but Glen Elgin is an eloquent and rounded malt, ideally suited to finding the sweetness in the cheese.

BRUICHLADDICH WITH SHRIMP Much is made of seafood with peated Islay whisky, but this is a more elegant partnership: the gentle salty taste of the shrimp contrasts with the fruity notes of the whisky but rides on its maritime qualities.

RITTENHOUSE RYE WITH PARMESAN

GLEN ELGIN WITH CHEDDAR

BRUICHALDDICH WITH SHRIMP

Making a meal of a whisky

The notion of whisky and food going together may be alien to some, but let's lay it to rest by starting with four tried-and-tested combinations sufficient to change anyone's opinion.

Rich fruity speyside whisky

with foie gras

It is not that many years ago that there was nearly a riot at a Whisky Live London tasting event staged by Laphroaig at which the brand owners dared to pair up the malt with cheese, appalling some people in the room who were there for Laphroaig and Laphroaig alone.

Whisky, though, is remarkably flexible when it comes to accompanying food. On the face of it, foie gras would seem ill-suited to a whisky accompaniment, but it works surprisingly well with a rich and fruity Speysider, with the whisky taking the place of a fruit compote with certain roasted meat dishes, and the fats and oils in the foie gras bringing out the flavours in the malt. Try Cardhu or Laphroaig for starters.

Spicy or peaty whisky

with seared scallops

Seafood and whisky are a marriage made in heaven. Langoustines and oysters suit a peated whisky such as Bowmore, the saltiness working well with seaweedy and seaside notes in the whisky. The peppery and spicy nature of Talisker also works well with seafood, giving it a salt-and-pepper tang. For a slightly more subtle and sophisticated pairing, try a robust whisky such as Clynelish with prawns, mussels or seared scallops. It's a more balanced pairing than some of the peaty whisky and seafood ones.

Actually, Clynelish is a very versatile single malt for food pairings. Amazingly, it works well with beef and mustard or horseradish sandwiches, and with spicy chicken dishes.

Fruity speyside whisky

with spring rolls

Perhaps unsurprisingly, much of the work in the area of food and whisky pairing has come from France, and in particular from the great French whisky writer Martine Nouet. Her whisky dinners, using a varied range of malts from Ardbeg to Aberlour, are legendary. She is at ease with using whisky as an ingredient and serving it to go with food.

Her advice: experiment with different foods and look for pairings that either complement each other or provide a contrast.

You would not necessarily expect a combination of Chinese spring rolls and a fruity malt such as Cragganmore to work but the whisky contrasts with the rolls, bringing out flavours in both, particularly ginger.

Big, sweet highland whisky

with desserts

Dalwhinnie is alcoholic bottled honey and it works extremely well with a whole range of desserts and sweets. Try it with a chocolate bar and you will be amazed.

Bread-and-butter pudding would not seem to have the guts for a malt whisky pairing but with Dalwhinnie it is like eating honey sandwiches, with the currants in the pudding adding an extra dimension to the flavour.

If you don't have a sweet tooth and would prefer to go for the cheese board instead, then a big peaty whisky such as Lagavulin with a strong-tasting blue cheese such as Roquefort is stunning.

Classic whisky cocktails

Whisky traditionalists don't hold much truck with cocktails either, which is a bit bizarre really.

Why? Well, the malt whisky produced in the Highlands a few hundred years ago tasted so awful that they added anything – mint, honey, heather – to hide the taste. The story goes that Bonnie Prince Charlie handed over the recipe to Drambuie to thank the people who saved him – a lot of old balderdash admittedly, but the point is that it is plausible that in the mid- 18th century whisky was served with flavourings – and that's all a cocktail is, after all. These days a good cocktail is not about concealing the taste of whisky, it's about showing it off. The classic, and longest surviving whisky cocktails, therefore, are the simplest and the ones that add a twist to the whisky.

The Old Fashioned
The first ever cocktail. Serve it in a lo-ball tumbler.

The Manhattan is always an elegant aperitif served in a Martini glass.

The Mint Julep works best in a squat lo-ball glass.

The Waldorf first appeared at the beginning of the 20th century at the Waldorf-Astoria bar.

The Whisky Sour is bourbon-based. Serve in a low fluted glass.

The Old Fashioned

1 sugar cube
2–3 drops angostura bitters
2 fresh orange slices
80 ml (3 fl oz) bourbon
Maraschino cherry for garnish

Place the sugar cube at the bottom of an old-fashioned glass. Saturate it with the bitters. Add orange slice. Muddle these ingredients, and then fill the glass with ice cubes. Add the bourbon. Stir well. Garnish with a second orange slice and a maraschino cherry.

The Manhattan

4 drops angostura bitters
50 ml (2 fl oz) blended Scotch whisky
25 ml (1 fl oz) Noilly Prat rouge
2 teaspoons juice from maraschino cherries

Pour the ingredients into an ice-filled cocktail shaker. Shake well. Strain into glass.

The Mint Julep

4 mint leaves
1 teaspoon caster sugar
37.5 ml (1 ½ fl oz) bourbon

Lightly muddle together the 4 mint leaves and sugar with a few drops of water in the bottom of the glass. Next, almost fill the glass with crushed ice and pour the bourbon over it. Garnish the crushed ice with a sprig of mint.

The Waldorf

8 ml (¼ fl oz) absinthe or substitute
50 ml (2 fl oz) rye whiskey
25 ml (¾ fl oz) sweet vermouth
2 drops angostura bitters

Pour the absinthe into a mixing glass and swirl it around to coat the sides. Toss out any excess. Add the remaining ingredients and ice. Stir well. Strain into a chilled cocktail glass.

The Whisky Sour

40 ml (1 ½ fl oz) bourbon (e.g Maker's Mark)
40 ml (1 ½ fl oz) lemon juice
25 ml (¾ fl oz) sugar syrup
maraschino cherry for garnish

Pour the bourbon, lemon juice and sugar syrup into a cocktail shaker with ice cubes. Shake well. Strain into a chilled sour glass. Garnish with the cherry.

Contemporary whisky cocktails

These modern takes on traditional whisky cocktails deliver a new twist to hip whisky drinking.

Whisky is to bartenders – or mixologists – what Mount Everest is to the climber: the ultimate challenge. Mix a cocktail with vodka and the spirit quietly goes under without a struggle, providing an alcoholic kick but giving the mixologist free licence to paint pictures. Whisky and especially single malt whisky doesn't do that. It's the untamed tiger of the drinks world and if you're going to work with it you're going to need a lot of patience.

In the early part of the millennium, *Whisky Magazine* held a cocktail competition that divided the room between those who made good cocktails despite having whisky in them, and those who made good cocktails because they had whisky in them. Things have moved on since then and here are five specially created whisky cocktails made by the some of the sector's hottest drinks makers.

The Pure Bard by Esther Medina Cuesta of Bureau Club, London.

The Broadmoor by Stuart Hudson of Viajante, London.

The Watermelon Smash by Nidal Ramini of Brown-Forman Spirits.

The Bonnie Blush by Alistair Malcolm of Lab, Soho, London.

The Cool Walker by Vamsi Putta of Salt Whisky Lounge and Dining Room, London.

The Pure Bard

25 ml (1 fl oz) *Talisker single malt*
25 ml (1 fl oz) *Noilly Prat rouge*
25 ml (1 fl oz) *Boudier Guignolet*
25 ml (1 fl oz) *blood orange juice*
Orange peel or zest

Shake the ingredients together, then fill an elegant tumbler with cubed ice and pour everything in. Garnish with a twist of orange peel and enjoy the flavours.

The Broadmoor

50 ml (2 fl oz) *Dalwhinnie 15-year-old single malt*
12.5 ml (½ fl oz) *Green Chartreuse*
10 ml (½ fl oz) *Sugar Syrup*
3 dashes of orange bitters

Stir over ice and strain into a coupette glass. Garnish with a star anise.

The Watermelon Smash

50 ml (2 fl oz) Woodford Reserve bourbon
8 mint leaves
½ a lemon
1 bar spoon of vanilla sugar or 20ml of vanilla syrup
Large piece of watermelon, sliced, to garnish

Cut the lemon into quarters, squeeze and add the lemon juice to the ice-filled shaker. Add the bourbon, mint and vanilla. Shake everything together, strain and garnish.

The Bonnie Blush

25 ml (1 fl oz) Johnnie Walker Black label
12.5 ml (½ fl oz) fresh lemon
12.5 ml (½ fl oz) Crème de mûre
3 bar spoons blackberry jam or conserve
High-quality Champagne
Fresh blackberry, halved, to garnish

Shake together all the ingredients except the Champagne. Half fill a flute with Champagne then slowly add ingredients from shaker glass to flute. Garnish.

The Cool Walker

40ml (1 and ½ fl oz) Johnnie Walker Black Label
15 ml (½ fl oz) Drambuie
10ml (½ fl oz) lime juice
10ml (½ fl oz) Gomme syrup
Ginger ale
Slice of fresh lemon

Pour the ingredients into a Boston shaker and add the ice. Shake and strain into a highball glass filled with ice. Top with ginger ale, and garnish with a lemon wheel.

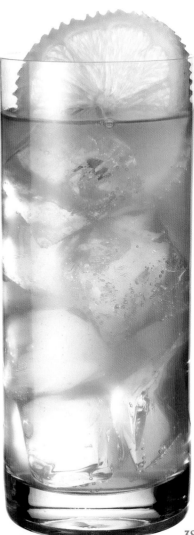

THE WORLD'S BEST WHISKIES

A WORLD OF WHISKY

A world of whisky

Whisky is now produced across the entire world, ensuring an even greater range of tastes to enjoy.

Making the selection

Keeping a tab on the number of whiskies available across the world is like counting leaves in the garden during a hurricane. The world of whisky is not only in a permanent state of evolution, but it is segregated, too, with Scottish blends, in particular, finding favour in certain territories but unavailable elsewhere.

If counting the number of whiskies has been extremely difficult, then picking a definitive 750 best whiskies is, if the truth be told, quite a challenge. You simply could not taste every single one, but even if you could, deciding which should and should not make the cut is an entirely subjective and deeply unscientific process.

What would be hard to do in any drinks category is made all the harder in the field of whisky because of the presence of independent bottlers. These are companies that buy up casks of whisky and then bottle them under their own labels, often in tiny quantities because they are the product of one, two or three casks. Every cask produces slightly different whisky to the next, so independent bottlers do not seek to produce uniform representative malt from the distillery in question, but rather offer the whisky lover a variation of it. If an official distillery bottling is to whisky what an official CD release is to a rock band, then the independent bottling is a live bootleg: often a rougher and rawer version, clearly by the same artist but reproduced differently; sometimes better than the original, sometimes not, but highly attractive to the true fan nonetheless.

As independent bottlers often bottle just one cask and produce only 250 or 300 bottles from it, many whiskies are literally gone before they can be written about, and are rapidly replaced by

another wave of bottles. This area of the industry is an ever-changing quicksand and for this reason many great whiskies produced even a couple of years ago by independent bottlers have had to be ignored because they have gone forever, though I have touched on this area in a bid to recognise the biggest and best independent bottlers.

The selection process can be simplified further by ignoring the scores of poor-quality drinks passing themselves off as whisky made outside the guidelines laid down by the Scottish (and therefore European) and American whisky industries. Both continents work to a code where the highest standards are maintained, and they provide a good base camp from which to work. While some rare whiskies are included, other extremely exclusive one haven't made it in.

But that doesn't mean the net has not been cast far and wide: it has, and there has been a conscious effort to include some of the most esoteric whiskies and to recognise countries where the whisky light has only just been switched on. Some of them are distinctly weird, others are a shock to the palate which has grown used to the finest Scottish malts and the tastiest bourbons. But every whisky mentioned in this book has been well made by a master craftsman and is included on merit. For ease of reference whiskies are listed by the country of origin with the biggest regions of Scotland and America to the fore. Within each country section whiskies are listed by whisky style; within these sections, brands and/or distilleries are listed in alphabetical order. The symbols are designed to help make selection and categorisation of each whisky easier. Each entry includes tasting notes but I've tried to avoid being too prescriptive. More importantly, I've attempted to capture some of the personality of the whisky, and the people or events that shaped it, to give it greater context and interest.

While everything possible has been done to ensure accuracy, the pace of evolution in the world of whisky inevitably means that some whisky distilleries and whisky brands will have changed or changed hands. Some will have been swallowed up, some closed, new ones opened. A significant number of the whiskies included here are produced by small independent distillers and might be hard to find. I have not deliberately attempted to be obscure, but on the other hand, I have had considerably more time and greater resources to seek out these whiskies, and if you struggle to find some of them, my apologies in advance.

Tasting symbols

The following symbols have been used in the whisky listings to help describe each of the 750 listings, from classic blends to special cask-aged bottlings. They correspond to the following defininitions listed below.

CONNOISSEUR CLASSIC
Cult or classic whiskies that should be high up the wish list for a whisky connoisseur.

SESSION SIP
Everyday whiskies that often feature in the cupboard at home.

PREMIUM TIPPLE
Special whiskies for occasional drinking or best reserved for celebrations.

OLD AND VENERABLE
Whiskies aged 25 years or more.

SUPER STYLE
Whiskies that exemplify a particular style of whisky.

FOR PEAT'S SAKE Whiskies whoses smokiness or peaty phenolic flavour is a major component of the overall taste.

MIND HOW YOU GO Whiskies bottled at the strength they came out the cask or at more than 50% ABV, 100 Proof.

A LITTLE UNUSUAL Quirky or unusual whiskies with a unique taste or featuring an unusual or unique aspect to their production.

RAREST OF THE RARE
Hard to find and very special whiskies.

GONE BUT NOT FORGOTTEN
Whiskies from a distillery that has closed.

The face of modern whisky

New distilleries, new whisky making nations and new marketing-savvy companies are ensuring that whisky looks as exciting and varied as it tastes.

It was not so long ago since buying a whisky either meant selecting from a weak and predictable selection of bottles and labels at the supermarket or liquor store or venturing into a 'specialist' shop for something more exciting. But whisky packaging has come on in leaps and bounds in recent years. If you like the formal, somewhat grandiose and elegant style of the traditional whisky bottle that's fine. There are plenty of them still out there such as the iconic names and iconic packaging of Glenfiddich, Johnnie Walker, Jack Daniel's and Jim Beam, pretty much unchanged. But these days a new generation of whisky companies such as Penderyn and Compass Box have helped transform the shape of packaging and companies across the world have adopted bottles in such a range of shapes and sizes that whisky shelves are as vibrant and colourful as those of any other drink product. The traditional qualities are now being served up in a modern context.

THE WHISKY LABEL

There are rules as to what can be stated on whisky labels, varying by country. Generally, if there is an age on the label, that age refers to the youngest whisky in the mix. There may be many older whiskies, but one drop of 12-year-old whisky is enough to 'age' the overall bottle.

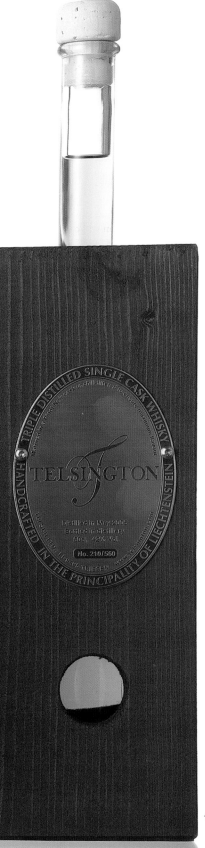

THE WORLD'S BEST WHISKIES

SCOTLAND

Scotland

When it comes to whisky, it all starts and ends with Scotland.

We can jet all over the world searching for great whisky and in Kentucky, Ireland and Japan we can find plenty of it – and even some that is better than a good proportion of Scotland's. We can marvel at the whiskies of distilleries such as Lark and Bakery Hill in Australia, Amrut in India, Mackmyra in Sweden, Blaue Maus and Slyrs in Germany, Millstone in The Netherlands and The Belgian Owl in Belgium. But when all is said and done, we always return once more to Scotland.

Why? Because not only does Scotland produce a breathtaking quantity of stunning whiskies but it seems to be setting the pace effortlessly for whisky as we go forward, celebrating its traditions but looking towards the next goal and challenge. And because overall the standard of its whiskies, blends, vatted malts, and grains as well as single malts, is consistently so high.

It is true that from time to time another nation will produce a whisky that is a match for the very finest from Scotland, but it doesn't happen every day. Scotland's whiskies are like the New Zealand All Blacks – they can be beaten but rarely, and over any era, they still dominate their field.

When choosing the 750 whiskies for this book, there was no pre-planned decision over numbers. Lists were made of all the potential candidates for inclusion, then they were tasted and chosen on their merit. The fact that about two-thirds of the final number should come from Scotland is down to quality alone. The proportion is spot-on.

There are just over 100 single-malt distilleries in Scotland, more than the rest of the world put together, and there are hundreds of single malts. Probably thousands. For that reason single malt is the dominant style and is reflected here by the largest number of entries. But it should also be remembered that 90 per cent-plus of all Scotch whisky sold is blended whisky, and most of it conforms to the same high standard as malts. You do not get to be a global household name such as Johnnie Walker or Chivas Regal by being average. Some blends go even further, using the finest aged malts and commanding the highest price tags as even the rarest malts.

Scotland is the home of whisky, where every whisky lover returns eventually. No matter what is happening elsewhere, that will not change any time soon. If ever.

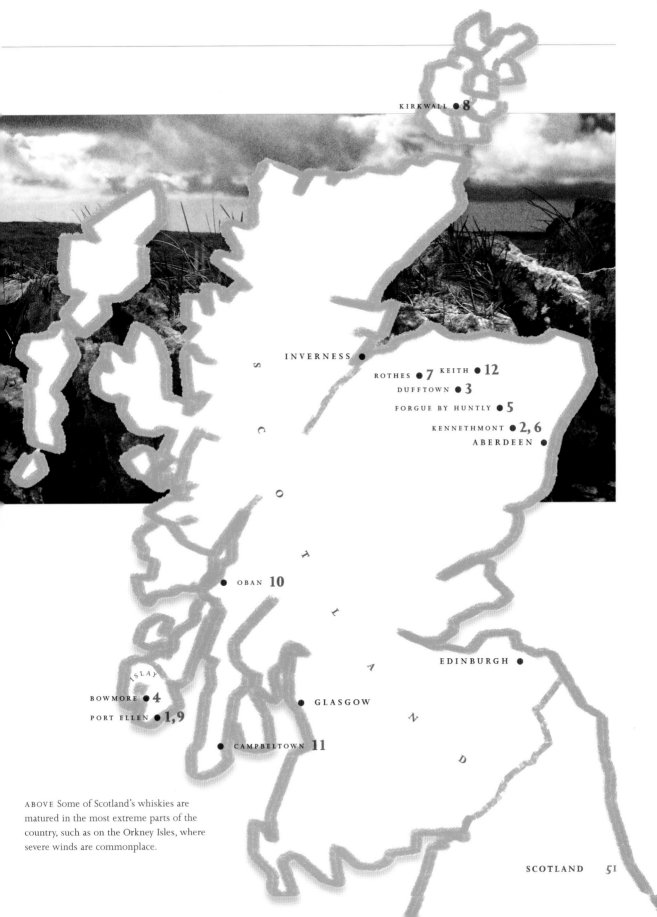

KIRKWALL ●8

INVERNESS ●

ROTHES ●7 KEITH ●12

DUFFTOWN ●3

FORGUE BY HUNTLY ●5

KENNETHMONT ●2,6

ABERDEEN ●

SCOTLAND

OBAN ●10

EDINBURGH ●

ISLAY

BOWMORE ●4

GLASGOW ●

PORT ELLEN ●1,9

CAMPBELTOWN ●11

ABOVE Some of Scotland's whiskies are matured in the most extreme parts of the country, such as on the Orkney Isles, where severe winds are commonplace.

Single malt

Scottish single-malt whisky is the world's most exciting, dynamic and complex spirit. While wonderfully diverse concoctions exist in the fields of rum, tequila and to some extent brandy, no other drink style can amaze and delight so consistently and so frequently as Scottish single malt does. And no other drink exhibits its qualities quite so flamboyantly and stylishly.

Single malts are now produced in a number of countries, but none of them can hold a candle to the better Scottish malts. If you are not convinced, line up a world selection of malts alongside the best of Scotland and taste them. Even if they match up in the first instance, add a few drops of water, leave them for 20 minutes and compare again. You can almost guarantee that a proportion of the non-Scottish malts will have fallen apart.

The attention to detail in production, the involvement of copper, the craftsmanship honed over centuries, the calm and patient maturation and the loving attention to detail all combine to form what is nothing less than a fortress in a drink. To you and me, it is a glass of whisky. To a scientist it is a feat of molecular engineering, a complex unyielding liquid that is so well structured it delivers on the palate every time you approach it.

There's an air of mystery and romance about Scottish single-malt whisky. Produced from the simplest of ingredients, it serves up tastes and aromas that really have no right to be there. How is this? And why is it that wine matches or outperforms beer in terms of diversity of flavour, and yet brandy comes nowhere near malt whisky when it comes to taste?

Scottish single-malt whisky as a hobby is still in its infancy. Most malt whisky is produced as a component for blended whisky, and only a handful of malts are widely recognised in their own right. A good number of malts have never or have rarely been bottled singly, and many have never had the chance to show off because they have always been stored in average wood on their journey to the blending room. But as interest grows, that may change, and there are many cases of distillery owners re-casking malt in order to give it a chance to shine in the future.

Much has been made of the growth of new whisky-making nations. Indeed, in this book a strong argument is made for a number of countries and why they deserve to be on whisky's highest tasting table.

But the head of that table is Scotland, and year after year the country serves up a feast of fresh single-malt whisky and it is a trend we will continue to see.

ABERFELDY
www.dewarswow.com

Drive through Aberfeldy distillery and up the lane beyond it and you will find, high up in the hills, a group of cottages that are available for hire. In the morning the cloud gathers in the valley below and you can watch golden eagles dip in and out as they swoop to find breakfast. Then you can walk down to the village with the distillery below you to the right. I'm not sure there is a better way to start the day.

Aberfeldy distillery lies in the village of the same name to the North of Perth and not far from Pitlochry. It is also the home of Dewar's World of Whisky, an excellent visitor facility telling the story of the Dewar family and its famous blended whisky. The distillery itself is kept in pristine condition and is also open to the public. There are enough interactive facilities to keep the children occupied too, though whether it's a good thing that my youngest son now knows how to blend a whisky and is, according to one machine in the centre, better at it than me, is up for debate.

The distillery – of course – also produces a great malt too.

Aberfeldy 12-year-old 40% ABV

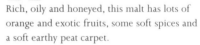

Rich, oily and honeyed, this malt has lots of orange and exotic fruits, some soft spices and a soft earthy peat carpet.

Aberfeldy 18-year-old single cask 59.6% ABV

A very recent addition to the range, this is an absolute stormer. It is a smooth, rich malt with honey, nuts, vanilla and spices, but best of all it has a weighty punch to it.

Aberfeldy 21-year-old 40% ABV

Rich honey is often a defining characteristic of Aberfeldy bottlings, and here it is at its most potent. But there are also some lovely orange notes, a little bit of peat and just enough oak to give the proceedings some gravitas. I wish it was bottled at a higher strength though.

ABERLOUR
www.aberlour.com

Of all the tours offered by Scotland's malt distilleries, Aberlour's is among the very best. Owner Pernod Ricard has several distilleries in the Speyside region and it seems that those involved sat down way back and thought about how they could offer the visitor a different experience at each. The Glenlivet, with its smuggling past and large visitor centre, looks after itself. Strathisla is the home of Chivas and that provides an obvious angle. And Aberlour? Well there are those of us who regard the distillery as Speyside royalty. VIP tours are commonplace now, but Aberlour was offering them years back. Today your visit will be a lengthy one, with knowledgeable guides. At the end you can taste the whisky, then pour an exclusive cask-strength version from a bourbon or a sherry cask and bottle it.

Aberlour 10-year-old 43% ABV

This is classic Speyside, with an emphasis on the green fruit end of the Speyside spectrum. Crisp, fresh and distinctive, with traces of trademark mintiness and elements from both bourbon and sherry casks used for production. Creamy on the one hand, red berries on the other. World class.

Aberlour 15-year-old Cuvée Marie d'Ecosse 43% ABV

Mainly sold in the French market, where Aberlour and Amour are two sides of the same coin, this comes from a mix of bourbon and sherry casks. It is delicate and flowery on the nose, with lingering toffee and liquorice notes, late spice and a smooth finish.

Aberlour 15-year-old Sherry Wood Finish 40% ABV

Another beautiful mix of sherry and bourbon with butterscotch, candy, tangerine and red berry fruits, all delivered on a gossamer light pillow, with some trademark mint and spices late on.

Aberlour 18-year-old Sherry Wood Matured 43% ABV

Most Aberlour expressions are akin to elegant ladies dressed in finery but this is altogether more fiesty. Think Nicole Kidman on horseback in the film *Australia*. Okay, any excuse. The 18 years in the cask and the fact that the casks in question are all sherry go a long way to explaining this one. Nutty, spicy and fruity in equal measure, this is a complex malt, bright orangey amber in colour, which ebbs and flows but ultimately leaves the oak and sherry in charge.

Aberlour a'bunadh ('The Origin')
BATCH 21 NO AGE STATEMENT 59.6% ABV

In Gaelic, *a'bunadh* means 'the origin' and it is the name given by Aberlour's owners to a series of malts released in batches. Each batch varies but the overall effect is the same – simply, these probably represent the best value for money malts in the market. Indeed, they seem to be well under-priced.

Each batch is a vatting of sherry cask Aberlours, with a range of whiskies aged from very young to more than 15 years old. The batches vary in strength but often tip over 60% ABV – that's one and a half bottles of standard 40% whisky.

The flavours are intense, with frequent whiffs of smoke and sulphur over concentrated redcurrants and blackcurrants, cherries, blood orange, nuttiness, spice and some mint. Each one is rich and elegant, almost liqueur-like and unforgettable. You would think that such big flavours would appeal only to committed malt lovers but I met a woman on a bus once who hated whisky of all types except this one. What's more, this one she drank regularly. Can't blame her.

Aberlour 16-year-old, Double Cask Matured 43% ABV

Fluffy apples and fruit crumble on the nose, green fruits, vanilla and mint on the palate, with a refreshing and more-ish finish. Almost a palate-cleanser this one.

ARDBEG
www.ardbeg.com

Could this be my nomination for the best whisky moment ever? Drinking cask-strength Ardbeg at the distillery after two days of a sponsored charity event which comprised travelling from Jura to Ardbeg by cycling 30 miles, walking 30 miles and rowing three miles from Bruichladdich across Loch Indaal to Bowmore. The first day went fine until lunch, when we collected our bikes at Bunnahabhain and started up the long hill from the distillery. A nightmare that wasn't helped by Bunnahabhain's distillery manager John MacLellan who insisted on sharing a couple of cask-strength malts just as we were leaving. Problem was I hadn't been on a bicycle for 35 years. By the time we reached Bruichladdich for the first stop I could barely walk. So the rowing – and that's another story – and the lengthy walk from Bowmore was a blistery nightmare. Worth it though – for those Ardbeg drams. It is hard not to love Ardbeg regardless. The distillery is known for its big, peaty whiskies, it is one of the prettiest distilleries in the world, and provides some of the best food on Islay.

Ardbeg 10-year-old 46% ABV

The distillery reopened in 1997 but it was only a couple of years ago that the standard 10-year-old, made of all new spirit, was first released. This is a humdinger of a whisky, big, oily, tarry and sweet, with wave after wave of solid peat. Awesome.

Ardbeg Corryvreckan 57.1% ABV

Corryvreckan is one the most violent and dangerous whirlpools in the world, and it lies close to the islands of Islay and Jura. You can only safely pass over it at certain times of the day during low tide and even then it's an experience – a wide stretch of small eddying pools making up a collective monster. With such a raw display of nature come countless fables and legends, but undoubtedly it has claimed many lives. The writer George Orwell is among the many people who had to be rescued after an encounter with it.

The whisky is like the reputation. Calm and placid on the surface, underneath it's dense, rich in plummy jam fruits wrapped in intense smoke, with citrus notes running through it. Wonderful.

Ardbeg Uigeadail 54.2% ABV

Named after the source from which Ardbeg takes its water, this is almost the definitive distillery bottling. Bottled at cask strength it is a hugely flavoured whisky, with all the rich, tarry and phenolic peat tones that the distillery excels at. But behind the curtain is a malt of sublime complexity. You will find sweetness, citrus fruits, earthy and astringent notes, smoked fish, seaside flavours and dark cocoa.

Ardbeg Almost There 54.1% ABV

Some distilleries are like soccer clubs – they have a group of supporters who were into it before the current managers, and will still be there whoever takes charge in the future. As a result they act like custodians, not shy of offering their views if anyone messes with their malt. Ardbeg is one such distillery and when Glenmorangie bought and reopened it, the move was obviously greeted positively but there was curiosity – and some concern – as to what the new owners might do to their beloved malt. To help reassure them, whisky-maker Bill Lumsden and his team released a series of works in progress – Very Young at six years old, Still Young at seven and a half years and this one at nine years. The first two bottles have pretty much disappeared and this one is not far behind it, so they are true collector's items. But if you find one, consider drinking it – peated whiskies as young as four years old can be excellent, and, while this one might be a little rough around the edges and slightly odd, the intense fruit and coal-like tarry smoke makes it a treat.

Ardbeg Renaissance 55.9% ABV

This is the fourth and final whisky in the 'works in progress' and is effectively a cask-strength version of what has become the standard 10-year-old. What a great moment when this was released. Few Ardbeg fans would have tasted this and been disappointed. It is undeniably vintage Ardbeg – lots of sweet and sour, and fruit and peat notes to compare and contrast.

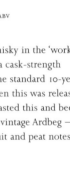

Ardbeg Airigh Nam Beist 46% ABV

All but disappeared now and replaced by
Corryvreckan, the name is another reference
to the area where Ardbeg is produced and is
pronounced Arry Nam Bayst. If you find a bottle
it's worth exploring because it has a soft vanilla-
influenced heart and the usual citrus flavour is
replaced by rounder, softer yellow fruit.

Ardbeg Blasda 40% ABV

This very nearly did not make the cut, but finally
made it through after an intense second round
of tasting. The problem here is that approaching
it as an Ardbeg is like going to see heavy-metal
band Motorhead and lead singer Lemmy playing
along to a string quartet. You want the volume
up to 11. You should bang your head to Ardbeg,
not tap your feet. And this is a muted toe-tapper,
with the peat turned well down and the strength
at only 40%. The name means
'sweet and delicious', which
says it all really. It is truly
delicious – it just doesn't taste
like Ardbeg, so bear this in
mind when you approach it.

Ardbeg Supernova 58.9% ABV

From the faintly ridiculous to the truly sublime. If
Blasda were acoustic Motorhead, then
this would be Motorhead with your
head stuck in the bass bin, the peat
scale turned to max. The oily coal-
like notes form a tsunami, crashing
over the palate into the throat then
refusing to budge. Liquorice and
cocoa appear, too.

Ardbeg 17-year-old 40% ABV

You rarely see this any more but it does come
up at auctions from time to time. It's included
here because it has reached iconic status but it
probably has more value as a collectable than
a drinking whisky – like Blasda, it's under-
powered and peat-lite.

ARDMORE

www.beamglobal.com

If there were any justice in the world Ardmore would be a
household name. It is a Highland distillery situated to the
South of Speyside and it makes a great deal of malt – one of
the few distilleries at the time of writing that was still in full
production as the rest of the industry slowed up a tad. Most
of its output goes in to Teacher's, a malty, rugged blend with
more character than many of its competitors. But now, under
the ownership of Beam Global, the single malt is becoming
known in its own right. Realistically, it will probably not
become as familiar as The Glenlivet or Glenfiddich, because
it is altogether more challenging. But I do not think I have
been to any distillery where the folk who make the whisky
are more proud of their product, and rightly so, because
Ardmore tastes like no other dram. It is the backbone of a
great blend and it wins new admirers by the month.

Ardmore Traditional Cask 46% ABV

A few years ago the previous owners of this
distillery, Allied, launched an experiment under
the watchful eye of a skilled team of whiskymen
including Robert Hicks and Michael Cockram.
The idea was to put a number of malts into small
quarter-sized casks, as would have been the
way a couple of centuries ago. The small
casks mean more interaction between
spirit and wood, and a faster process of
reaction and flavour absorption. Of the
several malts involved in the experiment,
only two worked out well – Laphroaig and
Ardmore. When Allied broke up, Beam took
Teacher's, Ardmore and Laphroaig, as well
as Cockram and Hicks. And here is the first
properly backed single-malt offering from the
distillery for several years – and the quarter
casks are included in the mix.

   This whisky is not an easy ride. It has a
rootsy, savoury, bamboo-like nose and on
the palate it's the whisky equivalent of a
delicatessen, with savoury flavours, olive and
artichoke, waves of grungy peat, oily, full and
demanding. It really grows on you, and the grungy brine and peat
finish are a delight. Do not try it after the ice cream and chocolate
sauce dessert, though.

   Finish: Delightfully peaty, briny, long and full.

ARDBEG DISTILLERY

Port Ellen, Isle of Islay, Scotland, PA42 7EA
www.ardbeg.com

As shards of sunlight pepper the broody inky–blue waters around Islay, the bows of the boat rise and dip in the swell, and the white walls of the distillery appear and disappear with each surge as seaspray cleans the pores and alerts all the senses.

It is an invigorating and exciting way to arrive on the Hebridean island of Islay and at the three great distilleries which hug its rugged southeastern shoreline.

If whisky were the music industry, Ardbeg and its neighbours Laphroaig and Lagavulin would be its big industrial heavy metal bands, the Metallica, Maiden and Motorhead of malts. For whisky lovers this compact two-mile stretch of coastline is a peaty paradise, unrivalled anywhere else in the world.

Of the three, Ardbeg is easily the most cherished. While its neighbours flourished, healthily supported by the international drinks companies that owned them, Ardbeg struggled, stopped producing on a couple of occasions, and was nearly lost entirely.

It was eventually bought and rescued by the Glenmorangie Company, who took it on 12 years ago. It was in a sorry state, its farmhouse-like still houses and production areas badly neglected, in need of some serious repair work. Since then the distillery has been restored to its full glory and it's not only a delight to visit, but it can now boast the best food on the whole island, produced in the delightful Old Kiln Cafe.

Like the distillery, the remaining whisky wasn't in great shape either. Stocks of whisky in the warehouses were, by any standards, no more than ordinary.

For these reasons what Glenmorangie's director of malts Bill Lumsden and his team have achieved with Ardbeg is nothing less than extraordinary. Unearthing a number of diamonds in the dust, they set about mixing old and new

Most of the buildings at Ardbeg, including the striking main building (opposite page), were built in the nineteenth century, and stand at the head of a protected inlet on the southern side of the beautiful Isle of Islay, an essential shelter from the North Atlantic.

KEY WHISKIES

Ardbeg 10-year-old 46% ABV	**Ardbeg Almost There** 54.1% ABV	**Ardbeg Blasda** 40% ABV
Ardbeg Corryvreckan 57.1% ABV	**Ardbeg Renaissance** 55.9% ABV	**Ardbeg Supernova** 58.9% ABV
Ardbeg Uigeadail 54.2% ABV	**Ardbeg Airigh Nam Beist** 46% ABV	**Ardbeg 17-year-old** 40% ABV

malts throughout the first years of the new millennium to produce malt gems such as Airigh Nam Beist and Uigeadail. But it wasn't until 2006 that the distillery properly qualified for whisky's Champions League and it hasn't looked back since. That year saw the launch of Very Young, a six-year-old whisky made entirely with malt produced since the reopening, and the awards have been pouring in on a regular basis ever since. By 2008 its flagship 10-year-old was being made with all new malt.

Ardbeg is small — making just over one million litres a year on one pair of stills, a tenth of the amount that Glenfiddich is capable of, and the new owners show no signs of messing with quantities, having stuck doggedly to the traditional way whisky is made here.

This, though, comes with its own set of problems. The stills are stubborn old beasts, unpredictable and untameable, regularly throwing tantrums and sulkily refusing to play along with the stillmen. They are, literally, high maintenance, but don't dare suggest the distillery could do with a new pair.

When they do decide to work properly they produce a complex, distinct, sweet and peaty spirit. It is matured on site in warehouses just a few metres from the shoreline. The debate over whether coastal maturation influences the flavour of the whisky has been going on for as long as Scotland has been making whisky and is never likely to be resolved, but the warehouses in Ardbeg put up a great argument for those who believe it does — their walls are caked with salt and you can taste the saline in the air. It is a whisky every bit as exciting as the sea-crossing journey to Islay.

WELL FANCY THAT...

Ardbeg Corryvreckan is named after a large and vicious whirlpool off the coast of Islay and close to the island of Jura. The third largest of its kind in the world, the Corryvreckan is actually a series of small whirlpools that form over a shelf on the seabed. During certain tides and at certain times of the year waves 10 metres high and travelling at high speed crash noisily through the narrow straits nearby. The whirlpool can only usually be crossed at certain low tides. It has claimed scores of lives over the years and wrecked dozens of boats. The writer George Orwell was left stranded by the whirlpool on Jura while writing the novel *1984*.

ARDMORE DISTILLERY

Kennethmont, Aberdeenshire
www.ardmorewhisky.com

When Queen Elizabeth embarks on her Diamond Jubilee tour in 2012, perhaps they will reopen the rail line up to Ardmore distillery for the occasion. The Queen and Prince Phillip stayed in the sidings during the Golden Jubilee tour in 1992, the very last people to use the line. Whether they had a glass or two of Ardmore is not recorded.

'John Campbell at Laphroaig goes on about his distillery's link with Prince Charles but we just tell him we don't muck around with princes, we deal with Queens,' laughs Alistair Longwell, Ardmore's manager. 'When she came they put down new tarmac for the caterers, so if you're the Queen, it's not just a new lick of paint which greets you.

'She isn't the only royalty we have had here, either. In 1906 the King of Spain, Alphonso XIII, came here after he and his bride survived an assassination attempt on their wedding day. There was a connection to here because one of the local lairds had links to Gonzalez Byass. The distillery has a rich royal history.'

It also makes fine whisky. Ardmore is a rugged, earthy Highland malt that plays a key role in Teacher's Highland Cream, both as a main component in the blend and as a

brokering malt to exchange for the many other malts that help give Teacher's its signature high malt content.

Since the distillery became part of Beam Global it has enjoyed considerable success in its own right. Ardmore Traditional has been partly matured in quarter casks in the same way that one of the expressions at sister distillery Laphroaig has.

'It doesn't work for all whiskies because it reinforces the sweetness so if the whisky is already sweet it can be too much,' explains Longwell. 'But with a whisky such as Ardmore it smoothes off some of the rugged edges and has a delicious mix of sweetness and spice.'

Ardmore may be a traditional distillery on the face of it, but it's never been afraid to experiment and this year saw the launch of Teacher's Origin, the first new version of Teacher's

Ardmore Distillery in the Highlands lies at the highest point of what was the Aberdeen-to-Inverness rail line and has its own sidings. It's one of the few passing points on the line. The line was used to bring coal to the distillery and to transport casks off towards Glasgow. It was used up until the early 1990s when the distillery stopped using coal.

KEY WHISKY

Ardmore Traditional Cask 46% ABV

BELOW LEFT Some of the casks used to mature spirit at Ardmore, including the quarter cask on the right.

BELOW Ardmore's stills make a weighty, peaty and savoury spirit unlike anything else in Scotland.

for well over a decade. It's a piece of creative genius that stems from the quarter cask trialings.

'We took the vatted malt for Teacher's and the grain for Teacher's but kept them apart,' says Longwell. 'Then they were sent back here to Ardmore where they were matured separately to each other for a further two or three years in quarter casks. Then the grain and malts were brought together just before bottling. It makes for a full-bodied and rich-tasting blend.'

The new Teacher's will be rolled out worldwide in 2011 and there are more plans for Ardmore as a single malt in the pipeline after that.

And who knows – maybe a Diamond Jubilee bottling in 2012 that is fit for a queen.

ARRAN

www.isleofarrandistillers.com

If you are an Elvis Presley fan you will know that the only time he set foot in the United Kingdom was when he landed very briefly at Prestwick Airport on Scotland's west coast.

Why Prestwick? Because back in the day it served as Scotland's main international airport, the airport most likely to stay open, because of the fact that it rarely freezes there or struggles with snow.

If you want to travel to the distillery at Arran, then you can fly to Prestwick and take a train to Ardrossan for the ferry crossing. And the moderate climate that the airport and the island have in common has a great deal to do with the whisky that is produced on the Isle of Arran.

There are palm trees on Arran. Really. The island sits slap bang in the middle of the Gulf Stream. The distillery itself, built only some 15 years ago, sits in a sun-trap, and all of this has had a profound effect on the whisky.

Every new distillery faces a dilemma. After three years you have whisky and you can sell it as such, but is it up to the job? How long can you afford to leave it? On the one hand, in the short term, the investors want some money and you have to keep shelling out for wages, fuel and so on; on the other, the short-term damage of bottling immature whisky may fatally impact your reputation in the longer term.

Some of Arran's early efforts were very poor indeed. But then something wonderful happened. Around seven years old, the malt went from ugly duck to beautiful swan, it took on a rich, creamy texture and the distillery started to bottle a wonderful malt that not only tasted different from anything else coming out of the islands, but it also tasted like nothing else on earth.

Isle of Arran 5-year-old 46% ABV

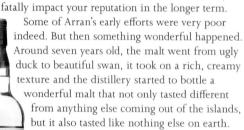

Young and zesty, with some sherbet, straw and flour on the nose, sweet zingy citrus notes on the palate. Overall this is a clean and fruity whisky, with cinnamon spice.

Isle of Arran Robert Burns 250th Anniversary Edition 43% ABV

Floral, with Parma violets and some perfume notes on the nose, and a very sweet taste, reminiscent of squidgy melon and tinned exotic fruits. Clean and refreshing on the palate.

Isle of Arran 10-year-old

46% ABV

Full and creamy in feel, with some butterscotch and spearmint on the nose, a big chunk of chewy barley, rich melon and sweet candy on the palate, and a gentle and rich medium-long finish.

Isle of Arran 12-year-old

43% ABV

A coming-of-age for Arran, but slightly disappointing because there is less of the buttery richness and more orange and mandarin notes, some ginger, barley and spice. It has a good finish though, which is almost liqueur-like.

Arran 8-year-old St Emilion Finish 50% ABV

This has a sugar-and-spice nose, with some rosehip syrup and fresh flowers but then blueberries, and earth roots, with almost putty-like notes. The taste is a strange mix of grape, green banana and plum and it all finishes well with some savoury but rich tones.

Arran 8-year-old Madeira Finish 50% ABV

Madeira finishes can go two ways – and there's a danger that the big dose of sweetness will be too much. Not here, though. This is an outstanding expression of Arran. The irresistible nose is of strawberry soda, sweet lime and exotic fruits, the palate is a refreshing mix of fruit Starburst, stewed apple and pear, and a topping of vanilla ice cream. Clean, summery, and guaranteed to have you reaching for another.

Arran Malt Fontallaro Finish 55% ABV

Another sweet, fruity delight, this time with mandarin notes joining the parade of citrus fruits on the nose, and a full and oily mix of tinned fruits in syrup on the palate. Not too much, though. This is not over-sweet and has a nice balance throughout.

Arran Moscatel Finish 55% ABV

The nose on this one is a little odd, with roses, old lady's perfume, lavender and toffee all popping up. Taste-wise it is equally intriguing: sugared almonds, apple peel, and some pepper combined with a certain oilyness make for a surprisingly agreeable overall package and a pleasant and warming peppery finish.

Arran 8-year-old Chianti Finish 55% ABV

Here you will find a powdery light and elusive nose, with traces of Parma violets, and a contrast on the palate, with savoury and rootsy notes and some olives and stewed plums. The finish is unassertive.

Arran 100 Proof 57% ABV

This is Arran in all its pomp and finery, and one of the distillery's very best bottlings. The 100 proof and a corresponding 50% ABV refers to the British proof system of measurement, equating to 57% ABV, and not the American one, which would be 100 proof and a corresponding 50% ABV. The British one relates to the spirit being able to ignite gunpowder.

Expect a grapey green apple nose from this, some chewy barley and highly attractive sweet lime on the palate and a creamy finish.

Arran Single Sherry Cask No. 96 / 1754
59.4% ABV

By rights I'm not sure a brutish cask such as this should work with a malt like Arran. It does though – and brilliantly so – a Little-and-Large combination with lots of kitchen pantry odours, Christmas cake mix and mouth-coating rain, red berry and orange fruits on the palate. It is surprisingly astringent, too, the oak sucking back the malt and making for a drying finish. A surprise all round.

AUCHENTOSHAN
www.auchentoshan.co.uk

When the distillers at Auchentoshan started making a beer last year, it may have been that they were completing a circle, for Auchentoshan is built on the site of an old monastery where the monks were almost certainly into brewing – another link between whisky and the Church.

Auchentoshan is something of an oddball. Once a wee rural distillery (the name means 'corner of the field') it is now part of the Glasgow urban sprawl, the city's motorways reaching out to it like gigantic tentacles. It can therefore lay claim to being Glasgow's distillery. It is unusual in other ways, too. It is a Lowland distillery but draws its water from Loch Katrine some six miles away in the Highlands. It triple distils, too, one of the few establishments to do so in Scotland. It could be that the distillery's time has come because owner Suntory has invested heavily in visitor and conference facilities, the brands got a makeover and a new 12-year-old was introduced a couple of years back. This is a beautifully maintained distillery.

Auchentoshan Select 40% ABV

This is Auchentoshan at its fruitiest and freshest, suggesting that it is young. Some citrus notes, some berries and a clean refreshing barley taste all reflect its young age.

Auchentoshan 12-year-old 40% ABV

Introduced two years ago to replace the standard 10-year-old expression, this is a big improvement, with the extra two years giving it a new dimension. Still quite light but with a nicely balanced fruit and malt taste and just enough spice to pep it up.

Auchentoshan 18-year-old 43% ABV

Not nearly as woody as you might expect, but the influence of sherry casks gives this a richness and spiciness and the slightly higher strength reflects a significant step up in quality.

Auchentoshan 21-year-old 43% ABV

Without a doubt this is the best of the range. You
would never know it was 21 years old, and the
wood certainly hasn't overwhelmed the Lowland
malt. This is zappy – all grapefruit and zesty citrus
with a touch of oak and spice. Very drinkable and
utterly irresistible, it is right up there with the very
best of the Lowlanders Rosebank and St Magdalene.

Auchentoshan Triple Wood 43% ABV

A rep for Auchentoshan was sat at a bar once when
the barman, a New Zealander, started explaining
the background of different single malts to an
American guest.

'The bar man was doing fine until he got to
Auchentoshan,' he recalls. 'The guest asked
him about Three Wood and he said "Oh that's a
special bottling for golf clubs. Auchentoshan do a
Seven Iron, too, and I think this summer they're
launching a Putter." I nearly fell off my seat.'

Three Wood actually refers to the Oloroso, Pedro
Ximénez and bourbon casks used in maturation.

AUCHROISK

The Singleton is a generic name that means
different things in different countries. Buy a
Singleton in Europe and the malt is Dufftown.
In the Far East it's Glen Ord. In the United States
it's Glendullan. But the original Singleton, and
the one that commanded the most loyalty,
was the Singleton of Auchroisk. When it
was launched in the 1980s anybody listed in
the phone book with the name Singleton
received a free miniature of it. It is now
bottled under its own name as a single
malt but you don't see it too often because
most of it goes into J&B blended whisky.

Auchroisk 10-year-old 43% ABV

Orange, lemon, a touch of smoke and a savoury
under-taste makes this more than just a 'me
too' Speyside malt. The light and refreshing
notes make it a good summer whisky.

BALBLAIR

www.balblair.com

Balblair is a Highland distillery sited on the Dornoch
Firth, very close to Glenmorangie. This is a region steeped
in ancient history, stone monuments and the remains of
dwellings from ancient races and tribes. Clach Biroach –
the sharp stone – is not exactly Stonehenge but it proves
that a race of people who predated the Picts by 2000 years
understood the moon and stars, because the stone is aligned
against the nearby hills and marks the summer and winter
solstice, giving guidance to the people
as to when to plant and harvest crops.
The Picts adopted the stone, too. Four
thousand years on it has been adopted as a
symbol of the distillery.

The whisky here is fresh, clean
and sweet but relatively unknown,
though owner Inver House has
recently rebranded the range.

Balblair 1997 43% ABV

This is like drinking an alcohol-soaked
tin of Del Monte tinned fruits. It is all
kicking off here in the
sweet fruit department –
mouth-coating vanilla, lime cordial, kumquat and
orange peel, with rich barley and a trace of sweet
pepper to finish.

Balblair 1990 43% ABV

More fruit here but this time from a
different bowl. The trademark vanilla is
there but also pineapple and green fruits
on the nose and a mix of tinned pears and
icing-sugar-like spices plus an oak finish.

Balblair 1989 43% ABV

As succinct as one of the truly great Tamla
Motown tracks, this is simple and to the
point, but quite perfect in its delivery and
execution. Lots of sweetness and vanilla
from the bourbon casks, sherbet fruits and
strawberry Starburst on the nose, then lots
of sweet barley, exotic fruits, sweet lime and
citrus candy. Not into dessert? Have one of
these instead.

Balblair 1975 46% ABV

The increased age of this bottling gives it considerably more depth than other expressions. There are all sorts of aromas coming from this one, including orange marmalade, vanilla, cherry, berries and some oak. the taste is wonderful – almost liqueur-like, with dark chocolate, cherry, orange liqueur, sweet fruits and oak.

BALVENIE

www.thebalvenie.com

Balvenie is the Jack Daniel's of Scotland – a big malt-producing distillery which has successfully managed to convince the world of whisky that it is a small, artisanal one, producing handcrafted small batch malts. It is in fact a Speyside whisky producer owned by William Grant and occupies the same site as sister distillery Glenfiddich. And it does seem small in comparison. It has its own floor maltings that produces a fraction of the malt it requires, and it sits next to Grant's traditional labour-intensive cooperage so you get a sense that it is from a different era. Balvenie is another distillery, like Aberlour, offering outstanding VIP tours. You will be shown around in small groups, often led by someone who has 30 years' experience in the industry. The tour is as thorough as it gets.

Balvenie DoubleWood 12-year-old
40% ABV

Matured first in American oak and then in sherry casks, this is the whisky equivalent to a show house. Everything is in its place, immaculate and well put together, but it is a house not a home, and does not exude the warmth you get from the great Balvenies. That said, there are some pleasant fruit notes and a sherry richness that make it an acceptable everyday dram.

Balvenie Signature 12-year-old 40% ABV

The nose here is complex, dry and woody, like pencil shavings, but with some satsuma and orange notes. On the palate there is fruit cake and orange fruits. The finish is medium, pleasant and fruity.

Balvenie Roasted Malt 14-year-old 47.1% ABV

Butter and praline on the nose, some dry woodiness and then a rich palate of burnt toffee, dark treacle, some spices and toasted oak. The finish is long and toasty.

Balvenie Single Barrel 15-year-old 47.8% ABV

This varies from barrel to barrel but the intention here is to pick the sweetest, most dessert-like Balvenie. There is lemon and lime and fruit Starburst in the mix, combined with sweet barley and zingy spice. The standard of these bottlings has been consistently high and this is another right up there with the very best of Speyside. This has fruit syrup dusted with icing sugar on a delicate oaky base. Enjoy.

Balvenie Rum Cask, 17-year-old 43% ABV

Yo, ho and indeed ho, rum is influential from the off here, with dark rum and raisin notes, some oak, plus all sort of exotic fruits thrown in for good measure, including apple and citrus fruits. Complex and curious, this is but another triumph from a very impressive distillery.

Balvenie 21-year-old PortWood Finish 40% ABV

An absolute masterpiece of a whisky, and arguably the finest port finish available. There are traces of oak that reflect its age, a good nuttiness and big lashings of fruit. This is wonderful in every respect.

Balvenie Vintage Cask No 6570, 1976 52.8% ABV

A cask-strength bottling, this is a very big whisky, with a fruit-cake mix, dense honey and hazelnuts on the nose. The texture is thick and mouth coating and on the palate, wood and spice battle against prune juice and melon, with the fruit just about going the distance. This is an altogether rather marvellous whisky experience.

THE BALVENIE DISTILLERY COMPANY

Dufftown, Banffshire AB55 4BB
www.thebalvenie.com

In theory, making single-malt whisky is the same process no matter which distillery you visit. But variety is the spice of life, and one of the great joys of Scotland's distilleries is the way the process is tweaked, making each different from the next. Sometimes the differences are considerable and brought into stark focus by their proximity to each other – never more so than on the site of William Grant's three distilleries at Dufftown in the beautiful setting of Speyside.

At one extreme is Glenfiddich, a funfair of a distillery with the warmest of welcomes for all the family to the home of the world's biggest single malt, multi-lingual tours by smart and smiling guides, an interactive and state-of-the-art guide to the malt's history and production, and support facilities

that include an outstanding café. It also has the most luxurious ladies' toilets in Scotland – take my word for it.

At the other end of the scale and buried deep in the heart of the site beyond the barrel sky-scrapers and the noisy and business-like cooperage is Kininvie, an anonymous malt factory that produces spirit targeted entirely at the company's blended whiskies. There are no visitor facilities here, little information to impart, and no whisky to try. Kininvie isn't bottled as a single malt, but it's the pumping heart of the worldwide William Grant success story.

And then there is Balvenie, a whisky-lover's whisky, and a distillery that is a whisky-lover's distillery. No whisky enthusiast should ever forget how much Glenfiddich has done for the single-malt category, or take for granted the qualities that have made it the world's number one malt. But let's be honest, it is to whisky fans what the Harry Potter franchise is to film fans: you respect its success, acknowledge its quality and if pushed, concede that it has played a leading role in bringing in thousands of new faces and introducing them to the endless possibilities the category has to offer. But for all of that, it doesn't excite the enthusiasts, does it?

Balvenie, on the other hand...

For a starter, it would seem to be pretty much everything Glenfiddich's not. It's a traditional, old-fashioned and slightly ramshackle distillery and is high-maintenance, demanding considerable hands-on love and care. It still malts a proportion of its barley in its floor maltings. Only a proportion, though.

WELL FANCY THAT...

Monkey Shoulder, which has successfully converted a new generation of drinkers to whisky, is made up of three malts – Glenfiddich, Balvenie and Kininvie.

ABOVE The traditional and charming Balvenie distillery in Banffshire is an essential destination for any whisky lover visiting Scotland.

Let's not get too carried away – for all of its rustic charm it is still one of Scotland's biggest distilleries. It is also capable of producing some of the most delicious of all Speyside malts, some rich and sherried, others intensely fruity and laced with vanilla, like tasting a bowl of alcoholic tinned fruit and ice cream in a glass.

Although acclaimed by whisky writers for some time, Balvenie has been relatively hard to find as a single malt until recent years, and it is only now just starting to enjoy a deserved place in the sun.

But any budding whisky enthusiast wanting to get under the surface of malt-whisky production should take time away from the glitz and glamour of Glenfiddich up the road, and set aside half a day to do the VIP tour at Balvenie. At the beginning you will be taken to the old distillery manager's office for an introduction and you will enjoy a vertical tasting through pretty much the entire Balvenie range at the end.

And in between you will spend most of your time as part of a small group in the company of a highly knowledgeable guide who has spent his life in distilleries. If you're lucky he will regale you with anecdotes stretching back four decades, providing a unique insight into whisky's past.

It is priceless stuff and it not only adds up to one of Scotland's very best tours, but ensures that once you've completed it, Balvenie will have carved a special place in the corner of your heart – one you'll return to again and again. Every time, in fact, you pour yourself one of the distillery's wonderfully distinctive whiskies.

KEY WHISKIES

Balvenie DoubleWood 12-year-old 40% ABV
Balvenie Signature 12-year-old 40% ABV
Balvenie Roasted Malt 14-year-old 47.1% ABV
Balvenie Single Barrel 15-year-old 47.8% ABV
Balvenie Rum Cask 17-year-old 43% ABV
Balvenie 21-year-old PortWood Finish 40% ABV
Balvenie Vintage Cask No 6570, 1976 52.8% ABV

ABOVE The team behind the production of Balvenie.

BELOW Four core malts from the Balvenie portfolio – DoubleWood, Signature, Single Barrel and PortWood.

BEN NEVIS

www.Bennevisdistillery.com

Fort William feels like it is the last outpost before you get to Scotland's Wild West. You can cut across country to Speyside from here, head up to the Isle of Skye and the far north, or take the scenic route along Loch Ness. But whichever way you go, it gets pretty bleak and desolate.

The Ben Nevis distillery, in the shadow of the mountain, is an odd one. Owned by Japanese company Nikka, it has a chequered stop-start history and it's not well known as a single malt. Much of the distillery's output goes into blends and it is one of the few whiskies that uses the same name for both a single malt and a blend. If you can source it though, it is a weighty, robust and complex malt.

Ben Nevis 10-year-old 46% ABV

A big and oily Highland whisky that tastes as rugged as the environment that produced it. Here you'll find attractive dark chocolate orange notes, chunky malt and exotic fruit.

BENRIACH

www.benriachdistillery.co.uk

It may be only a small distillery, but like Bruichladdich on Islay, BenRiach sure does make a hell of a lot of noise. BenRiach used to belong to Pernod Ricard and because the company didn't have an Islay malt it set about experimenting with peated whiskies here in the heart of Speyside. It did not release any of them but since a consortium fronted by Billy Walker took over, bottlings have come thick and fast, and some of the peated releases have been magnificent. The distillery is something of a dream for malt fans – small and farm-like, it has its own floor maltings that Walker has started using again, and the big fires have been back in action too, peating the barley. The whole place is in immaculate condition and all sorts of unusual casks are maturing in its warehouses, maintaining its history as a test distillery. Add to that a wide range of always interesting bottlings, and we are talking serious whisky heaven.

BenRiach Heart of Speyside 40% ABV

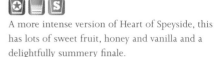

The distillery's entry-level malt is classic Speyside – lots of sweet fruit and vanilla on the nose, pineapple barley and citrus fruits on the palate, and an agreeably sweet medium-long finish, with a touch of spice.

BenRiach 12-year-old
43% ABV

A more intense version of Heart of Speyside, this has lots of sweet fruit, honey and vanilla and a delightfully summery finale.

BenRiach Curiositas 46% ABV

Not sure where the trend comes from, but the team at BenRiach seems to have a lot of fun coming up with Latin-derived names for their peated whiskies. This, at 10 years old, has been bottled at 46% and 40%, and if you can get the higher strength, do, because it's a growling monster of a malt. Acrid charcoal smoke and soot mix with lemon and cocoa on the nose, and on the palate there is a stunning mix of melon and peach on the one hand and diesel smoke and coal dust on the other. There is a slightly acerbic wet fire finale, but overall this is a corker.

BenRiach Dark Rum Finish 15-year-old 46% ABV

If you like your whisky sweet, this one's for you. On the nose it's all dairy chocolate, honey and caramel bar, on the palate it is rum-and-raisin ice cream, vanilla and exotic fruits. There is a touch of spice and oak coming through late on, but overall this is a one-trick pony.

BenRiach Madeira Finish
15-year-old 46% ABV

Another dessert whisky, this boasts melon, pear and vanilla on the nose. It tastes like chocolate lime bonbons at first, with some influence from the wood and a touch of pepper and spice late on. All in all, though, this is sweet and lingering.

BenRiach Pedro Ximénez
Finish 15-year-old 46% ABV

There is no doubt about the quality of the whisky-making on show here. The nose is quite restrained with some toffee apple and mince pie, but on the palate this is a mouth-coating and rounded malt, which elegantly unveils a procession of flavours including grapes, nuts, spice, some oak and marzipan. Sophisticated and seriously classy.

BenRiach Sauternes Finish
16-year-old 46% ABV

Another whisky with a curio for a nose, with stewed bamboo shoots, doughballs and a musty sweetness not selling the malt particularly well. But the taste is much better. It is a zippy whisky, with grape, berries and vanilla all vying for attention, some pluminess coming to the fore, and distinctive sweet pepper and oakiness towards the end. It is a bit of a tangy taste sensation, this one, with its rich orange syrup colour.

BenRiach Tawny Port Finish
15-year-old 46% ABV

What a weirdo! The nose is all over the place, with rosehip syrup, chestnut and dark coffee notes. The palate is something else again, with fresh clean soft fruit and barley and a charming and clean finish.

BenRiach Aromaticus Fumosus
12-year-old 46% ABV

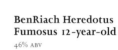

This is finished in a rum cask but of all this series it is the least affected by its finishing school. What we have here is a peaty monster, with lots of grungey smoke. The rum cask ageing gives it a nice sweet core, but really this one is for lovers of Islay.

BenRiach Heredotus
Fumosus 12-year-old
46% ABV

Well you cannot accuse the whisky makers here of playing safe. This is one of a number of peated whiskies finished in casks used to mature other drinks. It has the potential to taste like too many paints mixed together – a browny black mess. In fact, all four bottlings in the series work. This one is full, oily and peaty, with a soft yellow citrus and blackcurrant centre, like a smoky, liquid Turkish Delight. A long, smoky, fruit finish is exceptional.

BenRiach Importanticus Fumosus
12-year-old 46% ABV

Not quite reaching the dizzy heights of the last whisky, this one is still exceptional. The nose is a challenge, with brine and peat as well as vanilla, fruits and some floral notes, but the taste saves it, with port and lemon, grapefruit and smoke and a long finish.

BenRiach Maderensis Fumosus
13-year-old 46% ABV

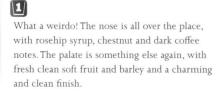

This one makes the claim that it is heavily peated and it is – so much so you can write your name in it, the whisky equivalent of a steam fair, but the 'spoonful of sugar helping the medicine go down' comes courtesy of soft pear and melon notes and a lemon flourish. The finish has all the classic BenRiach sootiness you could want.

BenRiach 16-year-old 40% ABV

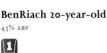

Back to classic Speyside malt, and the next step up from the 12-year-old. This offers a pretty straightforward journey from honey, vanilla and sweet fruit on the nose to a sweet and clean medium finish at the end, passing through apple crumble and vanilla ice cream. Late spices add depth, but this is about as far from the Fumosus bottlings as you can get.

BenRiach 20-year-old
43% ABV

This whisky is a bit shy on the nose, and you have to work hard to find grape, apple, pear and marzipan. The palate, though, is an elegant delight – a subtle and sophisticated marriage of fresh yellow fruits, vanilla, oak and honey. A slightly higher strength and the oak influence give it shape and a sense of purpose.

BenRiach Authenticus 21-year-old 46% ABV

The pick of the bunch from this great distillery, this Authenticus pulls off the rare feat of balancing rich fruit and intense peat and smoke. There is East Anglian Cromer crab and cured fried bacon on the nose, but also apples and peach. On the palate sweet tinned fruits and milk chocolate are wrapped in a wall of peat and smoke. Some astringency, an oaky influence, and a spicy bite lead to an oily, charcoal finish.

BenRiach 30-year-old 50% ABV

The age shows through significantly with this one, where the honey and citrus of younger bottlings are joined by dusty wood so that the overall effect is like a big oak-panelled office that has recently been polished. On the palate citrus and orange fruits give way to wood and spice. The finish is quite sharp but the orange fruits just about hold their own.

BENROMACH
www.benromach.com

Benromach lies close to Forres, to the north and west of the Speyside region. It is a small, rustic distillery now owned by independent bottlers Gordon & MacPhail, who bought it, invested heavily in it, and saved it from demolition. It was reopened at the turn of the century, which means that recent bottlings have contained spirit made since the reopening. Although classed as a Speyside distillery, the spirit produced here is varied but much of it has a distinctive peaty earthiness, and profile-wise it fits better with Highland distilleries such as Glen Garioch, Ardmore and Glencadam. Benromach was the first distillery to produce an organic single malt approved by the UK Soil Association. This meant stripping down all the equipment and cleaning it to an approved standard, and using organic oak barrels.

Benromach Traditional 40% ABV

The nose suggests youth, with grassy and viney notes, but also some smoke and oil. The palate is agricultural, cereally and earthy. When I was 16 we used to go out into the fields, chew barley husks and smoke roll-up cigarettes. This whisky reminds me of those lazy days in rural England.

Benromach 10-year-old 43 % ABV

Malty Ovaltine, sappy damp straw and flour doughballs on the nose, a savoury wave of peat and smoke on the palate at first, then a delicatessen smörgåsbord, with touches of cocoa and fruit. This 10-year-old is intriguing, challenging, different – and overall – worthwhile.

Benromach 21-year-old 43% ABV

Apple, pears and some prickly peat on the nose, with lime, guava and kiwi fruits on the palate. Overall this is sweet and clean, with some vanilla and marmalade notes. Later spice arrives and stays to the conclusion.

Benromach 25-year-old 43% ABV

Lemon and lime jelly bonbons to the fore on the nose, but backed by some spice, peat and oak. You just know from the aroma that this is going to be a treat. And it is – like a heavy metal band with three egotistical lead guitarists trying to outperform one other. Oak, spice and peat are all to the fore here, but it is the fruity rhythm section that holds it together and prevents a random mess. 'Freebird' in a glass.

Benromach Organic 43% ABV

This organic dram is softer and sweeter on the nose than the Traditional or the 10-year-old, but with oak and some toffee and mashed pear. With time there are hints of raspberry and blackberry sherbet. The palate is big and bold, with oak and blackcurrant squash, quickly followed by a wave of pepper so that overall it's a sweet and spicy treat. The finish is long, spicy and liqueur-like.

Benromach Organic Special Edition
43% ABV

Benromach goes to the seaside. A perfectly coastal nose that boasts salt, seaweed and shellfish in the mix. On the palate it's oily and fishy with plenty of peat. Soft and rounded, with little or no spice in evidence.

Benromach Origins
50% ABV

You have to reset your radar for this one. The nose is very odd and disconcerting, with some sulphur notes and then milk chocolate. It is intriguing more than off-putting, but you do wonder what it's going to taste like. The sulphur soon gives way on the palate, and you are left with a liqueur-like treacley malt, with sweet brown sugar in the mix.

Benromach Peat Smoke Batch 2 45% ABV

Lemon drizzled on grilled sole and barbecue wood chips on the nose, this is a charming mix of creamy lemon and feisty peat. All in all, a big fat and fishy peaty treat.

Benromach Sassicaia Wood Finish 45% ABV

The nose is a bowl of over-ripe fruit, resinous, with oak and peat vying for attention. On the palate there is chunky melon and the pleasant interplay between peat and oak remains. Yet another individual whisky from this intriguing distillery that has sailed down a little flavour creek all of its own making.

Benromach 1968 43% ABV

The aroma of this one is reminiscent of a church sacristy with incense, fresh flowers and polished oak. Maybe a Spanish one at that, where the priest likes fruit, because there's some Seville orange marmalade in the mix, too. And it is orange marmalade that dominates the palate, as the oaky tannins give the whisky a hint of astringency.

Benromach 1955 42.4% ABV

There are few distilleries that could age a cask for more than half a century and end up with a whisky as sublime as this. It comes from a cask that was laid down and cared for by a team of people many of whom are no longer with us, from the days before pop and rock music as we now know it had yet to be invented, before Elvis and The Beatles, before computers and moon landings. Mind-blowing. The whisky is delicate and subtle, with mandarin and tangerine fruits, together with traces of peat, oak and spice.

BLADNOCH

www.bladnoch.com

Bladnoch takes some getting to. It is tucked away in the southwest corner of Scotland, about as far from Edinburgh as Aberdeen is. But the Dumfries and Galloway region is well worth a visit, offering beauty and a more varied landscape than much of Scotland, its coastline rugged and Celtic. The distillery, in the renowned book town of Wigtown, is unlike any other in Scotland, coming over like a cross between a small cotton mill and a rural arts centre. Owner Raymond Armstrong is a free spirit and thinks outside the loop, too, so you can buy a range of malts from other distilleries at almost ridiculously low prices. In the warehouses there are casks from Scotland because the distillery rents out space at very favourable prices. Look hard enough and you will find several lesser-known malts maturing in top-quality casks. Some of them have been recasked and they are quietly maturing away now. Could these be the star names of the future?

Bladnoch 6-year-old Lightly Peated

58.5% ABV

You need to add water to prise open the nose but once you do you will find blackcurrant and sweet peat. The palate is multi-layered and sophisticated, with apple, pear and other soft fruits and then some peat smoke and spice. Towards the end, the peatiness still comes through but there are some savoury and earthy flavours, and even pine needles.

Bladnoch 15-year-old 40% ABV

The nose here is reminiscent of Irish whiskey, with delicate clean fresh fruit, especially pear. The palate is mostly apple and pear, but with some oak coming through and some marzipan-like apple pip. Overall this is a refreshing, fruity summery whisky, with the merest hint of spice and a pale lemony colour, with a greenish hue.

Bladnoch 16-year-old 46% ABV

This has an autumn garden of a nose, with some green fruit and delicate smoke. The taste is of tinned pears with ice cream, all wrapped in an earthy and peaty blanket. The finish mixes smoke and spice, liked tinned pears in ash. This is a good thing.

Bladnoch 18-year-old

55% ABV

Gooseberry, barley sugar, oak and grape on the nose, rich sweet fruit and sweet peppers on the palate, with oak and spice appearing towards the satisfying finale.

BLAIR ATHOL

www.malts.com

Blair Athol is a pristine, well-maintained Diageo distillery close to Pitlochry and this is an ideal base for a whisky lover with a less interested family. Blair Castle is only up the road, there is plenty to do and see, great walking and a handful of distilleries and whisky attractions within easy reach. This distillery is the spiritual home of Bell's and there is a small exhibition, though it pales alongside Aberfeldy (Dewar's World of Whisky) and Glenturret (the Famous Grouse Experience). All very pleasant but it is so well maintained that you can forget they make whisky here.

Blair Athol 12-year-old
Flora and Fauna 43% ABV

One of those single malts that feels as though it was intended for blending. It is a surprisingly full and fruity malt, rich and thick, with some pleasant fruit notes.

BOWMORE

www.bowmore.co.uk

Bowmore lies halfway up the island of Islay on the sea loch, Loch Indaal. It faces Bruichladdich, which is about three miles away across the loch. Each summer there is a swimming event across the loch but can I suggest you do not row it unless you've taken advice on tides. This comes from bitter experience. We did it for a charity event and became a little concerned when a fishing boat came alongside and the six lads on board told us that they were escorting us for our own safety. They were bluffing though, and were in fact a bunch of distillery workers led by Kevin Campbell out for a laugh. We did well for three-quarters of the crossing but then realised that Bowmore wasn't getting any closer. So as we struggled to row harder the boat crew passed along a flask and tried to curb their raucous laughter. Finally they took pity on us and towed us in. Kevin asked me to join the annual round-island row for charity after that, but I never did it, deciding I would be better off preserving what dignity I had left.

Bowmore 12-year-old 40% ABV

If Lagavulin, Ardbeg and Laphroaig are the Maiden, Metallica and Motorhead of whisky, Bowmore is its Bon Jovi. The whisky from here is peated but not so fully as the southern distilleries are – altogether a more mainstream taste. Bowmore can rock when it wants to, though, and this expression might be a lightweight but it is still a classic – a sort of 'Keep The Faith' or 'Livin' On a Prayer' for malt drinkers. A peaty and seaspray nose leads to a fruit and spice palate.

Bowmore 16-year-old Limited Edition Sherry Cask 53.8% ABV

This is very hard to find and I think there may have been a bourbon cask version of it, but if you can find it then this is a treat, a mix of big sherry notes and intense peat delivered at cask strength. Sherry and peat can be a disastrous mix but when it's right – BenRiach Authenticus, Compass Box Flaming Heart, Laphroaig 27-year-old, and this – it works for me.

Bowmore 18-year-old 43% ABV

I believe that everybody who discovers the joys of whisky will have an enlightenment moment, the point at which you cross the threshold from interest to passion. I remember vividly the first time I went to an evening soccer match at Filbert Street, Leicester some time around 1968. I remember walking up the steps to our seats and the pitch coming into view. I remember the sheer excitement and wonder of the bright green pitch illuminated by dazzling floodlights, the noise of the crowd, the sense of anticipation. It was the beginning of a lifelong love affair. The whisky equivalent to that for me was my first taste of Bowmore 17-year-old, with its distinctive Parma violet notes and weird fruit and peat mix. Sadly the 17-year-old has been discontinued and this isn't a patch on it, but the Parma violet notes are just about still there and there are enough positives to hold the attention, even if it is all a bit too slick and clean these days.

Bowmore 25-year-old 43% ABV

Surprisingly clean light and delicate for a whisky of such an age, most of the distinctive flavours here are sherry-influenced, with berry fruits and some citrus in the mix. It is all rich and chewy – a very pleasant experience.

Bowmore Legend 40% ABV

Vanilla, sweetness and as big a wave of peat and smoke as you will get from any Bowmore. There is also some lemon and orange in the mix.

BOWMORE DISTILLERY

School Street, Bowmore, Islay, Argyllshire PA43 7JS
www.bowmore.co.uk

There is no finer place to drink whisky than when sitting on the sea wall at the waterside Bowmore distillery.

In summer the view across Loch Indaal to Bruichladdich is a dynamic and colourful one. Gulls drift in the clear blue sky, sunlight flits off the waves in the loch, and bracing crisp wind caresses your face. You can smell fish and seaweed in the breeze. Sipping a strong, peated malt in such circumstances is an exhilarating and vital experience, and it is made all the more so by the knowledge that just below you some of Bowmore's most treasured whisky stocks are sleeping peacefully.

The wall is part of the town's sea defences but also forms the outer wall of warehouse one, the legendary warehouse that has stored some of the distillery's finest malts. While angry seas vent their frustration against the wall in winter, the casks rest in blissful tranquility on the other side. Part of the warehouse is below sea level and you can smell the salt in the air, see it encrusted on the walls alongside the black mould that is proof positive that the angels are taking their share. If you do not accept that malt matured in coastal distilleries is affected by its environment, then ten minutes here may just be enough to make you change your mind.

It was warehouse one that produced the malt used in the Bowmore Trilogy, which was completed last year with the launch of Gold Bowmore. The bourbon and oloroso casks were laid down under the stairs in 1964 and gave up their final treasures 45 years later.

'You never know exactly how

casks are going to mature and many are ready at 18 or 20 years,' says distillery manager Eddie McAffee. 'But we have areas of that warehouse where we know there is a chance of the casks doing something special. There was always something exceptional about those casks. Even in the early 1970s, when it was still the practice for distillery workers to take a dram from the cask to taste, the warehousemen would not let anyone touch those ones. And the whisky inside them just kept getting better and better over the years. It is quite the best malt I have ever tasted.'

Eddie joined the distillery in 1966, when the casks were just two years old and their contents were still too young to be called whisky. He is a week younger than whisky legend Jim McEwan and went to school with him. His appointment as Bowmore manager for a while meant that every distillery manager on Islay was born on the island. He is clearly proud of his career at the distillery and acutely aware of the responsibility of being its custodian. But he believes a combination of a good young team and an investment by the parent company in quality casks will ensure a bright future for the distillery.

'Bowmore always had good spirit but in the past there was an inconsistency in the wood,' he says. 'But about 15 years ago a decision was taken to put the spirit in to better wood and the 12-year-old coming through now is getting better and better. Some of us older ones will be leaving the distillery soon so it is important that we pass on our skills.'

If you take the VIP tour of the distillery you will be offered new-make spirit to try and a sample from one of the casks. The remains of the cask sample will be returned to where it came from, but the new make spirit will be thrown on the floor. 'We do it to ward off bad spirits' says Eddie. 'It's to ensure nothing bad happens to the casks.'

On the evidence of the 1964 casks it seems to be working. Without doubt more stunning casks will appear in the future. Sitting on the sea wall soaking in the splendour of the view is the perfect way to appreciate Bowmore.

KEY WHISKIES

Bowmore 12-year-old 40% ABV
Bowmore 16-year-old Limited Edition 53.8% ABV
Bowmore 18-year-old 43% ABV
Bowmore 25-year-old 43% ABV
Bowmore Legend 40% ABV

LEFT An old picture showing the jetty at Bowmore and the view across Loch Indaal, one of the most exhilarating places in the world to sip whisky and day dream.

BRORA

www.malts.com

The Brora distillery no longer exists, having been demolished some years ago. It was on the same site as Clynelish in the far northeast of Scotland, in the village of Brora. It is included here because in recent years Diageo has released a series of 30-year-olds and although they vary significantly from one to the next, they have been consistently excellent.

Brora 30-year-old 2008 Release 52.4% ABV

This whisky lies somewhere between the tobacconist, the florist and the fruit store, with big orange and soft fruit notes and waves of peat, with a rounded spice and peat finish.

Brora 30-year-old 2006 Release 55.7% ABV

This expression is defined by a drier, woodier nose than the 2008, with wood dust, spices, pepper, peat and peach to the fore on the palate and a long, peaty finish to distinguish it.

BRUICHLADDICH

www.bruichladdich.com

Reopened at the start of the millennium, Bruichladdich has proved itself a very 21st-century distillery ever since. Its smart packaging and distinctive sky-blue livery has made it instantly recognisable, and a large range of different and diverse bottlings, a good proportion of which are outstanding, has won it a loyal fan base across the world. The team at the distillery, which includes legendary Ileach whisky maker Jim McEwan, has never been slow to exploit a marketing opportunity or to promote itself, nor has it minded being Islay's maverick distillery and undoubtedly bizarre things have happened to it. Like the time the distillery was spied on by the Americans because they were worried that the distillery was actually making weapons of mass destruction rather than whisky.

Bruichladdich Laddie 2001 45% ABV

Here you will find stewed vegetables, noodles and beanshoots on the nose, and a highly unusual and provocative mix of sweet and savoury, peat, raw vegetables and delicate floral notes.

Yellow Submarine
46% ABV

A few years back, a fishing boat discovered a bright yellow mini submarine packed with high-tech surveillance equipment floating a few miles from Islay. It had 'MOD' on the side. At first the Ministry of Defence denied it was theirs and then implied that it had been stolen. For 10 days the submarine was left abandoned until eventually a Royal Navy mine hunter arrived at Islay and hastily removed the submarine. This whisky commemorates that occasion.

There is honey, soft melon and sweet plum on the nose, and on the palate there are green fruits and some clean malty, peppery notes. The finish is savoury with some pepper.

Bruichladdich 12-year-old 46% ABV

This has a very fresh and enticing nose, with vanilla, citrus and yellow fruits. The palate is a tin of exotic fruits in syrup, with vanilla ice cream for good measure. Soft and rounded, it is a very moreish whisky.

Bruichladdich 15-year-old Links
46% ABV

This is one of a series of releases named after classic golf courses. Not quite sure why. But this is very different from the last bottlings, with its earthy, wet grass and autumnal roots on the nose, and a challenging but not unpleasant mix of clean barley and grape on the one hand and some tannin and spice on the other. The finish is medium with wood, spice and some dryness.

Bruichladdich 3D The Peat Proposal
46% ABV

Cross the fields towards the coast for this one, where the nose is seaweed, barbecue and salt, the flavour comes from gooseberry and young green fruits, while barbecue and peat are on the palate, with a spicy finish.

Bruichladdich 10-year-old Oloroso Finish 46% ABV

Caramel, toffee apple, red berries and sweet fruits on the nose, soft tinned fruits, particularly melon, on the palate. This is all sweet and fruity, a rich golden brown colour with sugar dust coated on for good measure.

Bruichladdich Waves 46% ABV

On the nose it is like being in a fishing port when the tide has just gone out, with fish, seaweed and saltiness all in the mix. The taste of this one is a real delight – barley, rich plummy stewed fruit and smokiness all battling in the mix, with the sweetness winning through.

Bruichladdich 16-year-old Bourbon/Latour 46% ABV

Vanilla ice cream, soft melon and pineapple on both the nose and the palate, and apart from a touch of oak and some sweet pepper late on, that is it. This is simple, blemish-free, very palatable and sweet.

Bruichladdich Bourbon 16-year-old
46% ABV

Rich, sweet, honeyed and with vanilla on the nose, lots of bourbon candy and vanilla notes, masses of fruit and again, with a touch of spice very late on.

Bruichladdich Bourbon/Lafite 46% ABV

There are several other wine finishes in this range and to my mind not all of them work, but then again, I do struggle with some wine casks. This, though, is a beauty. There is a most welcoming butterscotch and vanilla on the nose, and a rich and full mouth-feel. On the palate the whisky changes direction sharply but thrillingly midway, with orange marmalade and dark chocolate cherry liqueurs at first and then a sharp astringency to give the malt structure. The finish is a mix of chilli, bitter cocoa and wood.

Bruichladdich 1998 Manzanilla 46% ABV

Flighty, wispy nose with tangerine and cocoa, but on the palate this is like a milk chocolate fruit-and-nut bar, with some honeycomb thrown in for good measure. The finish is short, soft and pleasant and leaves you wanting another sip.

Bruichladdich 18-year-old 46% ABV

The nose is grungey and rootsy, with stewed chestnuts reminiscent of Chinese food. The palate is savoury, with grape and clean barley, some chilli and a salt-and-pepper finale.

Bruichladdich 20-year-old 46% ABV

The nose is complex, with some mustiness and tannin kicking out at a flavour combination of fruit compote of date, dried apricot and tinned pear. The palate is clean and refreshing, with some peppermint, oak and traces of peat among candy fruits and fluffy apple. All very soft and subtle, with some sweet pepper and spice at the finish

Bruichladdich 35-year-old Legacy Series 40.7% ABV

A bit laid-back this, but cajole it and there are some good flavours here. Candy sweets and sweet nougat on the nose with sherbet-citrus lemon-and-lime combos on the palate. The whisky dries in the mouth before a peppery conclusion.

Bruichladdich Peat 46% ABV

Does it do what it says on the tin? Sure does, with beach barbecue and burnt fish on the nose; the most wonderful cheesecake palate of stewed sweet pear and apricot on top; a creaminess with wispy smoke in the middle and rugged biscuit base at the bottom. Total harmony.

Bruichladdich PC6 61% ABV

Port Charlotte is the little town close to the distillery and the whiskies using the name have come to mean intense and highly peated wonder-beasts. This has deep tar and strong coastal notes on the nose, and is oily and rich in the mouth, with the full range of peated flavours, from diesel engine to tarry rope, smoky barbecue and seaweed. It roars in like a lion but is a pussycat in the finish, with a long and gentle purring mix of fruit and smoke. Sublime.

Bruichladdich PC 7 60.5% ABV

Not quite what you might expect, with a damp wood and lighter peat attack, much more subtle and restrained than PC6. On the palate there is more tarry peat and growly smoke but the predominant flavour is stewed tinned strawberries. As with PC6 the finish is long and impressive, with fruit and smoke dancing around each other to marvellous effect.

Bruichladdich 21-year-old 46% ABV

The aromas here are rich, with dried fruits and some softer citrus candy notes. The taste is big, rich and bold, with the age of the cask adding gravitas while peach and apricot are enhanced by a polite level of pepper and oaky tannins. Astringent in the finish and a deep autumnal brown in colour, with a greenish hue.

Bruichladdich 40-year-old 40% ABV

This is light, clean and sherbety in flavour, with sweet pineapple on the nose and an assortment of exotic fruits on the palate. The finish here is mainly sweet and sugary but the drying tannins and spices stop it becoming too cloying.

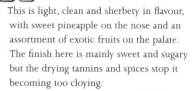

Bruichladdich Blacker Still 50.7% ABV

A dumper-truck-sized whisky this, with a tidal wave of prunes, sultanas and pantry spices on the nose. The taste is big and heavily sherried, with great spoonfuls of over-ripe fruit, a big oak hit and spices that dip in and out of the mix. It is like the sort of whisky the Japanese make and it is utterly seductive – a bit of a roller coaster, but by the finish it has slowed right down and delivers you safely and gently back to earth.

Bruichladdich Infinity 52.5% ABV

Here you will find an Islay coastline on the nose, with brine and seaweed. Tastewise it is like eating a tin of exotic fruits while smoking. Very sweet and smoky, this is yet another Bruichladdich that is all too easy to fall in love with.

Bruichladdich Octomore 63.5% ABV

This comes in stylish and very unusual packaging and is out-and-out Islay, with big waves of charry tar, barbecued bacon and grilled fish on the nose. A big oily whisky that needs water. Once unlocked it is a charmer – trout drizzled with lemon, playful phenols, a very sweet peat centre and a stunning finish.

Bruichladdich Redder Still

50.4% ABV

Remember dandelion and burdock fizzy drink? It is on the nose here, only with alcohol. Blackcurrant cordial and floral notes are also present. On the palate there are lots of intense candy fruits: lemon, lime and orange. A clean intense malt stormer this.

BUNNAHABHAIN

Kilchoman and Bruichladdich might be further west, but Bunnahabhain on Islay feels like Scotland's last malt outpost.

To reach it you drive pretty much to the end of the island and just before Port Askaig set off down a long sloping pathway. The distillery hugs the shore under the shelter of the cliffs, and the view out across the sound of Jura and towards the Paps is breathtaking. The distillery itself is a little weatherbeaten, the offices dated, but like a loveable scruffy mongrel, the friendliness of the welcome here makes up for the tatty appearance. Bunnahabhain promoted itself as the 'gentle taste of Islay' because its core brands have only a light peatiness. Within the distillery's warehouses, however, there are some stunning peated casks. And recently the distillery's owner has allowed some of the peated stock to be bottled, most notably Toiteach, meaning 'smoky'.

Bunnahabhain 12-year-old 40% ABV

Only lightly peated it may be, but this 12-year-old is a rugged, coastal malt, and there's salt and a nutty earthiness among some solid fruit notes. Late on a rapier-sharp barley spice hit welcomes in a hint of sherry trifle, adding sweetness to an otherwise savoury malt.

Bunnahabhain 16-year-old
Manzanilla Sherry Wood Finish 53.2% ABV

Limited to less than 3800 bottles, and bottled at cask strength, this is an example of the distillery letting some of its buried secrets out of the bag. Hopefully it will be suitably encouraged to do more. This is the distillery on a day out at the funfair, sacrificing discipline for big flavours – wine, cocoa, red fruits and brine.

Bunnahabhain 18-year-old 43% ABV

In some ways this is another departure for the distillery but something of a star nonetheless. This is rich and full, and there are some big fruity sherry notes, plenty of oak, and traces of citrus.

Bunnahabhain 25-year-old 43% ABV

The malt and salt you expect from a Bunnahabhain are in place but this is altogether a bigger, more lavish whisky than others in the portfolio. The fruits are rich and chewy, the oak influence is big and bold, and the core barley is delightfully full and sweet. Very good indeed, but whether I would trade three bottles of 18-year-old for one of these is a moot point.

Bunnahabhain Toiteach 46% ABV

Anything the other Islays can do... public proof that Bunnahabhain can do peat. The nose is quite shy though the peat's there, but on the palate there is a fascinating mix of sherry fruits, peat and pepper.

CAOL ILA

www.malts.com

Caol Ila is one of the fastest-growing of all Scottish malts and as people discover it, that growth might well accelerate. Despite the fact that it turns up in scores of independent bottlings, it has been something of an industry secret because a high proportion of it goes in to blends, particularly Johnnie Walker. Its emergence as a single malt in the early part of the millennium may have stemmed from an accounting mistake. Caol Ila is owned by Diageo and is one of two distilleries owned by the company on Islay. The other is Lagavulin, which was one of the original six Classic Malts that were sold together to pubs in a display plinth. A few years ago the company realised that they had miscounted their stock of Lagavulin and once the Classic Malt allocation had been dealt with there was not much left for everyone else. So Caol Ila stepped into the breach. Much of the output from the distillery going into blends is unpeated and occasionally appears as such in the form of special bottlings.

Caol Ila 12-year-old 43% ABV

One of the reasons Caol Ila is such a good blending malt is its oiliness, and this is oily – but in the nicest possible way. At this age it is a lively malt, with sooty peat and some citrus fruits as well as some burnt bacon rind all adding to a rich tapestry of flavours.

Caol Ila 18-year-old 43% ABV

There is a view that peat is at its liveliest and most expressive when it is young, and once it has been aged for more than 15 years it loses some of its effect. But the imperious Lagavulin 16-year-old provides a big counter argument to that view, the release of the Laphroaig 18-year-old last year kicks it into touch. This mix of age, sophistication and oily smoke show that a peated whisky never needs to be too old to rock and roll.

Caol Ila 25-year-old 59.4% ABV

An Islay classic – with the oils, seaspray, smokiness, barbecued trout with lemon, burnt bacon and oak all in evidence and all playing a role in making this one of the very best malts you can buy.

Caol Ila Cask Strength

61.6% ABV

The battering-ram strength of this one demands water but that in turn unlocks some sweet fruits among the oil, seaweed and smoke. They tell you on the bottle to mix this one-part whisky to two-parts water. Don't be tempted to do so. This should be three-parts whisky to one-part water, so that you are drinking it in the high 40s ABV and you are able to appreciate the full pepper and peat attack of the whisky. When it comes to this unmissable classic, you can take the responsible drinking theory too far, you know.

CARDHU

www.malts.com

Cardhu's main claim to fame in recent years has stemmed from an unholy row caused when its owners Diageo added malt from other distilleries to it and branded it as Cardhu Pure malt. That story has been regurgitated ad nauseam elsewhere so let's not bother with it here.

Cardhu is in Speyside and it makes the best 12-year-old malt in the region. The distillery is the symbolic home of Johnnie Walker and it has an amazing history. Originally founded by whisky smuggler John Cummings and his wife Helen at Cardow farm in 1811, it was run by first Helen, and then her daughter-in-law Elizabeth, who became famed for her whisky-making and marketing ability and who expanded the distillery into a major operation. This remains one of the few times that women have run whisky distilleries, made all the more amazing given that it happened during the Victorian era, when women tended to play a far more submissive role in society.

Elizabeth's son, John Fleetwood Cumming, took over from her and was the first person in Speyside to own a car. He was driving it back to the distillery when he encountered Willie, the distillery's handyman, coming the other way on his bike. Willie, who had imbibed a few drams of Cardhu and had never seen a car before didn't quite know how to avoid it, so steered first left, then right, before riding off the road altogether and ending up in a ditch.

Cumming stopped his car and rather than check to see that Willie was alright or to apologise for driving him off the road, unfairly berated him for being drunk instead: 'yer a disgrace to yersel', yer a disgrace to yer family and yer a disgrace to my distillery,' he said, to which Willie replied: 'It's a wonderful thing this whisky. It puts some of us in big flashy cars, and it puts others of us in the ditch.'

The number plate of that first car can still be seen in Speyside on a blue Mercedes. A few years ago the owner turned down an offer from London-based porn magazine and sex-show promoter Paul Raymond for the number plate. He had realised that if the number was attached to a car with the rivets in the right place the number SO110 would look very much like Soho.

Cardhu 12-year-old 40% ABV

Hard to find outside Spain, but this an absolute must for fans of Speyside malts. This is the whisky equivalent of the chocolate factory of Johnny Depp's Willy Wonka in the 2005 film *Charlie and the Chocolate Factory*: an oral mass of happy bright colours and an overdose of the sweetest, fruitiest most delectable flavours you could ever imagine.

Cardhu Special Cask Reserve

40% ABV

Fuller and with an added third dimension over the 12-year-old, this expression has some nuttiness among the malt. Vanilla and oak both make an appearance here in another very palatable malt.

CLYNELISH

The coastal road from Inverness to Wick has been described as Scotland's forgotten coastline, but it is home to a string of excellent distilleries, including Glen Ord, Glenmorangie, Balblair and Dalmore. Clynelish is here, too; a distillery that is sometimes not given the credit due to it partly because it's a relatively new distillery built in the 1960s and overshadowed by the ghost of Brora, which occupied the same site for a few years but was finally put down and replaced by Clynelish. Shame really, because it produces very good whisky. No doubt its day will come.

Clynelish 14-year-old 46% ABV

With green fruit and some melon on the nose, zippy lemon sherbet and fruits on the palate, this expression is given an extra dimension by its strength, together with traces of pepper and peat to round it all off.

Clynelish Distiller's Edition 46% ABV

This has been put into big sherry casks and it shows, with the Clynelish at the heart of the mix struggling to keep its head above the influence of the cask and just about succeeding. Arguably, Clynelish does not need this treatment, but it is worth trying because I suspect some people will fall in love with the unusual mix.

CRAGGANMORE

www.malts.com

Depending on how you define the region, well over half and up to two-thirds of Scotland's distilleries are in Speyside. We associate distilleries there with fruity, sweet, honeyed whiskies but it was not always that way. Before the Industrial Revolution, distilleries would have used peated fires to dry the barley. But Scotland's whisky has a long and close association with trains and as the railways spread into Scotland they brought with them cheaper commercial fuels such as coal. On the mainland peat was made redundant and its use only continued on the islands because trains do not generally travel through the sea.

Cragganmore was one of the first distilleries to build a railway siding into the heart of the distillery, ensuring an efficient method of bringing in supplies from the mainland and shipping out malt.

The distillery's whisky was chosen by Diageo to represent Speyside in its Classic Malts collection.

Cragganmore 12-year-old 40% ABV

If you are of the view that Speyside whiskies tend to be predictably fruity, easy drinking and unchallenging, then this should change your mind. It is a surprisingly complex malt, with heather and spring meadow on the nose, while on the palate you will find deep fruits, oak and wisps of smoke.

Cragganmore Distiller's Edition 43% ABV

This is Cragganmore finished in a port cask, and such a sympathetic extra maturation works well, giving the already-complex malt additional red berry and cherry flavours and an extra sweetness.

DALMORE

www.thedalmore.com

You know those signs that say 'you don't have to be mad to work here but it helps'? Well they were invented for places such as Dalmore.

The year 2010 marked the 50th anniversary of the distillery being part of the Whyte & Mackay stable. It is located in the northeast of Scotland on the Cromarty Firth and it's as wacky and kooky as a whisky distillery gets. While many distilleries are logically constructed and contain a balance of wash and spirits stills, Dalmore is anything but. Its stills come in a range of shapes and sizes and distilling is a hit-and-miss affair, with different runs coming off at different strengths. Making malt here is the whisky equivalent of flying a kite in a gale. It's a demanding process made more complicated by the unpredictable water supply. Water travels down to the distillery from a little reservoir but the sea water must travel over a wall. When the water levels fall below the level of the wall, the water stops flowing completely, so global warming, therefore, is not the distillery's friend.

Making spirit here is a tough ask, so you can excuse a certain degree of ordered chaos. The resulting spirit, though, is robust, fruity, and the starting point for some of the finest-tasting single-malt whisky in the Highlands.

The Dalmore 12-year-old 40% ABV

A burnt caramel, rich orange and mandarin taste and some oaky notes make this seem older than its 12 years, but it is a big, full malt with lots of flavour, most notably a sprinkling of cocoa dust and some charming spicy notes.

The Dalmore 15-year-old
40% ABV

The nose is reminiscent of a church on Easter Sunday morning, with polished oak, fresh flowers and a hint of sherry. On the palate there are bucket-loads of fruit, with tangerines and satsumas in the mix. Vanilla, cinnamon and some woody tannins all contribute to a big, bold and spicy whisky. Delicious.

The Dalmore 18-year-old 43% ABV

Released late in 2009, this is a step up for Whyte & Mackay because it's bottled at 43% ABV instead of the company's favoured 40% ABV. It has a bold and meaty nose with a trace of sulphur and then intense orange and red berry fruits. The palate is a big and busty mix of fruit, chewy malt, oak and spice – all rather wonderful. This is a heavyweight of a whisky.

The Dalmore Gran Reserva 40% ABV

A sort of Dalmore greatest hits package, with some creamy walnut-and-date cake dry fruit and tangy spice on the nose, and a sharper and fuller spiciness on the palate, with some pleasant fruit notes.

The Dalmore 40-year-old 40% ABV

Historically, whisky stills in the Highlands are small. While barley was in abundance in the Lowlands and big commercial malt stills were built to produce the volumes of malt needed to service the growing blended whisky market, in the Highlands barley is harder to grow so there was less of it to turn into whisky. Smaller stills also suited the illicit distillers because they could be transported or hidden from the gaugers more easily. But the more the spirit comes into contact with copper, the more fats, oils and flavour compounds are removed, creating lighter, more floral malts. Short, squat stills allow more to pass though into the final spirit, making for an oilier, meatier and fuller malt. Robust malt is better suited to standing up to the influence of the cask, and that's why you can get the likes of Dalmore and Macallan maturing 40, 50 and even 60 years and they still taste good. This has a shy nose at first, and you don't want to be adding water to a whisky this old, so work with it. Eventually there are some orangeade and lemonade notes. The taste is elegant, delicate and citrusy. Added to this there are some dark chocolate, nutmeg and plummy notes for good measure.

Dalmore 1263 King Alexander III 40% ABV

Legend has it that one of the Mackenzie clan saved King Alexander from death during a hunting trip and as a way of thanks he granted the Mackenzies the right to use the royal stag's head in its livery. When the Mackenzies became involved with The Dalmore, the stag's head emblem was taken up and now appears proudly on all bottles. In commemoration of this, whisky-maker Richard Paterson has married casks of The Dalmore of different ages and of different types. As a result the whisky has all sorts going on, with plums, red liquorice, vanilla and red berry fruits on the nose and a big hit of stewed fruits, oak, cherry and spice on the palate.

Dalmore 1974 45% ABV

If The Dalmore were The Beatles then this is Ringo Starr, the least charismatic and stylish of the bunch, but a Beatle all the same. Actually it's a bit of a weirdo, with milk chocolate, soft yellow fruit and some oak in the mix. The finish is long and fruity but it does not taste like it belongs in this company. Odd, but intriguing nevertheless.

Dalmore Sirius 45% ABV

Extremely limited 1951 malt, making it more than 50 years old. Unsurprisingly, it is rich and venerable, full of burnt oak, toffee and deep orange marmalade notes and surprisingly aggressive and robust for such an old boy. Pretty special but at about $15,000 a bottle it ought to be. I tasted my small sample during the second half of the thumping that New Zealand's All Blacks rugby team gave to France in Marseille – this was a super premium malt moment if there ever was one.

DALWHINNIE

www.malts.com

Arguably the funniest sign in the United Kingdom is the one that greets you at the tiny village of Dalwhinnie just off the A9 on the road up to Aviemore.

'Dalwhinnie – twinned with Las Vegas,' it says. In winter, when the snow is a metre deep and the icy gusts from the Cairngorms reach into your soul, the village is a remote and barren place and really far removed from the glitz and glamour of Las Vegas. Thankfully God invented whisky for such occasions, and the malt at Dalwhinnie is the ideal tonic for such extreme conditions. The distillery can no longer claim to be the highest in Scotland now that Braeval has reopened, but sipping a 15-year-old at altitude is a marvellous experience.

Dalwhinnie's sign is not the funniest I've ever seen. That honour goes to a house door near Cork in Ireland. It says: 'This is the back door. The front door is round the back.'

Dalwhinnie 15-year-old 43% ABV

Dalwhinnie does not come in a range of ages, but that is because its owners discovered long ago that its perfect age is 15. This is one of the truly great malts, traditionally part of the Classic Malts range. It is a rich, full and mouth-coating malt defined by two very different traits – intense honeyed sweetness wrapped around the fruit and malt centre, and a peaty earthy carpet to rest it all on. That combination – sweet and earthy – is what great Highland whiskies are about.

Dalwhinnie Distiller's Edition 43% ABV

Tasting this after the 15-year-old is like watching The Rolling Stones do 'Start Me Up' for an encore after they have ended their set with 'Jumpin' Jack Flash', 'Satisfaction' and 'Sympathy for The Devil'. It is perfectly fine, better than many other malts and you would not turn it down, but you have just pretty much experienced perfection so this cannot help but be a tad disappointing. That said, the oloroso influence does work well, and there is still plenty to enjoy, particularly for fans of the core whisky.

DEANSTON

www.burnstewartdistillers.com

It is cool to be green these days, so Deanston has an advantage over many of its competitors, one that its owner has hit upon and taken full advantage of.

The distillery is like no other. It lies beside a fast-flowing river and is a tall, foreboding eighteenth-century cotton mill of the dark satanic variety. It was founded by the great industrialist Richard Arkwright and it channels water from the river to drive a wheel and power its own electricity plant, so successfully that it provides light and heat for both the distillery and the local community.

The old Deanston sold very well in the United States a while back, but was not stunning. The new 12-year-old is an altogether richer, fruitier affair. It is like Speyside, with spicy, nutty notes and eco-friendly packaging.

Deanston 12-year-old 46.3% ABV

The new 12-year-old Deanston is a vast improvement on the original standard Deanston, with a softer and more rounded fruity palate and a longer finish.

DUFFTOWN

www.malts.com

Clever people, the malt marketing folk at Diageo. Having backed down in the row over Cardhu a few years ago, they came up with another way of spreading their limited stocks further afield by encouraging people to drink malts they might not have otherwise chosen. A few years back the Singleton of Auchroisk built up a considerable following before it was eventually withdrawn. Now the Singleton is back – but what you are drinking depends on where you drink it. In Asia the malt in the bottle is a sherried version of Glen Ord. In America it's Glendullan, while in Europe it is Dufftown you will encounter.

It is a clever ruse because many customers are drawn to the words The Singleton, which appear on the label in bold capitals. The distillery name is in light italics. In many whisky shops you will find it under S for Singleton, not D for Dufftown or G for Glendullan. The whole package is cleverly designed to encourage people who would never buy a Glendullan or Dufftown to do so by purchasing a Singleton.

Is this a con, and does it matter? Not really, especially if the customer ends up with a quality bottle of malt. And actually, you cannot help but admire Diageo's chutzpah.

Singleton of Dufftown 40% ABV

This is a bit like the quiet bloke who comes down to the pub to watch football with the lads. All perfectly pleasant and harmless but you would not really miss him if he was not there. This is a workman-like Speysider with nothing worthy of criticism but nothing to get excited about. It is included here, though, because it is an easy-drinking entry-level malt – a tame pony to teach novices how to sit in the saddle.

EDRADOUR
www.edradour.co.uk

Few distilleries command as much love and devotion as Edradour. This is partly due to the fact that is very small and perfectly formed. Production at the distillery is just 90,000 litres a year, a drop in the whisky ocean compared to Glenfiddich and Glenlivet, both of which can produce 10 million litres of spirit annually. The whole production process is housed in one small outbuilding though the site has grown in recent years with the addition of a bottling hall, a visitor centre and shop. Until recently Edradour was Scotland's smallest distillery though now Kilchoman and the new Isle of Lewis distillery match it.

Tour bus drivers love this pretty distillery, because it is an easy drive from Glasgow and Edinburgh and a good stopping point on the way to the Highlands.

Edradour 40% ABV

An attractive mix of lemon and lime and gentle spearmint on the nose, soft fruits, honey, vanilla on the palate with a lingering and pleasant finish and a hint of peat.

FETTERCAIRN

Fettercairn is a rustic Highland distillery that has not had the best press in the past. This is a little unfair. One celebrated whisky writer was so critical of the malt from here that he has not been invited back. Which in turn means he has never updated or reassessed his criticism. Perhaps he should. About 14 years ago the distillery replaced the old stainless steel condensers with copper ones, and over the last couple of years the 12-year-old has been made with spirit from after the change. Some of the whisky in casks at the distillery suggests that Fettercairn has a lot to offer as a single malt, including some sparkling new packaging and a new range of four malts. The malt has adopted a unicorn emblem as a reference to the Ramsays, distillery owners who were noted for their philanthropist tendencies. Fettercairn was sold on to the Gladstone family and Liberal Prime Minister William's familiarity with whisky led to legislative reforms that abolished the malt tax, allowing the sale of whisky in bottles to the public, and tax laws, so distillers were no longer taxed on the 'angel's share', the two per cent of spirit that evaporates during maturation.

There is plenty to thank this distillery for, so the Fettercairn fight-back starts here.

Fettercairn 24-year-old
44.6% ABV

An awkward malt, which initially hides behind a slightly rubbery, sulphury nose but in time gives way to a taste of tangerine and grapefruit, some cocoa and some prickly spices. It is like prising conversation out of a sulky schoolboy and finding he is remarkably bright and interesting – just lacking in confidence. A strange but ultimately worthwhile experience.

Fettercairn 30-year-old 43.3% ABV

The best of these three old releases is a delight: surprisingly young-tasting, with zest of red apple and soft pear, some melon and orange fruit and eventually a subtle wave of spice. The age only starts to make itself known very late on. In the finish there is blackcurrant sherbet. Fettercairn – poor? Oh no.

Fettercairn 40-year-old 40% ABV

Classic old Highland whisky without a blemish. Early on it is surprisingly soft and gentle, with grapefruit and lemon and some savoury notes, but it builds with oak and spice adding to the body and gives way to raspberry and glacé cherry. The finish is long but gentle, with spice and oak.

GLENCADAM

www.angusdundee.co.uk

The traditional view of a distillery setting up close to a primary water source is turned on its head by Glencadam. The Highland distillery, close to Brechin on Scotland's coast, pipes water 30 miles to meet its distilling needs but the malt made here does have a distinctive creaminess. Glencadam is a notably creamy malt, using unpeated malt.

Glencadam 10-year-old 46% ABV

Sweet strawberries with ice cream on the nose, pleasant and easy malt and spice on the mouth, with some raspberries, strawberries and redcurrants. The spiciness remains into the finish.

Glencadam 15-year-old
46% ABV

Arguably the definitive Glencadam bottling, here the extra age giving the malt a fuller and richer mouth-feel. The berry notes are still prevalent on the nose, but on the palate the oak makes its presence felt and with time tannins and spices battle against the berry fruits, leaving a long oaky and spicy finish.

Glencadam 25-year-old 46% ABV

A rare and unusual bottling of Glencadam because there are some distinctive sherry influences. Indeed, this is a classic big Christmas pudding of a whisky, with sherry-soaked raisins and mulled wine on the nose, leather, raisins, plummy fruits and spices on the palate, with tasty strawberries and ice cream in the fruity finish.

GLENDRONACH

www.glendronachdistillery.com

Talk to people with long memories in and around Huntly, and they'll talk of GlenDronach as a big, proud and dark sherried whisky, a million miles away from the somewhat anaemic 12-year-old that kept the brand's name alive. For many years the distillery's owners Allied Domecq did not seem to know what to do with it, and for years it seemed to drift, unloved and uncared for. When Allied was broken up, Teacher's and Ardmore went to Beam while GlenDronach, a key component in the blend, went to Pernod Ricard. It felt like a divorce, and the distillery's wretchedness was summed up on the quaint maltings floor, where cardboard figures had been placed to show visitors what a working maltings was like. But a couple of years ago the team behind BenRiach got its hands on the distillery and wasted no time in restoring the distillery to its former glory. A new range of standard bottlings and a number of special releases – yes, big dark sherried ones – has helped put GlenDronach well and truly back on the distillery map.

GlenDronach 12-year-old 40% ABV

Some mint toffee on the nose, with sherry, berries and citrus fruit. The taste is reminiscent of blackcurrant and cranberry, there is some pepper, and an earthy undercarpet so that the overall effect is not too sweet. The finish is savoury with some peat.

GlenDronach 15-year-old 2009 RELEASE 46% ABV

The new version of the 15-year-old is deep brown, leaving the drinker in no doubt what is coming next. There are distinctive wisps of sulphur on the nose but this doesn't detract from a grandiose and complex nose that includes sherry, floral notes and chicory coffee. The taste is also intense and challenging, with sweet fruit cake at first, then a wave of chilli and paprika, and finally some woodiness, astringency and plummy smoke. The finish is about three Ps – plums, peat and pepper. Wonderful.

GlenDronach 18-year-old
2009 RELEASE 46% ABV

Not for the faint-hearted this. You want big old-fashioned sherry cask malt? You've got it. There are earthy and rootsy aromas with some distinctive sulphur on the nose, but don't be too put off – the taste is all about plum, stewed fruits and raisins. There is some astringency from the wood late on, some peat and menthol and some spices in the finish.

GlenDronach 33-year-old 40% ABV

Here there is Kahlua and dark coffee on the nose, with raisins and mince pie filling. The taste at first is fruity, with peach in the mix, then tannins and spices come through. It is all ordered and rounded, with a long, soft finish.

GlenDronach Cask No 483 1971
Single cask batch 1 49.4% ABV

A classic example of the sort of weighty whisky we might come to expect from GlenDronach, with rich sherry, spice and earthy peat notes on the nose, blood orange, dark chocolate, espresso coffee and woody tannins. This is to malt whisky what Batista is to world wrestling.

GlenDronach Cask No 4424
1988 Gaja Barolo 54.3% ABV

Thinner and less sweet than the previous cask, this Gaja Barolo is much spicier, with orange marmalade some lemon and clear honey in the flavour mix.

GLEN ELGIN
www.malts.com

Several towns lay claim to being the 'capital' of Speyside but Elgin's claim is as good as any. Elgin is, according to its website, Scotland's smallest city and its friendliest, and has a fascinating history based around its cathedral. But it also lies close to several distilleries and is home to outstanding independent bottling company Gordon & MacPhail. The company's large shop in the town is well worth a visit if you are in the area, especially if you are looking for something different, whisky-wise. Glen Elgin distillery lies in a small village on a road into the town and has been long associated with the White Horse blend. It has a substantial following as a single malt, too, and its reputation as a rich, fully flavoured and honeyed malt has been enhanced by some special bottlings in recent years, including a cask strength bottling as part of Diageo's Manager's Choice series in 2009.

Glen Elgin 12-year-old 43% ABV

This is an example of classic Speyside at its best. You don't see it very often, but if you like clean, sweet, malty and plummy whiskies then you need to seek this one out. An unsung hero.

Glen Elgin 16-year-old 58.5% ABV

A lovely rich nose with a touch of sherry, blackberries and blueberries. The taste is big, sherried and intense with some stewed fruits, oak, spice and aniseed.

THE GLENDRONACH DISTILLERY

Forgue by Huntly, Aberdeenshire AB5 4DB
www.glendronachdistillery.co.uk

Visit the GlenDronach these days and you will quickly pick up on the positive sense of purpose. New facilities, fresh paint, happy staff and some great malts all contribute to the feel-good factor.

But it was not always this way. A few years ago a brooding black cloud of gloom hung over the stills and warehouses. It was a moribund, directionless distillery with its heart ripped out, the victim in a messy divorce when parent company Allied Domecq was broken up. Long a key malt in the make-up of Teacher's, it was split from the blend and sister distillery Ardmore when they passed to Beam Global and GlenDronach went to Pernod Ricard, a company that already had more than enough distilleries in the region. Unloved and uncared for, it started to look shabby and weather-worn, its visitor centre felt dated and irrelevant and it was all but ignored by the whisky-loving public.

Perhaps the most potent symbolism of all, though, came courtesy of a whisky bottle that is framed in the old wood-panelled boardroom.

The whisky was bonded in 1884 and bottled in 1913 and was one of three purchased by three friends. When war was declared the men signed up and decided to hold their whisky for when they returned from a victorious war a few months later.

It never happened. Two of the friends were killed and the owner of this bottle put it away in a cupboard, unopened. In the 1960s, when the owner of the bottle died, his family rediscovered it and handed it back to the distillery.

Did that old soldier ever look at the bottle again, or was the memory too painful? Did he often hold it and think about his fallen friends? Did he consider opening it in their memory but found that he couldn't bring himself to take out the cork? In 2007 that bottle epitomised GlenDronach itself; a wretched story at the heart of a wretched distillery.

Several years on, GlenDronach is going places. Now owned by the same team that owns BenRiach, it has taken on a new lease of life. New signs have been put up, everything has been painted and the old 1960s-style visitor centre and offices have been completely upgraded. Not, it has to be said, without a struggle.

'One of our major projects last year was to develop a brand-new visitor centre and shop,' says Kerry White. 'This we achieved but the distillery was badly flooded shortly after completion and much of the work was ruined so we had to restore it all over again. But we managed to do this for the tourist season in 2010.'

A little woods at the back of the distillery dedicated to the Gordon Highlanders is also being restored to its former glory to give ex-soldiers a memorial their families can be proud of, and the run-down brewers' house has been refurbished to provide accommodation for visitors to the site.

Best of all, though, is the flow of new and exciting bottlings. Managing director Billy Walker is determined to restore GlenDronach's reputation as a distillery producing the finest sherried whiskies and to this end, 2010 alone saw the launch of a 21-year-old, a 31-year-old, and a number of special finishes.

LEFT Under the distillery's new owners GlenDronach is returning to its rich sherried roots. This is a vintage bottling.

RIGHT Whisky supremo Billy Walker inspects a glass of malt from his new distillery. Walker has already restored the fortunes of BenRiach.

ABOVE RIGHT The pretty distillery at GlenDronach, now being restored to its full glory.

KEY WHISKIES

GlenDronach 12 year-old 40% ABV
GlenDronach 15-year-old 46% ABV
GlenDronach 18-year-old 46% ABV
GlenDronach 33-year-old 40% ABV
GlenDronach Cask No 483 1971 49.4% ABV
GlenDronach Cask No 4424 1988 Gaja Barolo 54.3% ABV

WELL FANCY THAT...

One of the buildings that the new owners of
GlenDronach have restored is the two-storey warehouse
– one of the few of its kind in Scotland. The warehouse
has been part of the traditional maturation process at
the distillery and while two storeys in the Highlands
isn't quite the same thing as the multi-storeyed
warehouse in Kentucky, lovers of GlenDronach believe
that the two floors do affect the way the spirit matures.

GLENFARCLAS
www.glenfarclas.co.uk

Glenfarclas is to whisky what Bentley is to cars – excellently made, to the highest standards, in the traditional manner. You do not mess with classic style, so there are no gimmicky finishes from the distillery, no malt alchemy in its labs. Glenfarclas is one of the last family firms still making whisky in Scotland and it survives by simply being the best at what it does. And what it does is to produce big, bold fruity sherry-influenced Speyside malts.

Much of the day-to-day management is handled by father-and-son team John and George Grant, with George very much in the front line. After several years of travelling the world promoting his malts, George may well be cutting back on the globetrotting. It is not all it is cracked up to be, he says, especially when you are detained at immigration in the Far East twice – once for carrying a plastic bag full of white powder, which turned out to be barley flour, and once for carrying a suspicious-looking lump of peat.

Glenfarclas 10-year-old 40% ABV

There is some orange and lemon on the nose here, followed by Christmas cake, rich malt, some orange notes and a warm and delightful finish.

Glenfarclas 105 60% ABV

A weighty, intense classic malt, and the epitome of clean and crisp sherried whisky.

Clearly you need some added water, and this releases raisin, date and plum flavours, sweet spicy orange notes and some delicious crystallised maltiness at the end.

Glenfarclas 12-year-old 43% ABV

A rich and full sherry influence here, with stewed plums and apricots, honey, cinnamon and nutmeg. This is a perfect winter warmer.

Glenfarclas 15-year-old 46% ABV

The extra strength and age adds another dimension to the malt here. Tangerine, marzipan and red berries complement the sherry trifle and Christmas cake mix. Some oak adds tannin and spice, to give the overall flavour balance and shape.

Glenfarclas 21-year-old
43% ABV

A slight departure from what has gone before, the intensity of previous bottling is replaced by a candy-ish flavour, less sherried and perhaps with more vanilla and yellow fruit notes.

Glenfarclas 25-year-old 43% ABV

Glenfarclas responds well to old age. I was given a small bottle of whisky from the year of my birth by John Grant at a Speyside festival. From 1961, 44 years old, it was sublime, one of the best whiskies I've ever had – toasty, spicy and fruity. I am saving my bottle for when England next win the soccer World Cup: a heady and happy day for sure.

Glenfarclas 30-year-old 43% ABV

The nose is surprisingly soft and rounded with some marmalade and oak notes. The oak is noticeable in the taste, too, with crystal barley, pepper and earthiness.

Glenfarclas 40-year-old 43% ABV

A big wave of pink grapefruit, burnt toast with chunky lime marmalade on the nose, and rich orange marmalade, dark orange chocolate and Turkish Delight on the palate. A very lucid flavour for one so old.

Glenfarclas Family Cask

Glenfarclas might not be experimenting with weird casks and strange finishes, but that does not mean it is not capable of being a pioneer in the world of malt.

The Family Cask range has no parallel in whisky – 43 single-cask bottlings covering 43 consecutive years from 1952 to 1994. This is the equivalent to the long-awaited complete archive set of recordings that Neil Young has been promising and which has been appearing in dribs and drabs – a chance to plot the complete history of a distillery. Unsurprisingly, over such a lengthy period of time, there is huge variety on display.

Among the casks are:

1952 ED2 Cask 2115 46.5% ABV
Nose: Herb garden, plums, raisins.
Palate: Sweet, salt and spice. Tannins.

1954 Cask 444 52.6% ABV
Nose: Chestnut, oak, root vegetables.
Palate: Cocoa, dark chocolate, bitter oak.

1957 Release III Cask 2 46.2% ABV
Nose: Stewed fruits, date, oak, dark treacle, nutty.
Palate: Intense marmalade, menthol.

1959 Release III Cask 3227 50.9% ABV
Nose: Mahogany polished office.
Palate: Dark chocolate, treacle toffee.

1962 Cask 2647 52.0% ABV
Nose: Dry sherry. Cocoa, dark chocolate orange and limes.
Palate: Rum-and-raisin chocolate, mint, sherry, cocoa, oak.

1969 Cask 3188 55.6% ABV
Nose: Spent match sulphur, toasty, candy, shrimps.
Palate: Sweet, metallic. Raisin, dark cherry, menthol.

1972 Cask 3546 51.1% ABV
Nose: Dusty and musty, smoky, resinous.
Palate: Mint. Sharp spices. Wood. Hot.

1975 Cask 5038 51.4% ABV
Nose: Blood orange, hot mince pie filling.
Palate: Orange fruits, liquorice, soft toffee.

1976 Cask 3111 49.4% ABV
Nose: Ginger biscuit. Date. Cake mix. European-style fruit.
Palate: Sweet, full and fruity. Dates and late pepper.

1978 Cask 587 50.3% ABV
Nose: Linseed oil, nuts, mandarin.
Palate: Rapier-sharp spice, bitter fruit, liqueur-like.

1979 Cask 146 52.8% ABV
Nose: Sweet, honey and sherbet.
Palate: Honey and lemon, smooth and rounded.

1981 Cask 29 52.4% ABV
Nose: Chinese spices, tingling.
Palate: Plum fruit, menthol.

1988 Cask 7033 56.3% ABV
Nose: Odd, herbal, oil paints.
Palate: Soft fruit, pear, liquorice

1989 Cask 11721 60.0% ABV
Nose: Powerful, rich orange, fruit cake, sulphur.
Palate: Rich, sweet, rounded and very fruity.

1991 Cask 5623 57.9% ABV
Nose: Almost European liqueur-like fruit, sweet.
Palate: Rich, mandarin orange, creamy, oak.

1993 Cask 11 58.9% ABV
Nose: metallic, sulphur.
Palate: sherry, sharp astringent oak, dark, intense finish.

ABOVE John and George Grant show off all 43 expressions of the Glenfarclas Family Cask collection, covering the years 1952 to 1994.

GLENFIDDICH
www.glenfiddich.com

Lovers of whisky have a great deal to thank William Grant and its number one malt Glenfiddich for. Familiarity breeds contempt and it is understandable that experienced malt lovers might feel the overwhelming urge to move swiftly on but please don't. Pause for a minute and pay tribute to the malt that kicked it all off.

Talk to family member Peter Gordon about how William Grant & Sons has consistently sensed the way the wind is blowing and continually got it right when making big make-or-break decisions and he'll modestly tell you it's been through luck rather than design.

I don't buy that. It's a bit like the 'lucky' fisherman who keeps catching the best fish because by chance he's always in the right place at the right time. And from the 1960s when the company set about putting single malt into the spotlight right up to the launch of cool and trendy Monkey Shoulder, William Grant has been instrumental in the development of modern-day malt whisky.

It's hard to believe now, but 50 years ago there was no real single-malt market. Single malts were sold in Scotland and close to the distilleries where they were produced, but their influence was minimal. But William Grant & Sons had a problem. To make its blended whiskies it relied on grain whisky from its rivals. So what would happen if the suppliers turned off the tap?

The company made two huge decisions in the early 1960s – it built its own grain distillery at Girvan, and it bottled Glenfiddich as a single malt whisky. It had already come up with the distinctive three-sided bottle. To help explain the world of whisky the company also opened up the very first visitor centre.

The rest, as they say, is history. But Glenfiddich was no pace setter, leading from the front then falling away to let bigger and stronger competitors get out front. Glenfiddich has held on to the top spot in the single-malt market ever since. If you can't get excited by the standard 12-year-old then the distillery offers all sorts of more esoteric releases, culminating with a remarkably delicate 50-year-old in 2009.

Glenfiddich 12-year-old 40% ABV

One of the things that the whisky industry rarely talks about is the way malt whisky changes over time. Better cask management and a greater understanding of production and maturation on the one hand, better yielding but arguably blander and more homogenous barley strains on the other, mean that the spirit in the bottle today will not be the same as it was 20 years ago. Booms and busts affect whisky, too. There will be times when a standard 12-year-old will contain more rare and aged whisky than at others, for instance, depending on malt supply and demand.

There is no doubting that this has changed in recent years and is now a better whisky than it used to be.

This well-made but unchallenging entry-level malt is fresh and fruity, with vanilla malts.

Glenfiddich 15-year-old Solera Reserve
40% ABV

Unfortunately, this whisky will always remind me of a prospective candidate for the British Conservative party who joined a group of whisky writers for a short leg of a sponsored walk from Glenfiddich to the Craigellachie Hotel in Speyside. I got stuck with the Tory, an Englishman who bemoaned the fact that he had been banished not just to the north, but to Scotland. As I walked with him he argued that we should not be raising money for Africa any more because everyone was so rich there now they all had sunstrips on their cars thanking the British for their new wealth and he thought that whisky would be a more viable product if the Scots just added flavourings to industrial alcohol.

A fine example of Speyside malt, this has a vanilla creaminess plus soft fruits, sweet barley and a touch of oak. It is beautifully crafted.

Glenfiddich 18-year-old 40% ABV

A full fruit bowl of over-ripe squelchy fruit, with plums, raisins, apricots and grapes all in the mix, and some toasty oaky notes make this a sophisticated and stylish drinking treat.

Glenfiddich 21-year-old 40% ABV

Many of my favourite whiskies are aged 17 or 18 years, but for some reason Glenfiddich does not seem to fully hit its stride until this age. This would probably be my pick of the entire core range, though there are some beauties in the rarer and older vintage range.

Boiled sweets, new office and lemon cleaner or polish on the nose, lemon and honey on the palate, plus sweet malt, oak and a touch of menthol. The finish is quite zingy, with lemon and grapefruit in evidence.

Glenfiddich 1983 Cask 10888 53.4% ABV

Big sherry notes on the nose, with Christmas cake, sweet spices and some nutty notes. The taste has lots of big fruit, mince pies, sweet pepper and oak, and there's a liquorice and hickory twist, too.

Glenfiddich 1975 Cask 15354 47.3% ABV

The aromas here are soft and welcoming, with vanilla, honey and boiled candy fruits. The taste is diverse and complex, with spearmint and chilli mixed among soft yellow fruits. The finish is balanced between fruit, oak, spice and honey.

Glenfiddich Vintage Reserve 1975 Cask 287 51.1% ABV

An odd rootsy and earthy nose here, but the taste is much better – it is a full, oily malt with grapes, prunes, pear and soft peach. Gentle spices arrive towards the end.

Glenfiddich Rare Collection 40-year-old

43.6% ABV

This whisky does not give up its treasures lightly, and you have to chase the nose a bit. But it is a surprisingly soft and subtle whisky, with some lovely yellow fruit flavours, as well as honey and vanilla. There are few signs of age, no negative oak or spice notes, and a lingering and lovely finish. Quite outstanding.

Glenfiddich 50-year-old 46.1% ABV

Should a whisky that retails at $15,000 a bottle and which has pretty much all gone anyway, be included in a book like this? That's a big debate and one to be held over a dram or two, though probably not with this particular whisky.

Ok, I'm there – yes it should. Once this has gone, it will have gone forever, and there should be a record of it somewhere. William Grant & Son invited people from all over the world to the launch of this. One bottle arrived accompanied by a piper, then guests were invited to swoon over it. We had songs and a dramatic and quite brilliant recital of *Ode To a Haggis* by Glenfiddich public relations manager Libby Lafferty. All this was in honour of one whisky.

It could have been a disaster, an overdose of sentimentality resulting in a massive anti-climax. But it wasn't, simply because this whisky is stunning. At 50 years old, it is imbued with spritely sweet grapefruit, honey and citrus. Amazingly, you can trace the thread of this malt all the way forwards to the petulant teenager that is Monkey Shoulder. It is like watching the scene in Martin Scorsese's *Shine A Light* when Mick Jagger upstages Jack White, the master showing the pupil how it should be done.

Is whisky ever worth $500 a shot? Of course not. Is this a blemish-free, perfectly matured piece of art in a glass and history in a bottle? Very much so. This was distilled before the age of single malt whisky had fully dawned – and it is an honour to have tasted it.

GLEN GARIOCH

www.glengarioch.com

Glen Garioch – pronounced *geery* – is a hidden gem, the unsung sibling in the Morrison Bowmore stable, though that might be changing. Having rebranded and repackaged Auchentoshan, the company seems to be turning its attention to this highly underrated distillery. You'll find it north of Aberdeen off the main road to Speyside in the village of Old Meldrum. It is a small but perfectly formed distillery with a smart, newish visitor centre.

Glen Garioch is a Highland whisky but it has had something of an identity crisis with a distinctive peaty note playing hide and seek. It is back, in spades, in the latest bottling – but for how long?

Glen Garioch 15-year-old 43% ABV

A Jekyll-and-Hyde malt, with heathery light and almost floral notes on the nose, and a fuller, earthier and eventually drying prickly taste with some smoke. The oak makes a fleeting appearance, too, just for good measure.

Glen Garioch Founder's Reserve
48% ABV

Crikey! A new bottling focusing on the fact that this distillery was originally established in the late eighteenth century but if Morrison Bowmore is keen to win over new drinkers to this malt, it sure is taking a difficult route. This is a true Highland laddie, dominated by big spicy, peaty and earthy notes. Easy it is not, but for me it sits in a special category of old-fashioned Highlanders along with Ardmore, Benromach and Glencadam. No bad thing at all in my book.

GLENGLASSAUGH

www.glenglassaugh.com

In the heady days of 2008, when malt was at its most buoyant and everybody and their dog was after a distillery, Glenglassaugh was snapped up by a private consortium. Its new owners inherited a distillery in a stunning location (it has access to a small private beach) but with virtually no stock at all and with a serious vandalism problem. But they are not messing about – they have recruited two top talents in the form of managing director Stuart Nickerson and former Glenmorangie and Scapa distillery manager Graham Eunson and have released limited quantities of aged Glenglassaugh (see below) and a couple of 'works in progress' including one called The Spirit that Blushes to Speak its Name and which tastes a lot like raspberry liqueur and nothing at all like whisky. Give it time, though...

Glenglassaugh 21-year-old 46% ABV

Boiled lemon candy and vanilla on the nose, this has a core taste of orange, citrus fruits and crystallised barley, with supporting roles for mint, cinnamon, chilli and oak. The finish is disciplined and polite.

Glenglassaugh 30-year-old 55.1% ABV

The pick of the bunch, with all the ducks lined up in a neat and balanced row. There's lots of delicious orange marmalade, stewed fruits and plums on the nose, and it has a zesty sherbety taste, with pineapple and melon up front and tannins and spices later. The finish is long and fruity with just the right amount of oak to balance it all up.

Glenglassaugh 40-year-old 44.6% ABV

Dark berries, fruit cake and plum on the nose, a creamy toffee and vanilla heart on the palate, with berries, chilli and tannins in the mix. The finish is refined and very long, with the plum and oak holding out longest.

GLENGOYNE
www.glengoyne.com

Glengoyne is Glasgow's other distillery, but it is located a few miles north of the city, straddling the Highland line – the distillery being in the Highlands, the warehouses across the road in the Lowlands. The distillery is owned by independent bottlers Ian MacLeod. Its Islay malt Smokehead, is currently enjoying some success among younger drinkers and rock fans, which is ironic, because for a long time Glengoyne has made an asset of the fact that it is peat-free. A few years back they even hired a luxury boat and sailed to the Islay festival with a banner that urged whisky fans to drink peat-free whisky – the real taste of malt.

Glengoyne is a lovely distillery and it employs some of the most charming people in the industry. It offers a comprehensive range of tours and whisky experiences from the basic tour to a blending course.

Burnfoot 40% ABV

Something of a victory for style over substance, though full marks to the owners for trying to do something genuinely different with the packaging and presentation. Subtle this isn't. There is no age statement and it tastes young and two-dimensional. But in its favour, it is a clean and robust whisky with some endearing sweet and malt notes.

Glengoyne 10-year-old 40% ABV

Another entry-level malt with a clean and crisp malt bite, very refreshing. Wet straw and heather give way to a touch of oak and sweet crystallised ginger, as pure as the water that tumbles down the rocks at the back of the distillery.

Glengoyne 12-year-old Cask Strength
57.2% ABV

Something is here.

This is an intense and pure version of Glengoyne but not as uncluttered or pure as other bottlings. There is plenty to delight here though, including cooking apples notes, apple pip/marzipan, and some vanilla. The malts eventually give way to pepper spices.

Glengoyne 12-year-old 43% ABV

A recent addition to the Glengoyne stable, having been launched in late 2009. This has a clean and refreshing green apple taste, lots of crisp barley and just a small amount of spice late on. This is a beautifully made malt whisky, with flavours all working at their cleanest and sharpest limits.

Glengoyne 16-year-old European Hogshead 52.3% ABV

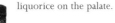

Clean, fresh straw and barley field on the nose, with crystallised ginger, chewy barley, a big oak hit and some hickory and red liquorice on the palate.

Glengoyne 17-year-old 43% ABV

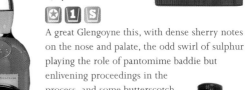

A great Glengoyne this, with dense sherry notes on the nose and palate, the odd swirl of sulphur playing the role of pantomime baddie but enlivening proceedings in the process, and some butterscotch, maple and vanilla lurking just below the surface. They like big, smelly browny-black sherried casks here – we know that because a while back each of the team was allowed to choose a cask for bottling and without exception they were sherry monsters. This is a happy compromise.

Glengoyne 21-year-old Sherry 43% ABV

Again, restraint is the order of the day, and this is a delightfully juicy mix of succulent barley, rich raisins and black grapes on the nose, and dried fruits, grapefruit marmalade and a wave of oak and pepper on the palate. The finish is a long-distance jog, featuring honey, red fruit and oak.

THE GLENLIVET

Ballindalloch, Banffshire, AB37 9DB
www.maltwhiskydistilleries.com

On my first day at work as editor of *Whisky Magazine* I received a letter of complaint from an outraged reader. Apparently the magazine had published a picture of a pair of pot stills that we said were at Bunnahabhain but were actually from Bruichladdich. I nearly resigned on the spot.

At the time it was beyond me how anyone could tell the difference between one pair of pot stills and another. And I felt there was something unhealthy about a grown man identifying two lumps of copper at one place over two lumps of copper down the road. This was, it was clear, obsessive – the whisky anorak's version of the Page Three photograph in the British tabloid *Sun* newspaper. But of course every distillery's stills are different, each

still room unique. Like the whiskies they make, distilleries have much in common with each other but we thrive on the differences between them. And while they all go through the same process in pretty much the same order, the differences between them can be vast.

One of the main differences is in atmosphere, created in part by size, in part by the layout, and in part by the noise, or lack of it. So while Bunnahabhain, say, or Pulteney, clatter and clang, others such as The Macallan or the Glenrothes seem to hum. The former are bustling and busy, the latter, calm and graceful.

I've always put The Glenlivet in the 'quiet' category. But if the old still room is relatively silent, nothing quite prepares you for the new still room, which in 2010 effectively doubled the distillery's output and made it the biggest single-malt distillery in Scotland. It is like a library.

Where once malt spirit production required several people with a number of skills, today the modern distillery can be operated by one person, and if health and safety regulations allowed it, he or she could run it from their living room and not come into the distillery at all. Modern computers have taken on so much of the burden of production that at the Glentauchers distillery everything has been maintained in the traditional way, so staff can be trained in skills that might otherwise become redundant.

At the Glenlivet the new still room is like something from a science-fiction film. There is only one desk, placed at an angle on a raised platform, to oversee the new stills. It has a bank of computers telling the operator exactly what is going on in the room. Nevertheless, just in front of the desk are the traditional spirits banks you would find in any distillery.

'When we were planning the new still room we involved staff in decisions as to where to put the desk and that sort of thing,' says Chivas distilleries manager Alan Winchester. 'It's not often you get the chance to include people in that way. They wanted the spirits banks where they could see the spirit flowing, even though the computer tells them that it is. It's a link to the old ways.'

They don't want to make much about their size, pointing out that all the company has done by reopening Braeval and Allt-a-Bhainne and extending The Glenlivet is replace the volumes it lost when it was forced to sell off Glen Grant and Ardmore during the purchase by Allied a few years back.

But it makes what is one of Scotland's most impressive distilleries even more so. It also produces some of the world's finest whiskies and some that pretty much define Speyside. A ridiculous pricing policy in British supermarkets may have devalued The Glenlivet 12-year-old but expressions such as the 15-year-old French Oak Reserve, the 16-year-old Nadurra, the 18-year-old and the 21-year-old are all heavyweight champion malts.

But there are other reasons to visit here, too. A small but beautifully executed interactive visitor experience is a highlight of one of the most charming visitor centres in the industry, and The Glenlivet is trading on its historical role as the birthplace of the modern Scottish malt whisky industry by opening up a series of smugglers' trails so you can relive more dangerous times for whisky while immersing yourself

KEY WHISKIES

The Glenlivet 12-year-old 40% ABV
The Glenlivet 15-year-old French Oak Reserve 40% ABV
The Glenlivet Nadurra 16-year-old 48% ABV
The Glenlivet 18-year-old 43% ABV
The Glenlivet 21-year-old 43% ABV
The Glenlivet XXV 43% ABV

in the unspoilt natural beauty of the Glenlivet valley.

Add to all of this a calm and not-too-noisy tour and there's an argument that The Glenlivet is the epitome of rest and relaxation. Oh, and if you are interested, some pretty distinctive pairs of stills, too.

OPPOSITE TOP The new stills were installed in the winter of 2009/2010 despite the worst conditions for a generation.

OPPOSITE The Glenlivet distillery is located by the banks of the River Spey in Laggan, Banffshire, Scotland.

ABOVE Glenlivet's new stills take shape at the Forsyth's foundry, where they were made.

GLEN GRANT

www.glengrant.com

One of five distilleries in the Speyside town of Rothes, Glen Grant is now owned by Campari and continues to enjoy immense popularity in Europe and particularly Italy. It would surprise many in Scotland to learn that it is one of the top five selling malts in the world. It is a lovely distillery to visit, particularly in late spring or early summer, because it has extensive gardens. By the side of a little bridge there is a safe built into the wall. Major Grant kept a bottle of whisky here and would take guests out for a dram among the flowers and trees. The house style may be described as light and soft. The Italians like it at five years old (probably because at such a young age it is the nearest that Scotch gets to grappa) but the 10-year-old is more suited to most malt lovers' tastes.

Glen Grant 10-year-old 40% ABV

Dry and shy on the nose, followed by a crisp, herbal and light fruity taste on the palate, with a medium-long finish to enjoy.

GLENKINCHIE

www.malts.com

The nearest distillery to Edinburgh can be found at Pencaitland and is a Lowland distillery making light, gingery whisky.

Glenkinchie 12-year-old 43% ABV

The nose is cereally and sweet here, with some damp straw and a hint of spice. The taste is distinctly spicy but rounded and smooth, with some ginger notes. This is one of the single malts that works as an aperitif whisky.

GLENLIVET

www.theglenlivet.com

A few years back Glenlivet's owners announced that it intended to challenge Glenfiddich for the number one malt spot but the claims were regarded by most of the cynical journalists present at the press conference as marketing bluster. In 2010, though, the distillery put the finishing touches to an expansion programme that now allows it to produce pretty much the same amount of spirit each year as Glenfidddich and Diageo's 'super distillery' at Roseisle.

The Glenlivet was already a big player, up there as one of the three great Glens, alongside Glenfiddich and Glenmorangie. It is a great distillery that produces fine malt – a shame, then, that its fine 12-year-old has been so badly devalued by years of discounting into the supermarket trade. Only Glen Moray has fallen further from malt's high table.

The Glenlivet 12-year-old 40% ABV

Another classic Speysider, with aromas of fresh green apples and a touch of grapefruit, and a soft, sweet fruity taste and a pleasant and clean finish.

The Glenlivet 15-year-old French Oak

40% ABV

Now we're motoring. This is an outstanding expression of Glenlivet, all zippy spice from some virgin French oak, and scattergun oak and malt, like a couple of playful kittens tumbling over each other. Feeling depressed and into rock music? Then get yourself an album by Australian cosmic rock giants Wolfmother (either will do but the debut album is easier to get to grips with), pour a weighty (but obviously responsible) glass of this, turn off the lights and listen to the Sabbath-Zeppelin hybrid while the spices zip about your mouth. Try not to smile until you've swallowed. There. Everything seems better now, doesn't it?

The Glenlivet Nadurra 16-year-old 48% ABV

There is a cask-strength version of this but this is the one to go for. You have to hunt for the Glenlivet characteristics because this malt is a law unto itself, a mix of ginger, paprika, white pepper and chilli, all sprinkled over ginger barley. You know how trendy chefs are into mixing pain and pleasure and creating egg-and-bacon ice cream and that sort of thing? Well this is whisky's answer to that – a sort of chilli-flavoured chocolate, with ginger wine in the mix.

The Glenlivet 18-year-old 43% ABV

If the Nadurra is a fun pillow-fight of a whisky, this is the sensible big brother asking you to keep the noise down. This is exactly what you would expect the 12-year-old to grow up to be, with some oak, honey and spice adding a sophistication not found in the younger malt. But the fresh apple fruit is still there.

The Glenlivet 21-year-old
43% ABV

Very rich and chewy, the flavour here is much fuller than in younger bottlings. If the 18-year-old is a fit athlete of a whisky, this is it with a beer gut, less disciplined, but fun to spend time with – a soft and smooth malt with citrus fruits, a nuttiness and some oak. Yet another twist to the Glenlivet story.

The Glenlivet XXV 43% ABV

This is a rich and enveloping malt with big candy, toffee and vanilla notes alongside the trademark fruits. Oak and spice give away clues to the whisky's age – but overall it is a sublime and enjoyable whisky.

GLENMORANGIE
www.glenmorangie.com

The lattice-work symbol on the Glenmorangie bottle is an image of an old Pict standing stone that you can go and see in a field close to the distillery. The images on it show female warriors on horseback, symbolising power and high rank, and suggesting that the Picts were a matriarchal society. Sitting at the foot of the stone with a glass of fine Glenmorangie such as this one is, without doubt, a special and spiritual experience and is throughly recommended.

There are plenty of people who will tell you that a few years back Glenmorangie was driving fast towards a brick wall, its warehouses full of inferior whisky going nowhere quickly. The change-around since then has been remarkable. Taking full advantage of the skills of whisky genius Dr Bill Lumsden, Glenmorangie has become the industry leaders in wood management. Spirit was put in better wood, and existing whisky was finished and transformed in a range of different casks. Glenmorangie is now synonymous with quality whisky.

Under the new ownership of French luxury company Louis Vuitton Moët Hennessy (LVMH), a new range of core malts and three finishes was introduced in ultra-modern bottles. More recently Lumsden, ably assisted by Rachel Barrie, has started to experiment with new whiskies such as Astar and Signet – with astounding results.

Some analysts predict that the company could be sold.

Glenmorangie Original
40% ABV

This is the original 10-year-old repackaged and it's as reliable as a Harley Davidson. There is a lot going on in this whisky, with a honeyed nose, sweet malty centre and candy-like core. Rounded, easy-drinking, characterful whisky with hints of orange and nuts.

Glenmorangie 18-year-old 43% ABV

Sharper than the 10-year-old, with clean citrus fruits on the nose and an overall taste that is a mix of orange, oak and citrus fruits. The finish is clean and lengthy.

Glenmorangie Nectar d'Or 46% ABV

Putting malt in a cask that has been previously used for wine, rum, port or madeira for the last few months of its maturation is a delicate and complex skill. Many such finishes are clumsy, at best making for a disjointed and confused whisky, at worst brazenly trying and failing to hide poor-quality malt. Glenmorangie's finishes, though, are exemplary. This whisky is finished in Sauternes casks – sweet white wine and some of the big French red wine casks are more of a challenge to a whisky maker. But the sweetness, cinnamon and spices take what was a great whisky in to an even more glorious place.

Glenmorangie Quinta Ruban 46% ABV

Here the finishing cask is port and again the lovely orange and barley core is enhanced by sweet fruit and an extra richness so that sweet and dry battle for attention, to pleasing effect. This is up there with the wonderful Balvenie 21-year-old as the best port finish available.

Glenmorangie La Santa 46% ABV

Okay, enough's enough. This is finished in sherry, which is fine and the whisky is perfectly palatable, but what's with the name? What on earth were they thinking? Actually it is pretty obvious. Some marketing team headed by someone called Tristan or Sebastian and with little understanding of Scottish malt whisky, its culture or its heritage, got carried away by the LVMH connection and went to town re-labelling the malt finishes, coming up with the wheeze of each name coming from the same country as the finishing cask – French for Sauternes, Portuguese for port, and Spanish for sherry. Nectar d'Or is just about okay, but Quinta Ruban is contrived and pretentious, and La Santa is meaningless and forgettable. Compare these names with the stylish and sympathetic though complex names given to the malts at sister brand Ardbeg and you realise what a road crash these names are.

Glenmorangie 25-year-old 43% ABV

If you are going to splash out for a whisky of this age you have got to be sure that it steps up a division. Without doubt this does – up there with Macallan 25 and Highland Park 25 as a monumental malt worthy of every one of its 25 years. This is stately, dignified and complex with a honeycomb heart, enough oak and spice to give the whisky shape, orange and stewed fruits in the mix and a dusting of cocoa.

Glenmorangie Signet 46% ABV

This is not so much a roller-coaster ride as the whole funfair in one glass. What's happened here is that Bill Lumsden and his team have thrown away the Genmorangie rule book and set out on an adventure, exploring every channel within the tight rules of whisky-making. They have used toasted and chocolate malt, virgin oaks to add spiciness, casks of different types and sizes. And they have come up with the most exquisite and hedonistic malt imaginable. It is rich and gloopy, and is whisky's equivalent of those hand-made boutique dark chocolates you get that have been infused with fruit flavours and aromatics. Awesome whisky-making and there's more to come. Dr Lumsden has just shared another 'work in progress' with some of us, and it's a different beast altogether. These are exciting times that we live in.

Glenmorangie Astar 57.1% ABV

On the face of it, another experimental departure for Glenmorangie, an intense barley-fuelled cask-strength malt. If Signet is all about urban sophistication then Astar on the face of it would seem to be all about rustic gruffness. Add some water, though, and the Glemorangie characteristics come flowing through, with a range of barley and honeycomb in evidence. The spices that make an appearance early, and then just keep popping up, are a big plus.

GLEN MORAY

www.glenmoray.com

I wonder if the LVMH folk reading the Glenmorangie notes just before this will glance down and feel just a tad ashamed. Glen Moray has been the ugly duckling of Scottish malt, or at least in its younger forms it has, wandering from supermarket shelf to supermarket shelf before 'quack! get out of town...'.

Hopefully all this will change. The distillery is located in the Speyside town of Elgin, tucked back at the end of a standard residential area. It's a dinky, pleasing distillery and it makes perfectly fine 12-year-old and some rather special older releases. But the distillery has been criminally undervalued, its 12-year-old sold at under half its market value through supermarkets. So let's look at this: you distil fine spirit, put it into quality oak casks, and mature it to the same standards as other malts for a minimum of 12 years. Then you flog it off as a cheap supermarket brand. What does that do for the morale of the talented team at the distillery? LVMH finally sold the distillery so it could focus on its more premium malts, and Glen Moray is under new ownership. It has been very quiet in recent times – and hopefully a reappraisal and repositioning process is underway.

Glen Moray 12-year-old 40% ABV

This defines a Speyside malt – plenty of sweetness, plenty of fruit, plenty of crystallised barley, and a blemish-free and pleasing mouth-feel, taste and finish.

There has been a series of distiller's editions that have been truly outstanding from this distillery over the years. They are extremely hard to find but if you do stumble across one, then it is definitely worth investigating. A limited-edition 1974 pot-finished malt is particularly recommended.

GLEN ORD

www.malts.com

Glen Ord is something of a hidden gem, occupying a site to the north of Inverness overlooking the Black Isle, and it has suffered from something of an identity crisis over the years, having been bottled under several different names. Most recently it has been reformulated to include a higher proportion of malt matured in sherry wood and bottled as the Asian representative of the Singleton range.

The Singleton of Glen Ord 40% ABV

Soft, sweet and very drinkable, this is more sherried than the usual bottlings of Glen Ord but none the worse for it. There are traces of nuts and flowers among the soft fruits, as well as the gentlest trace of oak in the finish.

The Singleton of Glen Ord 12-year-old
43% ABV

Glen Ord is located close to Inverness in the north east of Scotland and it has become quite difficult to find as a single malt because Diageo has used it as its Singleton malt for the Far East and particularly Taiwan. If you do find this version, expect a robust, fruity and reasonably sherried malt with some plummy fruits. The Singleton version, should you come across it, is sweet and has even more sherry. There is little evidence of an earthy Highland backbone, but this is pleasant enough.

Glen Ord 25-year-old 58.3% ABV

Wow. A gem of a whisky, with sweet and savoury in perfect balance – on the one hand there are green and exotic fruits, on the other just enough level of earthy peat fruit, and wrapped around the whole shebang are some oak and spice notes.

Glen Ord 28-year-old 58.3% ABV

Hickory, surprisingly youthful barley and some estery notes on the nose here, with a full and sweet taste combined with some cocoa and coffee notes. Late on some tannin and spice but it is all well-balanced and ordered. A revelation.

THE GLENROTHES

www.theglenrothes.com

You would struggle to find two places that have less in common with each other than Texas on the one hand and St James in Mayfair, London, on the other – but they do have a bizarre link.

St James Street is home to Berry Bros & Rudd, a traditional wine merchants with a long and colourful history at the heart of affluent London. In recent years it has added fine spirits to its offering, and it has the long-term rights to the outstanding Speyside Glenrothes distillery.

A few years ago, Berry Bros company director Christopher Berry Green was made a freeman of the state of Texas by the then governor George Bush Senior.

'Between 1842 and 1845 Texas was the Lone Star republic and had embassies and legacies across the world,' says Glenrothes ambassador Ronnie Cox. 'In London it was on the first floor of our offices in St James. So in recognition of this, in 1996, Mr Berry Green, who was a six-feet-four former Grenadier Guard and very British, was presented with a pair of garish cowboy boots and a 10-gallon Stetson which I doubt he ever wore. In return, he gave George Bush senior an unpaid invoice from 1845 for three months rent.'

Glenrothes is a big distillery – they call the still room The Cathedral – but most of its output has traditionally gone into blends. Now, though, it is being recognised in its own right, partly because of the quality malts it is putting out, and partly because of its distinctive grenade-style bottles with hand-written labels.

The people behind Glenrothes are not above having some fun with the brand, and like matching each vintage with music of different styles, including jazz, blues, new wave, Americana and rock. So in the spirit the company intended, here are some classic rock pairings.

The Glenrothes Robur Reserve

40% ABV

The aromas include apricot jam, some lemon zest, and honey. The creamy taste has citrus and yellow fruits and some soft spices. Very pleasant, very Speyside and very ordered.
Soundtrack: 'Make Me Smile (Come Up and See Me)'
Steve Harley & Cockney Rebel

The Glenrothes Select Reserve 43% ABV

This is a mix of various vintages and is therefore more consistent than some of the distillery's other malts and at the same time is something of a greatest-hits package. Sweet barley, vanilla, mince pies, sherbet and orange on the nose, dried fruits, spice, sugar and sherry on the palate, and a gentle pruney finish.
Soundtrack: 'Purple Rain' Prince

The Glenrothes 1994 43% ABV

This is reminiscent of a freshly cleaned dining room, with aromas of lemon cleaner and polish. The whisky is oily and rich in the mouth, with flavours of melon and lemon and some toffee. A breezy, summertime whisky.
Soundtrack: 'Made of Stone' The Stone Roses

The Glenrothes 1992 43% ABV

Another light and easy-drinking malt, with a flowery nose sprinkled with sherbet and fruit. The taste is rich and fruity, with pineapple, melon, liquorice and melon.
Soundtrack: 'Dancing in the Dark' Bruce Springsteen

The Glenrothes 1991 43% ABV

An enticing malt with some welcoming aromas that include soft toffee, vanilla, blackcurrant and blueberries. The taste has caramel, some tannins, cherry and redcurrant and stewed fruits. The colour is chestnut.
Soundtrack: 'Solsbury Hill'
Peter Gabriel

The Glenrothes 1987 43% ABV

Probably the least complex and most predictable of all vintages but that is not a criticism – this is floral and almost perfumey, with orange and grapefruit notes and a simple, medium long but pleasantly sweet finish.
Soundtrack: 'I Want You To Want Me' Cheap Trick

The Glenrothes 1985 43% ABV

A different Glenrothes to what has gone before, it has an earthy, savoury nose with chestnuts, apple core and mushroom. The taste is much more attractive, with overripe peach and apricot, honeycomb burnt toffee and a distinctive oakiness in the delicious mix.
Sound track: 'In the Evening' Led Zeppelin

The Glenrothes 1984 43% ABV

This is a more delicate example of Glenrothes, with delicate vanilla and wood sap. The taste is sweeter than you might expect, with sugary barley, vanilla ice cream and some caramel sauce. Ends with a pleasant dash of oak and spice.
Soundtrack: 'Wrecking Ball' Emmylou Harris

The Glenrothes 1981 43% ABV

The oddest of the Glenrothes vintages, this has some sulphur and cask vagrancies on the nose, reminiscent of stewed beanshoots. The taste is woody with some dried fruits and after a sweet start thins out and leaves a peppery finish.
Soundtrack: 'Welcome to the Machine' Pink Floyd

The Glenrothes 1978 43% ABV

The nose is a bit off-kilter, with a strange mix of sherbet fruits and earthy chestnut flavours but the complex taste makes up for it – with lots of fruits, liquorice, aniseed and vanilla. The finish goes on and on, and it is very pleasant.
Soundtrack: 'More Than a Feeling' Boston

The Glenrothes 1972 43% ABV

Another vintage that starts off with rootsy and earthy aromas reminiscent of stewed vegetables, but the malt is creamy and full in the mouth with fruit, vanilla and liquorice and some late spice and tannins. The finish is the best part – long and balanced with sweet fruits, spices and oak.
Soundtrack: 'Nice n' Sleazy' The Stranglers

The Glenrothes 30-year-old 43% ABV

This takes no prisoners, after a slow-burn start. At first there are damp leaves and faintly musty aromas on the nose and then some sherry and citrus fruits. But it explodes on the palate, with lemon sherbet, aniseed, sweet mint and some drying astringency. The finish is long and intense.
Soundtrack: 'Mistreated' Deep Purple

The Glenrothes 25-year-old
43% ABV

Here you will find a truly adorable nose, including sweet candy fruits, lemonade, orange and lemon rind, and spearmint. The taste is pretty extraordinary too – tropical fruits, some sugar-like spice and an oaky carpet. The finish is long and sweet, with fruit and spice.
Soundtrack: 'California Dreamin' The Mamas and the Papas

The John Ramsay Legacy 46.7% ABV

This was produced to mark the retirement of Edrington's master blender John Ramsay, the man responsible for Famous Grouse, among other things. What makes this special is the clever mix of some stately and old malt and some refreshing and spritely younger ones, making for a crystal-clear-but sophisticated and complex mix. Most of this release was snapped up on release but it is a fitting tribute for John Ramsay to go out on.

GLENROTHES DISTILLERY

Rothes, Morayshire AB38 7AA
www.theglenrothes.com

When whisky-maker Edrington and wine merchants Berry Bros & Rudd announced that they had struck a deal over the future of single malt Glenrothes and historic Scottish blend Cutty Sark, it was a bitter-sweet moment for whisky expert Ronnie Cox.

He is the international brand ambassador for Glenrothes and he has dedicated a good part of his life to promoting both that brand and Cutty Sark.

'The deal gave Berry Bros control over Glenrothes but at the same time Cutty Sark has gone to Edrington. That was a sad moment for me because I started at Berry Bros & Rudd on that side of the business, promoting it into South America, not always totally successfully I might add, because it's a light blend and not easy to sell in that part of the world. It's a blend with an amazing history and is very special.'

History is important to Ronnie Cox, and it seems to surround him – in the brands he works on, at the distillery and especially at the premises of Berry Bros & Rudd in St James Street, London. Here they still have the scales that were used to weigh the leading lights of society and there are wine collections in the cellars stretching back decades and generations. If you are really fortunate you can dine in Napoleon's Cellar, where there is an escape tunnel that was built as a quick getaway for Emperor Napoleon III, who took refuge there while in exile in the 1840s, when he lived in fear of assassins and used it as a base to plot his return to France.

If I were to pick a table for the perfect dinner party, Ronnie Cox would be among the guests – probably sat between English politician Tony Benn and the wonderful American crime writer James Lee Burke. Cox is a genial host, a wonderful raconteur – and as batty as a fruitcake.

Give him half a chance and he will tell you great stories about how Cutty Sark was designed as a peat-free alternative whisky for Berry Bros' wine customers who wanted to taste fine Scotch but did not want to taint their palates. He will tell of how Sam Bronfman, larger-than-life

American head of Seagrams, rudely burst in on a company lunch to demand to buy the business and was politely and firmly rebuked, and how, just over 20 years ago, the management approached Highland Distillers to ask if they could develop one of its whiskies that hadn't been bottled as a single malt before, thus starting the fruitful Glenrothes-Berry Bros partnership.

Then there's the story of how Mr Berry travelled on the same ship as Prohibition advocate Pussyfoot Johnson, how they had an altercation, and how Johnson wrote a letter of rebuke on ship's paper urging Mr Berry to train his son for the cloth rather than the wine trade, which he assured him, was 'a vanishing business'.

Cox is one of the whisky industry's true gentlemen and although you would not necessarily sense it from his educated accent and attire – he is more of a tartan trews sort of guy, rather than a kilt-wearing one – he has Scotland and whisky running through his veins, distilled and matured over generations.

It is fitting that he is the face of Glenrothes because he has an association with the town of Rothes stretching back to when he was a little boy. Indeed, the house the distillery owns brings back memories from his childhood.

'It was the old manse and I had been there as a boy,' he says. 'When I was six I got a three-inch rocket on a spring as a gift from a cornflake packet; with it I managed to hit the Presbyterian minister on the head right in the middle of a sermon – a frightening moment.'

That Glenrothes will be tied to Berry Bros and Ronnie Cox for many years to come is great news. With such a marriage of outstanding talent, the malt can't fail to go from strength to strength.

LEFT Rothes is an ancient crofting village and a popular destination for anyone following the malt whisky trail map.

BELOW The stunning Moray coastline provides breathtaking views and a beautiful backdrop to the five local whisky distilleries.

BELOW INSET The river Spey, known for its pure waters, runs close to the Glenrothes distillery.

KEY WHISKY

The Glenrothes Robur Reserve 40% ABV
The Glenrothes Select Reserve 43% ABV
The Glenrothes 1994 43% ABV
The Glenrothes 1992 43% ABV
The Glenrothes 1991 43% ABV
The Glenrothes 1987 43% ABV
The Glenrothes 1985 43% ABV
The Glenrothes 1984 43% ABV
The Glenrothes 1981 43% ABV
The Glenrothes 1978 43% ABV
The Glenrothes 1972 43% ABV
The Glenrothes 30-year-old 43% ABV
The Glenrothes 25 year-old 43% ABV
The Glenrothes John Ramsay Legacy 46.7% ABV

GLEN SPEY

One of several Speyside distilleries that exists primarily to provide malt for blending. It is not easy to find as a single malt, but Diageo did release a 12-year-old as part of its Flora & Fauna range.

Glen Spey 12-year-old 43% ABV

Full and sturdy fruity malt, with a spicy fencing and solid malty base. Smooth, honeyed and tasty.

GLENTURRET
www.thefamousgrouse.com

Glenturret is one of Scotland's oldest, most rustic distilleries but it is also home to the Famous Grouse Experience, a completely interactive family experience. The overall effect is akin to dressing a farmer in a space suit. The distillery itself is small and traditional. Much of the malt goes into the Famous Grouse, but there is a hard-to-find single malt, too.

Glenturret 10-year-old 40% ABV

Solid enough though somewhat two-dimensional Highland malt, with honey, crystallised barley and gentle oaky tones.

HAZELBURN
www.springbankdistillers.com

If Springbank is the scuzzy street punk of Campbeltown and Longrow is its salty sea dog, then Hazelburn is its dapper young gentleman, a triple-distilled unpeated and sweet malt on a day trip down from the northeast. It's not easy to find, but is a treat if you do.

Hazelburn 8-year-old 46% ABV

Hazelburn is triple-distilled at Springbank in Campbeltown, so the overall taste is smooth and rounded. This is a Malteser-in-a-glass, with honey flowing throught it.

HIGHLAND PARK
www.highlandpark.co.uk

Everyone should visit the Orkney Isles at least once in their life. The islands are littered with burial sites, ruins and stone circles, signposts to history are at every turn, and you can trace human struggle and suffering from the earliest settlers thousands of years ago, to the protected war grave in Scapa Flow. The islands are also home to two distilleries.

Highland Park is whisky's greatest all-rounder, its malts noted for the balance of peat, oak, fruit, honey and spice, making it easy to put up an objective argument as to why the 18-year-old and 25-year-old, in particular, can lay claim to being the world's greatest malts. The 21-year-old won best single-malt whisky in the World Whisky Awards.

In recent years the distillery's owners have started putting out unconventional and surprising expressions of Highland Park. For this reason new releases are always exciting.

Highland Park 12-year-old 40% ABV

The standard 12-year-old Highland Park is like a colourful fashion show featuring a number of different designers. You get honey and barley first, then fruit, a touch of wood and spice, and a sexy, sensual peaty smoke finale. Some performance.

Highland Park 15-year-old 40% ABV

Again, trademark honey to the fore and a support act of oak and smoke, but the extra years give the malt more of a caramelised toffee centre.

Highland Park 16-year-old 40% ABV

This is more restrained than the younger bottlings and the nose has developed some range and citrus notes. The honey is there on the palate but this time with some toasty, cereally notes, an orange candy centre and then some pleasant smokiness. The malt ends as it started, with a finish that is delicate and short.

Highland Park 18-year-old 43% ABV

Malt whisky's equivalent to rock band REM's 'Man on the Moon'. Loud bits, quiet bits, passion, and perfect harmonies – a little bit of something for everyone and as a whole, instantly familiar while different to everything else in its field. Perfect.

Highland Park 40-year-old 48% ABV

Another twist again. On the nose there is scented wax candle, pot pourri and sweet citrus fruits. The palate combines exotic and citrus fruits, honey and peat. The big five – peat, fruit, spice, oak and honey – face up to each other in the finish to see who can go longest without blinking. And it is the peat that wins.

Highland Park 21-year-old 40% ABV

Brought down from a higher strength but still a masterpiece, with the oak playing a big role but malt and honey still the dominant tastes.

Highland Park Vintage 1998 40% ABV

Surf and turf. A surprisingly farmyard version of Highland Park, with soft and mellow peat smoke and barley sap on the nose, and a fresh, playful and easy malty taste, with plenty of honey at first and then a Highland-style peat carpet to finish.

Highland Park 25-year-old 48% ABV

This has changed significantly from the big heavy fruit-and-oak driven 25-year-old from a few years back. With lemon flu-powder and grapefruit on the nose, it is quite delicate overall. And a game of two halves on the palate: first up there is honey and candy sweets followed by some citrus notes. Then a triple whammy of spice, peat and oak take your taste buds to a different place altogether. The finish is an intriguing amalgam of all that has gone before.

Highland Park Vintage 1994 40% ABV

Highland Park sails round to Islay with barbecued fish, chilli, brine and deli aromas. Just as Ardbeg Blasda is akin to heavy rock bank Motorhead playing acoustic with a gospel choir, this is poptastic Take That playing a set of Nirvana songs. Nothing necessarily wrong with that, but be prepared. As the popular British Old Speckled Hen beer advertisement would put it, 'very interesting, but it's not a hen...'

Highland Park 30-year-old 48% ABV

It seems that there are two very different styles of old Highland Park. This one, like the 25-year-old above, comes from the citrus stable, but this is an altogether more assured bottling than its slightly younger sibling. The citrus fruits dominate the nose, but there is some peat and honey there, too. Honey and vanilla dominate the taste, but there is enough oak and peat to prevent it from being too sweet and wispy.

Highland Park Vintage 1990 40% ABV

All change. This time there is toffee apple and vanilla ice cream on the nose, and the fruity apple and pear make it through to the taste. It is quite amazing that this and the 1994 vintage come from the same place. This is clean and sweet, with rumtopf, apple and pear, honeycomb and Crunchie bar in the mix. Oh, and to wrap it all up, a touch of icing-sugar late on in the spice.

HIGHLAND PARK DISTILLERY

Holm Road, Kirkwall, Orkney KW15 1SU
www.highlandpark.co.uk

Over the last five years or so Britain has lost a number of top-class beer breweries, each of them shut because they were considered 'economically unviable.'

This excuse has become depressingly familiar in the last quarter of the century, and reflects a sizeable shift away from culture and community and to the relentless and selfish pursuit of money. And as we increasingly try and trade and/or compete with nations that pay their workers a pittance and can mass-produce components for next to nothing, uncaring capitalism will grow stronger.

Next time someone tells you the local factory or business closure is inevitable, say two words to them: Highland Park. Truth is, when companies are committed to something beyond the cash figure at the bottom of the page, miracles can happen. Whisky is full of them. And when it comes to economics, how can it make sense to produce whisky on the tiny islands of Islay, Jura and Skye?

And most of all, what sort of business model allows for a regular convoy of vehicles to travel the full length of Scotland on narrow roads to its furthest point, then sail through rough northern waters to a group of islands best suited to sheep-rearing, and all for the sake of an alcoholic drink?

It is because distillery owners – and this includes giants such as Diageo and Pernod Ricard – are committed to maintaining a malt-whisky industry noted for its diversity and regional variations.

And Highland Park is a case in point – a malt distillery that makes no sense whatsoever until you taste the whisky that comes from it. Highland Park is Scotland's most northerly distillery and it is sited at the heart of a group of islands where history is marked out by archaeological sites, stone circles and ruined villages that pre-date Egypt's pyramids. The islands are characterised by wind and water and there are few trees due to the unforgiving climate. The surrounding seas are littered with wrecks, including much of the German fleet scuppered towards the end of World War 1, and that of the *Royal Oak*, which was sunk by a U-boat with the cost of more than 800 lives. You can still see the masts of fishing vessels sunk to block channels and stop U-boats entering Scapa Flow, and some of the islands are linked by roadways placed over massive concrete slabs that were piled

up in the narrow waterways by Winston Churchill to thwart the submarines when the fishing boats failed.

The distillery itself is a cosy dark brick distillery with twin working pagodas, a haven of warmth and welcoming aromas set in the harshest of environments. Owner Edrington has been investing heavily in it over the last couple of years so new pagoda roofs, a modern and stylish distillery shop and a smart tasting room sit next to old traditional stone walls and cosy but antiquated offices.

The beating heart of the distillery lies high up in the distillery's maltings, however. Here, in a forgotten and dusty room full of crumbling old distillery equipment is a rectangular window. Through it is a room illuminated in eerie orange. Wispy smoke wafts across it, and on the floor golden nuggets of barley feed on the peat smoke that is rising up to them. This is the honeycomb heart of the distillery and its whisky, and it is utter magic.

Honey is at the heart of Highland Park whisky, but so is the peat, which is cut from a moor close to the distillery. You can see it being cut in spring and drying in the fields over summer, an umbilical cord between the malt and the land on which it is produced. And if the sun shines and the sea turns Caribbean-turquoise blue, then grab a hip flask full of 18-year-old, head to the port and watch the procession of ships bringing barley and carrying away waste products and whisky spirit.

It is enough to have the accountants sweating in their sleep. And it is testament to how whisky-makers are committed to investing in their industry.

WELL FANCY THAT...

The Pictish village at Skara Brae consists of eight dwelling areas dating back to 3200 BC. Huge stones used to create ancient stone circles are not from the islands, but no one knows how they were transported there.

KEY WHISKIES

ABOVE The Orkney Isles are rich in history and spirituality. This is the Ring of Brodgar, made with stone not native to the islands.

BELOW Quiet...whisky sleeping.

Highland Park 12-year-old 40% ABV	**Highland Park 30-year-old** 48% ABV
Highland Park 15-year-old 40% ABV	**Highland Park 40-year-old** 48% ABV
Highland Park 16-year-old 40% ABV	**Highland Park Vintage 1998** 40% ABV
Highland Park 18-year-old 43% ABV	**Highland Park Vintage 1994** 40% ABV
Highland Park 21-year-old 40% ABV	**Highland Park Vintage 1990** 40% ABV
Highland Park 25-year-old 48% ABV	

JURA

www.isleofjura.com

Highland Park on Orkney might claim to be the most 'uneconomic' whisky distillery, but Jura can give it a run for it's money. It's not fashionable to say it these days, but there are more important things than the blind pursuit of money. Such things include happy communities, the dignity of honest labour, and an expectation that the state has a duty of care to its people. Many, many businesses would not survive without being subsidised, but what is and is not helped out financially, is the essence of politics. So Britain's coal mines, once central to the communities of all working-class Britain, were not helped, but farming, and most recently the banks, have been. The distillery on Jura makes no sense economically because it is on an island off an island. Great big lorries must negotiate little back roads and a feisty car ferry to ship in grain and ship out spirit as well as effluent, because the distillery's wastage cannot just be dumped offshore. But it is thanks to distilleries such as Jura that the world of whisky is such a diverse and stimulating one.

Jura has a lot of deer, even more adders, and the most bolshy cows in Britain. If you go there, they will remind you that you are the visitor by refusing to get out of the way.

The whisky has been changed and improved in recent years and repackaged. The whisky is clean and un-peated but the new and quite pricey Prophecy suggests that the distillery can give Islay next door a decent sparring partner.

Jura 10-year-old 40% ABV

A soft and unassertive malt, with a sweet and fruity backbone. The abrasive tangy notes and 'baby sick' notes have gone, so if you were put off in the past, it might be time for a revisit. That said, it continues to be quite two-dimensional and unexceptional, apart from the well-designed packaging.

Jura 16-year-old 40% ABV

This is a step up from the 10-year-old expression, with more malty cereal, oak and honey, and some nutty notes. It is still a bit timid though.

Jura Prophecy 40% ABV

Some years ago while sailing down the Sound of Jura, the captain let me take the helm. I'll never forget the excitement of that moment, the sun shining, the wind whipping up the spray, the feeling of power and control. Then fellow traveller and whisky writer Dave Broom gave me his iPod and played me Alabama 3's 'U Don't Dans to Tekno Anymore'. I've got a lot to thank Mr Broom for, but introducing me to Alabama 3 and the album *Exile on Coldharbour Lane* is up there with the best of them. A blast of this album and a sizeable (but obviously responsible) dram of Islay malt remain my 6 pm Saturday evening treat. Throw in a few favourable soccer results, and the weekend truly starts here.

This whisky is a revelation. As with my sailing experience it has salt spray in its face and finds itself somewhere between Jura and Islay, its big peatiness ensuring it can hold its head up high when mixing it with the big boys from the other island. At last an assertive, aggressive malt from Jura, which seems to have grown tired of having sand kicked in its face and has struck out with the same sort of rich peaty vein that the outstanding, but very rare, Jura 5-year-old had. Don't miss this one.

Jura Superstition 43% ABV

The addition of peated malt to a mix of different aged Jura whiskies is akin to adding salt and vinegar to an ordinary piece of cod – it brings it on in leaps and bounds, but not necessarily for all the right reasons.

KILCHOMAN

www.kilchomandistillery.com

The launch of whisky from Islay's first new distillery for more than 100 years was some occasion. Representatives from all of Islay's other distilleries were there, friends travelled across the world, whisky writers and enthusiasts rubbed shoulders and the whisky arrived on a tide of emotion. For the team behind the project its arrival was greeted with relief – successfully overseeing the birth of a new whisky takes blood, sweat, nerve and very deep pockets.

Kilchoman, though, is on its feet and starting to run and all the indications are that it will go from strength to strength.

The distillery lies to the west of the island and is a pretty, dinky operation, complete with a small shop.

Kilchoman 3-year-old 46% ABV

Young and aggressively peated, this whisky is vindaloo curry in a glass – quite sharp and fiery, but with sweet malt and charcoally peat just starting to make friends.

KNOCKANDO

www.malts.com

Knockando is something of an enigma. Not a particularly large distillery, it is the core malt in J&B but it has a surprisingly big fan base of its own. Fans are drawn to its complexities – nuttiness and floral notes, honey and an engaging earthiness, that all contribute to a fascinating malt.

Knockando 12-year-old 43% ABV

Like being out in the long grass on a summer's day, with light grassy and heathery notes, some sweet fruit and a dry and brittle malt.

KNOCKDHU

www.ancnoc.com

Knockdhu is owned now by Inver House, but when the company bought it from Diageo it agreed to change the name of its malts to An Cnoc to avoid confusion with Knockando. It is a Highland distillery but sits right on the boundary of Speyside, its postal address is in Speyside although the distillery is not.

An Cnoc 12-year-old 40% ABV

This is an interesting malt. Taste it in isolation when you have had nothing else to confuse your tastebuds and it is quite rugged, with clean-cut barley, some herbal notes and a rising crescendo of spices before a long, complex conclusion. Taste it after a meal and it can flounder. Overall, though, an impressive whisky.

An Cnoc 16-year-old 46% ABV

Pineapple candy, vanilla and crystallised barley on the nose, lots of citrus and yellow fruits in the centre, and a long spicy-sweet conclusion.

An Cnoc 1994 46% ABV

A real dessert of a whisky, with rich vanilla ice cream and butterscotch sauce, deep sweetness and summery malt.

An Cnoc 1993 46% ABV

More oak and spice than the 1994, but otherwise this is from the same stable – clean, sweet barley with candyfloss and ice cream after.

An Cnoc 1975 50% ABV

The nose is subtle and sophisticated, with citrus fruits, noticeably lime, vanilla and honey. A pleasant mix of balanced flavours on the palate, with berries, honey and gentle oak and spice.

LAGAVULIN

Lagavulin is one of Islay's holy trinity of big peated whiskies and lies in the southeast of the island, hugging the shoreline. It doesn't go for lots of different expressions but that is because once you have got to where the 16-year-old is, the only place to go is down, and there is not much room on the tasting ledge for anything else.

Lagavulin 12-year-old Cask Strength
56.4% ABV

Intense, sharp and peaty with the odd citrus note on the nose, a full and mouth-coating peat, and oil hit in the mouth. The finish crackles and flares with peat and fruit.

Lagavulin 16-year-old
43% ABV

Up there with the very best whiskies in the world and a place in my personal top 10, Lagavulin 16-year-old has a nose that flies like a butterfly and stings like a bee, with some sweetness on the nose and palate but a sledgehammer punch, with big peat and some brine. Salty seaweed lingers, giving way to sensational oily grilled bacon and an exquisite smoky conclusion. As with Miles Davies, you either get it or you don't.

Lagavulin Distiller's Edition 43% ABV

To continue with the music analogy, would you add an orchestra to a definitive Miles Davis track? Messing with this malt is like playing pontoon and twisting on 20. Lagavulin lovers fall into two camps. The traditionalists who argue you do not dance with the devil no matter how good the moonlight, so leave this well alone. And those that argue that this is indeed the extra ace to give you what you need to make the score up to 21. Sherry casks give this a rich intensity and some extra sweetness, but remarkably none of the peat is lost.

LAPHROAIG
www.malts.com

Quite possibly the least subtle of the Big Three, It is still hard not to love Laphroaig if you like peated whisky. There has been a debate among lovers of this malt about whether it has been 'dumbed down' in recent years. But there is plenty to be encouraged about. The Quarter Cask bottling is an intense heavy hitter and does not break the bank, the weak 15-year-old, has been replaced with a storming 18-year-old, and a truly remarkable 27-year-old has been added.

Laphroaig 10-year-old 43% ABV

A classic iodine-charged medicinal and peaty nose, with big, grungey taste and through the brooding clouds of peat, some sweet and succulent barley. The finish is long and peaty.

Laphroaig 10-year-old Cask Strength 57.3% ABV

Restrained peat, salt and tar on the nose, but a firecracker of a taste, particularly with a little water. This is a sort of scorched-earth policy of the mouth, with hot chilli peppers flattening the few taste buds still standing after the peat has jumped up and down on them a few times. It is the oral equivalent of soccer hooligans running riot. When the peat and pepper depart, you can still hear them chanting, out of sight.

Laphroaig Quarter Cask 48% ABV

After about six years of maturing, the whisky is put in to smaller casks, increasing the amount of contact between wood and spirit. This leads to speedier maturation but more importantly it intensifies the flavours in the whisky. So that by eight years and maybe a bit more, you have all the flavours of a 10-year-old but with the volume turned up and better still, you retain some of the youthful barley at the core.

Laphroaig 18-year-old 48% ABV

Sometimes the best whisky moments come when you least expect them. Somebody recently gave me a CD by Soulsavers, a band who I knew nothing about at all, beyond the fact that the line-up features Josh Homme, of The Screaming Trees and various dreamy solo albums. I tasted this while watching out of my window as the snow fell when fifth track 'Some Misunderstanding' came on. It's eight minutes long, mixes dreamy beautiful interwoven vocals, rolling sludgy bass lines and sharp, twisted gritty guitar. Just like this whisky, the music mixes pure sweet grist and grain, sludgy liquorice and hickory and growling pepper and peat. Quite possibly the best whisky and music match I have ever experienced. And this is quite possibly one of the best-ever whiskies.

Laphroaig 25-year-old 50.9% ABV

Be warned: the age of this whisky means that the peat has not only been tamed, but it cowers back for a good part of the drinking experience. That is not necessarily a bad thing because there are plenty of pleasant and sweet directions in which the core malt takes you. The nose is almost grapey, and on the palate there are some oak and dark chocolate notes. When the peat does arrive, it crashes over the palate like a spring tide crashing past the harbour walls and swamping the beach with frightening speed.

Laphroaig 27-year-old 57.4% ABV

An extraordinary, exceptional and unusual malt. The nose is earthy, rich and intensely sherried, with some winey, floral notes for good measure. The taste is an oral double whammy, with stewed fruits and over-ripe berries on the one hand, and intense smoke and peat on the other. They batter tannins and spices back and forth between them, like some form of demonic tennis match and let go very, very slowly, leaving a long mouth-coating fruit and smoke after taste. Truly unforgettable.

Laphroaig 30-year-old 43% ABV

Hard to find, but the age has imparted a complexity which you rarely see in Laphroaig. It has a full rich taste and the peat still sits at the head of the table but is surrounded by oak, fruit and spice.

LINKWOOD
www.malts.com

Linkwood's output is mainly used for blended whiskies and, in particular, Johnnie Walker, but occasional single-malt bottlings do emerge, however, and these are surprisingly refined and floral on the palate.

Linkwood 12-year-old 43% ABV

If you have got a good imagination, then you could describe the St Andrews area of the English city of Norwich as the Soho of the east (London's Soho, that is). OK, a very good imagination. It has a shop selling Chinese food and drink, a Sinsin's Love Shop, and an Ali Bongo's so that's sort of like Soho isn't it? But it also has a great pub, the Rumsey Wells, run by brother-and-sister team Dan and Katie. On the one hand it is a traditional boozer, with great Adnams ale and a sausage and pie menu. On the other, it puts on great live music and attracts a cool student crowd. It is also where the Norwich Whisky Club meets. I tasted this whisky for the first time at a club meeting while world-class saxophonist Snake Davis played soprano sax for us. Snake has appeared on recordings by Take That, M People and Heather Small, and has toured with everyone, most recently Annie Lennox and George Michael. To taste a new whisky while listening to such sublime music guarantees a relationship with that whisky for life.

This is ideal for sax-fuelled jazz – a summery Speyside malt with green pear and apple notes and some clean and fresh barley notes – until, that is, a sharp wave of pepper arrives late on. Utterly irresistible.

LAGAVULIN DISTILLERY

Port Ellen, Isle of Islay PA42 7DZ
www.discovering-distilleries.com

It is a late summer's evening on the western whisky island of Islay, and darkness has shrouded the distillery in darkness.

On the far side of a pretty courtyard, pictures of sailing boats, whisky tastings and impromptu parties are being beamed on to one of the walls. In the courtyard itself there is laughter, the babble of chat and the sound of tinkling glasses. The whisky is flowing liberally, and around the courtyard revellers help themselves to an impressive buffet of local cold meats, shellfish and seafood. Later Islay's finest choir will entertain the guests.

This is Lagavulin hosting a céilidh to mark the end of the Classic Malts Cruise, an annual three-leg, three-week pleasure sail that attracts up to 1000 boats and which brings the world together for a celebration of whisky and sailing, linking up the distilleries of Oban on the mainland, Talisker on Skye and Lagavulin on Islay. Speak to anyone who has taken part in the cruise and they will talk of new friendships, the thrill of sailing on Scotland's wild western waters, and the fun and laughter of it. But even by the Classic Malt Cruise's standards the final céilidh at one of Scotland's most magisterial distilleries would be intoxicating, even without the whisky.

We had arrived by boat into Lagavulin bay by sea earlier in the afternoon, our boat bobbing wickedly as an increasingly ashen-faced skipper battled to steer us through two posts marking the only section of waterway deep enough to let us in to the natural harbour.

The sense of history is all-encompassing. When the Lords of the Isles ruled the western waterways they made their home here, and the ruins of their castle lie close to the distillery. The prominent white walls and bold black lettering of the distillery itself are seen to be carved deep in to the land, and there is evidence of several distilleries in the region stretching back to the time of the Jacobite uprisings. Savour the craggy shoreline and you cannot help but feel little has changed geographically in the ensuing 275 years.

Lagavulin is the centre-piece of Islay's holy trinity of peated whiskies, all lying within a couple of miles of one another. It sits between Ardbeg on one side and Laphroaig on the other. If Islay is to whisky what heavy metal is to rock music, then Lagavulin is its Led Zeppelin, a loud battering ram of a whisky but with nuance, subtlety and sophistication if you look for it. This mix of 'volume to 11' peatiness and rich vein of fruity sweetness stems from the long maturation period and the use of selected sherry casks. Unusually for any malt but especially for a peated whisky, where old age isn't necessarily a friend, the standard Lagavulin is aged for 16 years, though a cask-strength 12-year-old has teasingly been drip-fed in limited batches on several occasions in recent years. Blink and you will miss it though.

For all its majesty and charisma, Lagavulin is actually a dinky, intimate distillery, where the emphasis is on quality rather than quantity. Owners Diageo has Caol Ila at the other end of the island geared up for large-scale production. Here the emphasis is on quality. The year 2010 may well be regarded as a pivotal year for the malt, too. During the 1990s, the distillery started producing a malt with a phenolic content of 50ppm, but reverted back to the original formula of 35ppm awhile later. The heavier 50ppm was bottled throughout the first decade of the millennium, but 2010 saw the first 35ppm whisky complete its 16-year maturation journey and arrive in the bottle.

There is one word of warning about the tour at Lagavulin. While the warehouses are a highlight, do not be taken in if the guide talks about the whisky maturing here. Only a tiny amount is stored in those warehouses, mainly for show, and Diageo takes virtually all its new-make spirit away in tankers to be matured on the mainland - not very romantic, but practical. And as anyone familiar with Lagavulin can testify, there's no discernible negative effect on the final whisky. Sipping a glass of it on the deck of a sailing boat in front of the distillery as the sun sets is right up there as one of my favourite whisky experiences.

ABOVE The stills at Lagavulin produce the distinctive rich and peaty spirit that characterises the final whisky after it has undergone 16 years of maturation.

RIGHT Lagavulin is one of the holy trinity of peated distilleries that are located next to one another on the southern shores of Islay.

LONGMORN

Iconic single-malt whiskies enjoy the same sort of loyalty as sports teams or rock bands do. Mess with the whisky at your peril, as the owners of Longmorn found out. Longmorn enjoys cult status, or at least its 15-year-old expression does, made all the more intense and perhaps charismatic by the fact that the distillery is usually closed to the public. So opening the distillery and launching a new expression at one Speyside festival made for a major event. I bet Pernod Ricard wishes that it had not bothered. What should have been a celebration turned sour as die-hard fans of the 15-year-old rounded on the people unveiling the new premium priced 16-year-old and roundly rejected it. They had a point.

I was first introduced to Longmorn by the French whisky writer Martine Nouet, who passed me a glass and uttered the immortal, Gallic-inspired: 'Let me introduce me to your new mistress...'. Since then, it has all gone very quiet on the Longmorn front and the mistress has become a dowdy madam. Pity.

Longmorn 15-year-old 45% ABV

Hard to get now, but definitely the expression to go for from this distillery. It's one of those malts where the age is not reflected in the whisky. The oak is held back by the juicy, grassy and green fruity centre. Balanced and refreshing, Speyside-style.

Longmorn 16-year-old 48% ABV

Considered by some as a blatant attempt to take advantage of the growing market for premium malts, the 16-year-old is bigger and fruitier than the 15-year-old but is in some respects flabbier and less focused. There are no negatives here and the whisky is good but not like the original.

Longmorn 17-year-old Cask Strength 49.4% ABV

Apple, pear, maple and vanilla on the nose here, with yellow and apple fruits on the palate, plus custard, toffee and some oak. Spices arrive later.

LONGROW

www.springbankdistillers.com

Longrow is the name of the heavily peated phenolic whisky made at Springbank in Campbeltown.

Longrow 10-year-old 46% ABV

An oddball this, where smoky peatiness and a sweet barley core work side by side, but never totally in harmony. Intriguing though, and worth investigating because it is distinct from the peated island malts.

Longrow 10-year-old 100 Proof 57% ABV

This one is much more like it. An earthy, rootsy flavour underpins a rich intense and very oily mouth-coating mixture of sweetness and malt. Water lets the smoke out.

Longrow 14-year-old 46% ABV

Smoke and peat on the nose here, as well as fudge, but the taste is coal tar, peat and bonfire. Distinctive seaside notes, too, make for another deli of a whisky for savoury malt lovers. Oak and spice are a late showing.

Longrow CV 46% ABV

Arguably the best of the Longrow range, with a proper charcoal peat delivery and a delightful oily and downright rustic note – tastes as if it is hand-crafted by artisans. Funny that...

Longrow Gaja Barolo 55.8% ABV

I have a problem with whisky and red wine, and think that as a rule they prove that, while you can mix the grain and the grape, you have to keep them at arm's length much of the time because they will fight like cat and dog. But this is an example of a puppy and a kitten rolling about in playful abandon. Lots of smoke flavour, lots of wine flavour, and a totally original taste. The whisky here is only seven years old, so it is untamed. It works very well.

THE MACALLAN

www.themacallan.com

Will the real Macallan please stand up?

On the one hand, there is the iconic gilt-edged Speyside distillery which has few equals when it comes to special and rare collectable bottles; the distillery that has been capable of commanding more loyalty than almost any other and that has consistently sat at the very head of the *premier cru* Scottish distilleries. And on the other is the one that seems to have lost its way in recent years, partly through bad luck and partly through bad judgement.

Having for years based at least part of its reputation on exceedingly well-made spirit using Golden Promise barley and the finest sherry casks, it has had to move away from Golden Promise because there is none left, and it is trying to move European customers away from sherry because of their limited supply due to the demands from Taiwan and Southeast Asia. The argument by the distillery's owners that European drinkers want lighter spirits and have moved naturally to its Fine Oak range of malts does not hold any water when you look at trends in dark spirits generally and the success of the likes of Glenfarclas and GlenDronach distilleries in particular.

Macallan also lost a great deal of respect when it first denied that it had fallen victim to forgers, as every other company had, then tried to spin its way out of the mess in which it found itself when tests showed some of its special bottles were indeed fakes.

For all its recent problems, some of the world's best whiskies still come out of the distillery, and the Fine Oak range contains some expressions that easily outshine their sherried counterparts, showing off whisky-maker Bob Dalgarno's outstanding skills to great effect.

So, still a distillery very much in credit. You just wish it would throw off the marketing claptrap.

The Macallan 10-year-old 40% ABV

The original 10-year-old punches well above its weight, dripping in style and sophistication without commanding a premium price. A bottle of this, a bottle of Aberlour, and a bottle of BenRiach 12-year-old and you have a pretty good cross-section of the different Speyside styles. This is sherried with orange, red berry and plum fruits.

The Macallan Fine Oak 10-year-old 40 % ABV

The Fine Oak range marked a radical departure for the Macallan, and offered a lighter version of what had always been a full sherried malt. A higher percentage of bourbon cask whisky in the mix works remarkably well, showing off the malt craftsmanship. Clean barley, cedar-wood and orange on the nose; citrus and spice to taste.

The Macallan 12-year-old 40% ABV

Rich Christmas cake, fruit crumble and spice, with some orange in the mix and a taste shaped by toffee and candy notes.

The Macallan Fine Oak 12-year-old 40% ABV

This has aromas of butterscotch, vanilla, orange fruits and other citrus fruits. The taste is of grapefruit and orange before a big wave of spices arrives. A great example of how sherry and bourbon casks can perfectly complement each another.

The Macallan Fine Oak 15-year-old 43% ABV

A soft nose with squidgy yellow fruit, a big mouth-coating taste of ginger barley, tinned peaches and some oak and spice late on. Altogether, this is a rich and satisfying malt, and proof positive that the Fine Oak concept can be every bit as rewarding as the other traditional Macallans.

The Macallan Fine Oak 18-year-old 43% ABV

The nose is soft and mushy and not very impressive, but the taste is much better, with a sweet and sour one two, rich fruit and chewy barley giving way to intense pepper and oaky tannins. It all pulls around, however, for a most pleasant finish.

The Macallan 18-year-old 43% ABV

This is another contender for the title of the world's best single malt, whatever that means. There are plenty of Macallan lovers who will tell you that this is not the heavyweight it once was, more of a David Beckham than a Wayne Rooney. I could not tell you, as I do not get this expression at all and do not have a long enough history with it. Undoubtedly, though, this is premier league stuff all the same – lots of sherry, oak and spice.

The Macallan Fine Oak 21-year-old 43% ABV

An ideal whisky for warm summer days this one, it has lots of playful barley and zippy citrus fruits on both the nose and the palate. Very refreshing, and the oak very much takes a back seat.

The Macallan 25-year-old 43% ABV

Venerable old-boy whisky, with rich sherry, plenty of oak and a clean orange core.

The Macallan Fine Oak 25-year-old 43% ABV

An assertive nose, this combines stewed fruits, dark chocolate and cocoa, plus summer berries. The taste is a Ferris wheel of flavours, with all sorts of sweet exotic fruits, ordered and pleasant spices, hickory and liquorice, and just enough oak to give the whole shebang some weight.

The Macallan 30-year-old 43% ABV

Christmas in a glass, not just because of the big sherry and fruitcake notes, but also because of the spicy aromas of clove and cinnamon-laced punch and Liquorice Allsorts at its centre. If the Macallan is the Rolls Royce of whiskies, this is its Silver Cloud, an ageing, classy model.

The Macallan Fine Oak 30-year-old 43% ABV

This is no slouch either, a slightly sleeker but not so stylish and elegant old whisky, the Rolls Royce Silver Shadow perhaps? The sherry and red berry notes are all present and correct, but there are some notes of yellow and citrus fruit, too, and on the palate it's all about chunky orange marmalade and oak. Heady stuff that is rich and golden in colour.

The Macallan Select Oak 40% ABV

Like a great Beatles song – short and perfectly formed, with lots of honeyed and sweet notes. There are aromas of honey, wood sap, toffee and fruit; on the palate there are hints of soft pastille fruits, the gentlest spices and oak imaginable, and a soft, gossamer-like conclusion. An elegant lady of a dram, and a fine example of blemish-free whisky-making.

The Macallan Whisky Maker's Edition 42.8% ABV

Do not add water to this. It is gentle on the nose, with some aromas of fruit gums. Some oak, grape and spice appear too. On the palate, the citrus fruits are matched by a delightful woodiness and some hot chocolate notes. Spice wraps it up. A traffic light of a whisky, changing as it unfurls in the mouth. A delight.

The Macallan Estate Reserve 45.7% ABV

Dried orange peel, marmalade, gingery spice and some woodiness on the nose, blood orange, toasted barley and burnt oak on the palate. The whole ball game is wrapped up with creamy toffee.

MILTONDUFF

www.maltwhiskydistilleries.com

Miltonduff is one of the two key distilleries for the production of Ballantine's, the other being Glenburgie, which was rebuilt a few years ago and can now be run by just one operator, who can see every part of the production process from his desk. Technology has now reached a point where, were it allowed, a distillery need not be manned at all, but can be controlled by an operator with a laptop. To counteract the obvious de-skilling, one whisky company invested in one of its distilleries as a training ground for traditional distilling skills.

Miltonduff 15-year-old 46% ABV

A perfectly palatable and enjoyable Speyside whisky with a twist. It is sweet and fruity for the most part, but it takes an odd salty, nutty turn half way through. Like finding a knot in a rope.

MORTLACH

www.malts.com

One of Scotland's most enigmatic distilleries and one that produces a whisky that is always worth getting excited about. The distillery is not open to the public, little of its considerable output is bottled as single malt, and what is bottled is either as a 16-year-old or occasionally as a 32-year-old. But this is a core whisky in Johnnie Walker, it's a whisky anorak's dream because the distillation process is unique and includes a triple-distillation process for at least a sizeable fraction of the distillation. The distillery has worm tubs – the traditional condensation method which is thought to ensure a meatier, more robust spirit. It often appears in specialist bottlings as intensely sherried and is unpredictable: oily, meaty or sulphury.

Mortlach 16-year-old 43% ABV

On one level this is a street urchin, but get past the unkempt nature of the malt and it is surprisingly sophisticated. There is sherry, spice, oil, menthol and an endearing, welcome touch of sulphur on both the nose and the palate, with fruit, cocoa and chilli late on. Not for softies.

Mortlach 32-year-old 50.1% ABV

Some light citrus fruit on the nose battles against a wave of sherry and cordite. The palate is grungey – the oral equivalent to the smogs they used to get in industrial cities and which you see whenever a Jack The Ripper film is shown. There's something quite Highland peat about it all, but the taste is so intense it is hard to know what is caused by oak, smoke or spice. The taste changes in the mouth but it is always savoury and what little sweet fruit there is gets squeezed by prickle on the palate. It is a total delight – but only if you like rollmop herrings, Scandinavian salted fish and kebab-shop chilli sauce.

OBAN

www.malts.com

Oban is a port on Scotland's west coast and is the gateway to the Western Isles. The distillery is small and compact, hidden behind the towen's main street. Nearly all of Oban's output is bottled at 14 years.

Oban 14-year-old 43% ABV

Another quirky and unique malt, big on fruit and sherry on both nose and palate but with at least a smattering of west coast and Highland earthiness. Sweet conquers peat here, but there are enough smoke and peat to stop the sweetness elsewhere becoming too dominant in the mix.

Oban Distiller's Edition 43% ABV

The debate about whether you should mess with a special whisky too much is assuredly kicked in to touch by this distiller's edition, which uses sherry casks and adds a spiciness and clean green fruitiness to the sweetness of the standard 14-year-old. It succeeds in pulling off that trick of still being distinctly Oban, but is very much a quality whisky in its own right, with its own personality and character.

OBAN DISTILLERY

5 Stafford Street, Oban PA34 5NJ
www.discovering-distilleries.com

If you travel up the west of Scotland on the A82 from Glasgow, it is hard not to feel that you are on holiday, no matter what time of the year it is or the reason for your journey.

ABOVE Oban is well known as the town from which ferries set off for the Western Isles, off the northwest coast of Scotland.

RIGHT The Oban distillery nestles in a side street in the town. The location of the distillery makes expansion very difficult.

You don't want to be in a hurry. The road has a habit of dragging you in to Highland time, and the procession of caravans and cars pulling boats ensures that progress is slow. Rucksack-carrying hikers line the route, whatever the weather, and to your right-hand side Loch Lomond provides the backdrop for numerous bed and breakfasts, cafés and water sports centres.

You eventually arrive at the The Green Welly Stop at Tyndrum, which is a sort of Highland version of a motorway service station, with a café-restaurant, convenience stores, gift and outer clothing shops, a petrol station and a whisky shop that warrants investigation because it often stocks gems that have long been sold out elsewhere.

The road divides here, the right fork heading off for Glen Coe and Fort William, the left to Oban, a bustling seaside town that serves as a main gateway to the Western Isles and is home to one of Scotland's few town-based distilleries – and one of its quirkiest.

Oban is a relatively small distillery and is nestled in a side street behind the bustling sea-front shops, in the shadow of a steep cliff and what looks like the remains of a Roman coliseum. The distillery's location means that it cannot be expanded, and because the standard 14-year-old malt was part of Diageo's original Classic Malts series, it is very rare to find any other expressions of it – although limited stocks of older expressions have appeared from time to time. Such is the demand for it that everything Diageo can bottle it does. So much so that in 2003, exactly 14 years after the distillery was closed and production halted to build a visitor centre, Oban malt was all but impossible to find.

There are a few peculiarities about this cramped, characterful distillery, and one of them pertains to the way in which the spirit is condensed.

It is something of a sad whisky-obsessive joke to ask a distillery tour guide if he or she has worms. Oban has. This is, in fact, a reference to the condensing method used at the distillery. These days, the vast majority of distilleries cool their spirit through a condenser consisting of a pipe within a pipe. The vapour passes through the inner pipe, and cold water through the outer one, in the process condensing the spirit back into liquid.

But there is another more traditional way of condensing spirit liquid. A worm tub consists of a water pool, normally placed externally on a roof, filled with flowing cold water. Under the water's surface, a long copper pipe snakes from

KEY WHISKIES

Oban 14-year-old 43% ABV
Oban Distiller's Edition 43% ABV

one end of the pool and back again. Spirit passes through the coiled pipe and is cooled by the cold water covering it. Very few distilleries have these anymore, but there is a view among some experts that condensation is gentler by this method and enriches the spirit.

Certainly, Oban single malt is like no other, deliciously combining a sweet fruitiness with a hefty peaty base and a pleasant spiciness.

If you are, indeed, passing though Oban on the way to some resort elsewhere, take the trouble to savour an Oban while watching the CalMac ferries heading off to Mull and beyond. The holiday starts right here.

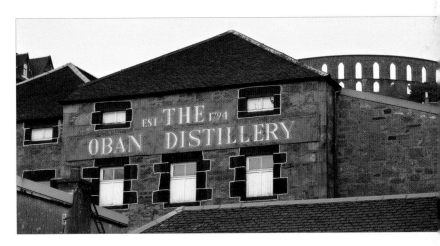

WELL FANCY THAT...

The coliseum building is special to the people of Oban and is called McCaig's Tower. John Stuart McCaig is said to have started work on a family monument in 1895, to provide much-needed employment for local stonemasons and builders. But after spending some five thousand pounds – a fortune at the time – on a model of the Roman coliseum, he died with the work unfinished. He is remembered by the local people as a caring, altruistic merchantman.

OLD PULTENEY
www.oldpulteney.com

Pulteney is Scotland's most northerly distillery and, if you travel by road, you go so far through the Highlands you come out the other side and the landscape goes flat again.

Old Pulteney 12-year-old 43% ABV

This was once described by whisky writer Dave Broom as the ultimate whisky for which you should throw away the cork – and he is spot-on. I know several people who have set out on an (obviously responsible) afternoon or evening session with a group of friends and a bottle of this, and belatedly discovered that they had all but drained the bottle. It is the saltiness in this easy-going citrusy malt that does it, coupled with a spectacularly short finish. As someone pointed out to me, it is a bit like Pringles crisps – the whisky seduces you with its sweet and sour combination. You want to resist, but it's futile.

Old Pulteney 17-year-old 46% ABV

Many years ago, the herring were so plentiful around Wick that the sea turned silver, hence the distillery's, and this whisky's, gold and silver theme. You could walk across the harbour by stepping boat to boat. The herring created a buoyant and thriving industry, and at one time Wick had the biggest port in Europe. So great was the trade that the area known as Pulteney was built to house the hundreds of immigrant workers who moved here. Thomas Telford built roads and bridges to service the trade. And the Scottish fishwives followed the herring as they travelled all the way down the east coast and into England. Today you can visit the Time & Tide museum in Great Yarmouth and learn of the link between Wick and East Anglia, and occasionally you can meet someone of Scottish descent whose grandmother followed the fish and fell in love with the region, one of its inhabitants, or both.

There is nothing left in Wick now, of course, except this distillery. But this whisky is a fitting salute to another lost part of great British industrial history. It's a much more intense version of the 12-year-old, with some oiliness, chocolate, soft toffee and rich fruit notes.

Old Pulteney 21-year-old 46% ABV

The tide was well and truly in with the 17-year-old and while this is a wonderful whisky, it is like going back to the 1960s and asking Hank Marvin to follow Hendrix. Lots of honey, just enough wood, and some orange and candy fruit, salt and treacle toffee. Very good indeed.

Old Pulteney 30-year-old 45.8% ABV

Hard to know what to make of this – it is a very different Pulteney, adding more to the distillery's admirable diversity. This is very delicate and soft, with lemon and grapefruit that belie its age. It is all a little fragile, but more spritely than it has any right to be. The spice is still there but it plays quite a back role.

PORT ELLEN

Increasingly rare now as the last stocks dwindle away, the whisky has taken on iconic status and the distillery at Port Ellen on Islay has been demolished. So it is hard to decide whether to save it or drink it. My advice? Save for a special occasion then drink it.

Port Ellen 2nd Annual Release 24-year-old 58.35% ABV

The history of whisky is littered with the remains of closed and silent distilleries. In Scotland, Ireland and the United States, the winds of economic change have skittled scores of famous distilleries. Where once there were thriving businesses, now there are car parks and shopping malls. The town of Port Ellen is on Islay, and today you will find maltings there. But there was a distillery once, too.

So why do the likes of Port Ellen, and other closed distilleries Rosebank and St Magdalene, warrant their own listing in books like this and scores of others do not? The answer is because Diageo finds enough whisky in its depleted stocks to still put out well-priced special

bottlings, partially because there is a highly active market for them. Indeed, there is very little Port Ellen left, and when it's gone, it's gone. Practically the only real guide to the value of what is left is on eBay. So an independent bottle retailing for US$150 sells on eBay for US$200 and overnight the retail price shoots up to US$180. I know of one store where a Douglas Laing bottle went from US$120 to US$200 through three price-hikes in less than 12 months. Now that is a highly investable whisky.

ROSEBANK

I admit that I never really got Lowland malts, but I blame my mother. As a child, I was allowed to dip my finger in her whisky, and I remember vividly the taste of bonfire and smoke. So unsurprisingly my route in to malt was through Islay and the Islands, with the Highlands not far behind, partially because of the peat that popped up in many of them, but also because I am big on chilli and Madras curries, and big bold flavours work for me.

So pity the poor Lowlands, where nuance and subtlety are key components. Rosebank, though, was a breakthrough. The distillery is demolished, but there is still a fair bit of whisky around. Good expressions, like those at the Scotch Malt Whisky Society in Edinburgh, are great.

Rosebank 20-year-old Rare Malts 62.3% ABV

Floral and heathery on the nose, with sherry trifle, custard and Dundee cake on the palate, this has a soft, honeyed and rounded heart.

ROYAL BRACKLA

Royal Brackla was bought by John Dewar & Sons 12 years ago, but no stock was included in the deal, so only very young malt exists. But the promise is certainly there, so this is one to watch in the future.

Royal Brackla 10-year-old 40% ABV

Youthful, fresh sappy malt with some heather and floral notes, a touch of spice and a sweet core. It is included here because it is one of the best examples of young and untainted barley.

ROYAL LOCHNAGAR
www.malts.com

This distillery lies close to the Balmoral Estate, Scottish home to the Queen.

Royal Lochnagar 12-year-old 40% ABV

Royal Lochnagar is one of only three distilleries allowed to include the word 'royal' in its title, thanks to the patronage of Queen Victoria. The distillery is small and traditional, with worm tubs and old wooden washbacks, and it makes a traditional Highland whisky. The 12-year-old provides easy drinking, a rich honeycomb heart, sherry fruits and a warm finish.

Royal Lochnagar Select Reserve 43% ABV

I happened to be tasting this when my brother called me to say Bobby Smith had died. That name will mean little to most people, but Smith played football for Leicester City in the 1980s (and for Edinburgh side Hibernian for many years too) and was part of the great Jock Wallace City sides of yesteryear. Years before I fell in love with whisky, Leicester had a special relationship with Scotland. Wallace, who had been a legend at Rangers, gave Leicester one of its greatest spells. He brought in fiercesome fighting Scots such as Gary McAllister, Ally Mauchlen, Iain Henderson and personal favourite Alan Young. He mixed them up with a bunch of enthusiastic puppies including one Gary Lineker, future England international player.

I lived in Market Harborough and our crowd knew one of the players, Andy Peake, so we always felt we had a direct line to the heart of the club, and we went home and away, often travelling with the exiled Glaswegians from Corby, whose parents had been moved en masse from Scotland to the English Midlands to work in the steel factories, but who faced mass unemployment and poverty when the industry declined.

Bobby Smith was a journeyman Scot who had a flash of genius. We loved him.

When I am in Scotland talking to taxi drivers, I often bring up Leicester City's Scottish link. Bobby Smith died of cancer in 2010. Just like music, you associate whisky with special moments, happy and sad. So Bobby Smith, this honeyed, rich and spiced apple whisky is forever yours.

ST MAGDALENE

Is single-malt whisky a male preserve? There are scores of women who would emphatically say not. Indeed, the likes of Glenmorangie's Rachel Barrie and Annabel Meikle and French *Whisky Magazine* editor Martine Nouet, are among the very best nosers in the business. Annabel, who was once nicknamed the 'Lowland Queen', is responsible for introducing scores of people to the delights of malts such as St Magdalene, including me.

St Magdalene is another great and lost Lowland malt. All over the Highlands, there are distilleries that have reopened after being mothballed for years. They were saved because, once they stopped producing whisky, the land they were on was of little use to anyone else, so they were never knocked down. When the economy picked up, they were re-opened.

St Magdalene 23-year-old Rare Malts
58.1% ABV

It is likely that fine whisky was produced at the St Magdalene distillery for well over 200 years before its doors were shut forever in 1983 and the land was converted in to apartments.

Not surprisingly, there is very little whisky left from this distillery, and you have to be very careful with it – some independent bottlings are on the dodgy side. Diageo still has some stocks, however, and the releases in its rare malts series are worth checking out.

This particular bottling has some vegetal and grassy notes but develops in to a pleasant mix of stewed fruits, clean and sweet damp barley, and some clear honey. Subtle and pleasant.

SCAPA
www.scapamalt.com

Witnessing the resurrection of a whisky distillery is rare, and an experience not to be missed. And so it was that I found myself on the Orkney Isles, clambering over bricks and debris with industry good guy Michael Cockram in driving wind and rain. The roof for the main part of the distillery was off, and birds had taken over the still room to messy effect. But two features stood out: the large window, which overlooked the brooding Scapa Flow and the black buoy marking where the sunken *Royal Oak* had come to rest, and the big Lomond still in the centre of the still room. The Lomond still was a feature of some distilleries in the

1960s. It fell in to disuse, because its plates often clogged up and were difficult to clean. Today the distillery is refurbished and the still room is fully functional. The Lomond is in place, but functions as a conventional still these days.

Scapa 14-year-old 40% ABV

This is now a rare bottling because the 16-year-old has replaced it, but it is worth getting hold of. This is an easy-drinking malt which twists and turns on the palate, with light floral and citrus notes and a delicate dosing of salt and pepper. Irresistible. And very quaffable.

SPEYBURN
www.inverhouse.com

Speyburn is owned by Inver House and has been used as an entry-level malt. It is not seen very often, but an occasional older bottling suggests that this distillery is an undiscovered gem. Time – and the plans of the parent company – will tell.

Speyburn 25-year-old 46% ABV

This has an unusual aroma, with a slight off note nestled under lemon, grapefruit and orange and hints of oak. The taste is soft, honeyed and rounded with some oak and spice. The finish is refreshing and really quite fruity.

SPRINGBANK
www.springbankdistillers.com

Once there were scores of distilleries in Campbeltown, which is the peninsula running down the west coast of Scotland. Whisky was exported across to the United States from there, but over time the quality of the malt deteriorated, people stopped wanting it, and one by one the distilleries disappeared. Today there are three distilleries in the region. This is the biggest and most successful.

It is actually three distilleries in one, because the triple-distilled Hazelburn and the intensely peated Longrow are also produced here. Springbank itself enjoys iconic status, with serious whisky drinkers attracted by both its unique taste and the rustic and boutique nature of the distillery.

Springbank 10-year-old 46% ABV

As complex as a whisky this young gets, with honey, barley, candied lemon, earthy peat, and salt and pepper all contributing to a malt which has an appealing bitter-sweetness to it.

Springbank 100 Proof
57% ABV

Like the 10-year-old with the volume turned up. This is an oral orchestra, and although each section is working in harmony overall, it is fun to focus on each component part individually, particularly the peat and spicy notes which give the whisky its character. There are some vanilla and soft toffee notes in the mix too.

Springbank 15-year-old 46% ABV

An outstanding, rich and full-flavoured malt, with a soft and sweet crystallised peach nose, and a full oily, fruity palate that again pulls the impressive trick of being sweet and savoury all at once. Red and tropical fruits can be found in the taste and a rustic grunginess provides weight to the whole drinking experience.

Springbank 16-year-old Rum Wood
54.2% ABV

Arguably the best bottling of Springbank there is, with all the exotic fruits, vanilla and coconut cranked up to the highest level and almost in conflict with big peat and pepper notes, like duelling fencers scampering across our mouth. A big, mouth-coating and assertive whisky and not one for wimps.

Springbank 18-year-old 46% ABV

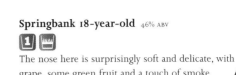

The nose here is surprisingly soft and delicate, with grape, some green fruit and a touch of smoke. The taste, on the other, hand is massive, with an early hit of black pepper, some unripe banana in the centre and some cocoa and smoke towards the end. Peat is most noticeable in the finish. Not much impact from oak for the age, but the overall effect is less sweet than some other bottlings.

Springbank Vintage 1997 54.9% ABV

Toffee, vanilla, peat and green banana on the nose. The taste is very intense and needs unlocking with water, but when you do so there is oak, smoke, vanilla ice cream with soft toffee sauce and tropical fruits.

STRATHISLA
www.maltwhiskydistilleries.com

Flooding in November 2009 forced its owners to give the visitor centre a complete makeover. But this is a very pretty distillery anyway, and one of Scotland's most photographed. It is also home to Chivas Regal.

Strathisla 12-year-old 43% ABV

Another definitive Speysider with a delicate ginger barley and grapey nose and a rich, sweet yellow fruit taste, with some red berries and barley at its core and a wisp of smoke towards the finish.

SPRINGBANK DISTILLERS LTD

85 Longrow, Campbeltown, Argyll PA28 6EX
www.springbankdistillers.com

Springbank is special. Very special. It is one of those distilleries that seems to tick all the right boxes without trying.

Marketing departments in companies with one hundred times the money to throw at image-making cannot touch it for credibility, and must eye it enviously. For no matter how much money you throw at something, it either has that *je ne sais quoi* or it doesn't. In Mastercard-speak: New stills: a million pounds. An interactive visitor centre: five million. A new brand launch with full marketing and advertising support: ten million. Genuine atmosphere and authenticity: absolutely priceless.

And it's not just its small-scale (750,000 litres – no Edradour, but still a 'wee bairn') or the fact it remains independent, or that it happens to possess a delightful mix of ramshackle disorganisation and admirable shrewd professionalism – there is a heroic element here, too.

It is whisky's equivalent to an ageing but trusted deep-sea trawler – it operates alone in the harshest of economic swells on the Campbeltown peninsula, the last survivor in a region where once there was a monstrous fleet of distilleries, now alone and buffeted by the swirling waves of economic fortune. Where distilleries in other areas cling to each other and seek solace through shared experience when times get tough, Springbank seems to stand alone. This point was illustrated vividly during the boom of 2008, when the industry did not seem capable of meeting demand worldwide for malt, and seemingly all was good with the world. The demand, however, was matched by shortages of wood and escalating fuel prices. While others spoke misguidedly of the boom to end all booms, Springbank surprised everyone by acting alone in battening down the hatches against the huge seas of spiralling costs and riding out the storm, taking the opportunity to build new warehouses and shape up for the next wave it was set to ride.

It's doing that now – and how!

Of all whisky stories, Campbeltown's rapid and hideous decline is among the most tragic. Back in the day, the region boasted the biggest and most important whisky-making region in the world. Its distilleries went all out to satisfy the thirst of the booming industrial heartlands of Glasgow, spewing its waste in to the water with little regard for its environment.Then trains arrived and opened up the Speyside region, providing a doorway for the region's whiskies. The

big, heavy, oily and peaty style of whisky from Campbeltown fell out of favour with drinkers, who turned to the sweeter and fruitier creations from the northeast. No matter: the region turned to North America.

But the region's distillers had grown bloated and complacent, and they paid scant regard to the spirit they were making and selling. 'Campbeltown' became synonymous with 'bad malt', and fell out of favour even further and in to decline. When Prohibition gripped the United States, the end for Campbeltown was fast and furious.

Through it all Springbank, owned by the Mitchell family for more than 150 years, never once compromised on quality and survived.

What clinches the deal for this wonderful distillery, though, is the fact that on the one hand it is a traditional boutique distillery where there are few nods to modernity and progress. And on the other, someone somewhere knows his onions as the distillery continues to put out exciting and challenging whiskies with the same sense of commercialism as any of the big boys.

Not just under the Springbank moniker, either. This is a three-for-the-price-of-one distillery, bottling heavily peated whiskies under the name Longrow, and sweet, rounded triple-distilled malts under the name Hazelburn.

Today the light is still on for whisky in Campbeltown. Springbank's owners have a hand in keeping Glen Scotia alive in the region too, and now there is another distillery producing whisky under the name Kilkerran.

Meanwhile, Springbank goes from strength to strength, its flavoursome and unique whiskies acclaimed across the world.

Yes, very special indeed.

ABOVE Part of the new-look springbank range, combining a modern marketing approach to traditional production.

RIGHT AND INSET Whisky enthusiasts are drawn to the traditional methods used at Springbank. Here the malt is being turned.

STRATHISLA DISTILLERY

Keith, Banffshire AB55 3BS
www.maltwhiskydistilleries.com

Our timing was perfect.

The roads through the Glenlivet valley, many unsurpassable just days before, after the heaviest snow falls for 30 years, had reopened. Elsewhere the landscape was dominated by snow, metres of it, turning the region in to a stunningly still winter wonderland.

We went up to Tamnavulin and then Braeval, the sun shining across the valley, the snow dazzling and elegant. It was both breathtakingly beautiful and disturbing, the snow and silence intense, reinforcing the desolation of the bens and glens in these parts, the enormity of the snowfall and the extremes of nature making you feel meek and vulnerable.

There is something very disconcerting about miles of virgin snow where no human has ventured, and something wistful about the occasional trail of footsteps heading out to the hills. It is a miracle that anyone travelled to and manned Braeval distillery through the weeks of snow and ice, and it's hard to imagine a more lonely or isolated workplace.

All very beautiful yes, but snow comes with a price – and during the winter of 2009-2010 it played havoc with the Scottish whisky industry. A combination of heavy snow, intense ice and no wind – unheard of in these parts – meant that snow piled up on the roofs of whisky warehouses across the Speyside region and eventually it exacted its toll.

Chivas, owners of among others Strathisla, Glenlivet, Longmorn and Aberlour, lost 38 of its 67 warehouse roofs. They collapsed down on to racked casks of maturing whisky, making the warehouses unsafe to enter and the whisky unobtainable. That in turn created a major headache for the Chivas team who needed mature stocks for Chivas Regal.

'It has been a major problem,' says brand ambassador Ian Logan. 'They said that when the first roof went down it sounded like a bomb had gone off. And as others followed nobody was sure which warehouse would be next so there was the whole safety issue. They did everything they could to prevent further damage. They brought in helicopters to drop salt on to the roof to shift the snow and ice. Heaven knows

ABOVE Strathisla is one of the prettiest distilleries in Scotland, particularly when lit up at night. It also features on the elegant bottle design.

Strathisla 12-year-old 43% ABV

what it will cost but it will run in to millions to sort it out. The insurance people will pay but they will also insist that steps are taken to make sure that it does not happen in the future. And it is not just the roofs. There is one warehouse at Glenlivet where walls are leaning by 20 per cent.'

The logistics of how to move stock to keep the blends flowing is just the sort of problem the team at Chivas could have done without, because nature had already given them one major problem in 2009. In November the river close to Strathisla burst its banks after heavy rain. The Strathisla team was able to put sandbags across the entrance of the distillery but they just diverted the water further down the road, where it flowed in to the visitor centre. So substantial was the damage caused that the centre had to be completely stripped out and refurbished and was effectively out of commission for five months.

Perhaps a total refurbishment is just what Strathisla needed. The spiritual home of Chivas, it is one of the most photographed distilleries in Scotland, its buildings and pagoda roof almost defining what a Scottish distillery should look like. It is also home to the malts stored for use in Chivas, and although officially no-one will tell you what goes in to the blend, you only have to look around you to work it out – casks of Laphroaig, Aultmore, Longmorn and Tomatin are all stored here.

Neither are the casks of ultra rare 40-year plus whisky locked in a cage in the corner of the warehouse. One is to be bottled when Prince Charles becomes king, another, filled on the day Prince William was born, will be bottled on the day he gets married or when he becomes king, whichever comes first. The combination of dark aroma-rich traditional warehousing, the presence of such an array of whisky stock and the collection of iconic and ultra rare casks make this warehouse almost temple-like. The refurbishment provides the distillery with a fresh start and an environment fit, if not necessarily for a king, certainly for a prince.

And it is the future that drives this distillery and the others in the group. Despite all the recent trials the team at Chivas is bullish, looking forward with confidence. Barring any more catastrophes, the future looks bright. These have been abnormal weather patterns, nature's wake-up call, telling us that time's almost up for our planet. Scotland's whisky distilleries are in the frontline, reliant on weather patterns to produce their spirit, vulnerable to the whims of nature. More than most, the industry respects the environment. Perhaps nature understands that. And after such a rough and tumble period, it's about to give Speyside a break.

TALISKER
www.malts.com

You should not trust the Internet. It has no editor, and it can circulate information at an awesome speed, even when that information is wrong. When I first became editor of *Whisky Magazine*, a new James Bond film portrayed the hero as a Talisker drinker. Judi Dench as M also sipped single malt, so I thought it would be a good cover story. Talisker, was, I was told, James Bond's preferred tipple in the Ian Fleming books.

So we did a cover story, after some difficult negotiations with the management of Pierce Brosnan, as the actor did not want to be associated with a strong spirit.

A few years later I was telling a group of people how drinking single-malt whisky had started in the 1970s when someone asked me how it was that James Bond would have sipped single malt when the Ian Fleming books were written in the 1960s, before Talisker would have been generally available. Good question, so I consulted the Internet.

There are thousands of references to Bond and whisky. Trouble is, they all stem from my original feature. There is no reference to Talisker in the Fleming books. It is not true. By the time of the next James Bond film, our super spy was drinking Finlandia Vodka. It is called product placement.

Talisker 10-year-old 45.8% ABV

An electric storm of a malt, cackling with pepper and spice, and flickering with cocoa and sweet barley. It has an almost metallic quality, and it bounces around the palate like savoury sherbet, as uncompromising, unforgettable and unique as the island of Skye from where it comes.

Talisker 18-year-old 45.8% ABV

We've opened a bottle of this for Father Christmas for the past three years because, in our house, we know how seriously Santa takes his whisky. No more needs to be said about it. This is one of the world's very best whiskies, richer, fuller and with more depth than the fiery 10-year-old but with the pepper and peat still very much to the fore and an intensity to die for.

Talisker Distiller's Edition 45.8% ABV

The extra maturation in sherry casks makes for an intriguing and ultimately rewarding malt, with fruit filling out the flavour over the 10-year-old but without sacrificing the peat and chilli burst so important to Talisker. Like the 18 year old, this expression is richer and fuller than the standard bottling.

Talisker 57 North 57% ABV

This is a cask-strength bottling which is sailing somewhere between Skye and Islay (which is exactly where I first tasted it), so the trademark pepper and peat are still there, but they are joined by sea breeze and brine, smoke and seafood. This is a rough and rugged malt as big and hardy as a Scottish trawlerman.

Talisker 25-year-old
54.2% ABV

The nose is reminiscent of cracked pepper and salt on lemon-drizzled trout, and on the palate the pepper is still there, but sits snugly alongside citrus, ginger barley, vanilla and some oak. The tearaway ten-year-old has settled down in to an old man that still has some attitude.

Talisker 30-year-old 49.5% ABV

The peat and pepper have settled down in this whisky and have taken more of a back seat, making it one of the most intriguing and unusual Taliskers you will ever taste. Oak is unsurprisingly in the mix, and there are some light, even floral notes, alongside the spice.

TAMDHU

www.edringtongroup.com

Most of this sizeable distillery's malt goes into blends, including the company's Famous Grouse. Pity, because the malt is quite wonderful. If you like your whisky fruity and sherbety, and you see a bottle of this, go for it. Trouble is, most of the sizeable stock from here goes in to blends. The distillery has its own commercial maltings.

Tamdhu 40% ABV

No age statement, but this is clearly young, with fresh barley, sweet honey and a thrilling lemon and lime sherbet core. Outstanding.

Tamdhu 25-year-old

43% ABV

Oily, sweet, plummy and with enough oak and spice to hold the honey and sweet fruit in check. Very under-rated and worth seeking out.

TAMNAVULIN

www.whyteandmackay.com

Tamnavulin is now owned by Whyte & Mackay and was reopened in 2007, but since then it has struggled after being badly damaged by snow in the winter of 2009-2010. Stock is limited and most of the pre-2007 output tends to be reserved for adding to blends.

Tamnavulin 12-year-old 40% ABV

Another malt that is more often than not destined for blends and therefore hard to find in its own right. Owner Whyte & Mackay does little to support it. The taste is of digestive biscuits, light spices and a menthol note making this the ideal early summer's evening whisky.

TOBERMORY

Tobermory is the only distillery on Mull, one of the few places where you can see both sea eagles and golden eagles, though some local farmers would like to put a stop to that because they somewhat bizarrely claim that the birds are carrying off their livestock. Tobermory is only lightly peated, but the distillery produces the peaty Ledaig (pronounced *Led-ching*) for about six months of the year, though the official bottlings are nothing to write home about.

Tobermory 10-year-old 40% ABV

You expect the big peaty whiskies to divide opinion, but not something as simple and straightforward as this. And yet there are people who choose this slightly salty, very subtly fruity and faintly smoky whisky above all others. Equally, there are just as many who cannot stand it. As with Jura, the reason may lie in the dairy-ish nose, although the taste is thoroughly fresh and fruity.

Tobermory 15-year-old 46.3% ABV

This is rich in sherry and Christmas cake flavours, with spice and orange dominating the nose and taste. Some oak prevents the malt from being too one-dimensional, but if you do not like sherry you really will not like this.

TOMATIN

www.tomatin.com

You rarely hear much about Tomatin, but in its heyday it could produce more than 12 million litres of spirit a year, making it Scotland's largest distillery. Even today it is one of Scotland's bigger producers, but much of the spirit goes back to Japan. The distillery is in the north of the Speyside region. It is not the prettiest Scottish distillery, but it does welcome visitors.

Tomatin 12-year-old 40% ABV

The aroma of this whisky is light and delicate, the flavour surprisingly rich and robust, with a nutty malt. There are also some noticeable sherry tones and a pleasant fruity, malt finish.

Tomatin 18-year-old

43% ABV

Juicy currants, sweet spice and vanilla on the nose. The malt is rich, oily and mouth-coating, with lots of sherry fruit, red berries and oak. The finish is fruity and woody.

Tomatin 25-year-old 43% ABV

Fluffy apple, vanilla and lemon on the nose, and the taste is of vanilla ice cream sundae, with chocolate and hazelnuts, with a wave of late pepper and an ordered and balanced finish. This was a revelation – a very good whisky indeed.

Tomatin 30-year-old 49.3% ABV

Baked apple, cinnamon and cloves on the nose, and a complex and intriguing mix of spice, oak, orange, citrus and nuts and sherry with a long, characterful finish.

Tomatin 40-year-old 42.9% ABV

A big and bold nose here, with mint Battenberg cake and red apples. The taste is a mix of baked apples with mincemeat filling, nutmeg and cloves, oak and spice. The finish is long and surprisingly zingy for such an old whisky. Another dram straight out of the top drawer.

Tomatin 1997 57.1% ABV

This is young and totally different from what has gone before, with all the sweet fruits and soft banana suggesting bourbon casks, and a very pleasing taste of soft toffee, yellow fruits and vanilla ice cream. A welcome addition to the family. Not so much the black sheep but the yellow one in the family.

Tomatin 1991 57.1% ABV

Sweet clean barley, and buttery, like corn on the cob dripping with butter. There is also a big wave of caramel, making for a full and enjoyable whisky.

Tomatin 1980 47.4% ABV

Starts off shyly but eventually blossoms out with a big wave of orange and lemon. On the palate the fruit theme continues before a wave of paprika draws a curtain over proceedings. Quite delightful.

TOMINTOUL

www.tomintouldistillery.co.uk

Way back before Highland and Speyside whisky went legitimate, the reputation of malt from the region became known as far away as London. There was a thirst for the rich sweet malts in the bars and taverns of Glasgow and Edinburgh, and smugglers would bring whisky on horseback through the Glenlivet valley. The story goes that on one visit the king of England asked for a glass of Glenlivet, shocking his Scottish hosts and elevating the reputation of the distillery. Other distillers, keen to cash in on its perceived reputation, added the word 'Glenlivet'.

Tomintoul still includes the descriptor 'Speyside Glenlivet' on its label, and has every right to do so, because the two distilleries are sited very close to each other and some distance from other Speyside producers.

Tomintoul 10-year-old 40% ABV

A light easy-drinking malt and so gentle it could be from the Lowlands. Perfectly drinkable but a little underwhelming and with some decidedly sweet toffee notes. This is malt for people who do not like malt whisky perhaps, or whose experience is in blends?

Tomintoul 16-year-old 40% ABV

This one is much, much better, with lemon, orange and green fruits on both nose and palate, and a pleasant level of spiciness probably from the wood. It does not hang around long at the end, though, but is pleasant and rounded.

Tomintoul 27-year-old 40% ABV

A stocky and rich malt, with orange marmalade on the nose and a pleasing taste which includes fudge, vanilla and light fruits. Given the age, there is not a great deal of oak coming through, but it is noticeable at the finish.

Tomintoul Peaty Tang 40% ABV

More than just a tang of peat, but not a full-blooded Islay-style whisky either. This is a two-trick malt, with an earthy rustic character from the peat and green fruits from the Speyside malt. It all tastes a little like a smoky Irish whiskey (they do exist) or a peaty Bladnoch.

TORMORE

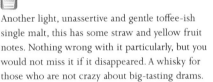

This is a really weird distillery. It is only just over 50 years old and when it was built, its owners were happy to splash the cash and produce not only a state-of-the art distillery, but an ornate and showy one too, one that almost begged for visitors to come and marvel at it. It has ornate clocks with moving parts and four different Scottish songs to mark each quarter hour. And yet it is not open to the public and never has been.

Tormore 12-year-old 40% ABV

Another light, unassertive and gentle toffee-ish single malt, this has some straw and yellow fruit notes. Nothing wrong with it particularly, but you would not miss it if it disappeared. A whisky for those who are not crazy about big-tasting drams.

TULLIBARDINE

Tullibardine was reopened by a consortium in 2003 and since then there has been a flood of different bottlings as well as extensive tours and the release of other products such as whisky beers. But the future of the distillery is uncertain and there has been talk of a sale.

Tullibardine 1993 40% ABV

A restrained nose complete with floral, almost perfumey notes. On the palate there are delicate spicy notes, some honey and oak. The finish is polite and ordered.

Blended whiskies

Single malt might be the John McEnroe, Muhammed Ali or Meatloaf of Scotch whisky, but the country also produces three other styles of whisky that are happy getting on with what they are doing without shouting loudly about it at every single opportunity.

By far and away the biggest category of these is blended whisky, the category that put Scotland on the map worldwide and that still accounts for the vast majority of whisky sales. One of whisky's greatest ironies is that while most whisky lovers pay homage to single malt and are dismissive of blends, which they consider inferior, in fact most single malts only exist because of the blended sector. Our ability to enjoy a single malt in its own right is made possible by the economic realities of selling a great deal of blended whisky to fund the single-malt process.

It is quite understandable that single malts should grab the headlines. For single malts read individuality, variety, unpredictability and stimulation. For blends read reliability, consistency and palatability. Single-malt whiskies are Angelina Jolie or Johnny Depp, blends more often than not are Jennifer Aniston or Hugh Laurie.

To ignore the category, though, is to overlook whisky-making at its very best. Blends are like the circus – there is a lot of tired, clichéd and uninspiring rubbish out there, but just occasionally you stumble on the Cirque du Soleil, a perfect blend of balance, strength, creativity and grace.

If you buy a bottle of 'Clan Sporrantosser' for less than the price of a can of strong lager from a dodgy corner shop, then expect it to be little more than caramelised vodka, matured for three years and a minute in a cask that has been filled more times than a window cleaner's bucket. Splash out for a special blend, though, and you get more twists and turns than a season of 24 and more layers than a boxful of onions.

Blends do not have to mean blands and indeed, at their best they are every bit the match of the very best single malts. Once you have found a favourite, the one that has you 'ooo-ing and aah-ing' every time you come back to it, then those values of consistency and reliability do not look quite so frumpy, do they?

To make blended whisky you need grain whisky, which is made in a different style of still to single-malt whisky, known as the continuous, column or Coffey still. The resulting spirit has a less defined taste than new-make malt spirit, but when mixed with malt it smooths and rounds its rough edges. On its own it can be pretty uninspiring, but it has been described as like a blank canvas, so if you can add enough colour through a top-quality oak cask it is possible to create something that is fresh, new and vital. The best examples of these are found in the independent sector and are often more than 30 years old.

The final style of Scotch whisky is a mixture of malts from different distilleries. In more sensible times, these were called 'vatted malts' but the term came to be considered to be too 'industrial'-sounding.

For reasons best known to itself, the Scotch Whisky Association ignored suggestions of alternative names such as mixed malts, married malts, mingled malts or just malts whisky, spuriously claiming with a somewhat amazing chutzpah that its research indicated support for a new term – blended malt whisky. This is a different category to blended whisky because blended malts contain no grain whisky.

Got that? Don't worry, you are not alone. No one has.

100 Pipers 40% ABV

The traditional Scottish song '100 Pipers' was written about Bonnie Prince Charlie and the Jacobite Uprising of 1745 and tells of how the clans marched on England, swimming across the Esk.

'His bonnet and feathers he's waving high,
His prancing steed naist seems to fly
The nor' win' plays wi' his curly hair
While the pipers play wi' an unco flare'

I can't help wondering whether if they had stopped looking at what his hair was doing and concentrated on fighting with swords, rather than playing with pipes, the Uprising might not have been such a total disaster. The song this blend is named after has survived the centuries, though, and with a symbolic 45 years (the Uprising was called the '45) behind it, the blend is in pretty good shape, too. It's light and toffee-ish and is used by owners Chivas as a good entry blend for new markets.

Antiquary 12-year-old 40% ABV

At 12 years old, this contains a mix of premium spirits and aged grain, and it really is something of a stonker. It's from Tomatin distillery, a large Japanese-producer, and is big, full and peaty – easily among the best in class for the price. The Antiquary, with its reference to the writing of Sir Walter Scott, used to be a superior premium blend but now, stylishly packaged and immensely pleasant to drink, is one of the best whisky deals you can come across.

Antiquary 21-year-old 43% ABV

Good golly! Intense, big mouth-feel, the sort of full taste you expect from a Japanese blend but without the earthiness. There is peat though, along with lots of sherry and berry. Excellent indeed.

Antiquary 30-year-old 46% ABV

This comes in a deep blue velvet box that is a bit like the interior of an old Victorian theatre: designed to be voluptuous and lavish but bordering on tacky and dated. Not unlike the blend actually. This is a whisky that is akin to hitting the cross bar with a 30-yard scorcher in soccer – nearly brilliant, but in the end dropping frustratingly short.

Bailie Nicol Jarvie 40% ABV

This is made by Glenmorangie and it's another big-bang-for-your-buck blend. The vital ingredients for good-quality malt whisky are: good quality malt, a big proportion of it and a a skilled blender. You get all of that in this, Look hard enough and you will find a Scottish road tour in the glass, with Speyside, Highland and Island malt in the mix. This is mainstream malt that stands up on its own, with the citrus notes, in particular, a total delight.

Ballantine's 12-year-old 40% ABV

Years ago there was a British beer advert that ended with the slogan 'the pint that thinks it's a quart'. This is the whisky world's equivalent, a blend so well made and established that it is produced in a range of expressions in the same way as single malts. This is a honeyed, creamy and stylish entry-level blend, with some oak.

Ballantine's 17-year-old 43% ABV

There is an argument – supported by this writer – that 17 and 18 years are the ideal age for Scottish whisky. By this age the cask has given up most of its secrets, the oak has added enough to the whisky's body but is not beating up the smaller and weaker flavours, and everything has reached a perfect pitch. It is the equivalent of a band at the peak of its powers, playing in perfect harmony.

Ballantine's 21-year-old 43% ABV

This one is almost as good. Here there is plenty of melody and harmony, but perhaps a little more individuality creeping in. This has some truly scrummy candy bourbon layers, and lots of shifting shadows – smoke, oak, spice, hickory and red berries.

Ballantine's 30-year-old 43% ABV

This is to whisky what Paul McCartney is to the modern rock scene. It sits on a pedestal, one of the few really great stars, to be treated with the greatest of respect and a degree of reverence.

There are times when a vertical whisky-tasting – a tasting of different expressions from one brand – is akin to climbing up a castle on top of a hill. Each time you reach a new level you gasp at the view in front of you and spend a few minutes immersing yourself in the beauty. Then you head on up again and it gets even better. This is the view from the highest parapet.

SANDY HYSLOP OF BALLANTINE'S

Pernod Ricard, 12 Place de Etats-Unis, 75783 Paris Cedex-16, France
www.ballantines.com

Wentworth, Surrey, winter, and this is England at its very best. It's bitterly, bitterly cold but the sky is clear blue and a bright wintry sun is casting shadows over the immaculate fairways. A faint hint of wood smoke and damp vegetation hangs in the air.

Over on the 17th hole a convoy of golf buggies is snaking its way up the fairway. In front of them are Graeme McDowell, up-and-coming professional golfer and last year's winner of the Ballantine's Championship in Korea, and Neil Coles, who won the event in 1961 and whose achievements include eight Ryder Cup matches and 28 European Tour titles. McDowell is dressed in 1960s golf gear and is using clubs from that era. We're all here to launch this year's Championships.

Among the party is Sandy Hyslop, master blender for Ballantine's. Later he will unveil his latest creation – a Ballantine's 36-year-old developed with golfer McDowell as part of his prize for winning last year's tournament. There are just 20 bottles of it, and some will be auctioned off for thousands of dollars. Hyslop is an amiable and accommodating man but like many in the whisky business, he admits that he's not at his most comfortable among the razzmatazz of this sort of marketing event.

'I get invited all the time to do different events but this is the first one I've done for eight months,' he says. 'I'm happier being involved with the production side of things. I'm very hands-on and like to be involved. You could easily get wrapped up in all this stuff and perhaps lose touch with what's happening on the production process. I like the fact that when I walk into the distilleries I know what's going on, and have a relationship with everyone involved with making the whisky.'

In some ways the interest in whisky has grown at such a pace in recent years that jobs such as 'master blender' and 'master distiller' have gone in different directions in different companies and different distilleries. In some cases the job title covers a big ambassadorial role.

Not for Hyslop. Now 44 years old, he's been making whisky for 27 years, 19 of them with Ballantine's, which means that a good proportion of the whisky in the iconic 17-year-old was produced during his time with the company.

He's a production man through and through, a hands-on

whisky maker who likes to be in the distillery and among the casks. He takes his job very seriously but is delightfully passionate about it, too. And while he is at the helm making Ballantine's there will be not the slightest compromise in quality. At every stage of the process he expects as close to perfection as it is possible to get. To this end he and all his staff have their skills tested annually. Every one of them must identify rogue samples from a batch.

'They can fail for picking out too many rogues as well as failing to spot the bad ones,' he says. 'The tests vary for different departments but we all do them. It sounds tough but it involves everyone and they feel very much part of the family. They all know that at any time if they think there is something wrong they can say so. What I want are people who stay with us. The key to everything is consistency. I always say that it takes years to build up loyalty but it only takes one rough batch to lose that loyalty. Customers won't complain, they will just stop drinking our brand.'

Hyslop says that within his team he has the whisky industry's equivalent of the Great White shark, able to smell even the tiniest level of peat or gin aromatic in any given sample. It is a skill honed over years and for Hyslop the consistency aspect is essential. That, he says, comes from working with the whisky for long periods of time, so that every single member of the team is familiar with every aspect of the blend.

The result is a whisky that continues to enjoy massive success, from the bars of Europe to the golf courses of Korea. Making a limited edition whisky is quite simply the icing on the cake, he says.

'Ballantine's is all about maintaining a consistently high quality,' he says, 'so that it delivers every time. Doing a tiny blend like this is a chance to have some fun, and to play about a bit. There are whiskies in the mix going back 50 years. It's all a bit special.'

And you just know he can't wait to get back in to the distillery where he belongs.

KEY WHISKIES

Ballantine's 12-year-old 40% ABV
Ballantine's 17-year-old 40% ABV
Ballantine's 21-year-old 43% ABV
Ballantine's 30-year-old 43% ABV

Bell's Original 40% ABV

One of the very great names in blends and therefore
included here on the strength of provenance and
history. But if I am honest I am none too sure
about this at all. A couple of years back, Bell's
8-year-old was replaced by this, which has no age
statement. The company argues that this blend did
well in taste tests and has been made to reflect the
original Bell's recipe. Two questions then: was the
quality of whisky really better 150 years ago, and if
it was, why was it disposed with in the first place?
Truth be told, this is a perfectly acceptable medium
blend, in more ways than one.

Ben Nevis Blended At Birth 40-year-old 40% ABV

This is a unique whisky that deservedly picked up a Masters Award
in the 2009 *Spirit's Business* Whisky Masters Awards. It is different
because the grain spirit and malt spirits are mixed together as
new-make and then matured together for 40 years, as opposed to
the normal method of blending the finished whiskies. It is soft,
rounded, sophisticated, fruity and with cocoa and oak.
Another blend that almost demands a chance to be
tasted alone rather than mixed. Outstanding.

Black Bottle 40% ABV

Pound for pound quite possibly the best value
Scotch whisky on the market. It is a feisty
rugged Islay-soaked blend with whisky from
the seven older island distilleries. Now owned
by Burn Stewart and although repackaged,
still somehow fails to win the
adulation it deserves. All in all
this is a cracker.

Black Bull 12-year-old 50% ABV

Speyside is much in evidence in this wonderful
blend from Duncan Taylor, with green apples,
toffee, vanilla, pear and eventually some
sherbety fruit notes that you often get with
Tamdhu (which I know is in the 40-year-old
but I am not sure is here). This is a zingy, zippy
summer delight of a blend and well worth
seeking out if you can.

Black Bull 40-year-old 40.2% ABV

'It's a blend Jim, but not as we know it',
Containing a sort of malt whisky 'greatest
hits' including Highland Park, Glenlivet,
Bunnahabhain, Springbank and Glenfarclas as
well as some zesty Tamdhu, this is 90 per cent
malt and tastes it. This is a monster of a whisky,
with strong apple and pear up front and then a
wave of other fruits and spice. The oak is there
but is not in the least bit dominant. Exceptional.

Black & White 40% ABV

Glenrothes brand ambassador Ronnie Cox used to
work on Black & White and was once asked to attend a
promotional event in America.

'They flew me over on Concorde and I went straight
to the event,' he recalls. 'And the bloke organising it
goes "we have someone specially flown over from
the UK to talk to you now. Ron Cox!" So I get up
to talk and have just started when someone stands
up and says "are you gay?" "No I'm not," I say "I'm
as heterosexual as you are." "That's my point," says
the man. "I'm gay and this brand is a dead horse
but I can sell it to my gay customers." At this point
the organiser stands up and says "Shut the hell
up! Just shut up." So the poor man sits down and
I attempt to carry on. But another man stands up
– a big black man. "This brand is totally dead but
I can sell it and you know how?" he says. "I say to
the white bartender give me one of you and one of me. I'm black
and you are white, so give me a Black & White. That works." I knew
at that point I hadn't got a chance with that crowd.'

This is a sturdy, old-fashioned blend with a hearty malt core and
some well-crafted peat and smoke around it.

Blue Hangar 30-year-old 45.6% ABV

A blend put together by Berry Bros & Rudd that has been
consistently excellent over the last few years and has caused a
degree of confusion because it is also bottled as a vatted, sorry,
blended malt. This unfurls like a good-quality single malt, with oak,
oil and a fruity centre. Quite sharp and spiky, too and therefore a
blend for people who do not like blends.

Buchanan's 12-year-old 40% ABV

Buchanan's is a premium blend owned by Diageo that does well in South and North America. This 12-year-old is something of a whisky sandwich, its nose and finish rich and full, its centre citrusy and with some grape and sherry notes. Pleasant though.

Catto's Rare Old Scottish 40% ABV

Catto's is not a household name in the way that some of the old family blends are, but it still has a pedigree stretching back some 140 years. Inver House now owns the distillery and the range has been given a facelift so we might be seeing more of it in the future. This standard version is fresh and juicy with distinctive cidery apple and citrus notes in mellow grain.

Catto's 12-year-old 40% ABV

The citrus is still there and this is refreshing and enjoyable enough, but there is not a great deal of depth and little evidence of the 12 years in wood.

Catto's 25-year-old 40% ABV

Delicious rich and sherried whisky, with burnt fruit cake, dark caramel, oak and spice. Full and assertive yet gentle and mellow on the finish. Excellently made – a venerable old whisky.

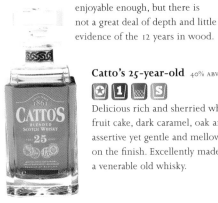

Chivas Regal 12-year-old 40% ABV

Another of the truly great blends, Chivas is owned by Pernod Ricard and has pretty much worldwide distribution. With Speyside whiskies such as Strathisla and The Glenlivet at its heart, this is unsurprisingly very clean and fruity and nicely honeyed. The finish is too restrained for this palate overall though.

Chivas Regal 18-year-old 40% ABV

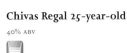

The distinctive Speyside green fruits are in place here, and there is a honeyed, creamy mouth-coating feel about the whisky, too, with some heather and floral notes. It is nicely balanced, mellow and polite.

Chivas Regal 25-year-old

40% ABV

Undoubtedly the best in the range but then you would expect that. Strangely enough it is the most lively and zingy, too, despite its age – with green, red and orange fruits, an elegant layer of spices and clean, chewy barley at the finish.

Clan Campbell 40% ABV

Launched just over a quarter of a century ago, this is a new boy on the block. Owned by Chivas it contains Aberlour and other Speyside whiskies and has been successful in some countries where young, light and fruity whiskies are popular. A refreshing whisky, begging to be served with ice, and therefore suited to warmer climes.

The Claymore 40% ABV

A Whyte & Mackay second-division brand sold in the standard market, but if you take that into consideration it is not bad at all. It is traditional and Highland in style, which means that it is full and fruity, possibly because of the inclusion of Dalmore in the mix. A solid 'centre-back' or 'prop forward' of a blend.

Compass Box Aylsa Marriage 40% ABV

John Glaser set up Compass Box more than 10 years ago with a vision to take whisky into new and exciting areas and he has succeeded in abundance. Many of his creations, call them boutique whiskies if you want, are blended malts but this is a blend, albeit not a normal one. It is exceptionally sweet, reminiscent of vanilla slice with squidgy cream, or perhaps traditional Bakewell tart.

Crawford's 40% ABV

You do not see Crawfords too often in the major markets so presumably it is doing licence-holders Whyte & Mackay a job in developing some overseas territories. This has an intriguing lemon and pepper combination going on.

Cutty Sark Original 40% ABV

There are few more famous or iconic brands than Cutty Sark, and 2010 marked an important crossroads when control of it was handed over to Edrington (owners of Famous Grouse, Highland Park and The Macallan) and the long-term lease of The Glenrothes was given to Berry Bros & Rudd instead. Berry Bros originally introduced the blend for its wine-drinking customers who wanted to drink whisky but were put off by the prevalent peatiness because it ruined their palates. So Cutty Sark was designed to be fresh and clean and it was the world's first light whisky. This version meets the bill perfectly, with clean fruit, honey and vanilla.

Cutty Sark 12-year-old 43% ABV

Sadly the Cutty Sark visitor experience is only open to trade visitors. It includes the Berry Bros London shop, where Mr Berry will talk to you, or enter a speakeasy and listen to an American World War II soldier tell you 'You can get a Cutty Sark down the street, buddy, but you'll have to wait in line'. Also on display are advertisments used to sell the brand over the years, so you get a strong sense of how big it once was. This version is full and fruity, with honey at the finish.

Cutty Sark 15-year-old 40% ABV

It is possible that Cutty Sark was the reason for the St Valentine's Day Massacre. During Prohibition, the gangs running the illegal drinking dens and having to make do with poor-quality bourbon mixes, welcomed the opportunity to bring in Scotch. One supplier, William S McCoy, based in Bermuda, supplied Cutty Sark to many parts of the United States. His product was known for quality and his name is credited with the expression 'the Real McCoy'. Whisky would also travel down the Great Lakes from Canada. And it was after a shipment of whisky was stolen that it is thought Al Capone ordered the attack as revenge.

Cutty Sark 18-year-old 43% ABV

Oak and sherry notes drift around the edges, woody and honey notes mix at the middle and there is a nice mix of sweet molasses, some spice and a sharper lemon note to end. Pure style from start to finish.

Cutty Sark 25-year-old 45.7% ABV

Another classic example of how great blended whisky can be, this includes a good mix of everything, including smoke, all coming together in a perfectly balanced blend. Honeycomb malt and chocolate-like Maltesers flavours form the core of the whisky but there are significant spices too. A real treat.

Dewar's 12-year-old 40% ABV

The impact that the Dewars family has made on whisky has been considerable, and none more so than Tommy Dewar. He was only the third person in the country to own a motor car, was a pioneering champion of whisky and travelled across the world promoting his brands. He had a less attractive side to his personality, too, as a Conservative MP who campaigned vigorously on behalf of an immigration law aimed particularly at London's East End Jewish community. But he actively supported sport initiatives and was responsible for the building of the Aberfeldy distillery where today you can visit the excellent and informative Dewar's World of Whisky.

The standard version of Dewar's is pleasant and sweet, with Aberfeldy trademark honey singing through a robust fruity body. Stylish.

Dewar's 18-year-old 43% ABV

This is a fine and fairly assertive blend, with sweetness from the grain to the fore, and just enough citrus fruit, oak, hints of smoke, hickory and spice to create a noisy big band sort of a whisky.

Dewar's Signature 43% ABV

Based around an aged 27-year-old Aberfeldy malt, this is one of my very favourite whiskies and absolute proof to any doubters that blends can feature among the very best Scottish whiskies. Perhaps it is the malty feel of the whisky upfront, but it is more than that. It unfurls in the mouth like someone turning over cards, a Jack of citrus fruit here, a King of spice there, the Queen of oak and an Ace of sweet honeyed chewy grain. Good heavens – a Royal Flush of flavour.

Dimple 12-year-old 40% ABV

Now owned by Diageo, this brand was known as Haig Dimple and it has a long and glorious history as a premium blend. Dimple is a triumph of marketing and few brands inspire as much sentimentality as this one. The distinctive bottle and the advertising slogan 'don't be vague, ask for Haig', along with some definitive brand adverts from the 1950s to the 1970s, has created an army of people who all but equate Dimple with quality blends. This whisky expertly mixes dried fruits, spice, toffee and a little bit of oak.

Dimple 15-year-old 43% ABV

The 12-year-old's big brother is just what you might expect, a full, fruity whisky with some cocoa notes and hints of smoke. Worthy of the name – and the brand's premium status.

Famous Grouse
40% ABV

Owned by Edrington, owners of Highland Park and The Macallan, Famous Grouse is Scotland's number one blend and has been triumphantly competing with the leading blending houses over the last 125 years. It is a surprisingly full and robust blend and a surprisingly sophisticated one, with the emphasis on the balance between rich meaty malt and delightful soft and sweet grain.

Famous Grouse Black Grouse 40% ABV

A fascinating aside for the Famous Grouse this, with smoky and peaty notes that join a toffee fruit and caramel base. The overall effect is altogether more grungey and chewy. The name refers to a threatened rare species of grouse found on the west coast islands and owners Edrington are working with the Royal Society for the Protection of Birds to help conserve the bird via whisky sales.

GORDON MOTION OF THE EDRINGTON GROUP

The Edrington Group, 2500 Great Western Road, Glasgow G15 6RW
www.edringtongroup.com

Distillers and blenders never seem to retire properly.

It says much about how much distillers and blenders love their jobs that there are countless examples of whisky men working into their 70s, 80s and even 90s rather than hanging up the boots and sitting back with a large glass of something special they created.

That said, though, the whisky industry is at a crossroads, as a whole generation of great whisky-makers have stepped down in recent years or are set to.

The list is a formidable one – Iain Henderson, Robert Hicks, John Ramsay, Hedley Wright, Jim McEwan, David Stewart, Colin Scott and Richard Paterson in Scotland, Elmer T Lee, Jimmy Russell, Parker Beam and Jim Rutledge in Kentucky – these are all larger-than-life characters who worked their way up from the maltings floor to the very top of their business. When they have all moved on there will never be another generation quite like them, a generation in which the secrets of the stills and the skills of distilling were learned among the malt and the mash.

The new generation is likely to have been educated at university and have a science background, and there are plenty of people who have concerns over where whisky will go under them. So should we be worried?

Probably not, for a number of reasons. Firstly, knowing more about the science of whisky and precisely why what happens does so, is a good thing. Secondly, the call of whisky is no less vocational necessarily just because it is pursued through the classroom. And thirdly, because many of the new faces may come armed with a chemistry diploma, they have also benefitted from having the best of both worlds, serving under the tutelage of the masters.

And of course the new generation is able to hold fast to the traditions that matter while looking at new ways to take their whiskies forward. Maintaining heritage and evolving are

not mutually exclusive, as the likes of Dr Bill Lumsden at Glenmorangie and Chris Morris at Woodford Reserve have demonstrated in recent years.

Then there is Gordon Motion, master blender at Edrington and now the man responsible for Famous Grouse and Cutty Sark. He comes with the science education and non-distillery background, but he worked alongside previous master-blender John Ramsay for close to 10 years. Yes things are changing, he says, but not so you'd notice.

'I learned a great deal from John and know how much integrity he has and how much effort he put into his whiskies,' he says. 'I have learned from him so my approach isn't going to be so radically different. I don't have any radical plans for the whisky though it's natural that I take a more modern approach. I'm starting to use more technology than John did for information-gathering but it won't influence the whisky.'

Motion has 13 caps as a small-bore rifleman for Scotland, but says that his hobbies have been put on hold somewhat by the challenges of the job. The modern whisky-distiller is expected to produce far more expressions of whisky than would have been the case in the past, and the pressure is constant.

But that is another thing he has learned from the grumpy old men of the past – being grouchy in defence of your whiskies is ultimately to the benefit of everyone.

'John would never have put out a whisky he wasn't happy with no matter what the pressure is, and I'll hopefully do the same,' he says. 'One of the many valuable things I learned from him was that it was acceptable to stand firm and say no to the marketing men from time to time.'

Yep, it looks like whisky is more than safe for some time yet.

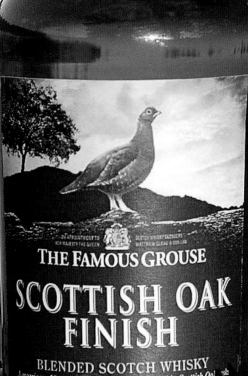

Famous Grouse 12-year-old Gold Reserve 40% ABV

Not sure what the future holds for this expression of Famous Grouse because it is quite hard to find and its owners were not particularly enthusiastic about supplying samples of it. A shame really, because the mix of orange and lemon fruits with some hefty oak, sweet toffee and wisps of smoke makes for a winning combination.

Famous Grouse Scottish Oak Finish 44.5% ABV

Whiskies matured in Scottish oak are exceedingly rare, not least because when they built the Scottish Parliament a few years ago the nation's oak reserves were all but swallowed up. But I cannot think of any of them that were not outstanding, and this is no exception. The effect of the oak seems to be to add a spiciness to honeycomb. Imagine a chilli-flavoured honeycomb bar and you are getting there. The grain softens the impact in this blend but nonetheless is pretty awe-inspiring stuff. This is a limited edition and very hard to find. If you find one, though, don't miss the opportunity to try it.

Grand Macnish 40% ABV

With its distinctive, quaint bottle and the fact that there are 40 whiskies in the blend, this makes for a good choice if you are looking to provide the blend drinker in your life with something a little different to their standard tipple – specialist whisky shops such as The Whisky Shop chain stock it. It is made by Macduff International and has a sweet fruity taste.

Haig Gold 40% ABV

Like Mickey Rourke in The Wrestler, this blend has seen better days. Indeed, it was a champion once, the leading whisky for a generation. Now it is a bit-part player, part of the vast Diageo stable, and only thriving in some of the remoter southern European markets. It is a perfectly palatable but light blend, with soft touches of fruit, spice and wispy smoke.

Hankey Bannister 40% ABV

Amazingly Mr Hankey and Mr Bannister's wine merchant business has its roots stretching back more than 250 years to the middle of the 18th century. The name is now owned by Inver House, and is the umbrella for a range of blends that, at the higher end, are of extremely high quality and continue to win world whisky awards and critical acclaim. This entry level blend is another good choice if you are looking to break from the norm, with a pleasant and rounded fruity taste and mellow finish.

Hankey Bannister 12-year-old 40% ABV

Speyside United, with fruit, vanilla, honey, a touch of spice and oak, and a balanced and attractive finish.

Hankey Bannister 21-year-old 43% ABV

This is an excellent but surprising blend. Fresh green fruit and a vigorous combination of flavours disguise its age until late on, when malt oak and spice arrive and give the overall taste a developing complexity. The finish is swan-like – seemingly graceful, but with flavours working hard beneath the surface.

Hankey Bannister 25-year-old 40% ABV

Tastes like the big brother of the 21-year-old, with the same array of flavours but with the intensity and quality turned up a notch. The oak and delightful vanilla notes make this a stand-out, however.

Hankey Bannister 40-year-old 43.3% ABV

This was voted the world's best blend by an impressive cross-section of the whisky industry a couple of years ago, and promptly disappeared, though another version has been put out since. It has enough weight and body to appeal to single-malt lovers, with rich oak, malt and spice. But it is a complex beast, too, with deep orange and yellow citrus notes and an appealing long, rounded finish.

Islay Mist 12-year-old 40% ABV

Another blend from Macduff International, this mixes rich peaty malts from Islay with some Speyside and Highland ones, and rounds them all up in a smooth grain net. It is a stylish piece of work, though, and pulls off the clever trick of delivering on rich flavour – both medicinal and linctus notes are present here – offering up 'a spoonful of sugar to help the medicine go down'.

Isle of Skye 21-year-old 40% ABV

The best of a range of Isle of Skye blends from Ian Macleod, this is whisky's Artful Dodger, a street urchin with a cheeky mischievous streak, and charming good nature at its heart. Sugar and spice are there, and the malt annouces its presence, though how much Talisker is here is unclear. Keeps you interested, though.

J&B Rare 40% ABV

J&B stands for Justerini and Brooks, but today the company is part of the Diageo empire. It has always been a bit cutting-edge, this version having been launched as a light whisky for a new type of drinker in the 1930s, and Diageo has used the brand for a series of innovative launches. There was a clear version, for instance, aimed at appealing to younger vodka drinkers, while Nox was a triumph of style over substance, packaged to stand out on nightclub shelves. And then there was Ultima, which was just that – a mix of more than 125 whiskies.

This version is hugely popular in many markets across the world and has sweet tinned fruits, vanilla and honey as well as a very appealing smokiness, all held in check by the grain.

J&B Jet 40% ABV

Wonderfully packaged in sleek black with red touches, this looks the part. Taste-wise there is a distinctive Speyside influence, some assertive notes, and a mellow and rounded finish.

John Barr 40% ABV

If this had originally been produced by anyone else other than the company which became Diageo there would be a case for 'passing off', because everything about it screams Johnnie Walker Red. It was introduced to replace that very brand when Diageo's predecessors DCL got into a dispute with the European Union and withdrew Red Label. Now with Whyte & Mackay, the blend most likely includes Fettercairn and Jura. A curiosity found only in selected markets.

Johnnie Walker Red Label 40% ABV

Funny what sticks in your mind. I remember clearly my father's indignation at no longer being able to buy this version of Johnnie Walker, and how he was being presented with a choice of paying more for the Black Label, which he did not like (too peaty) or changing brands. It says masses about the power of a top brand that my father seemed genuinely offended that his loyalty could be repaid in this way. I think of him standing in the kitchen complaining to anyone who would listen (me) every time I hear of an American football franchise upping sticks to move cities. He blamed 'the grey gnomes of Europe' and I've been cynical ever since about Britons blaming Europe for everything.

Nowadays this does pop up in British airports and specialist shops. Srangely the peaty taste my father objected to in Black Label but presumably wasn't there in the late 1960s is key to the current Red Label.

Johnnie Walker Black Label 40% ABV

As editor of *Whisky Magazine* a few years back I asked 10 blenders to name their favourite blend by a rival company. I recall eight said Black Label, and one of the two blenders who did not was the blender for Black Label.

This really is an iconic blend, a masterclass in blending, with a touch of everything in the mix, including a delightful wave of spice from Talisker and peat from Caol Ila. I do not claim to be any sort of expert on blending, but I am told Caol Ila is loved by blenders because it is oily and full-flavoured, so makes a successful foundation for a blend.

There is Speyside fruit here, and it is clear that only top-grade 12-year-old-plus whiskies are present. A heavy hitter for sure.

Johnnie Walker Gold 40% ABV

Diwali is the Hindu celebration of good over evil and marks the return of Lord Raama to his kingdom after defeating the demon king. It is known as the Festival of Lights because it is celebrated with the lighting of small lamps, and it is traditional to exchange gifts with loved ones. One of the ultimate gifts a son can give his father at this time is a bottle of Johnnie Walker, and sales to the Indian market at Diwali are huge, so much so that when a batch of home-made whisky passed off as Johnnie Walker led to the death of several people, Diageo put out advertisements written in a number of Indian languages across the British trade press, reassuring Asian customers that the official bottlings were not tainted.

The Gold label contains whiskies that are at least 18 years old, and you get the impression that someone opened the 'very special' cupboard and said 'fill your boots, boys'. No expense has been spared here. I can't help thinking that when people moan about the fact that one company owns so many distilleries they should consider whether this blend would exist if the situation was different, and whether the world is a better place for its presence. It most certainly is, and worthy of a top place on whisky's highest table – and that's all whisky, not just blends. Initially, this is surprisingly youthful, rich and zesty, then the full fruit, berry and smoke notes kick in and kick off. Diageo's marketing people suggest you keep the bottle in the fridge and serve it chilled. Then hold it in the mouth, and let it warm so the flavours reveal themselves one by one. Yep, you could do that. Or just take it as it is, sip it and enjoy. World class.

Johnnie Walker Blue 40% ABV

The journalist and presenter Piers Morgan annoys a lot of people but I love him. He is opinionated, brave and an outstanding journalist, prepared to stand up for his principles and with the uncanny knack of being able to get people to open up to him, and not only tolerate awkward and difficult questions, but answer them.

A few years ago he was approached by Johnnie Walker Blue's marketing people to do some work for them, which was, as he said in one of his books, a bit of a a no-brainer – why would you not take money (and no doubt some whisky) to say nice things about a blend he drinks anyway?

As part of his ambassadorial duties he

interviewed the world-famous Italian referee Pierluigi Collina (you know, bald with bulging eyes) in front of an invited audience, the idea being that if you take different components and bring them together, you create something new – geddit?

Halfway through the interview Morgan asked Collina what it was like to send off a world-renowned soccer superstar. The Italian gave a lengthy answer about the regret at ending the performance of an artist and depriving the crowd of a craftsman...all very Italian and dramatic.

'Oh come on,' interrupted Morgan after a minute or so, 'when you've got that red card in your hand, and you're waving it in his face...well it must be better than sex isn't it?'

Priceless Piers.

Beforehand the guests were invited to numb their mouths with chilled water, then to put Johnnie Walker into the mouth. As the whisky warmed the mouth, its flavours took over.

The most expensive of all the Johnnie Walker range does not have an age statement because the age on the label must refer to the youngest whisky in the mix. Here there is a proportion of very young whisky but it is there to pep up some very old grand malts indeed. This is an oral kaleidoscope, with peat giving way to pear and melon, sherbet dip and liquorice and some oak notes. Not cheap, but sublime.

The Last Drop 52% ABV

Johnnie Walker is a snip next to this. This will set you back some US$1750 minimum, and there is not much of it (hence the name). But if anyone ever tells you that at the high end premium whisky cannot match the world's best cognacs, tell them about this. It is another curiosity. There are 12 grains and something like 70 malts in the mix here, and they all date from 1960 or earlier. But they were blended in 1972 when they were a minimum of 12 years old, and then returned to the cask for a further 36 years, when the whisky was rediscovered by accident and bottled at 48 years old. Its price comes from its rarity but it is the most honeyed, rounded, smooth and wonderful blend I have ever tasted. Amazingly, every oak note is positive and good, with no sharpness or unpleasant tannin at any point.

If you buy a full bottle they give you a miniature so you can try it and decide whether you are going to keep the big bottle as an investment or drink it. That's not a choice, that's torture.

Lauder's 40% ABV

This does not claim to be anything it is not. In fact it is a straight-ahead well-made session blend good for mixing. It's made in the heart of Glasgow and it is a far better prospect than the cheap blends you find in supermarkets and corner stores.

Old Parr 12-year-old 43% ABV

A juicy, fruity and exceptionally well-balanced blend this, with raisin, toffee and an earthy underbelly with a whiff of smoke.

Old Parr Superior 43% ABV

I tasted this while listening to Johnny Cash's final recording, *American Vol VI: Ain't No Grave*. By the time he made the CD he was so ill he could only record on certain days. Clearly close to death and struggling to find the strength to sing, you can tell. I defy anyone not to have a lump in the throat or a tear in the eye by the time he sings Kris Kristofferson's 'For the Good Times': 'Don't look so sad, I know it's over. But life goes on and this old world will keep on turning. Let's just be glad we had some time to spend together. There's no need to watch the bridges that we're burning'.

This whisky is a fitting tribute to the great man – big and old-fashioned, rich and fruity. There is sherry all the way through this. A little rough round the edges but a class act right until the end. Yep, this is good enough for Johnny.

Pig's Nose 40% ABV

Pig's Nose was part of the same management buy-out from Whyte & Mackay as Sheep Dip, and while on the face of it both brands might appear to be novelty acts, they both reflect high-quality whisky making by W&M's master blender Richard Paterson. Find a stockist for either or both brands and you will also find a loyal fan base. This is smooth, tasty, gentle and well constructed.

Royal Salute 21-year-old 40% ABV

Royal Salute is owned by Pernod Ricard and is all about top-quality premium whisky. Lavishly packaged in royal blue and gold, this blend includes some of the company's finest Speyside malts, but don't assume it will be a softly, softly honey and fruit medley. Whether consciously done or not, this occupies a different place to older bottlings of sister blend Chivas Regal, and there is some real bite, and creamy chocolatey tones that give an identity all of its own.

Royal Salute Hundred Cask Selection
40% ABV

Another big, big blend that would hold its own in any malt company, not least because it knocks the spots off most malts simply because of its complexity. The chocolate theme remains here, but there are all sorts of twists and turns, from fresh and zesty malt notes and from splashes of spice, oak and smoke. This is a rollercoaster ride of a blend and delightful on every level.

Scottish Leader 12-year-old 40% ABV

This is owned by Burn Stewart and, like Lauder's, it does not claim to be anything it is not. Indeed it is whisky's answer to AC/DC singer Brian Johnson – a salt-of-the-earth, no frills, honest-to-goodness blend that delivers exactly what you would expect it to.

Something Special
40% ABV

Another Pernod Ricard blend, but this one is aimed at the premium blended market, particularly in South America – and is impressively packaged. It also has Longmorn as its core malt and as you might expect there is rich fruit, though soft fudge and vanilla ice cream are not far from the surface. Spice notes add to the pleasant overall experience.

Stewarts Cream of the Barley 40% ABV

Has probably seen better days, but among a certain generation of Scotch drinkers, in Scotland, this remains king. It once enjoyed wide distribution as a 'rack whisky' and is surprisingly malty. It is also young but it captivates because of a touch of chilli and smoke in the mix. In fact it occupies a little niche all of its own.

Teacher's Highland Cream 40% ABV

One of Scotch whisky's old bruisers, this is a heavyweight blend from another era and one that divides opinion. The high malt content and gritty, grainy heart are welcomed by lovers of robust whiskies, but many naturally drawn to blends find it too rough and aggressive. I would argue that it is one of the few blends that can be enjoyed neat, not for the subtleties or nuances of an aged Johnnie Walker or Dewar's Signature, but because of its malty, craggy honesty. Like sitting on rocks by a rugged coastline when the wind is up – not for everyone, perhaps, but for some eminently more preferable to sunbathing on a sunny day.

Teacher's Origin 42.8% ABV

Teacher's was, for a long time, a silent giant, and even when Allied broke up and it ended up as part of the Beam empire, little was heard of it. But that started to change in 2010 with the launch of two new Teacher's products and a general increase in its media profile. The move is long overdue and I for one am delighted. Of the two new releases this is the one that is cause for the greatest excitement. Teacher's Origin is genuinely different and a blast of fresh air for blended whisky.

It is based on four principles – a high malt content of about 65 per cent as opposed to many blends that are 40 per cent malt or less; a bold and characterful core malt, in this case the savoury, peaty and challenging Ardmore; quality barrels including the same quarter casks that have produced stunning Laphroaig and Ardmore malts – and a range of aged whiskies, in this case from five to 13 years. It is not an easy ride – the Ardmore means there are oily, peaty, fishy and savoury notes to contend with – but give it a chance to grow on you and chances are you will be locked in for good. Tasting is like fishing – for every big catch you have to land a few minnows. This is like finding a monstrous brown trout after a day catching sprats.

Te Bheag Connoisseurs Blend 40% ABV

And talking of unusual fish, this is a west coast sea bass, fat and fleshy, dripping in brine, reeking of sea, oily and slinky, and utterly irresistible. There is some peat, some spice and some soft fudge. Oh, and if you are wondering, you pronounce it *Chay Veg*.

VAT 69 40% ABV

My dad's favourite joke in the 1970s was 'what's the Pope's phone number?' and this is what he used to drink once Johnnie Walker Red Label ceased to be an option. Is it still going? A million cases say yes, though only in a few selected markets. This is a medium-bodied and very drinkable blend with a nice one-two between sweet grain and chewy malt.

White Horse 40% ABV

My father's second favourite joke involved this whisky and ended with the punchline: 'What? Derek?'

No one has done more work with matching whisky with food than Diageo. Many of the pairings in the early part of this book were put together with the company's help. And a few years ago the company used to stage large dinners with a different malt for each course.

One meal, based around curry, was held at Terence Conran's Bluebird Café in Fulham, London, specially memorable for me because it was the night when Diageo's Nicholas Morgan introduced me to what is now my favourite pairing, Lagavulin and Roquefort. The evening was also memorable because at the dinner was Charles MacLean, whisky writer, after-dinner speaker and genial *mein host* beyond compare.

This evening, though, he had a bee in his bonnet. He had issues over the way I was editing *Whisky Magazine* as a consumer magazine rather than trade one. That's because that's what it is, I told him.

'Oh no it's not,' he replied, and thus began a five-hour debate that started at the restaurant, continued in the taxi and ended in the hotel bar over several drinks. Gradually everyone went to bed until it was just us, but still Charlie wanted to continue.

Then suddenly he sat bolt upright and said 'there's a mouse!' I turned round but there was nothing there. Five minutes later it happened again. Same thing. And again. And by this time I was having serious doubts about Charlie's state of mind. But on the fourth time I turned round and there was a mouse, staring intently at us and eating a crisp

'Look Charlie,' I said. 'Even the hotel mouse has got fed up waiting for us to leave so let's go to bed and tomorrow send me an email and I'll address your points.'

'Tomorrow,' says Charlie. 'Good golly, man! I won't remember any of this in the morning!'

No email arrived and the matter was never referred to again.

White Horse is another Diageo blend and it's a big and busty whisky, with plenty of fruit, honey, smoke and spice. Spot-on.

Whyte & Mackay Special 40% ABV

Charlie MacLean is a lot of things, but if you asked most people who know him to make a list, 'AC/DC fan' would not be on any of them. So I was a bit surprised when Whyte & Mackay's international PR manager Rob Bruce told me he had got tickets to see the band and that Charlie would be coming along. Charlie looks like a World War I bi-plane pilot, complete with moustache, is a gentleman in

the best sense of the word, and is in his element in fine dining rooms surrounded by articulate wealthy bon viveurs. But Charlie is also a chameleon, and from the off it was clear he was going to have the time of his life. The image of AC/DC's Angus Young writhing on his back on a platform underneath a 60-feet high busty Rosie while Charlie guffawed heartily at the madness of it all, will be with me forever – and comes back to me

every time I hear the words 'Whyte & Mackay'.

This is an easy-to-like blend, unchallenging and very palatable, with lots of over-ripe fruit and a rich, sweet and pleasantly lengthy conclusion.

Whyte & Mackay The Thirteen 40% ABV

Orange and citrus fruits suggest Dalmore, red berries suggest some sherry influence and there are yellow fruits, some spice and a rounded and full grain backbone.

Whyte & Mackay 30-year-old 40% ABV

A big, rich, venerable blend packed with oaky, spicy flavours, good old-fashioned Highland malt and a substantial sherry hit. In many ways this is traditional in style, but whichever way you look at it, this is an impressive blend in an impressive bottle.

Whyte & Mackay 40-year-old 45% ABV

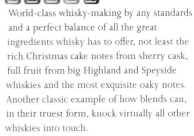

World-class whisky-making by any standards and a perfect balance of all the great ingredients whisky has to offer, not least the rich Christmas cake notes from sherry cask, full fruit from big Highland and Speyside whiskies and the most exquisite oaky notes. Another classic example of how blends can, in their truest form, knock virtually all other whiskies into touch.

ROBERT HICKS OF BEAM GLOBAL

Beam Global UK Ltd, Dalmore House, 310 Saint Vincent Street, Glasgow G2 5RY
www.beamglobal.com

Read about Scotch whisky in most books or attend tasting events and you could be forgiven for thinking that the only type of whisky is single malt.

It is the category that attracts the most attention, which provokes all the excitement and through its diversity, generates the dynamism that is driving the whisky market forward.

But pity the poor blends. They still account for more than 90 per cent of sales of Scotch whisky, most of the recognised brands are made to a high and impressive quality, and at least a proportion of them are not only excellent, but are more than a match for most single malts.

So will the better blends ever get the attention they deserve? If Robert Hicks has his way they will. He's a feisty fighter, and since he officially retired from his job as master blender at Allied Domecq in 2005, he's been on a mission to help get people to look at the blended category afresh. Now working as an ambassador for Beam Global, he is playing a key role in bringing Teacher's in particular, and blends in general, back into the public consciousness.

'Nearly all the books and articles over the past 15 to 20 years appear to concentrate on single malts and have relegated blended whiskies to the state of, if not the poor relation, then that of a distant cousin,' he says.

'Considering that blended whiskies contain many single malts with all their unique flavours this does seem very hard, especially when it was blended whisky that kept the industry running for the past 150 years.

'I expect that it's much simpler to write about a specific single-malt distillery which has been producing for many years and where there are numerous stories to be got, while to write about a blend is much more difficult.'

Despite the problems, though, Hicks is optimistic that as knowledge about whisky in general grows, people's attentions will turn to blends and there will be a renewed interest in how they are put together.

'I really hope there will be a future resurgence in the popularity of blends,' he says.

'If we hadn't started producing and selling blended whisky and relied solely on single malts we would still be a cottage industry, if an industry at all. It has been blended whisky that's made the fame of Scotch Whisky worldwide and many people have forgotten this.

'Consumers are becoming more knowledgeable with all the books and articles that have been written over the past couple of decades. The problem is that 99 per cent of the books and articles have been written are about malt whiskies and that's where the knowledge base is increasing. When I do Teacher's seminars I am often surprised how low the knowledge about blends is. Over the years I've received many letters and phone calls from people asking where a blended whisky is distilled and whether could they visit. That still happens occasionally today.'

Hicks realises the category has a long way to go, but he relishes a challenge, and he's been playing his part of late. Take Teacher's Origin, a groundbreaking blend that may one day be seen as a crucial milestone in the journey back to acceptance. It is a big, rugged and pulsating peaty whisky that

KEY WHISKIES

Teacher's Highland Cream 40% ABV
Teacher's Origin 42.8% ABV
Ardmore Traditional Cask 46% ABV
Laphroaig 10-Year-Old Cask Strength 57.3% ABV
Laphroaig Quarter Cask 48% ABV

swims strongly against the tide of bland blends.

Hicks agrees. 'If you look back at the styles that Teachers have produced in the past there has always been an emphasis on two main points, the malt content and having a distinct peated style,' he says.

'So when I was asked to produce a new style it was relatively easy to set the baseline: a high, 65 per cent malt content with a distinct Ardmore tang. Once I had thought of this I realised that it could very well have been similar to the styles that would have been produced by the early blenders, especially William himself.

'They all knew and understood malt whiskies, but with grain whisky being a newer style, they may have been a bit reluctant to have used large quantities, so therefore a high malt/low grain content blend may have been the norm. It was also quite traditional to marry the whiskies in the way we do now. In our case, we marry the malts and grains separately, and from that starting point, what other casks could we use for the marrying but quarter casks?'

'The difference is that we don't marry for just a couple of months but for more than a year at Ardmore in the Highlands, in the traditional earthen-floored warehouses, again harking back to the old days. From all these clues it was then comparatively easy to come up with the brand name – Teacher's Origin.'

Hicks is optimistic about the future for whisky in general and believes that blends will be part of the future not just as the dull and worthy component, but at the cutting edge.

'I find it exciting every time I see a new brand or style of blended whisky, whether that be blend or blended malt' he says. 'Anything breaking the mould of what's gone before and that stretches the boundaries of aroma and flavour. As has been proved over the past 10 years we've not discovered everything there is to know about whisky, or about distillation, maturation and blending. That is what interests me the most, trying to come up with something that no one else has tried before, or if they have tried, they didn't succeed with it.'

William Grant 12-year-old 40% ABV

William Grant owns Glenfiddich and The Balvenie and the company knows more than its fair share about blending. Unsurprisingly, then, even in its relatively young guises its blends fly. This is a tango between malt and grain, with the malts showing both the citrus and green fruit zestiness and a creamier fuller fruit, and sweet and clear grain. The result is sweet, rounded, full and fruity.

William Grant 15-year-old 43% ABV

Basically the 12-year-old with the volume turned up. The extra age adds texture and a fuller oak influence, but basically everything else is perfectly balanced and in its proper place.

William Grant 25-year-old 43% ABV

Outstanding. A distinct sherry nose, a healthy level of spice and plenty of oak but wrapped up in the sweetest, softest grain imaginable, so the result is a gossamer-like blend that coats the mouth with honeyed fruit, then leaves behind a woody and wonderful aftertaste. It is like a musical concerto in three movements.

William Grant Ale Cask 40% ABV

If you have ever tasted Innis & Gunn beer, then this is where it originated from. William Grant made beer to season the casks for this blend and then threw the beer away. That was until someone in management spotted staff siphoning off the beer and drinking it. It was tasted, found to be excellent, and the rest, as they say, is history. By such happy accidents are some great inventions born.
This is great. The beer takes away a level of sweetness and adds a malty, earthy and slightly savoury level to the blend, leaving all its core characteristics intact. It is the whisky equivalent of a Rugby Union team playing a Rugby League team at league. Odd but fun...

Blended/vatted malts

For many the world of whisky is an intimidating one. The large number of distilleries, the many expressions emanating from many of them, the age statements, special finishes, complex and involved wording on the label... it all adds up to the drinking equivalent of map-reading in Tokyo.

So when a group of friends came up with the idea of throwing out the baggage, presenting whisky in modern and simple packaging, and focusing purely on taste, it offered Scotch whisky a route into the future that would bring on board a new generation of whisky drinkers.

The vehicle to which the friends chose to hitch their idea was the category of vatted malts, where whiskies contain a mixture of malts from different distilleries. Marketed under names such as the Smoky Peaty One, the Rich Spicy One, or the Smooth Fruity One, these new-look whiskies were introduced to a fresh audience at outdoor sports events and good food shows rather than the more traditional whisky shows. Although there was nothing new about the category, the new whiskies looked like they had the potential to revolutionise our approach to whisky drinking.

Then the Scotch Whisky Association got involved, imposed a new term for a mixture of malt whiskies from different distilleries on the trade and in the process caused so much confusion that the progress of the category ground to a complete halt.

The new term – now enshrined in law – for these mixed malt whiskies is blended malt whiskies. This is different from the category known as blends or blended whiskies because blended malt whiskies are made using only malted whisky, whereas blended whiskies have a large quantity of whisky made with a grain other than malted barley. The new terminology is utterly ill-conceived, misleading and clumsy because the vast majority of the population know little or nothing about whisky beyond the fact that they think single-malt whisky is better than blended whisky. Leaving aside the fact that this is in itself wrong, if they do opt to buy a 'special' whisky they tend to bracket the blended malt whisky category with blends.

This is a big shame because some of the most exciting experimentation is going on in this category. Compass Box, in particular, has taken malt whiskies into exciting new areas. At one point the company launched a series of more than 20 single cask vattings under the collective name Canto, with different territories receiving a different version.

It is a category of whisky worth watching – often offering great value and some seriously fine whisky.

Barrogill 40% ABV

I'm no royalist but it is hard to immerse oneself for eight years in whisky and not grow a sneaking respect for the Prince of Wales. He loves whisky. He has visited a good number of Scotland's distilleries and has casks maturing in most of them. And if he seems stuffy and formal when meeting the suits, that is not the case when he is out among the workers. Talk to a warehouseman or distillery worker who has met him and they will tell you of his genuine interest, his knowledge of whisky, and his enthusiasm to hear and learn more.

He does not like fuss. Distilleries expecting a visit are instructed to make sure that invited guests arrive well before he does and are given a drink. Guests are told to carry on chatting and not to stop what they are doing when he arrives.

Barrogill is a mix of malts from the northern Highlands and is endorsed by the prince, who is Duke of Rothesay as well as Prince of Wales, and it is liveried in the royal colours. It is a robust, full and weighty whisky, with some peat, lots of savoury tones and some tingling spice at the finish.

Big Peat 46% ABV

Do not be put off by the somewhat tacky label – it cost independent producers Douglas Laing a fair few sales over Christmas

because the whisky comes without a box and looks a bit amateurish. But the whisky is amazing and it deservedly won the best blended malt category in the 2010 World Whisky Awards. It contains Ardbeg, Caol Ila and Bowmore and the extremely rare Port Ellen. Big, rich, peaty and very good indeed.

The Big Smoke 40% ABV

Released by independent bottler Duncan Taylor and another heavy hitter for Islay lovers, with smoke, peat, seaweed and barbecued fish.

Blue Hanger 4th Release 45.6% ABV

Blue Hanger is made by Berry Bros & Rudd, and this suggests that whisky-maker Doug McIvor was given free rein to produce a whisky worthy of such a respected wine house. He has succeeded. This is a wonderfully intense mix of sherry trifle, tangerine, heavy spice and some seriously old whisky, with tannins in the mix. It has plenty of dark chocolate and chilli and is not for the faint-hearted, but is excellent.

Blue Hanger 25-year-old 2nd Release 45.6% ABV

In the mid 1980s I saw the legendary Hüsker Dü at the Sheffield Leadmill, just when they had hit their musical peak. I don't know if they always played that way or they had misjudged the size of the venue, but they began the set with an unbroken string of five songs in about 20 minutes. By the end of it there was a 10-feet gap at the front of the crowd and people were being scraped off the back wall. It remains the most intense and memorable live performance of my life. This whisky is similar. It marches on, plugs in and fires a volley of menthol, liquorice, hickory, spice and oak before you can gasp. Awesome.

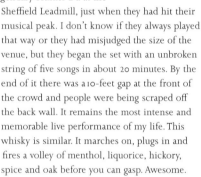

Clan Denny Islay 46% ABV

A fantastic big, rich, sweet and peated mix of four great Islay distilleries – Bowmore, Bunnahabhain, Caol Ila and Laphroaig. If you have ever asked yourself why you would bother buying a vatted malt of your favourite distilleries when you could just as well buy a single malt bottle of each, this is your answer. I'm drawn back to Islay time and time again, and often sit with a dram and debate in my head about which is my favourite distillery. This is in many ways greater than the sum of its parts, like watching four jazz musicians playing together and bringing out something new and fresh in each other. Sure, if you are in the mood for Coltrane or Davis nothing else will do. Sometimes a medley is enough, though. This is a malt medley and then some.

Clan Denny Speyside 46% ABV

Like the Clan Denny Islay but this time substitute peat for fruit. Again, big, clean, rich and tasty, this is every bit the match of the Islay bottling, though more mainstream. Less Coltrane and Davis and more Clapton, Beck, Page and maybe Jack White of the White Stripes (there is some younger stuff in here, I am sure of it).

Compass Box Flaming Heart 48.9% ABV

Quite close to being my perfect whisky, this is stunning stuff, using the finest mainland and island whiskies. What we have here is blackcurrant, melon and tropical fruits all wrapped up in a ball of smoke and peat and kissed away with liquorice, hickory, chilli and cinnamon, and an oiliness that coats the mouth – absolutely the 'business'. Compass Box makes this in limited batches and it sells quickly each time. Hopefully, though, the company will come back to it again and again.

Compass Box Oak Cross 43% ABV

This is another personal favourite, but for altogether different reasons. Here the heads of the bourbon cask have been replaced with new French oak (the cross reference in the title). The effect is a dusty, dry, fruity and highly spiced whisky. Late on there is some Battenberg cake and milk chocolate. Tastes like it should be expensive. It is not. Oh, and as with all Compass Box products, it is beautifully packaged too.

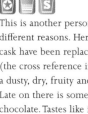

Compass Box Optimism 44% ABV

A limited-edition whisky so it is hard to know whether you can still find it, but this was released as an antidote to all the depression that a recession brings and could be described as 'happy juice'. It is all bright, zingy, refreshing and sherbety malts and has a rich and sweet taste, with some delicious peaty notes.

Compass Box The Peat Monster 46% ABV

Does what it says on the tin – lots of big and bold smoke and peat flavours, and among the char and oil there is some very pleasant fruit and spice too.

Compass Box Spice Tree 46% ABV

Every time I write something nice about the Scotch Whisky Association I get a wave of negative replies from whisky enthusiasts who despise the organisation. Does it have any idea what a large number of whisky enthusiasts think of it? We try to be nice about it, we really do, but the feeling is that it always goes after the little guy, wielding a sledgehammer to crush a nut. This is a case in point. The original version of this was matured in casks where some fresh oak staves were put inside the existing cask. You cannot do that, said the SWA, because you are adding oak. It would have been okay to replace existing staves with new oak, and Compass Box legally replaced the heads of casks with new oak for Oak Cross. But the company could not put extra staves in. Now John Glaser and his team have come up with a new and legal way to bring Spice Tree back. This is another extraordinary whisky not least because we really do get a spice rack of flavours – from clove, ginger, nutmeg and cinnamon at one end of the spectrum, and chilli, paprika and black pepper at the other.

Compass Box Lady Luck 45% ABV

Another limited edition which was still available at
the time of writing, this is very much in line with
what is becoming a Compass Box house style –
lots of fresh, open-air fruitiness wrapped in
dense smoky or peaty surrounds. The higher
price suggests that there are some rare and older
malts in here, but such is the skill of the whisky
maker, an irresistible youthfulness is also a
dominant theme of the flavour.

Famous Grouse 10-year-old 40% ABV

If you are an English Rugby Union fan, turn
away now. Ever since I first went to Eden Park in
Auckland in 1988, shared beers with Welsh and
Kiwi fans in the gardens of total strangers close
to the ground, and watched the best sporting
team on the planet, then and since, annihilate
Wales, scoring more than 50 points for the second week in a row, I
have loved the All Blacks. My love of their way of playing the game
has led to countless great shared rugby moments with fans across
the world and to the consumption of far too many whiskies with
knowledgeable and intelligent fans of the game. But there is one
exception: the English. Maybe they are not the arrogant public
school fans of old, but English rugby is dull and their fans remain
superior and blinkered. When they win they crow, when they lose
they whine about the cheating opposition and the poor quality
referee. I am no fan of English rugby even though Martin Johnson
went to my school. In fact I am responsible for him playing rugby.
When I was a prefect at Robert Smyth in Market Harborough and he
was a new boy, I said to the young Johnson, 'no, lad, you can't play
netball. Netball is for girls. Go and play rugby with the big boys. And
blow your nose.'

This might be a lie.

So I was delighted when Famous Grouse invited me up to a
Calcutta Cup game in 2006, showed me round the Famous Grouse
Experience and introduced me to this blended malt. Then off we
went to the game – or rather off to the bar first before the game. It
did not kick off until early evening by which time the Scottish fans
had consumed pretty much the entire beer and whisky allocation
for Great Britain for that year. And frankly, the English did not have
a chance. The Scots built up to the game by filling the pitch up with
bands and pipers, sent on a whole army of fire-waving Bravehearts,
and banished the English team to a small corner of the pitch.

When they actually got around to the rugby the Scots won – a
famous victory; remember, this was when the English team was
actually very good. I recall sitting in the corridor of my hotel (so as
not to disturb the family, who were in bed by the time I managed to

find my way back from the celebrations) and toasted
the day with a glass of this and a big juicy rare steak.
Great memories.

This has blackcurrant and soft fruits in the mix
and is nowhere near as good as it tasted that night.
But that's whisky for you.

Famous Grouse 15-year-old 43% ABV

Lots of vanilla, summer fruits and soft spices,
with a degree of smokiness and a pleasant and
easy-going finale.

Famous Grouse 18-year-old 43% ABV

A whisky-drinking experience
can be soured by external
events that have nothing
to do with the whisky itself. I first tasted
this at a Whisky Live show in Glasgow.
The trouble was, the Famous Grouse
had a 12-feet-high grouse wandering around
the event repeating the tune from the advert –
'duh duh duh duh de-de-de duhhhh' it went.
For two days – two whole days. By the end
several people at the event, both
paying customers and other
exhibitors, were scouring the
city for shooting rifles and
organising a grouse hunt.

This is rich in fruits and has
a layer of honey and oak to
give it depth and character.

Famous Grouse 30-year-old 43% ABV

If you have ever wondered what it would be like
to drink old Highland Park with old Macallan,
this may well be the chance to find out. The
rich and full Speyside fruit are at the core of
this, with orange in the mix, but there are some
honey, oak, spice and peat notes too – almost
trademark Highland Park. Very well made
indeed, and another example of how a vatting
can add up to more than the sum of its parts.

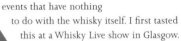

JOHN GLASER OF COMPASS BOX

Compass Box Delicious Whisky Ltd, Chiswick Studios, 9 Power Road, London W4 5PY
www.compassboxwhisky.com

On the face of it, it doesn't look much – an incongruous blue building with art deco pretensions in a faceless industrial estate off the Chiswick High Road in west London.

Through the doors, though, and you are in a whisky Aladdin's cave. It's a spacious open-plan room with desks down the left-hand side, advertising hoardings and posters down the middle, and bizarrely, keyboards set up in the corner. But the main act is in the middle. Slap bang in front of you is whisky. Bottles and bottles of it, including full demi-johns and scores of sample bottles.

This is the home of Compass Box, Britain's only true boutique whisky-maker, and before company founder John Glaser has even defined the terms for our meeting, he's off, bubbling with enthusiasm and reaching for the sample glasses.

First up is a Laphroaig from 1998, taken out of the wood before its 10th birthday and the product of a wonderful cask, he says, and he's right – it's rich in vanilla and has peat to die for. He follows it up with a quite stunning Glen Elgin, one of the three distilleries he never fails to recognise. I'm coming to the end of a 750-plus whisky marathon, but the nose, rich liqueur-like tropical fruits, is like nothing else I have come across. It turns out it is a vatting of various Glen Elgins he has got his hands on over the years. Five minutes in and Glaser has offered up two world champions, surely he must be tempted to bottle both these outstanding samples as they are?

'That would be so me-too,' he says. 'What would be the point of that? We attempt to do something a bit different rather than just do independent bottlings. Better to keep hold of these whiskies just for our friends.'

Compass Box was formed at the start of the millennium by Glaser, then in his mid 30s, to create new and exciting whiskies and present them in stylish, upmarket packaging. Compass Box remains small but it has been punching above its weight for years now, giving whisky enthusiasts such stunning whiskies as Flaming Heart, Oak Cross, Peat Monster, Lady Luck, Spice Tree and

Optimism, all included elsewhere in this book.

Armed with a supply of fine-quality malt from some of Scotland's best distilleries he has pushed the whisky envelope outwards, experimented into new taste channels, and tested the very boundaries of Scotch whisky. Not without controversy: occasionally he has fallen foul of the Scotch Whisky Association but inadvertently he has become a champion for the small producer and of the craftsman.

'Perhaps it's my background and I should get on with just making whisky,' he says with a shrug, 'but it's important that a line is drawn between artisan producers and brands and the big brands and mass producers speaking the parlance of artisan producers while making industrial products.'

Glaser believes firmly that as whisky drinkers learn more about whisky there will be more of a demand for small-scale whiskies from across the world and this in turn will lead to an influx of small companies who will chip away at the dominance of the enormous international drinks companies.

'If you think of the hegemony of French wines over the rest of the world 30 years ago versus the world of wine today, you'll get the picture,' he says. 'We'll see more people who love whisky cross from avid consumer to whisky producer. We'll see continued growth in small, entrepreneurial whisky-making companies. The consumer perception of what whisky can be, stylistically, will evolve, as new producers push at the envelope of the craft.'

The message is clear: Compass Box is doing fine but if you fancy joining it, come on in. In the meantime Glaser is living his dream, crafting fine whisky. We lunch at a local pub but before we leave he asks the barman to pour

us a Sipsmiths, a small-scale gin produced on a tiny still down the road, in the offices where Michael Jackson used to run his beer and whisky business.

Micro-distilling: you can see the temptation in his eyes.

'We have looked at distilling ourselves,' he says 'but we decided against it because we're so small. But it remains a dream and I'm not against distilling in London or somewhere else in England. We have started filling our own casks with new-make spirit so we have greater control over the process, so who knows?' Then a cheeky gleam enters his eye.

'If we took a cask of Clynelish and matured it in London, what could we call it? It wouldn't be Scotch if it was matured in England, but could we call it whisky? Or English whisky? Or Scottish malt spirit matured and bottled in England?' He laughs but I swear I hear something else, too.

Not a bunch of Scottish Whisky Association lawyers spluttering into their Scotch on the rocks perhaps?

full

half full

OPTIMISM

BY THE **COMPASS BOX** WHISKY C^o
MALT SCOTCH WHISKY

A SOFTLY SMOKY *malt Scotch whisky*
AGED in a combination of **AMERICAN**
and **NEW FRENCH OAK CASKS**.

BOTTLED
BY HAND ON... **27 & 28 FEB 2009**
BY THE *John Glaser*
WHISKYMAKER

BOTTLE NUMBER
173
COMPASS BOX
WHISKY COMPANY

44% vol.
70cl

YES, WE HAVE managed to bottle OPTIMISM.

We have done so as a *HOPEFUL* antidote to the
current global economic malaise.

We believe that the more people are *optimistic*
about their future, the faster we will be able to pull
ourselves out of this depressed economic state.

THE PURPOSE OF this bottling is to *REMIND*
and *INSPIRE* people to be *optimistic:* make the best
of any situation, *DISCOVER* the *OPPORTUNITIES*
in adverse circumstances, be *BRAVE* but pragmatic,
envision wild success.

Also, remember not to spend more than you take in.

Enjoy this bottled *Optimism*, our small effort to
help the world economy.

Here's to a bright future!

John Glaser
Whiskymaker, February 2009

COMPASS BOX
WHISKY COMPANY

Johnnie Walker Green Label 43% ABV

Green by name and green by nature. Diageo relaunched this as its big hitter in the blended malt category shortly after the SWA had declared victory for the new terminology well before the votes were metaphorically even in, let alone counted, and just before most of the ballot boxes went missing. I seem to remember we were taken to a big stately home or castle and played lawn croquet in the pouring rain. And am still not really sure why. But Diageo's point was that this was an 'outdoor malt', the sort of whisky to take hiking through the forest. Spot-on. Whenever I taste this – and I really love it – I'm reminded of steep, muddy forest paths by gurgling brooks in the shadow of mountains on a wet spring day. As you'd expect from Johnnie Walker, this is a masterclass in whisky-making and just about as good as vatted malts can get – give or take the odd Compass Box offering (which, interestingly, tend to use a similar range of malts). It is refreshing and clean whisky, with a weighty dose of Clynelish and some to-die-for smoke. Truly outstanding.

Monkey Shoulder 40% ABV

The vatted malt sector has the potential to bring a whole new generation of drinkers to whisky, and this brand provides the proof. Because a mixture of malts can come baggage-free and it does not need to have intimidating labels that many people don't understand, it is possible to present whisky in a totally different way. When the whisky in the bottle tastes like this, then the job is twice as easy.

The name sounds slightly off-beat and zany but is actually as traditional a reference as you could possibly get, referring to an old distillery affliction that was effectively repetitive strain injury in the shoulders caused by manually turning the malt, causing sufferers to hunch. The whisky in the bottle is a mix of un-aged Balvenie, Glenfiddich and Kininvie and producer William Grant has deliberately focused on the soft, sweet pear and apple flavours in its malts, making for a light, refreshing and easy drinking whisky that tastes great when chilled. It is great neat, but of course youths being youths, they will insist on mixing it, so the company has created an

impressive and inventive list of Monkey cocktails. So successful has the Monkey Shoulder campaign been that in some areas bars apply to become Monkey bars – preferred stockists for this malt. So, in effect, bars are asking to be allowed to sell Monkey Shoulder and to pay William Grant to do so. That is very clever and, if it is not the future, I don't know what is.

Sheep Dip 40% ABV

Another wacky name, and another one that has a stronger link to whisky's heritage than at first it might appear. It has been the patriotic duty of Scottish whisky-makers over the last 1000 years to avoid paying tax to the English, and they have demonstrated considerable skill at doing so. One way was to mark casks of whisky as sheep dip, for ridding sheep of vermin and infestations before shearing. If there was duty due on sheep dip it was far less than it was on whisky. Simple really. And again this is young and fresh, with a range of Speyside and Highland malts brought together without blemish and with the meekest touch of spice. Now marketed independently.

The Six Isles 43% ABV

As the name implies, this blend takes malt from six of the whisky-making islands of Scotland, which when it was launched was all of them, though now there is a new distillery on Lewis. You associate the islands with peaty whisky but this is not always the case –Tobermory on Mull, Arran on Arran and Scapa on Orkney all make predominantly peat-free whisky and Islay has its share of unpeated malt too.

That said, though, this focuses on the peatier end of the spectrum. The nose does not give too much away but, boy, does this kick on the palate. There are some citrus notes, a rich, oily undercurrent and some pepper spices late on.

Wemyss Peat Chimney 43% ABV

Wemyss is an independent bottler and it has picked up where Dave Mark & Robbo's Easy Drinking Whisky Company left off some years ago, mixing malt together to create a whisky based on a flavour profile. So this is self explanatory. It is actually not as peated as it might be, but that is not necessarily a bad thing, and the unusual tangy and nutty notes, some pear, a sprinkling of pepper and a mocha-like sheen to the proceedings all make this an intriguing and deliciously different whisky.

Wemyss Smooth Gentleman 43% ABV

I am not totally convinced that smooth is quite the right word for this – perhaps sleazy is more appropriate. There is something vaguely fishy here (in more than one sense of the word) and although you get apples and pears on the taste and a pleasant sweetness, it sort of slides in and out without making a huge impression. That said, it is pleasant enough and worth investigating.

Wemyss Spice King 43% ABV

You have to wait for the spices but they are not necessarily the dominant theme. If this whisky were in the Spice Girls it would not be Spicy Spice so much as Oily Spice or even Fishy Spice (which is better than Greasy Spice). It is likeable enough, like eating tinned mackerel with a dollop of soy sauce on it. What do you mean, yuck?

Grain whiskies

There is a view that single-grain whisky is lining up for its place in the sun. If you find an old grain whisky that has been matured in a good-quality cask, it can be quite sublime, bringing the finest elements of Scottish grain with the rich vanilla and candy notes of an American oak cask, a Scotch-bourbon hybrid to die for.

Aged grains of 30 years are less expensive than their single-malt whisky counterparts. Look out for independent bottlers such as Duncan Taylor and Gordon & MacPhail.

Compass Box Hedonism 43% ABV

Most grain whisky goes into blends and what little ends up being bottled on its own is mainly produced by independent bottlers, and much of it is very old. This is a vatting of grains, from the grain distilleries Cameron Bridge, Carsebridge and Cambus. There is nothing younger than 14 years old and some of the grain is more than 25 year old. By this time the grain has taken on some of the flavours of the bourbon casks they have been matured in. This is a delightfully sweet, vanilla and coconut dessert whisky with some gentle oil and oak. A pleasant change.

Snow Grouse 40% ABV

Unsurprisingly from the Famous Grouse family, though you would be hard pressed to make any real connection. This is another one of Edrington's experimental releases, and is a whisky designed to be kept in the fridge and served chilled. It's a refreshing enough drink, has a sweet two-dimensional taste, and has very little to do with whisky as we know it. Make of that what you will.

THE WORLD'S BEST WHISKIES

USA

United States of America

Of all the great whisky regions of the world, the United States is potentially the most exciting.

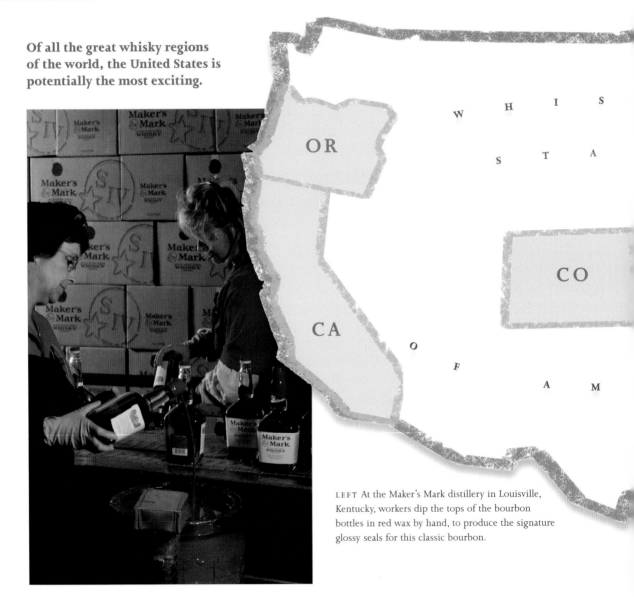

LEFT At the Maker's Mark distillery in Louisville, Kentucky, workers dip the tops of the bourbon bottles in red wax by hand, to produce the signature glossy seals for this classic bourbon.

Not only is United States whiskey in rude good health as we enter the second decade of the millennium, but it is sitting on the brink of a whiskey revolution as well. All sorts of weird and wonderful whiskeys currently maturing across the country are set to revolutionise our perceptions of the nation's spirit.

The United States has form in this area. A few years back, a new wave of micro-breweries did for its beer industry what punk rock music did for bloated corporate rock: shook it by the throat, scornfully cast it aside, and replaced it with something altogether more vibrant and exciting. Now, it seems, the same might be happening to whiskey, albeit on

a smaller scale. In the United States, whiskey has tended to mean bourbon and a few add-ons, and bourbon has tended to mean Kentucky. These days, though, new micro-distilleries are starting to pop their heads above the surface, unfettered by tradition and convention and not afraid to take whiskey in whatever direction they see fit. They are just starting to pick up awards domestically and in time their reputation will spread overseas.

So a classic case, then, of out with the old, in with the new? Actually, no. They're built of sterner stuff than that down in Kentucky. You know that song which goes 'I get knocked down, but I get up again...'? That's Kentucky.

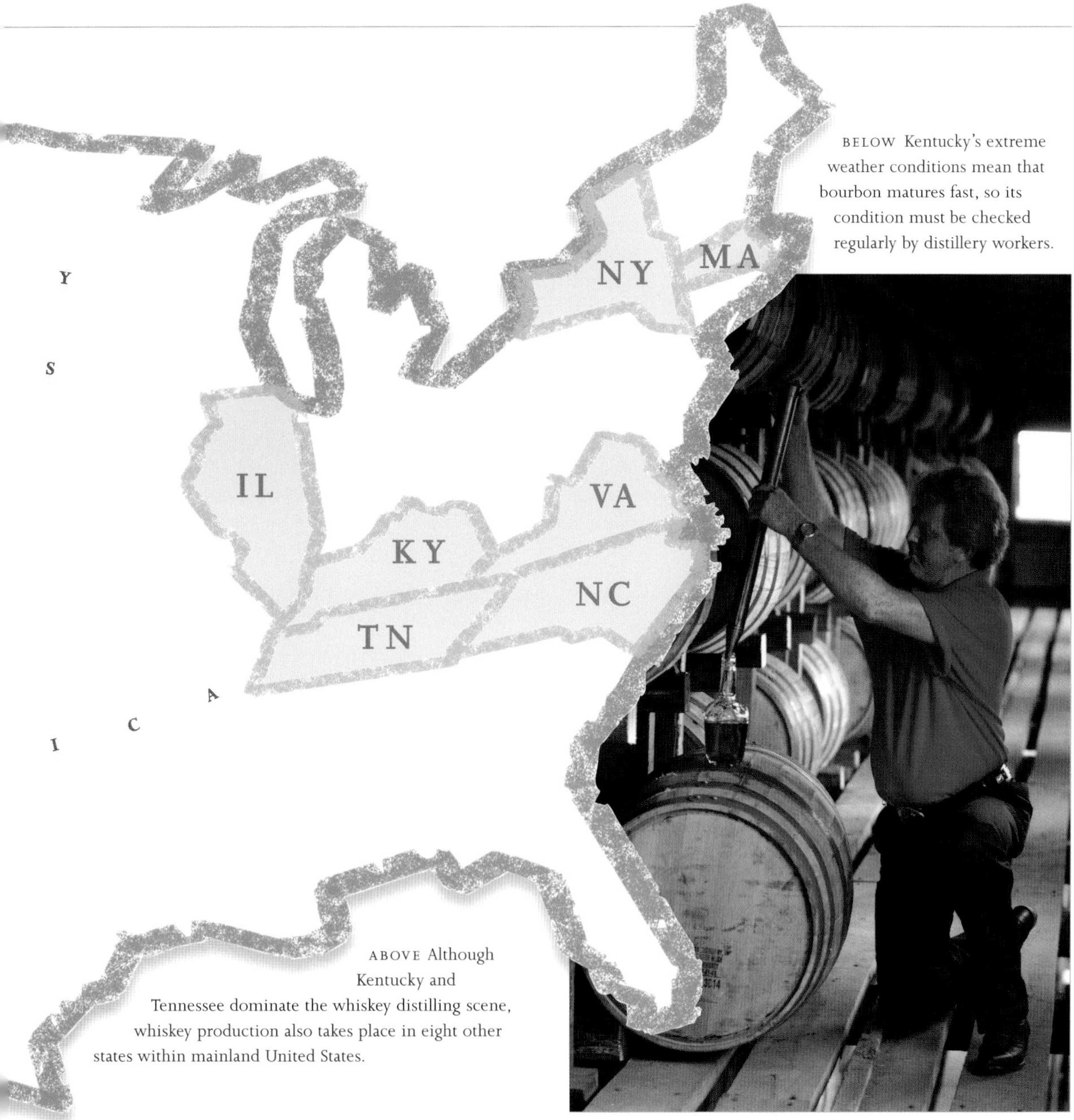

NY MA

IL

VA

KY

NC

TN

C

A

BELOW Kentucky's extreme weather conditions mean that bourbon matures fast, so its condition must be checked regularly by distillery workers.

ABOVE Although Kentucky and Tennessee dominate the whiskey distilling scene, whiskey production also takes place in eight other states within mainland United States.

It is a state littered with the crumbling remains of fallen distilleries, its history books packed with great whiskey-making names that have been battered and broken, but have a habit of still popping up again within the portfolios of the surviving distillers. Economic tornados and social hurricanes have battered Kentucky's whiskey industry, but this is a state built on limestone rock, and it will take much more than a few upstarts in Portland, San Francisco, Colorado or New York to rock it off its axis.

Indeed, Kentucky has risen to the challenge. Across the state there are casks made of maplewood, ash, and hickory filled with maturing spirit; there are barrels containing single malt, pure wheat and rye whiskey, and spirit made with oats and even white (sweet) corn. And then there is the more traditional bourbon: rich, flavoursome, magnificent – and in as good a shape as it has ever been.

Only Islay in Scotland can match this wonderful state for its cohesive sense of purpose, its intensity, the quality of its whiskey, and its empathy with, and understanding of, grain spirit. Just as single-malt whisky will be dominated by Scotland for generations to come, so, too, will Kentucky dominate American whiskey – and aided by the new wave of exciting new distilleries elsewhere, play a key role as it moves forwards to a new level on the world stage.

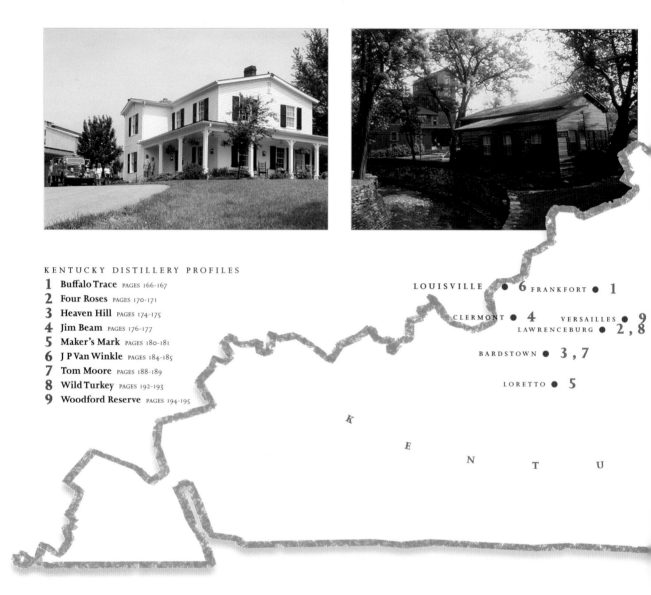

KENTUCKY DISTILLERY PROFILES

1 **Buffalo Trace** PAGES 166-167
2 **Four Roses** PAGES 170-171
3 **Heaven Hill** PAGES 174-175
4 **Jim Beam** PAGES 176-177
5 **Maker's Mark** PAGES 180-181
6 **J P Van Winkle** PAGES 184-185
7 **Tom Moore** PAGES 188-189
8 **Wild Turkey** PAGES 192-193
9 **Woodford Reserve** PAGES 194-195

LOUISVILLE ● 6 FRANKFORT ● 1

CLERMONT ● 4 VERSAILLES ● 2,9
LAWRENCEBURG ●

BARDSTOWN ● 3,7

LORETTO ● 5

K

E

N

T

U

When you think of Kentucky the state you tend to picture green fields, glistening chestnut geldings, fields of corn and picket fences – and, in part, this is true. The distilleries of Woodford Reserve, Maker's Mark, Four Roses and Wild Turkey are situated in deepest rural Kentucky, and Tom Moore, Kentucky Bourbon Distillers and Heaven Hill are a stone's throw from the historic town of Bardstown.

But there is another Kentucky, too. Louisville lies to the very north of the state, the historic and symbolic Ohio river that separates north and south flowing through its heart. It is a growling, vibrant city, a mix of old down-and-dirty industry and modern skyscraper-based business, faceless retail malls and independent student-dominated suburbs. Whiskey first reached out to the world from here. Today, Brown-Forman and Heaven Hill have their biggest distilling operations in the centre of the city, and the historic Whiskey Row, bourbon's historical trading front line, is still in evidence. In the battered rough-and-tumble Shively, spirit still sleeps in large industrial whiskey warehouses and the brooding but long-closed distilling giant Stitzel-Weller is a monument to the past. It smells of another era.

But regeneration is in evidence, too. The urban bourbon trail boasts world-class restaurants and bars such as Revue and Proof, where bourbon is served in salubrious

Jim Beam, Maker's Mark and Buffalo Trace distilleries are popular on the Kentucky whisky tourist trail.

Bourbons

The United States' native spirit must contain at least 51 per cent corn, although it would usually have considerably more, and it must be matured in new white oak barrels which may be toasted and charred. Straight bourbon must be matured for at least two years, and the drink is bound by strict rules on distilling strengths and the strength is can go in to the barrel. Nothing can be added at all beyond grain, yeast and water, meaning that the rules for bourbon are stricter than those governing Scottish single-malt whisky.

Ancient Age 10-year-old 40% ABV
www.buffalotrace.com

'Ancient Age' is the old name given to what is now Buffalo Trace. The site, on the banks of the Kentucky river and close to the state capital, is where the traditional world of Native Americans and the new settlers met head-to-head. Buffalo Trace is so named because it lay on the old buffalo trails. The vast herds had to slow and stop in numbers to cross the river, providing plentiful opportunity for the Cherokee. But the region offered the settlers much, too, and their arrival and eventual settlement was not without bloody incident. Frankfort is named after Stephen Frank, who was killed by a Native American party while camping with other settlers.

This bourbon is a delicate balancing act of soft corn, spicy rye and chunky fruit, particularly citrus ones, all held together by some delightful oils.

Baker's Aged 7-year-old 53.5% ABV
www.jimbeam.com

One of four whiskeys in Jim Beam's small-batch collection, Baker's is named after Baker Beam, Jim Beam's great-nephew and a master distiller in his own right. This is made using a 60-year-old yeast strain and is matured for seven years, an age at which some would argue that the bourbon has taken all it can from the wood in terms of fruit, vanilla and sweetness. The recipe is the same as the standard Jim Beam, but this spirit comes off the still at 125 proof. This strength gives a big, upfront bourbon flavour with anisette and liquorice notes and a crisp, fruity heart while the seven-year maturation gives it a chunky fullness.

surroundings alongside the state's finest cuisine. In just a few short years, the producers of bourbon have given the drink an image overhaul. While still very much a people's drink, bourbon's big name brands no longer occupy the bottom shelf in liquor stores.

It is in this context you realise that bourbon is looking forward and not back. Its distilleries might still be monuments to hospitality, history, polite manners and gentle country ways, but here in Louisville the business men are finding new ways to sell their whiskeys, and marketing an increasingly diverse portfolio that includes everything from newly bottled White Dog to 25-year-old rye.

Basil Hayden's 8-year-old 40% ABV

www.jimbeam.com

When Basil Hayden travelled to Kentucky from Maryland the state had been in existence for just four years and George Washington was still president. The marketing material reckons this bourbon is made to a recipe perfected back then which is, of course, fantasy. What is true though, is that the recipe is that of Old Grandad, which was originally distilled in the 1880s by Richard Heydon – note the different spelling – who named it after his grandad, Basil. It is Basil's picture that appeared on the old Old Grandad label. What you will find in the bottle is a healthy amount of tasty rye, as much as a third of the mashbill. The spirit is taken off the still at 120 proof, much lower than Old Grandad, and is casked with no water. There is a distinctive pepperiness about this, but the lower strength means more fruity flavours, particularly citrus, and the eight years maturation ensures some delicious woody notes.

Benchmark Old No. 8 40% ABV

www.buffalotrace.com

A curiosity, this. The bourbon has appeared as just Benchmark, and as Benchmark Old No. 8. Some but not all bottlings have the word 'McAfee's' before the name. That's the case here. It is said that the McAfee Brothers travelled to Kentucky as early as 1773, identified a site near Frankfort and then left surveyor's benchmarks for subsequent settlers to find. This bourbon was part of the Seagram stable before its demise and has ended up at Buffalo Trace near Frankfort – not far from where the McAfees laid down their markers. This version of the bourbon is an easy-drinking and inoffensive tipple, with strong, sweet vanilla and some soft toffee notes.

Blanton's Single Barrel No. 209 46.5% ABV

www.buffalotrace.com

Arguably the first single-barrel bottling and therefore the very first drops of what has become a torrent towards premium bourbon. Bottlings of this sort are to official whiskeys what bootleg CDs are to the music industry. Every barrel is different and, certainly in the case of Blanton's, differences between them are significant, which is where the fun lies.

This particular series of bottlings was started by former distiller Elmer T Lee, who is now in his nineties. To this day he has free rein to seek out fine casks for future bottlings. He is one of a number of people still associated with the Buffalo Trace distillery who worked with Colonel Albert Blanton, who spent more than 50 years making fine handcrafted bourbon. Most bottlings are taken from casks stored high up in warehouse H, but they vary in age and so the bottle carries no age statement.

This one has a soft nose with exotic fruits upfront. Next follows a big wave of spicy rye, a dark treacle undertow and ends with a honey and liquorice combination that is to die for. Excellent.

Booker's 6-year-old 63.5% ABV

www.beamglobal.com

Number three in Beam's small batch quartet and arguably the best – but what a great argument to have. Booker Noe died a few years back and is sorely missed by anyone who came across him. His son Fred still works with Beam and a few years ago he was forced, against his better nature, to speak to a group of festival visitors while the PR people replaced some faulty samples that had been poured out. For 10 minutes he spoke about his father, about the special qualities that made him so loved, and about his legendary generosity. Finally he told how they went to him one night as he lay sick and offered him a whiskey, but he declined. 'That's when we knew he was leaving us,' said Fred. 'Because he no longer cared for a bourbon.'

This is a fitting tribute to him. It is a big, characterful bourbon just like Booker, rich in vanilla, fruit and spice and with a honeycomb-candy heart that is battered, but withstands the influence of the oak. All in all this is everything that a sledgehammer bourbon should be.

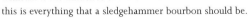

Buffalo Trace 45% ABV
www.buffalotrace.com

Ever had an experience that you will always associate with a particular whiskey?

For me it's this bourbon – and the day I interviewed Jon Bon Jovi and he referred to our chat on stage in front of 12,000 people.

It was in Sydney, Australia, during the Keep The Faith Tour. I was working for the New Zealand Herald and had seen the first of three Sydney shows the night before the interview. He was a journalist's dream. He spoke of how he had nearly tripped over a dead body as he jogged through Sydney's King's Cross that morning. He spoke about how much he missed home life while on the road. And he spoke about how he'd trade his rock-star status for a few nights playing guitar for one of his and my heroes Southside Johnny as a member of the Asbury Jukes, in front of 200 people.

That night he referred directly to our conversation on stage and mentioned me by name, and at the after-show party I toasted him with Buffalo Trace. Two weeks later he rang me to say he'd gone on the road with Southside Johnny and the Asbury Jukes. What a star.

This bourbon is, like Bon Jovi, pretty damn good. It rocks when it wants to but a sweet fruitiness makes it pretty mainstream too. Easy on the palate, but that doesn't mean that there isn't greatness here.

Bulleit 40% ABV
www.bulleitbourbon.com

A few years ago Tom Bulleit, great-great-grandson of original Bulleit distiller Augustus Bulleit, held a party for journalists in the suburbs of Bardstown. One small group of journalists arrived to find that Tom wasn't there yet, so they went back to the Bourbon & Cigars event happening elsewhere, planning to return later. When they came back two hours later, they walked into the house where the party was, to find no one there. After some moments wondering about, they heard laughter and talking in the neighbouring garden. They had entered the wrong house.

'That could have gone either way,' one of the Bulleit entourage said later. 'In Kentucky if the householders had found you they would have pulled a gun – or offered you dinner.'

Bulleit is made at the Four Roses distillery and the fruitiness suggests so. The recipe is said to be is based on Augustus's original one. This is populist bourbon with lots of honey and vanilla.

Eagle Rare Single Barrel 10-year-old 45% ABV
www.buffalotrace.com

Eagle Rare is another single barrel bottling and, while there are big differences between each bottling, you can be pretty confident that what you are going to taste will be outstanding. Originally launched by Seagram and now part of Buffalo Trace, Eagle Rare was arguably the first super premium bourbon. A new version is released every autumn but demand tends to outstrip supply; you have to move fast to get hold of it because it is hard to find. When you do, you will encounter a citrus and orange nose with an almost liqueur-like quality. Exotic fruits, floor polish and sweet grain make it an easy-drinking bourbon with just enough oak to lend shape and structure.

Eagle Rare 17-year-old 45% ABV
www.buffalotrace.com

Named after the great American symbol, the Bald Eagle, Eagle Rare is meant to share similar values – the pursuit of life, liberty and happiness. When it soars, the 17-year-old is up there with the very best bourbons. But there is considerable variance. This one has the trademark woodiness and substantial rye spice, but there is also a grassy and almost floral thing going on too, making it a surprisingly soft and gentle version of Eagle Rare. That is not a criticism, but it is slightly surprising.

BUFFALO TRACE DISTILLERY

113 Great Buffalo Trace, Frankfort, Kentucky 40601
www.buffalotrace.com

Distilleries are to whisky writers what children
are to teachers – you know you should not have
favourites but sometimes you just can't help it.
And even by Kentucky's exceptional standards
the visitor experience at Buffalo Trace is
special. No matter which of the three tour
options you take, youare in for a world-class
whiskey treat.

ABOVE Past, present and future: the stylish Buffalo
Trace bottle is a perfect example of old meeting new in
bourbon's quest to appeal to a broader market.

RIGHT Buffalo Trace distillery has traded
under various names since it was opened.
It backs on to the Kentucky river, once
used to ferry resources and whiskey.

If you have the time, though, and are in good health, make sure that you take the hard-hat tour. It does exactly what it says on the tin, and is a delightful trek up and down ladders and rickety staircases, into the heart of the distillery and through its warehouses.

Buffalo Trace occupies an immense site on the edge of Frankfort, the state's capital, and is another of those places with links to some of the great names of bourbon. Formerly called Ancient Age, the roll of honour at this distillery includes George T Stagg, William Larue Weller, Colonel Albert Blanton and Thomas H Handy. Tennessee whiskey-maker George Dickel was based here for a while, the Van Winkle range of old bourbons are maturing on site, and bourbon legend Elmer T Lee, now in his nineties, still pops in regularly to check on stock. They of course make Buffalo Trace here, but also Sazerac Rye, Eagle Rare and Hancock's.

If you think that once you have seen one distillery you have seen them all, then Buffalo Trace and its amazing guides will make you think again. Strange artwork, stunning views and a quirky micro-still, now used to create all sorts of single-barrel experimental whiskeys – all add to the colour. Recent additions to the tour include a visit to the barrel room and a meeting room that looks like a classroom in a nineteenth-century schoolhouse.

'You might think that what a distillery fears most is fire, but it's not,' says Freddie Johnson who, like his fellow guides at the distillery, is a gushing font of bourbon knowledge. 'The biggest fear is a bad cooper. You get the barrels wrong or end up with leaks, and it can wipe out your whole profit.'

At the back of the meeting room is a bookcase that turns out to be a secret door leading into warehouse C. It's whiskey's answer to Harry Potter's Room of Requirement and, once through it, you will find all manner of mini casks and strange creations as the distillery team test new whiskeys for future release.

But the best part of the tour is the visitor centre, which tells the story of the distillery and includes some stunning photos stretching back 150 years. On one wall there is a list of every distillery ever opened and/or closed in Kentucky, including scores that never reopened after Prohibition.

Close by there is a full-size picture of a worker inspecting barrels for leaks with a torch. This is Jimmy Johnson, Freddie's father.

'He's in his nineties now, but the distillery still involves him in celebrations and events, and it makes him feel wanted,' says Freddie. 'They brought him in to roll out the

KEY WHISKEYS

Ancient Age 10-year-old 40% ABV
Benchmark Old No 8 40% ABV
Blanton's Single Barrel No 209 46.5% ABV
Buffalo Trace 45% ABV
Eagle Rare Single Barrel 10-year-old 45% ABV
Eagle Rare 17-year-old 45% ABV
Elmer T Lee 45% ABV
George T Stagg 70.7% ABV
Hancock's Reserve Single Barrel 44.45% ABV
Old Charter 8-years-old 40% ABV
Old Charter 10-years-old 43% ABV
WL Weller 7-year-old Special Reserve 45% ABV
Weller Antique 53.5% ABV
William Larue Weller 67.4% ABV

six-millionth barrel since Prohibition and it's thought that he is the only man alive who touched the millionth barrel all those years ago, and the second-, third-, fourth- and fifth-millionth since.'

Freddie's grandfather also worked at the distillery, working alongside Colonel Blanton, and the distillery has several other families where generation after generation has helped to pour out the spirit and roll out the barrels. No other distillery quite captures such a sense of history. When you look at the black-and-white pictures on the visitor centre wall, at the workers from 140 years ago, and you read the list of great distilleries, many of which are now reduced to rubble, you feel like you're passing through history on a conveyor belt that was here before you stepped on to it and will continue to roll on by when you step off.

LEFT The imposing red brick walls of the distillery's warehouses in Frankfort are home to many a fine bourbon

WELL, FANCY THAT ...
Buffalo Trace is so named because the distillery is sited at a point where once-great buffalo herds, following a traditional migration route, slowed down to cross the Kentucky river, at a natural ford, making them perfect targets for native American Indian tribes.

Elijah Craig 12-year-old 47% ABV

www.heaven-hill.com

The nose is surprisingly wispy and subtle, with traces of cherry and mint, and some pine and forest flower notes. Given its age, this is nowhere near as bold as it might be, but the oakiness holds in check the sweet vanilla heart; the overall taste is rounded, smooth and more-ish. With its traces of glacé cherry and spearmint, this is very much a band effort, with no soloists.

Elijah Craig 18-year-old 45% ABV

www.heaven-hill.com

Is it only age that makes this bourbon significantly more assertive than the 12-year-old? Or could it be that it is made with whiskey distilled and matured at the old distillery, while the 12-year-old is made with stock from the Bernheim plant? Time will tell. Let's hope nothing happens to this though – it puts up a strong argument against those who say bourbon doesn't work older than 10 years. You should be a fan of oak in your whiskey to appreciate it, but this is no wooden battering ram, with plenty of spicy rye, peach, tangerine and liquorice notes, and a squelchy, oily base to carry it off. Stunning.

Elmer T Lee 45% ABV

www.buffalotrace.com

Elmer T Lee is a bourbon legend. After serving in the armed forces for four years after Pearl Harbor he returned to university in Kentucky, before starting work in 1949 at what was then known as the George T Stagg distillery. There he worked with two bourbon recipes that have remained largely unchanged, as well as a rye recipe.

We tend to think of Single Barrel and Small Batch bottlings as relatively recent developments, but Elmer T Lee can be credited with starting the trend 25 years ago.

This one has lemon, orange and sour apple notes, then a wave of spice, before a smooth finish marked by a perfumey quality and some soft fudge. Dangerously quaffable.

Evan Williams 43% ABV

www.heaven-hill.com

Heaven Hill's Heritage Center on the outskirts of Bardstown was built a few years ago and is a good introduction to bourbon in general and the Heaven Hill story in particular. A large barrel-shaped tasting room is the ideal place to sample the distillery's bourbons, and a well-stocked shop ensures that you can take one of the iconic brands away with you. Here you will find the stories of Evan Williams and Elijah Craig. But make sure you maintain a healthy dose of cynicism when you read them. Williams was born in Wales, settled in Virginia and moved into the unchartered territories within the state during the 1780s, some years before they were renamed Kentucky. Whether he was the state's first distiller is questionable, but he was certainly among its pioneers, providing the United States with a rich and evolving distilling heritage that stretches back 220 years.

This standard black-label bottling is a big seller and as good an entry-level bourbon as you'll find. But it is bourbon for people who have discovered Jack Daniels or Jim Beam and want to move on – this is easy going, sweet and toffee-ish, with some pear and apple flavours – unchallenging and pleasant enough – the bourbon equivalent of mainstream country singer Garth Brooks perhaps?

Evan Williams 12-year-old 50.5% ABV

www.heaven-hill.com

Twelve years old is a weighty age for a bourbon, and the strength of this bottling is just above the traditional industry standard strength of 100 % ABV. This is made up of casks specially selected by Parker and Craig Beam from Heaven Hill's iron-clad warehouses at the Bardstown site and is not widely available.

It is a bold and assertive bourbon and drier than many of its competitors. There is a juicy berry fruit aspect to it, as well as just enough tannins to keep everything in check, moderate vanilla notes and a delightful wave of spices courtesy of the rye.

Evan Williams 23-year-old 46.75% ABV
www.heaven-hill.com

The Watson Twins from Louisville record torch-song country and blues songs. The perfect way to enjoy their music is to pour a glass of something like Evan Williams 23-year-old, dim the lights and let the music and bourbon dazzle your senses. This is therapy of the highest order; after 30 minutes, no problem seems too great.

This whiskey is hard to find, but great to savour. You'll encounter kiwi fruit, guava, then hickory and finally sweet chilli and cayenne pepper. As delightful, complex and varied as the twins themselves, this is a heaven-made match.

Evan Williams Single Barrel 2009 43.3% ABV
www.heaven-hill.com

These special bottlings from Heaven Hill are released annually and have been consistently excellent. But a couple of years ago the distillery began using nine- or 10-year-old whiskey from the new Bernheim distillery rather than from the pre-fire Bardstown site. Despite this major change I cannot agree with those hankering back to a 'no longer an option' past, nor do I think that the changes have taken these releases downhill. The bourbon has lots of exotic fruit, some caramel, chewy candy, nutmeg and sandalwood, plus the right level of oak and spice. Pretty faultless really.

Four Roses 40% ABV
www.fourroses.us

The sentimental story of how this bourbon got its name involves a marriage proposal from the distillery founder to a southern belle being accepted by the symbolic wearing of four roses on a ballgown. More interesting is the fact that it stands out from more assertive bourbons like a ballerina stands out in a rugby scrum. It's very fruity, with orange in the mix, some fruit peel, cinnamon and creamy vanilla. You have to look for it, but there is enough rye there to provide a solid backbone. Bourbon's equivalent to Annie of 'Get your Gun' fame – quite feminine but pretty feisty too. Often accompanied by a rendition of 'My Old Kentucky Home' at the annual Four Roses Let's Talk Bourbon Breakfast.

Four Roses Small Batch 45% ABV
www.fourroses.us

There's nothing wrong with the standard yellow label, but when you move to the single barrel and small-batch versions you start to realise how very good this bourbon is. Four Roses uses two recipes and five different yeasts to create 10 different whiskeys within its walls. Just three of those are used for the Small Batch version.

The citrusy notes from the standard version remain but this is like mixing alcohol with fruit jellies and is far removed from big woody and ryed bourbons. This is bourbon's answer to Scotland's Monkey Shoulder, bringing a new generation to the world of bourbon.

Four Roses Single Barrel 50% ABV (VARIES)
www.fourroses.us

For many years you couldn't buy Four Roses bourbon in the United States beyond the regions where the workforce lived. Its rollout in the past three years has therefore been dramatic. But people still need convincing that this is a very different whiskey to the blend that dominated liquor-store shelves when the Bronfman family and Seagram took over. It was not an uncommon sight to find master distiller Jim Rutledge handing out samples in malls most Saturdays.

Bland blend this most certainly isn't. This is Four Roses at its sharpest and cleanest, with all the grains playing an active part, the fruits giving it the chewiest of centres, and just enough oiliness to hold it all together.

Four Roses Mariage 58% ABV
www.fourroses.us

Based on the French wine concept of taking two different wines and blending them to create something new and better, this Mariage from 2009 is bottled at a weighty 58% and is arguably the fruitiest bourbon ever made. It's like chewing on alcohol-soaked orange jelly babies, with a liqueur-like intensity. Also present is a charry, toasty aspect and plenty of oak tones to calm the sweetness. Best of all, there's a gloopy oiliness that coats the mouth so the flavours linger long after swallowing.

FOUR ROSES DISTILLERY

1224 Bonds Mill Road, Lawrenceburg, Kentucky KY 40342
www.fourroses.us

**Every September the historic town of Bardstown hosts the Kentucky Bourbon Festival,
a week-long celebration of all things bourbon, culminating with the prestigious Kentucky Gala.**

One of the best-attended events, however, is Let's Talk Bourbon, held early on the Friday morning, miles away from the Gala, south of Lawrenceburg, at one of the state's most remote distilleries,.

Four Roses distillery is like no other. Its butterscotch-yellow Spanish bodega-style buildings complete with bell tower and terracotta awnings, suggest it should be making wine not bourbon. This pretty, delicate distillery is surrounded by ugly and imposing warehouses that are now filled with Wild Turkey bourbon, distilled down the road. It's as incongruous as a Madonna in a muddy field.

Every year, as the humidity rises and summer mist drapes the distillery lawns and surrounding trees, guests gather under a large gazebo to hear master distiller Jim Rutledge explain how bourbon is made. Beforehand they tuck in to crisp bacon, grits and eggs, and sup freshly squeezed orange juice and strong rich black coffee.

'But I must be a pretty lousy teacher, because the same folk come back year after year,' he says about his seminar with a chuckle.

And of course no one is there for the science. They are there to see friends that they have not caught up with since last year's Gala, to partake in what is becoming a Gala institution, and to wait for those golden-nugget moments when Rutledge breaks from any pre-prepared script and indulges his 200 guests with anecdotes and stories that reflect his deep love of bourbon in general and this historic distillery in particular.

These are heady time for Four Roses. Five years ago you could barely buy the bourbon in America. Now it is available in close to 40 states and rising. New distribution deals in Europe suggest its future is healthy there, too. The change in fortune stems from the purchase of the distillery by Japanese company Kirin in 2002, after years as part of the Seagram stable.

'The problem with Seagrams was that the Bronfman family were in to blends,' says Rutledge. 'Four Roses was sold as a blend in America and the bourbon was removed from the shelves. Way back it was not only the most recognised whiskey in America, but probably its most recognised distilled spirit. But it was a totally different type of whiskey. So we have a big job to do, not only to re-establish Four Roses in America, but also to show people who remember it that this is something totally different – a good-quality bourbon. Thankfully there is a new generation coming through who do not remember the old Four Roses at all.'

Four Roses is unique among bourbons in that the pretty distillery operates more like a Japanese operation than an American one. It creates 10 different whiskeys within its walls, based on two recipes and using five different yeasts. The whiskeys are then mingled together to create the standard Four Roses bourbon. Of those 10, four recipes are selected for the Small Batch, and one for the Single Barrel. Where Four Roses is really catching up lost ground, however, is through its annual special and limited releases. Started in 2007 to mark Rutledge's fortieth year in the industry, it was followed in 2008 by Mariage, a bourbon built around the wine concept of combining two very different wine styles to create something new and better. Since then a limited-edition bourbon has been launched each year at the festival, and they have all been consistently outstanding.

'We're genuinely creating different whiskeys here, not just taking from different warehouses or from different parts of the warehouse or from different years,' says Rutledge. 'We're making bourbon of fine quality as part of the Four Roses stable but also offering a range of styles and tastes. People are starting to understand this and it's very exciting for us.'

It's exciting for everybody. Four Roses is definitely one of the distilleries to watch.

KEY WHISKEYS

Four Roses 40% ABV
Four Roses Mariage 58% ABV
Four Roses Single Barrel 50% ABV (VARIES)
Four Roses Small Batch 45% ABV

ABOVE & BELOW Four Roses distillery now and then. Its distinctive facade makes it unique in the world of whisky.

OPPOSITE The Four Roses are a symbol of acceptance of a wedding proposal from the distillery's founder.

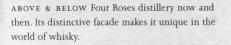

George T Stagg 70.7% ABV
www.buffalotrace.com

George T Stagg is one of those characters who ducks and dives through early bourbon history. The whiskey bearing his name today is fittingly distilled on the site that he once owned and which bore his name. But he appears in the history of Labrot & Graham, and within the Jim Beam empire through his links with Colonel Edmund H Taylor.

The bourbon that carries his name today is part of the Buffalo Trace Antique Collection and is, frankly, the star quarterback. Each autumn a new bottling is put out and each autumn there is a mad rush to get hold of it. Little makes its way into Europe and what does is considerably more expensive than in the United States. But if ever there were a bourbon worth shelling out for, this is it. One of the world's truly great whiskeys, the Big Brown of bourbon, is a true thoroughbred with no obvious weaknesses whatsoever.
So take your pick of the flavours – Stagg is rich in honey, oak, cinnamon, cloves, orange peel, marzipan, cocoa, sandalwood, tobacco pouch and candy stick. For me, though, it's all about cherry in dark chocolate, hickory, red liquorice and pepper dust. Sip and savour it without water. For the ideal accompaniment, play Whiskeytown's *Faithless Street* CD – perfect Americana for an all-but-perfect bourbon.

Hancock's Reserve Single Barrel 44–45% ABV
www.buffalotrace.com

This expression has an oily, slightly winey note at first, almost Scotch-like, but it gives way to a spiky, spicy note and some vanilla. The palate is dominated by the rye, and could just about pass for a rye whiskey, but then a wave of sweet vanilla, some cocoa and dark chocolate notes arrive before an astringent, oaky finish. It is the oral equivalent of one of those fireworks that goes through the colours of a traffic light. If Elmer T Lee selected this, then he sure is a complex individual.

Heaven Hill 40% ABV
www.heaven-hill.com

Bourbons such as Heaven Hill are matured first and then charcoal-filtered before bottling. In this case, the bourbon process of distillation and maturation is unaffected. Jack Daniels, on the other hand, cannot be called a bourbon because it is put through a wall of maplewood charcoal to mellow it after the still and before being casked. In this case the process affects the distillation and maturation of the bourbon.

This bourbon is mellow, as well as inoffensive and under-whelming. Best served as an early evening aperitif on a summer's night.

Henry McKenna Single Barrel 50% ABV
www.heaven-hill.com

Single barrel, so nothing's guaranteed when you buy a bottle, but if it's anything like this, then you're in for a treat. It has an applejack nose, and is liqueur-like, with pruney-rumtoft notes. Intense. The taste on the palate too is full, concentrated and intense with baked apple and concentrated syrup. The ideal music to accompany it? Try Kentucky's Broadfield Marchers, comprising brothers Mark and Dustin Zdobylak. They play jangly post-Byrdian pyschedelic rock reminiscent of REM at their best. Their mix of exuberant youthfulness and respect for tradition is a perfect foil for this wonderful whiskey.

Hudson New York Bourbon 46% ABV
www.tuthilltown.com

For more than 200 years, the gristmill at Tuthilltown used water power to grind grain in to flour. About ten years ago, a small group of whisky aficionados acquired the property and converted one of the mill granaries in to a micro-distillery and set about learning the craft of distilling. It took them a couple of years to negotiate the legal hurdles put in their way, but by 2004 they were making spirit and today the range includes vodka, brandy, rum, fruit infusions and several whiskeys.

Tuthilltown's main achievement has been in getting some of New York's trendier drinkers to take a fresh look at rye and bourbon.

IW Harper 43% ABV
www.fourroses.us

Some whiskeys are for sipping, some for slugging – but only responsibly of course. Some are for daytime, others for evening or late at night. Some are reflective, some raucous; some passive and subdued, others edgy and active. IW Harper, if you can find it, is smooth and elegant and one that should be sipped while listening to something left field and special. For this whiskey my suggestion is the CD *Face a Frowning World*, a tribute to Estil Cortez Ball, an Appalachian country singer from Virginia who sang secular and gospel country songs. An hour of this compilation of country greats with the complex IW Harper – now that's a classy night in.

Jefferson's 8-year-old 45.1% ABV (VARIES)
www.mclainandkyne.com

Some non-distiller producers refer to a distillery where one doesn't exist. McClain & Kyne, now part of Castle Brands in New York imply they make bourbon in Bardstown. They don't, but that doesn't mean they're not buying good-quality bourbon, and this small batch uses just eight to 12 barrels for each bottling. This is perfectly palatable, with hickory, rye spice and a pleasant sweetness. Tastes mature without being over-oaky, and has a delightful fruity finish.

**Jefferson's Presidential Select
Fall 2009** 47% ABV
www.mclainandkyne.com

Rare as hen's teeth, but this may well be one of the last chances to taste bourbon from Stitzel-Weller. It is 17-years old and is taken from the last casks ever filled at the old distillery. Some of the final Stitzel-Weller inventory went with Weller to Buffalo Trace, some went with Old Fitzgerald to Heaven Hill. Diageo, which uses the distillery for storage now, may have retained some. No one really knows what's left but they need to think about bottling it. This is woody and wilting, and another couple of years in the barrel might stamp out the grain notes entirely. After the oak is soft wheat, plummy fruit and rich fudge.

Jim Beam 40% ABV
www.jimbeam.com

Like Jack Daniel's, Glenfiddich, Famous Grouse, Teacher's and Jamesons, the standard Jim Beam suffers from contempt because of its familiarity. This is grossly unfair. World-class whiskies become world-class for a reason. Next time you walk in to a bar and you realise your whisky choice is limited to the above, make a point of going for one of them anyway. It will be then that you remember just how good each is, and how you'd forgotten about it. With Beam you'll get brown sugar, a significant alcohol bite and a sweet corn centre that is not so obvious in many other bourbons.

Jim Beam Black 8-year-old 43% ABV
www.jimbeam.com

Proof if ever it were wanted that big does not necessarily mean bland. This is aged for twice as long as the standard white label version and it is premier-league stuff, capable of holding its own in a blind tasting against any mainstream bourbon under 10 years old. Christmas cake, ginger drizzle and liquorice come into play here; juicy berry fruits and raisins dip in and out of the mix; and there are just enough wood and rye notes to make this a complete experience. Incredibly complex and well balanced, this is exhibit A for those who think eight years is the perfect age for bourbon.

Johnny Drum 43% ABV
www.kentuckybourbonwhiskey.com

A bit of a curiosity comes from the Kentucky Bourbon Distillers, which bottles for a range of other brands. Johnny Drum varies in strength, is normally bottled at four years old, and is rare. But it is a jolly bourbon, made, we are told, from small batches of top-quality barrels, and it is rich, fruity, spicy and zesty.

Johnny Drum Private Stock 50.5% ABV
www.kentuckybourbonwhiskey.com

This has an intense and fruity flavour with hints of strong candy stick, leather, tobacco pouch and over-ripe fruit, together with a pleasant woodiness.

HEAVEN HILL DISTILLERY

P O Box 729, Bardstown, Kentucky KY 40004
www.heavenhill.com

Visit California, Louisville, when it is raining, and you can't help thinking that whoever named it had a sick sense of humour.

ABOVE TOP The visitor centre at Heaven Hill is located in the Bardstown heartland of Kentucky bourbon production.

ABOVE Like father like son: Craig and Parker Beam, continuing the family line, in one of the distillery's warehouses.

RIGHT The Heaven Hill bottle retains a traditional-style label that fits perfectly well with its traditionally produced Kentucky bourbon.

It's a grim, run-down inner-city suburb that has nothing in common with the Sunshine State on the US West Coast, and there are few reasons to stop by. But it is home to Brown-Forman's big distillery and the Bernheim plant where Heaven Hill now produces its spirit – not without incident. The plant flooded a couple of years ago and more recently some local youths opened fire on it with a gun.

'They had been over at Brown-Forman and the security guys had chased them off,' says Heaven Hill's head of corporate affairs Larry Kass. 'They came down here and fired two bullets into the fermenters. They were caught by the police but the fermenters had to be emptied to be repaired because they were leaking. The slugs were never found.

'Now that's what you call bullet bourbon!' and he bark-laughs in distinctly Kass-like fashion.

Life at Heaven Hill is not usually as lively. Nevertheless it is hard to imagine a whiskey distillery more removed from the standard country image on show throughout Kentucky. Heaven Hill moved here about 12 years ago after its distillery was destroyed by fire. They bought the site from United Distillers, which was merging with spirits giants UDV to form Diageo, and it inherited a distillery that is both huge and high-tech. And there is something distinctly incongruous about finding a check-shirted Craig Beam, broad Kentucky accent and all, seated in an office surrounded by computer screens and automated production equipment.

Craig and his father Parker's role within the company is to ensure that the passage from grain delivery in Louisville to whiskey maturation out at Bardstown and then back for bottling is a smooth one and all the traditional values of brands such as Evan Williams, Elijah Craig, Rittenhouse and Henry McKenna are maintained. They oversee the second-biggest quantity of ageing bourbon in the world.

They do it by bringing the old production skills and methods into the modern environment. It is a classic case of old meeting new and hopefully taking the best from both. For instance, across from Beam's office is the refrigerated room where the yeasts are kept. There is always an air of mystery about yeast, because it is at the heart of whiskey-making magic, and it contains a whiskey recipe's deepest secrets. That applies just as equally in a high-tech monster plant as much as it does in a farm-hut micro-distillery. At Bernheim, two buckets on the floor contain the raw yeasts. But, on the refrigerator itself, there are scores of packets of dried yeast. Made in Belgium.

'I'm not too sure how Craig and Parker feel about dried yeast but it works for the plant,' says Kass. 'The original yeast is sent all the way to Belgium because this place is considered the best. Only Parker and Craig know the exact yeast strain though. It was handed down by Parker's father Earl from the old days, when they would have to weigh it

down and drop it to the bottom of the lake to keep it cool in summer. Earl would make up the yeast in a bucket and then cover it with a cloth and put a monkey wrench on top to hold it down. And that monkey wrench always faced the same way. You didn't mess with the monkey wrench.'

The way distilling skills and habits are handed down through the generations are much in evidence here. Craig shares his grandfather's obsession with cleanliness, too, even in the new plant. That is how it all started for him, he says.

'There was this old building which needed cleaning down so I got to do that with some friends,' he says. 'Pigeons had been roosting in there for years so we had to wade through the muck to clean it out. We'd come out looking as black as coal miners.'

Craig represents the eighth generation of family distillers and his great-grandfather was the brother of James, better known as Jim. He is immensely aware of the dual responsibility of carrying such a famous bourbon name and being responsible for some of its most famous brands.

'But that's why we take such great care doing what we do,' he says.

Kass agrees: 'Heaven Hill has strong family connections through the Beams and through the Shapira family that owns it. It is important for everyone to keep the old traditions alive, not just with bourbon but with rye, wheat and even corn whiskey – no matter where it's made.'

JIM BEAM DISTILLERY

526 Happy Hollow Road, Clermont, Kentucky 40110
www.jimbeam.com

If you are in a fighting mood and you fancy kicking up a storm while downing a few whiskeys with bourbon lovers at the Talbott Tavern in Bardstown, bring up the issue of small-batch bourbon.

On paper it would seem to be a simple-enough concept. Small batch, in theory, is exactly what it says it is – bourbon made from a small number of casks, with the emphasis on only using whiskey of the highest quality.

Problem is, there is no legal definition of the term. And one man's small shack is another man's castle.

At the big distilleries such as Jim Beam, they probably make in a minute what Maker's Mark manages to make in a day, so how small, exactly, is small? Are distilleries such as Maker's Mark by definition small-batch? And if a distillery makes 10 million litres (2,641,720 gallons) of spirit a year and directs 10 per cent of it – one million litres (264,172 gallons) – into its 'small batch' range, can that really count? Indeed, so vague is the whole concept that one respected whisky writer has even declared 'there is no such thing as a small batch.'

He's wrong, because there is. Or more exactly, there are. Smaller volumes of specially selected bourbons that are superior to their standard versions do exist. It is just that they exist under a number of different definitions.

The confusion arises from the fact that many assume that the term small-batch refers to the size of the production run, but this is not the case. If it were, Maker's and Woodford Reserve (if stock taken only from the new distillery were bottled), would qualify as small-batch distilleries.

At Four Roses, they have their own definition. The distillery produces 10 whiskeys from two recipes and five different yeasts and marries them together to produce its standard bourbon. For its small-batch runs, Four Roses selects just four of the 10. That may still well be a massive amount of whiskey.

The term 'small-batch' was introduced back in 1988 by Jim Beam as a way of describing a special whiskey Booker Noe had created to set it apart from standard Jim Beam. This was at a time when there was no great market for premium bourbons as there is now, and when single-barrel selections were few and far between.

Beam has two huge distilleries producing millions of litres of spirit every year, and although the company website is not above some smoke and mirrors when it talks of returning to small-scale, hand-crafted bourbon with its small-batch range, the company's whiskey professor Bernie Lubbers is more forthright on the subject.

'We have big distilleries and production is 24/7 and so in this sense production could never be small-batch,' he says. 'But that doesn't mean we can't make a small batch bourbon.' The issue here is over barrel selection. 'If you pre-plan what you are going to mature as single-batch before you start maturation and put a part of your spirit production in a set number of casks in specific areas of your warehouse, then that constitutes small-batch.'

It makes sense, particularly in Kentucky where temperature extremes mean that there are areas that will produce honey barrels – ones producing spirit of particularly high quality.

'It's not just a marketing trick,' continues Lubbers. 'In 2008 we ran out of Knob Creek and there were shortages of it. If you look at the figures from the Kentucky Distillers' Association for that year and you'll see we had 23,000 barrels of nine-year-old bourbon, but we didn't pull any of it out and call it Knob Creek because those casks weren't part of the planning for the small-batch run.'

Perhaps we should not get too hung up on definitions, anyway. The likes of Jim Beam, Brown-Forman, Tom Moore and Heaven Hill may be big, but they produce bourbon to the same exacting standards as even the smallest producers. Are Booker's and Knob Creek mighty fine bourbons? Yes, sir, they sure are.

And as someone put it while sipping moonshine at a barbecue a while back: 'Don't matter if it's one barrel or one thousand. Fine bourbon's fine bourbon, and rotgut is rotgut. No marketing man can ever change that.'

Then he smiled and refilled my glass – with fine, very small batch, bourbon.

ABOVE RIGHT Visitors to Kentucky can visit the Jim Beam American Outpost close to the distillery. It includes a tasting room housed in a traditional clapboard building.

KEY WHISKEYS

Booker's 6-year-old 63.5% ABV
Knob Creek 9-year-old 50% ABV
Jim Beam 40% ABV
Jim Beam Black 8-year-old 43% ABV
Jim Beam Rye 40% ABV

WELL FANCY THAT...

A version of Jim Beam has been sold in one form or another since 1795. Today it is the world's most popular bourbon and the company's two distilleries can make 40 million litres of spirit per year.

Kentucky Gentleman Straight Bourbon 40% ABV
www.heaven-hill.com

The nose here is soft and fruity, like tinned pears, with soft fudge in the mix. The makers claim that rye is higher in the mix than is sometimes the case, and certainly the overall volume of the other blended grains is turned down. This whiskey is fine but it won't kick or punch, preferring to make peace in the mouth, not war. Greener and fresher than classic bourbons and with shades of eucalyptus, it is still very drinkable and ideal for sultry summer evenings.

Kentucky Tavern 40% ABV
www.bartonbrands.com

If you want a great Kentucky Tavern, head on over to the Talbott in Bardstown. It is as old as the state of Kentucky, puts on great live music from time to time, serves some fine beer and has a marvellous selection of bourbon. Easy-going and fun and a great place to meet bourbon folk, especially at festival time, this was my nomination for inclusion as one of the world's great whisky bars in *Whisky Magazine*. They say that Jesse James held court here.

The whiskey, which is actually named after a totally different tavern, is quite endearing. Sweet apple and pear on the nose, not unlike Kentucky Gentleman, some very gentle spice on the green fruit palate – bizarrely it is not dissimilar to some of the stuff they are bottling at Bladnoch in the Lowlands of Scotland, or at Cooley in Ireland.

Knob Creek 9-year-old 50% ABV
www.knobcreek.com

There are two Knob Creeks in Kentucky. One is next to a gun range, the other is the creek running through the farm where Abraham Lincoln grew up. His father made whiskey, too.

The bottle is designed to look like a bootleggers' version, with newsprint on the label to ape the old newspaper that the distillery used for wrapping.

The oldest and best of the Jim Beam small-batch range, Knob Creek is full of flavour, with endearing cocoa and dark chocolate notes, honey sweetness and rye and oak as well.

Maker's Mark 45% ABV
www.makersmark.com

This is one of the most distinctive and softest of all bourbons, and so it should be, as it is designer-made and aimed to appeal to people who don't like bourbon. It is the creation of William Samuels, who bears the name of one of the great bourbon families but had retired from whiskey-making in the 1940s. When he decided to come back into the business he wanted to do something new and different and consulted Pappy Van Winkle, and hence he settled on a high wheat recipe. The story goes that it was his wife who persuaded him to drop the family name from the bottle, to go for a distinctive wax seal, and to model the product on the jewellery industry, with a stamp representing the maker. William's son Bill is still the brand's figurehead but these days the distillery is part of the Beam empire. Only Maker's Mark is made in relatively small batches. Nevertheless, bottlings tend to be pretty consistent, probably because this is the only Kentucky distillery that rotates its casks during maturation. This is an angel's delight of a whiskey, with soft bread and custardy notes.

Bill Samuels claims that every member of the bottle-dipping team has his or her own wax 'signature' and he can tell who dipped each bottle just by looking at it.

Noah's Mill 57.15% ABV
www.kentuckybourbonwhiskey.com

The Willett distillery has a long and chequered history in Bardstown and news that it was being restored was greeted with enthusiasm. But its owners agreed that they would not get into debt reconstructing it so over the last few years they have been building a new still-house brick by brick. Now it seems the project is complete and the new Willett distillery is accepting visitors again.

Over the years the company has bottled bourbon for a number of companies and has had its own bottlings too. This one is an award-winner and arguably the best from the Bardstown stable.

Another small-batch whiskey bottled by hand and containing some rare and special bourbon, Noah's Mill is a robust and full-tasting bourbon that is aged for about 15 years and has strong woody notes. A dash of water opens up an Aladdin's cave of flavours, however – banoffee pie, vanilla ice cream with hot fudge sauce and crumbly fruit cake.

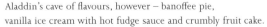

Old Charter 8-year-old 40% ABV
www.buffalotrace.com

This is another great, iconic bourbon brand with a history that stretches back close on 140 years. In that time the company has been buffeted by economic fortune and circumstance, with both the owner and the recipe changing more than once. Now it is a bit like an old steam engine – you keep it on the tracks for sentimental and historical reasons but it doesn't really cut the mustard any more in terms of performance and style. That said, if you are looking for a sweet, honest and unsophisticated whiskey, you could do a lot worse.

Old Charter 10-year-old 43% ABV
www.buffalotrace.com

Two years and a few units more alcohol, and this steps up a division. There is lots of rye, some grapefruity citrus notes and a nice slab of oakiness to this – although it does not taste as if it is anywhere near 10 years old.

Old Crow 40% ABV
www.beamglobal.com

One of the greatest names in bourbon, 2010 saw Old Crow given a new lease of life when its owners Jim Beam relaunched it as a four-year-old, gave it new packaging, and pitched it up against Evan Williams. For some years before that it had been neglected, available in limited quantities as a not-particularly exciting three-year-old, though there was something to be said for its youthful exuberance.

James Crow was a physician who became a leading figure in the development of bourbon, developing many of the techniques employed by bourbon-makers today to ensure consistency and quality. He was a skilled and charitable doctor, spent more than two decades at the Labrot & Graham distillery, and is remembered as one of the pioneers of modern bourbon. However, he never owned his own distillery, and the Old Crow distillery sited in Glenns Creek was not constructed until several years after his death.

The new version of Old Crow has some strong liquorice notes, retains its freshness and is clearly aimed at the mainstream, but it works as a session bourbon and is one to look out for.

Old Fitzgerald Prime 43% ABV
(www.buffalotrace.com)

Most bourbons that feature a name in their title tend to take it from a particular distillery owner or distiller. But not in this case, according to Sally Van Winkle. This is named after a security guard who used to help himself to bourbon from select casks to give to friends. He had excellent taste and his reputation for identifying good casks became well known. So when a good-quality bourbon went down to the blending room, it would be known as a Fitzgerald. Eventually it was applied to a brand. There is fudginess here, plus sweet pepper and cinnamon.

Old Forester 43% ABV
www.brown-forman.com

Old Forester's roots lie in the very earliest days of distilling. This was the whiskey – then spelled Forrester – that George Brown made at the distillery he founded in Louisville and today is at the heart of the Brown-Forman empire. The whiskey's claim is that it was the first bourbon to be bottled. Before this time whiskey was sold in barrels to wholesalers and retailers. This tipple is a bit of an A-Z of bourbon flavours and covers everything from fruit-and-nut chocolate bar and vanilla ice cream to nutmeg, cinnamon, sandalwood and chilli spices. Class in a glass.

Old Forester
Birthday bourbon 2009 Edition 48.5% ABV
www.brown-forman.com

A special limited-edition Old Forester Birthday Bourbon has been released each September since 2002 to mark the birthday of George Gavin Brown, a founder of Brown-Forman, and each release has become something of an event, because the quality has been consistently good.

This release, tasted in Proof on Main earlier this year, and not under strict tasting lab conditions, did not disappoint. It is the bourbon equivalent of a Muse gig – a three-pronged assault on the senses, breathtakingly ambitious, and with the volume up. There are peppery rye qualities, chewy oily corn and some fresh green fruit notes to give a stylish drinking experience.

MAKER'S MARK DISTILLERY

6200 Dutchmans Ln 3, Loretto, Louisville, KY 40205-3285
www.makersmark.com

As you travel from Louisville in Kentucky to Loretto you pass a number of houses that have statues of the Virgin Mary standing in upturned bath tubs.

The story goes that a bath salesman visited these parts a few years back but couldn't get the local folk interested in investing in new washing facilities. But he found out that this region of Kentucky is devoutly Catholic, so assuming the locals were more into spiritual than personal cleansing he hit on the shrine idea, sold his entire stock of baths, and retired a wealthy man.

Loretto is home to both Maker's Mark distillery as well as some of the world's most expensive thoroughbred horse-breeding facilities. That's no coincidence either: the whiskey and the horses are here for the same reason. Kentucky is rich in limestone that enriches the grass with vitamins, making it ideal for developing healthy and strong bones in the horses. And it hardens the water and makes it ideal for distilling top-quality bourbon.

One of Kentucky's smallest and prettiest distilleries, Maker's Mark is very much at home amongst the wealth and beauty of the region.

It was launched some 65 years ago but distilling has been carried on at the site next to Hardin's Creek for more than 200 years, making it the United States' oldest working distillery. It was established on farmland deep in rural Kentucky, and when you arrive there you are struck by how sedate and tranquil the neighborhood is.

The distillery is a sedate and calming place, too, even when it is in full production. That's partly because everything is done on such a small scale. While the debate rages as to what constitutes 'small-batch bourbon', it remains a fact that at Maker's they produce as much bourbon in a month as sister distillery Jim Beam does in a day.

The whiskey-making process is gentler than at other distilleries, too. The corn is crushed, not by hammer as elsewhere, but by roller, because Maker's owners believe that the heat generated by hammering scolds the grain and makes it bitter. The grains are cooked for longer, too, and brought to their cooking temperature over a longer period of time, and a higher proportion of wheat and lower proportion of rye is used than for other bourbons, giving the whiskey a softer, sweeter and less spicy flavour.

Traditionally Maker's only made one expression of bourbon, and it's about six years old. The distillery has argued that this is the perfect age to bring out the full flavour of the bourbon.

Once matured to the distillery manager's satisfaction the barrels are dumped on site and filled in a small bottling hall. Then each bottle is dipped into the red 'wax' to give it its trademark cap, labelled and boxed by hand.

ABOVE Bill Samuels, the quirky founder of Maker's Mark. He has played a key role in the renaissance of the bourbon category in the United States.

Maker's Mark 45% ABV

LEFT Maker's Mark Distillery,
Set amid deep countryside
in Loretto, is a National
Historic Landmark and one of
Kentucky's longest established
sites for bourbon production.

Maker's Mark Distillery

Old Forester Signature   50% ABV

www.brown-forman.com

Old Forester with the volume turned up, this is an intense and robust version of the standard bottling made up from a number of specially selected casks.

Old Pogue   45.5% ABV

www.oldpogue.com

Old Pogue is produced by another non-distilling company, despite the fact that the website displays a lovely old photograph of a Kentucky distillery and its home page claims that the bourbon is bottled in Bardstown by the Old Pogue Distillery. Pogue is an old bourbon name and the people behind this bottling are descendants of the original distilling Pogues. A mainstream bourbon launched a few years ago, this manages to find a niche all of its own – and that is because it's thinner and less sweet than many other bourbons, having an almost aperitif-like dryness and unusual barley meadow quality.

Old Rip Van Winkle 10-year-old   45% ABV

www.oldripvanwinkle.com

Sounds like a character from a nursery rhyme and indeed 'Rip Van Winkle' is the name of a short story by Washington Irving. It tells of Rip Van Winkle who escapes his nagging wife by wandering off into the Catskill mountains and encounters some strangely dressed men who are playing nine pins and drinking liquor, which Rip shares with them. Doesn't sound so odd if you have downed a couple of glasses of this bourbon, and maybe this bourbon is meant to be the liquor in the story. It is aged to perfection and uses the distinctive Van Winkle wheated recipe, so it's soft, mellow and rounded with a rich, creamy toffee flavour to it, and perhaps some chocolatey notes. There is a stronger 53.5% ABV version of this available, too.

Old Taylor   40% ABV

www.jimbeam.com

I reckon that, if you asked 100 film buffs to name their favourite stars, Jeff Bridges would not figure very highly. Over his career, though, he's produced some absolute storming performances – *Arlington Road*, *Thunderbolt & Lightfoot*, *The Fabulous Baker Boys*, *The Last Picture Show* and *The Contender* are all great films. The Dude, his character in *The Big Lebowski*, has reached cult status.

In his most recent Oscar-winning offering, *Crazy Heart*, he is exceptional as a washed-up back-bar country singer who slugs whiskey while watching his former band partner hit the big time with country-and-western slush. The soundtrack is by T-Bone Burnett, Stephen Bruton and Ryan Bingham, the film is a study in Americana, and if you are a fan of the new country genre, this hits all the right buttons.

I like to think that Bridges' drink of choice in the film is based on Old Taylor, because it's every bit as wizened, honest, genuine, traditional and soft at its centre as Bridges' character. A loveable old rogue of a bourbon, perhaps out of kilter with the smarter marketing whiskey world we now live in, but one to look out for and to savour at least once. It reminds me of Battenburg cake – all jam and marzipan. Good old bourbon as it should be.

Pappy Van Winkle's Family Reserve 15-year-old   53.5% ABV

www.oldripvanwinkle.com

Julian P Van Winkle was born in 1874 in Danville, Kentucky, and he didn't come from a whiskey-making family. But he fell into the industry, spent more than seven decades in it, helped shape the modern world for bourbon by putting emphasis on quality over quantity, and in the process started a whiskey dynasty. If it has the name 'Van Winkle' on it, you can be assured that the whiskey is going to be of the highest quality. There is a good chance, too, that it's going to be woody – these whiskeys are a challenge and are not for everyone.

Pappy Van Winkle's Family Reserve 15-year-old is an oddball when it comes to flavour; it's intense, toasty and oaky, but with a rumtopf-like rum-and-raisin heart and some citrus fruits in the mix. It is the whiskey equivalent of a Mad Hatter's tea party, with so much going on you may miss it all the first time around. So, a perfect excuse to go round again, then.

Pappy Van Winkle's Family Reserve 20-year-old 45.2% ABV
www.oldripvanwinkle.com

Van Winkle's lovely old labels picturing Pappy with a cigar provide a rosy view of Southern life back then. Take the new offices built in 1949. Instead of a door knocker to gain entry, there were five heavy brass keys, one for each stage of the bourbon-making process.. They also served as 'a link between Stitzel-Weller and the old Southern traditions of warmth, hospitality and enjoyment of the finer things in life,' writes Sally Van Winkle.

This is not for the faint-hearted. There are some green fruit and red berry notes, but also sharp, burnt wood and astringent spice.

Pappy Van Winkle's Family Reserve 23-year-old 47.8% ABV
www.oldripvanwinkle.com

As you progress up the ages of the Van Winkle range it's a bit like running a marathon, and hardcore. By 23 miles all the clowns and part-timers have been left way behind and it is only the serious contenders that are left. After 23 years of maturation you have to be pretty serious about your bourbon, and here wood is a big part of the mix. For this reason you can't talk about balance because there isn't any – but this is a worthwhile, iconic bourbon, providing an important link back to a different distilling era.

Parker's Heritage Collection 64.8% ABV (VARIES)
www.heaven-hill.com

The growth of new micro-distilleries across the United States has perhaps created something of a dilemma for Kentucky's distillers. On the one hand, there has been a clear and growing need to respond to the fleet-footed creativity of the new boys, but on the other, you do not want to be throwing the baby out with the bath water – what makes bourbon great will always make bourbon great, and anyway, they have seen it all before in these parts. So what do you do? Increasingly Parker's Heritage Collection, like Woodford Reserve's Master's Collection, is being used for experimental and front-line whiskeys, giving bourbon fans an annual treat to look forward to. Each one has been a godzilla, a roaring over-sized beastie.

Rebel Yell 40% ABV
www.rebelyellwhiskey.com

Once sold only below the Mason-Dixon line, Rebel Yell had a brief flirtation with international stardom some 20 years ago when it made its way to Europe accompanied by a free rock tape. Yep, before CDs were the main musical vehicle. Now you don't see it so much, but it is still palatable enough and the one to choose if you want to tear it up with some Southern boogie. Right now your best option for that comes courtesy of Kentucky boys Black Stone Cherry, who strut with the panache of Skynyrd and insult anyone who doesn't buy in to their brand of good time Southern rock and roll: 'Roll with Elvis in his Cadillac, Rode with Jesse on horseback, slingin' guns and raisin' hell, Livin' our life with a rebel yell' they sing on *We Are The Kings*. For those of us who don't buy in to the Confederate thing, we take that as a reference to bourbon. Way to go.

Ridgemont Reserve 1792 46.85% ABV
www.bartonbrands.com

The launch of this bourbon a few years ago signalled that times were a-changing at what was the Barton distillery. It is a premium bourbon, aged for at least eight years, and when launched, its modern packaging was a clear statement of intent. Its birth wasn't without controversy, however. Originally called Ridgeford Reserve, it attracted the wrath of Brown-Forman, owners of Woodford Reserve, and its owners had to change its name.

The date refers to the year when Kentucky broke from Virginia and became a separate state, though a sizeable number of settlers had already arrived in the region and whiskey was already being made.

While the name and packaging might have attracted accusations of plagiarism, the bourbon itself is something else again. It is a full-bodied and highly tasty whiskey, with just enough rye and oak to give it weight, but it is the creamy centre with vanilla pod and stewed apples that really delights. Some chicory coffee and hickory are in the mix, too. If it were a sports star, it would be the tennis great Roger Federer – immensely powerful and hard-hitting, but charming, soft and likeable too.

J P VAN WINKLE & SON

2843 Brownsboro Road, Louisville, Kentucky KY 40206
www.oldripvanwinkle.com

When Eli Boone Van Winkle was born in the last week of 2009, a new chapter started for two of Kentucky's most famous families.

Eli is the first child of Preston, who has taken up the baton of the illustrious bourbon-making Van Winkle family and his wife Whitney, who is a descendant of Daniel Boone, the pioneer and folk hero who established the state of Kentucky in the late eighteenth century.

You would struggle to find a more famous name in this part of the world than Boone, but the bourbon-makers are giving it a go. No family name excites bourbon fans more than that of Van Winkle. No family name more evocatively recalls the highs and lows of bourbon history or the struggle for survival endured by the bourbon dynasties in a changing world. And no name better symbolizes the link between the old bourbon industry of 50 years ago and the modern one geared up for the challenges of the twenty-first century. With good reason.

In her excellent book *But Always Fine Bourbon* about her grandfather, the legendary Julian 'Pappy' Van Winkle and the Stitzel-Weller Distillery he founded, Sally Van Winkle quotes a sign that hung at the distillery: 'We make fine bourbon. At a profit if we can, at a loss if we must. But always fine bourbon.' This is as true today as it was more than 75 years ago, when Prohibition ended and the Stitzel-Weller distillery was founded and started producing what is still some of the world's finest whiskey.

These days Van Winkle bourbon enjoys a special status in Kentucky. The company is run from a couple of small offices in a suburb of Louisville by Julian III, Sally's brother and grandson of Pappy, and increasingly by Preston, who is yet to reach his mid thirties but is already close to celebrating his 10th year in the business.

They do not distil any more. Stitzel-Weller shut its doors many years ago, and today only the warehouses are used for maturing spirit owned by Diageo. But the magic remains, and it is created in the cask, not the still.

RIGHT The Pappy Van Winkle labels feature old photographs that are both nostalgic and classic, summoning up a past era when most bourbon distilleries were family-run.

What sets the Van Winkle portfolio apart from the competition is its age. Van Winkle whiskeys range from 12- to 23-year-olds – monster ages for bourbon, especially when you consider that a bourbon such as Very Old Barton is just six years old and very few bourbons pass the 10-year mark. Maturing bourbon to this age is no mean skill. Kentucky's traditional metal-clad warehouses of seven storeys or greater sweat under the baking Kentucky sun in summer and are ice boxes during its sharp, brutal winters. On a hot day temperatures from top to bottom can vary by 15°C (27°F), and in the crow's nest at the very top it is not unusual for the thermometer to pass 45°C (113°F). Effectively the spirit cooks here and maturation is rapid.

There are other factors, too. It is often stated that while the alcoholic strength of whisky spirit will decline during maturation in Scotland, it rises in Kentucky. This is only part of the story. Higher up in the warehouse, the spirit does indeed get stronger as water in the cask evaporates out towards the hot, dry air outside at a faster rate than alcohol vapour does. But at some point further down there will be a 'neutral' floor, and at the lowest, moister and cooler levels bourbon may behave just as malt does in Scotland – it will decline in strength. There are even anomalies found within each floor of the warehouse.

To successfully steer selected casks past 10, 15, 20 or more years without turning their contents into stewed wood or losing them altogether, is an impressive skill. Today the Van Winkles have their stock scattered across the lowest floors of the warehouses at Buffalo Trace with whom they are in partnership. They're using a Weller whiskey made with a wheated recipe similar to the one Pappy used to make.

Fine whiskey, all right, but the elitist status of the Van Winkle range lies partly in its rarity. After 15 years, each cask contains little liquid. Few casks make the marathon journey. 'So it is our oldest problem,' says Julian while sipping on Van Winkle 12-year-old in Louisville's Proof on Main. 'We don't have enough whiskey and we spend much of our time having to disappoint people or else trying to justify to one bar account why they have not got any Pappy and the bar down the road does.'

As drinkers learn more about bourbon and seek out its heritage brands, it is not likely that the problem will go away soon. The plus side, though, is that with the involvement of a giant such as Buffalo Trace, at least some supply is guaranteed and the future for Van Winkle looks secure.

He doesn't know it yet of course – but that's good news for little Eli of the next generation.

RIGHT Julian III, grandson of Pappy, and his son, Preston Van Winkle, still run the family firm. The secret of Van Winkle's success comes from the maturation process.

KEY WHISKEYS

Old Rip Van Winkle 10-year-old 45% ABV
Pappy Van Winkle's Family Reserve 15-year-old 53.5% ABV
Pappy Van Winkle's Family Reserve 20-year-old 45.2% ABV
Pappy Van Winkle Family Reserve Rye 23-year-old 47.8% ABV
Van Winkle Special Reserve 12-year-old 45.2% ABV

Sam Houston 42.8% ABV
www.mclainandkyne.com

Sam Houston is one of the great characters in
American history. He is the only man ever to be
governor of two states, and he made a remarkable
impact on the state of Texas. He has no obvious
links with Kentucky, having been born near
Lexington in Virginia and spending his life in
Tennessee, Texas and Mexico. He was a slave-
owner and anti-abolitionist, but like the state
of Kentucky, didn't want to secede from the
Union and refused to sign for the Confederacy.
He spent time with the Cherokee nation and
married into it, then emigrated to Mexico
before becoming the leader of the Texas
Revolution. And of course the city of Houston
was named after him – as is this whiskey. A
10-year-old premium small-batch whiskey, it is a robust big hitter,
with plenty of rye and oak, a delicious raisin heart and caramel and
toffee notes at the finish.

Ten High 40% ABV
www.bartonbrands.com

In Kentucky many of the warehouses used to mature
whiskey are tall, ugly buildings that dominate the
skyline. They contain seven floors or more, and are
wooden constructions. Given the huge weight of
the scores of full barrels they contain, they are
feats of engineering.

Each floor will differ from the next, with the
hottest and most active ones at the top of the
building, and the cooler ones lower down. At
Tom Moore the warehouses have three ricks
(or stacks) per floor, and they do not use the
bottom three floors for bourbon at all. So the
first rick used for whiskey is ten high (the first
rick of the fourth floor) – hence the name of this
bourbon. But of course they are well aware of the
incidental gambling pun too.

'I'd like to bottle a bourbon using barrels from
the crow's nest at the very top of the warehouse'
says Greg Davis. 'We could call it Black Jack because it
would come from the 21st rick.'

No doubt it would be nearly black in colour, too.

This bourbon is a delight – very easy to drink, fruity and sweet.
Great with ice and a perfect example of what some folk refer to as a
sippin' whiskey.

Tom Moore 40% ABV
www.bartonbrands.com

Tom Moore is perhaps not as well known as some
other historical distillers but now that Barton
has restored the old Tom Moore name to its
Bardstown plant, this may change. Moore
was a successful businessman who set up
the Mattingley & Moore distillery in 1876 a
couple of hundred metres from where the
Tom Moore distillery sits today. By the time
the first whiskey was bottled, however, he had
already set up his own distillery and it's been
producing quality bourbon for 120 years.

Moore was a devout Catholic and a keen
horseman who at one time owned the
Talbott Tavern in Bardstown. A newspaper
article of 1889 said of him: 'Tom Moore is
one of the cleverest distillers in Kentucky, and makes a whiskey fine
enough to set before a king.'

I am not sure that the current bottling could justify that claim
but I have a real soft spot for it – there are fluffy red apples on the
palate to start with, some marzipan and stewed pear in the centre
and a dusting of white pepper over caramel at the end.

Van Winkle Special Reserve
12-year-old 45.2% ABV
www.oldripvanwinkle.com

Prohibition, introduced in 1920, was part of a moral
crusade that ended up nearly destroying a Kentucky
bourbon industry employing good, honest and
steadfast men, while creating a skilled and
exploitative class of bootleggers, moonshiners
and gangsters. Bizarrely, a number of distilleries
were allowed to stay open to make bourbon for
medicinal reasons, and at the same time the
number of people being prescribed bourbon
by their doctors grew massively. Whiskey may
well have been the cause of the St Valentine's
Massacre, when five members and two associates
were shot dead by members of Al Capone's gang
and hired help.

To replace his bourbon empire Pappy Van
Winkle went into business selling farm parts for a
while – not very successfully.

This is the most accessible of the Van Winkle
stable, a perfect after-dinner whiskey with a distinctive orange
marmalade and sweet taste. There is also summer pudding and
cream with some paprika and cinnamon spice in the mix.

Very Old Barton 6-year-old 50% ABV
www.bartonbrands.com

A few years back whiskey writer Charles Cowdery and I were invited to a barbecue held by Bettye Jo Beam. She is well known in whiskey circles, and has been a keen competitor in the barrel-pushing competition at the annual bourbon festival. She married a Beam and her maiden name is Boone, so she's linked to two of Kentucky's most famous families. On hearing that we were coming, she asked Chuck if she could tell all her friends.

'No, Bettye, because that would be half the state of Kentucky,' replied Chuck. 'Okay then, what about family?' she enquired.

'That, Bettye, would be the other half,' said Chuck.

That barbecue was some event, but before we went I asked Chuck, who knows masses about bourbon and whose opinion I respect greatly, what bottle I should take with me. He suggested this one, because it enjoys the respect of almost everyone.

'Very Old' in this case is just six years, and strangely the whiskey is bottled at three separate strengths. If you can get it, though, this is the one to go for. It is complex and challenging but never sharp or over-aggressive, and has a distinctive berry fruit centre in a pepper and candy wrap. Another solid backliner of a bourbon, this is as solid and reliable as a Swiss watch.

WL Weller 7-year-old
Special Reserve 45% ABV

William Larue Weller was one of the great early pioneers of bourbon. He was particularly noted for two things – using wheat in the grist rather than rye, creating a softer and more rounded bourbon, and for long ageing of his whiskey. Weller and later the Stitzel-Weller distillery became synonymous with aged and top-quality bourbon, and all of the current bottlings from Buffalo Trace live up to the name.

This is the youngest expression of Weller and it has a soft, fruity nose, a rounded and soft honeycomb centre together with gentle ebbing and flowing waves of mild chilli. It is as soft and delicate as bourbon gets, but none the worse for that.

Weller Antique 53.5% ABV

This bourbon is all about contrasts, with the soft honeyed and wheaten notes associated with Weller whiskies meeting their match from an elephant-sized chunk of oily corn and oak flavour. There is no obvious winner between the two sides but the effect in the mouth is captivating and as it slips down the throat it is tempting to pour another drop so you can go through the boxing match experience again.

Whenever I have a glass of this I also toast the late great Keith Weller, who is something of a legend among Leicester City soccer fans and who was my hero and role model. He is remembered most for playing an English cup game wearing white tights – an act that echoes this bourbon with its confusing mix of macho brawn and effeminate gracefulness. He was something of a pioneer in American soccer, too, playing and/or coaching in a number of places including Fort Lauderdale, New England, Tulsa, Houston, Dallas and San Diego. He died of cancer in 2004 at just 58 years old.

William Larue Weller 67.4% ABV

Every autumn, Buffalo Trace releases a group of special whiskeys under its Antique Collection series and they are snapped up within days. They are all exceptional. This year's offering from William Larue Weller is significantly stronger than normal, and unlike the George T Stagg release, requires water to truly reach its heart. Even with a considerable dash of water it is x-rated stuff, the soft wheaten notes are swatted aside by huge high-cocoa-content dark chocolate, hickory, molasses and espresso coffee notes. Work with it and you will find some mint notes, and some plummy fruit. But you cannot escape the fact that it is to bourbon what the Indianapolis Colts are to American football – tough, uncompromising, ruthless and thoroughly brilliant in equal measure.

TOM MOORE DISTILLERY

300 Barton Road, Bardstown, Kentucky
www.bartonbrands.com

Kentucky's bourbon distilleries are scattered across the state, but the industry's heart is in Bardstown, about 40 miles south of Louisville.

ABOVE TOP The world's biggest whiskey barrel. And no, it doesn't have any whiskey in it

ABOVE The parkways in Louisville, near Bardstown, typify the pleasant landscape found in the state of Kentucky.

Bardstown is a sleepy traditional Kentucky town which hosts the annual bourbon festival each September and it is also home to the Oscar Getz museum, which tells the history of Kentucky's famous spirit. Most of the year, though, there is little evidence that this is bourbon's capital.

Once the region boasted dozens of distilleries. Today, bourbon production barely figures here. Close by, Heaven Hill stores its bourbons in vast warehouses and has a state-of-the-art visitors' facility that is well worth the journey, but the distillery was destroyed in an infamous fire some 15 years ago, and production now takes place in Louisville. Close to Heaven Hill on the site of the old Willett distillery, the Kentucky Bourbon Distillers Company is rebuilding a distillery brick by brick. But the only proper distillery is on the other side of town.

These are good times for the Tom Moore Distillery. Until a few years ago, it was known as Barton Brands. It did not welcome visitors and it tended to trade on its former glories. Latterly though the distillery's owners launched a premium bourbon called Ridgemont Reserve 1792. Some time later, the decision was taken to revert to its original name, it was sold to Sazerac, and it joined the Kentucky Bourbon Trail, allowing visitors to get up close and personal at one of the bigger industrial-like facilities.

With the affable Greg Davis at the helm as master distiller and the tireless champion of bourbon, Pam Gover, fronting up the visitor experience, Tom Moore has had a facelift – at least in terms of perception and attitude it has. Its problem, though, is that what really needs a facelift is the distillery itself: it is old, grimy, and ugly. How do you sell that to the bourbon tourist?

Easy. By telling it like it is. You make a virtue of the fact that it is an old, working distillery. So when you go to Tom Moore, be prepared: you are about to get a definitive nuts-and-bolts tour. Literally.

And it is fascinating. Pam takes small groups by minibus around the sizeable estate, commentating as she goes. It is an engineer's dream, this place, a mass of pipes welded together in improbably complicated patterns, all linked by dozens of taps, spigots and tanks. The huge column stills down which the fermented beer runs before meeting a blast of high pressure and scalding-hot steam are a particularly memorable and impressive sight.

LEFT Barrels of spirit mature at the Tom Moore distillery in Bardstown, Kentucky. It is now on the Kentucky Bourbon Trail and well worth a visit.

RIGHT This eponymous bourbon is one of several expressions produced at the distillery.

KEY WHISKEY

Tom Moore 40% ABV

The warehouses are run down too, their white exteriors covered in black fungus.

'We could paint them but that would affect the way the whiskey matures because the heat would be absorbed in a different way,' Pam explains. 'The fungus is totally harmless but it's produced by the evaporating spirit – the angels' share – so it's part of the process. That's how they used to catch moonshiners. They just looked for where the trees had turned black.'

She points out the little hills around each warehouse, giving each building in effect its own moat. This is a legacy from the great Heaven Hill fire in the 1990s.

'The reason they lost so many warehouses is because burning whiskey spirit flowed from warehouse to warehouse. These hills would help stop the contents flowing if ever there was a fire.'

To be fair, the Tom Moore site is not without some attractive parts. You can go down close to the distillery entrance and see the old spring where the original Mattingley and Moore distillery once was, and there is a point where you can see the spring water that serves the distillery flowing through limestone to nearby Teurs Lake.

Overall, though, the distillery is like most of the whiskeys it produces – solid, dependable and unglamorous. It is, like the people who work within it, big-hearted, sure-footed and honest.

'In 1945 there was a fire here so when they refurbished this place in 1946 they spent a lot of money on it and made it a state-of-the-art distillery,' Pam Gover explains. 'And today it's still state of the art. We're still using state-of-the-art equipment from 1946.'

And she laughs heartily. They make whiskey the way it should be made here, warts and all. I think people respect that. And for this reason Tom Moore is a welcome addition to the Kentucky Bourbon Trail.

Wild Turkey 40% ABV
www.wildturkeybourbon.com

The story goes that Wild Turkey was named
after the sport of hunting wild turkey, which is
one of the most dangerous sports in the world.
Not because wild turkeys are very vicious –
although you would not want to mess with one,
especially when it finds out that the sexy bird
cooing at them is actually a human dressed up
as Thanksgiving Day and about to blow his head
off. No, the problem comes from 'friendly fire'.

To steady the nerves, you could do worse than
this. It is uncluttered, unchallenging and sweet.
Nice with ice.

Wild Turkey 101 50.5% ABV
www.wildturkeybourbon.com

Wild Turkey 101 is the ultimate rock-and-roll
bourbon, and to fully enjoy it you need to crank up
Lynyrd Skynyrd's 'Tuesday's Gone' or Blackfoot's
'Good Morning', sit back in your favourite
chair, close your eyes and wallow in nostalgia.
This is also the official passport to good times
and friendship south of the Ohio, certainly. If
anyone in a check shirt asks you if you'd like a
bourbon, just say '101'. Nothing else. Can't fail.

The bourbon is a big and balanced mix of
spice, candy, over-ripe yellow and orange fruits,
dark chocolate, vanilla and cigar box, all held
together by some chewy and oily undernotes.

Wild Turkey American Spirit 15-years-old 50% ABV
www.wildturkeybourbon.com

This is way out in the wilderness age-wise but it is not what
you might expect. Wood is there, certainly, but it is not over-
domineering and is not the taste that you will take away. That
comes from the Christmas cake and almost floral fruity heart, the
dagger-like rye hit, and the gentler vanilla heart. A departure for
Wild Turkey, this is certainly not to everybody's taste, but it is an
interesting diversion nevertheless.

Wild Turkey Kentucky Spirit 50.5% ABV
www.wildturkeybourbon.com

There may well be a few bourbons
from Kentucky that are not what they
claim to be, but when Wild Turkey
claims that Jimmy Russell personally
selects the casks that go into this single-
barrel offering, you can bet your last
dollar he did. His nose for great bourbon
is undiminished, repeatedly he dips into his distillery to produce a
gem. This has trademark citrus notes, rye, sweet vanilla and spice.

Wild Turkey Rare Breed 51.4% ABV (VARIES)
www.wildturkeybourbon.com

To catch a wild turkey you need to get close enough
to it to shoot it. The best way to do this is to disguise
yourself, strap yourself to a tree and then summon
a male turkey by impersonating a female. If you
are good enough, it will strut toward you
and start showing off. But turkey calling has
become a sport in its own right, and there are
competitions, many of them televised, where
you can win big bucks. There are various
categories and sounds include clucking,
yelping, cutting, putting and cackling.

This whiskey is a complete fruit bowl of
flavours mixed with butterscotch, vanilla ice
cream with soft toffee sauce, liquorice root
and menthol notes.

Wild Turkey Russell's Reserve 45% ABV
www.wildturkeybourbon.com

Jimmy Russell is one of the world's true great whiskey
personalities and he is a bit like his bourbons
– pleasant, soft and gentle on one level, but
hardy, determined and with a great sense of
purpose. He does not believe that bourbon gets
better after 10 years of maturation, hence the
age of this beauty. But his preferred bottling
strength is 101 proof – 51.5% ABV. Odd, then,
that this is 45%. No matter, because it is a
corker – an oral roller-coaster that takes you
slowly up and up, the flavours building and
then whoosh – a crash of vanilla, citrus fruit,
waves of sweet spices and some polished wood
in the mix. Very lovable.

Woodford Reserve
Distiller's Select 43.2% ABV
www.brown-forman.com

The Kentucky Derby is not just one of the
world's greatest sporting events, it is
the highlight of the social calendar in
Kentucky. The race itself is short and
sweet, particularly for a country that
likes to drag out its sporting events, but
the pomp and ceremony that surrounds
the race at Churchill Downs would
be hard to match. The drink most
associated with the event is the Mint
Julep and revellers raise their glasses of it
while singing 'My Old Kentucky Home'
with a religious fervour. According to Wild
Turkey's Jimmy Russell, though, you can spot true Kentuckians from
visitors as soon as the singing is finished. While visitors drink their
Mint Juleps, he says, local folk reach for their favourite bourbon.

High on the list is Woodford Reserve, used to make Mint Juleps,
but it stands apart as a fine straight drink, too. With higher-than-
average rye content, a triple distillation process and about eight or
nine years in the barrel, this is a full and rich fruity bourbon with
delightful spiciness and enough oaky astringency to prevent cloying.

Woodford Reserve Four Grain 43.2% ABV
www.brown-forman.com

In recent years the makers of Woodford Reserve have
taken to launching an unusual annual release under
the name Master's Collection. Each one is effectively
small-batch, using barrels taken just from the
Woodford Reserve distillery (unlike the standard
version, which is mixed with spirit from Brown-
Forman's Louisville distillery) and each is a
twist or take on standard bourbon. Each is rare.

Four Grain was the first and effectively
second release in the series. Most bourbons
are made using three grains – predominantly
corn, but with a proportion of other grains,
most often some malted barley because it is
an efficient catalyst in the process of converting
sugars to alcohol, but also rye, wheat or unmalted barley.

Here four grains are used and the resulting bourbon is intriguing
and very different. The first version was sappy and oily, with grains
battling against each other. Another year on, though, and the oily
corn and spicy rye have made friends, there is an earthy but highly
attractive base to the whiskey, and a delightful linseedy note sets it
apart from any other bourbon.

Woodford Reserve Seasoned Oak 43.2% ABV
www.brown-forman.com

Ah, that's much better. The best of the Master's
Collection, so far, by some considerable distance.
This is a punchy, sharp, well-shaped bourbon with
a delicious spiciness from the oak. There is a
muskiness to it, too, and the oils make sure that
it coats the mouth and stays there, alongside a
suitable amount of the trademark Woodford rye,
too. A classic in the making?

Woodford Reserve
Sonoma-Cutrer Finish 43.2% ABV
www.brown-forman.com

Not strictly a bourbon because the final part of the
maturation process is carried out in a cask that has
been used previously for wine. The technique of
using wine casks is common enough in Scotland, but
does it work with bourbon? Well, of all the Master's
Collection series so far, this is the one I struggle
with most. That's probably because it doesn't taste
very much like a bourbon, and the grapiness
of it takes it to a whole new place. I'm not
convinced but it raises some interesting
questions and might be a signpost to the future.

Woodford Reserve Sweet Mash 43.2% ABV
www.brown-forman.com

One of the cornerstones of bourbon-making is the sour-mash
process. At the end of distillation there is a stillage
made up of liquid and spent grain, with all the sugars
stripped out and converted to alcohol. This stillage is
known as backset and is the soured, sugar-free remains
of this mash. By adding this backset to the next mash it
is possible to prevent bacterial infection and to ensure
a consistency in the solution's ph levels and therefore
consistency in the mash – and eventually the new
spirit. It follows, then, that every time a distillery is
shut down and restarted, the first run will be a
sweet mash, and it is rejected.

This is one example of what it tastes like. If
you are a bourbon geek then it is an interesting
exercise. As you might expect it is sweeter than
the standard Woodford, but it is also flabbier,
blander and less complex, too. It's a sort of
Woodford Lite.

WILD TURKEY DISTILLERY

1525 Tyrone Road, Lawrenceburg, Kentucky KY 40342
www.wildturkeybourbon.com

Nobody rushes in Kentucky, and when it comes time to retire, there seems to be no hurry to hang up the boots and head out on to the porch for a well-earned cigar and a bourbon or two.

In fact if you want proof that bourbon-makers live for their work and love what they do, just look at how many of the industry's senior citizens are still turning their hands to making whiskey.

Elmer T Lee celebrated his 90th birthday in 2009, but still comes in to check on stock at Buffalo Trace, while Parker Beam and Jim Rutledge show no sign of letting up in their posts at Heaven Hill and Four Roses any time soon, even though both have passed the 40-year service mark.

And then there's Jimmy Russell at Wild Turkey. He has been making bourbon for more than 50 years and is moving into his late 70s. When his beloved distillery was sold by Pernod Ricard a couple of years ago, you would have thought that would be the perfect time to call it a day. Not a bit of it.

'The owners have got plans and they want me to go to New York, Chicago and San Francisco in the coming weeks,' he says when we meet at the distillery visitor centre. 'This is what I like to do, meet people who enjoy my bourbon, see the pleasure it brings them, travel to places to talk.'

'Mind you, you know you're getting old when you start working with your grandchildren, and I sometimes wonder when we fill the casks whether I'll still be around to see the whiskey being bottled.'

Russell is on site almost daily when he's not travelling, and splits his time between greeting visitors ('I try to personally say hello to everyone who visits here,' he says), and playing an active role in producing spirit, which he now does with his son Eddie.

There are few people anywhere in the world who understand their spirit the way Jimmy Russell does. He can tell how long the mash has been fermenting by the size of the bubbles, for instance, and he knows instantly if a batch of bourbon has strayed from the correct recipe or is the wrong strength. He also has a very precise idea of what great bourbon is. He doesn't care for spirit that has been aged for more than 10 years, for instance, and his preferred bottling

strength is 101° proof, not the more common 100° proof, which was the industry standard for a good while. The bourbon's name and its strength are inter-related, he says.

'The distillery was once owned by the McCarthy family and Thomas McCarthy was a keen wild turkey hunter,' he recalls. 'They used to go on shoots and everybody would contribute something to the food and drink for the trip. The story goes that Thomas McCarthy took a barrel of his bourbon one time and it happened to be at 101 proof strength and everybody enjoyed it very much.

'The next time they asked him to bring some more bourbon, so he found some the same strength and he referred to it as the wild turkey bourbon. Finally he christened it that way.'

Wild Turkey 101 remains one of the great old bourbons, but the distillery hasn't sat back and let progress leave it behind. Certainly, 101 is still going strong, but over the years the distillery has released a single-barrel bourbon, a rye, a liqueur and a number of special bottlings including Tradition and Rare Breed. At the heart of everything, though, is big-flavoured Wild Turkey whiskey, because, says Russell, sooner or later everyone comes back to it.

'A few years ago they started experimenting with light whiskey and I never thought it would work,' he says. 'If I had not been wrong then, I would not be sitting here today. It's good that new things come along and keep people interested but what goes around comes around, and folk always come back to proper well-made bourbon.'

What new owners Campari plan for Wild Turkey next is anyone's guess, but whatever it is, you suspect Jimmy Russell will be involved right at the very centre. 'For sure,' he says.

'I'm in good health and I've got the energy,' he says. 'As long as that's the case I'll be here.'

ABOVE Wooden bourbon barrels are stamped with identifying information while they are left to mature on racks at the distillery.

A distillery fire at Wild Turkey at the start of the millenium sent burning spirit into the Kentucky river, and this was blamed for an environmental disaster soon after. More than 200,000 fish were killed by a blanket of algae that was thought to have fed on the alcohol and drained the river of oxygen. Wild Turkey was faced with a bill for nearly half a million dollars.

KEY WHISKEYS
Wild Turkey 40% ABV
Wild Turkey 101 50.5% ABV
Wild Turkey American Spirit 15-year-old 50% ABV
Wild Turkey Kentucky Spirit 50.5% ABV
Wild Turkey Rare Breed 51.4% ABV
Wild Turkey Russell's Reserve 45% ABV
Wild Turkey Russell's Reserve Rye 45% ABV
Wild Turkey Rye 50.5% ABV

ABOVE Legendary bourbon maker Jimmy Russell, who has been making bourbon for more than 50 years, keeps a watchful eye on the maturing whiskey.

LEFT Wild Turkey Kentucky Spirit – one of the fine bourbons produced at Wild Turkey's remote distillery – also has one of the most distinctive bottle designs.

WOODFORD RESERVE DISTILLERY

7855 McCraken Pike, Versailles, Kentucky KY 40383
www.woodfordreserve.com

At the pretty Woodford Reserve distillery, situated in Kentucky's famed bluegrass country, they are ringing in the changes and looking firmly to the future.

History seeps from every pore here. James Crow carried out some of the pioneering scientific work into bourbon on this site. He may not have invented the sour-mash process but he mastered it and laid down the blueprint for consistency that is still maintained today. This was home to Elijah and Oscar Pepper too. Major history.

That may well be the case, says master distiller Chris Morris, but Woodford Reserve is a premium bourbon that looks to the future rather than the past.

'Sure this distillery is associated with Oscar and Elijah Pepper and with James Crow. But whatever they were making then was not what we know as bourbon now. We make Woodford Reserve here so we've taken down some of the displays about the past and replaced them with information on Woodford Reserve and we're focusing more on what we're doing now. That's what's important.'

Maybe, but it's not just Crow and the Peppers who haunt the distillery. George T Stagg is said to have distilled here, as well as Colonel Edmund Taylor, who was to later create Old Taylor at a distillery he built just down the road. The remains of distilleries are scattered around this part of Kentucky,

known as Versailles, a few miles from Frankfort. Some of them, such as Old Crow and Old Taylor, have taken on legendary status among bourbon enthusiasts.

It is like a ghostly bourbon hall of fame here. Combine this with the sublime charm and beauty of the place and there are few distilleries on the planet as magical and mystical, few so entwined in such a rich tapestry of history.

Woodford Reserve is situated close to Glenn's Creek and to reach it you must venture into the heart of Kentucky's bluegrass country, negotiating tree-lined country lanes and fields containing many gleaming chestnut brown thoroughbred horses.

In summer birds of prey circle overhead, wild turkeys strut nonchalantly, and red cardinals, the state bird, frolic from picket fence to picket fence. In winter chilly mists create eerie shrouds across the hills and icy rain helps cast a pall over the terrain. This really is the heart of rural Kentucky and nothing can quite match the marriage of culture, history and beauty of the new Woodford Reserve distillery. But such a heady combination can be a swamp and you cannot blame anyone from trying to break free from the ghosts of history.

What Morris and his team are keen to stress is that this is a new distillery making a sophisticated and stylish premium bourbon ideal for the 21st century. It might be built from the ruins of Labrot & Graham, but owners Brown-Forman spent a small fortune on renovating this site. They do not even use the old name any more.

Woodford Reserve is Kentucky's smallest distillery, and its least typical. Instead of the standard industrial-like column-still method of production, for instance, it has pot stills from Scotland. It distils three times, too. There is only one standard expression of the whiskey, but even then the distillery cannot make enough bourbon to meet the demand, so the new distillery's output is mixed with a significant – some would say high – proportion of nine-year-old whiskey made to the original Old Forester recipe at Brown-Forman's Louisville distillery.

But the real draw for bourbon fans is the Master Collection series. Each year for the past five years a limited-edition bourbon has been made purely with pot-still whiskey from the Woodford distillery, each one testing out a new angle.

ABOVE Brown-Forman's Wayne Rose checks a new bottling at the Woodford Reserve distillery.

Woodford Reserve Distiller's Select 43.2% ABV
Woodford Reserve Four Grain 43.2% ABV
Woodford Reserve Seasoned Oak 43.2% ABV
Woodford Reserve Sonoma Cutrer Finish 43.2% ABV
Woodford Reserve Sweet Mash 43.2% ABV

The first used four grains, for instance, one was finished in a wine cask, and another dispensed with the sour-mash process. Not all of them have worked, but they are always interesting.

'The last one was a big, weighty oaky bourbon after a couple of lighter ones,' says Morris. 'So in 2010 we went with a sweeter bourbon finished in maple wood. We have 100 per cent rye whiskeys and single malts maturing, whiskeys made with white corn and oats, and whiskeys maturing in hickory and ash. Some will not work and we will not do them, some will be outstanding.'

At their best, the special releases are enhancing an already greatly respected bourbon reputation. Morris and his team are tinkering on the margins, testing and experimenting as they look for new channels in the future. They are looking forward rather than back. But you know what? James Crow would surely have approved of what is happening right now.

LABROT & GRAHAM

WOODFORD RESERVE

DISTILLER'S SELECT

ABOVE OPPOSITE The visitors' centre includes a room devoted to distilling methods and history.

ABOVE The Woodford Reserve distillery, with its smart visitor reception area and well-maintained buildings and grounds, is a highlight of any whiskey lover's trip to Kentucky.

Tennessee whiskey

It is one of American whiskey's greatest ironies that the brand most people would cite as its most famous bourbon is not a bourbon at all.

Jack Daniel's is a goliath of a brand and the whiskey world's most accomplished grifter, able with ease to bottle and sell millions of gallons of spirit while fooling its audience into believing that a few good ol' boys in Lynchburg, Tennessee are making and bottling whiskey exactly as Mr Jack used to. In fact, this is a huge operation, with close to 200 million litres maturing on the vast site at any one time, and three bottling plants in operation. Not that you would know it from visiting – as millions do, because no other distillery enjoys an iconic status quite like this one. You know it's vast, of course, but this is Disneyland for whiskey drinkers and a million miles away from the hard-hat tours at Barton or Buffalo Trace.

Jack Daniel's is made in almost exactly the same way as a bourbon, but it does not qualify as one. Not because it is from Tennessee, but because at the end of the distillation process its producers break bourbon's strict rules by pouring the new spirit through a wall of maplewood charcoal. This process is a form of filtration and is known as the Lincoln County process, thus defining the whiskey as a Tennessee one and not a bourbon.

Some people say Jack tastes like bourbon and the technicalities do not matter. They do, though – especially to the people in Tennessee and Kentucky. Jack is not the only distillery in the state. George Dickel is a relatively large operation in its own right and produces whiskey using the Lincoln County process but with a small difference – it chills the spirit before passing it through the charcoal, a process that allows even more mellowing.

George Dickel No 8 40% ABV
www.dickel.com

This lighter version of Dickel is probably aimed at the mixing market but it is pleasant enough on its own with ice. It is a smooth, easy-drinking whiskey with a balanced but laidback mix of fruit, vanilla, rye and burnt oak. A lazy summer afternoon of a whiskey.

Jack Daniel's Gentleman Jack 40% ABV
www.jackdaniels.com

The problem with spending years telling the world that Mr Jack got his whiskey right first time and you do not mess with a winning formula is that you leave yourself no room for manoeuvre when it comes to brand extension. So this version of the famous whiskey divides the room like no other. While Single Barrel is just regular Jack unplugged and acoustic, Gentleman Jack is a different expression because an extra level of mellowing has been introduced. This is the alcohol equivalent of Diet Pepsi.

George Dickel Superior No 12 45% ABV
www.dickel.com

The Dickel distillery is only a short drive from Jack Daniel's and is now owned by Diageo, though the drinks giant seems to have a problem with American whiskey and has struggled to establish a foothold for this in the international arena. This is a perfectly decent whiskey, with floral and vanilla notes, soft sweet corn and toffee and chocolate in the mix. It also has a big mouth-feel and a surprisingly long finish.

Jack Daniel's Old No 7 40% ABV
www.jackdaniels.com

Whiskey enthusiasts get sniffy about this but really they shouldn't. It is quite remarkable that a strong-tasting dark spirit of any sort, let alone whiskey, should have established itself as the world's biggest spirit. Bland it most certainly isn't. It is true that most people mix it, but next time you get the opportunity to do so, sip it neat or mixed with a little ice. The vanilla, oak and liquorice triple whammy is impressive whichever way you cut it. This, then, is the Harley-Davidson of the drinks world – a big, growling, rugged and iconic symbol of blue-collar working man's America.

Jack Daniel's Single Barrel

www.jackdaniels.com

If Jack Daniel's is a Rolling Stones tour – a huge, glitzy worldwide greatest-hits package that delivers just what its audience expects – then Single Barrel is a Keith Richards solo gig – recognisably from the Stones but altogether rootsier, rougher, more intense and less predictable. It offers you the chance to get up close and personal. Each barrel not only differs from the next but also differs significantly and every barrel is chosen from the best parts of the best warehouses and every batch reinforces the view that Jack is a very well made whiskey indeed.

It would obviously be impossible to provide notes for a large number of different single-barrel bottlings, but here is a snapshot:

Jack Daniel's Single Barrel 8-15-08 8-2886

Liquorice allsorts on the nose, with hickory, red liquorice, glacé cherries and orange and grapefruit marmalade. The palate has anisette, liquorice and a big dollop of orange marmalade before an intense wave of pepper and spice. A big, growling monster truck of a whiskey, with all its lights on full beam.

Jack Daniel's Single Barrel 9-30-08 8-3531

The nose is dusty and powdery, almost flighty, with some grapefruit and lemon, caramel and faint spearmint. The palate is quite gentle, with banana skin and green melon. The citrus notes give it freshness and there are some late spice and oak notes towards the end.

Jack Daniel's Single Barrel 8-29-09 8-0267

Less masculine than some other expressions, with sweet tobacco and saddle leather on the nose, some floral notes and Christmas pie filling in the mix. There is toffee on the palate at first, then some sharp apricot and orange fruits, traces of cocoa and some late chilli.

Rye whiskey

Rye has a long and proud history in American whiskey but until relatively recently its popularity had declined and it had been marginalised. Over the past couple of years it has been enjoying a new wave of popularity, rediscovered by whiskey enthusiasts and bartenders who see it as an ideal base for several different cocktails.

In actual fact, there are three very different types of rye. Canadian whisky, which for a long time was actually referred to as rye, is often made up of several ryes produced in Canadian distilleries but these are blander and less spicy than American rye. American rye whiskey is made in the same way and to the same regulations as bourbon but must contain at least 51 per cent rye in the gristbill. There are also a few examples of 100 per cent rye whiskey. In this case the rye is malted so it is effectively a single-malt rye.

Cougar Bourbon 37% ABV

This is a curio. Cougar is distilled by Foster's, the Australian beer-maker, but although a rye has existed in the past, it is rarer than the brown-ringed blue-spotted cougar after which it is named. Those who swear they have tasted it talk of it as a stunning elixir. For this reason it warrants inclusion here. I, however, have been unable to track it down. And even those close to the subject admit that it seems to have gone to ground of late.

Devils Bit 47.7% ABV

www.mcmenamins.com

McMenamin's is a small pub and hotel company that runs its establishments in a quaint and old-fashioned manner, including its own micro-distillery that produces a range of spirits. It is exactly this sort of whiskey that shows the future is very bright indeed for the new wave of American distillers. What makes rye such a stunning drink when it gets it right is the way it packs spikes and spices at its heart but delivers on a crest of oil and oak, as is the case here. It is bold, assertive stuff. No drink can match it on its day.

Hudson Manhattan Rye 46% ABV
www.tuthilltown.com

New York was once famous for its rye, which was the whiskey used in the original Manhattan cocktail. So it is fitting that now small-batch distilling is taking place in the city once more, the whiskey-makers should turn their hand to a proper, edgy rye.

This has an odd nose – aromatic wax candle, floral and with floor polish notes – all quite pretty. On the palate it is initially rootsy, with linseed oil coming before some orange jelly notes. This is all a bit odd until the spices arrive to pull it back on track.

Jim Beam Rye 40% ABV
www.jimbeam.com

This isn't Beam's best bottling but it has its place because beyond the tough, robust and grainy nature of the core drink there are aromatic and floral notes, and as a result it's a good starting point for anyone wanting to get to grips with rye. Very reasonably priced, too, and I understand that Beam is upping output after some initial supply problems.

Old Potrero 18th Century Style Whiskey
62.05% ABV
www.anchorbrewing.com

According to Anchor, single malt rye made back in the 18th century called for heated oak wood chips to be used to heat the staves to bend them. The heat would have toasted but not charred the inside of the barrel. That's what is done with the barrels here. This is another amazing and totally incomparable whiskey. What a big nose you have grandma! Sort of

Campbeltown with liquorice. The taste is bold and mouth coating, with oily hickory and cloves and lots of peppery spice. I reckon this would not only numb tooth ache but would go some way to curing it too. The medicinal notes are balanced by anisette, treacle toffee and apricot. Complex.

Old Potrero Hotaling's Single Malt Whiskey 50% ABV
www.anchorbrewing.com

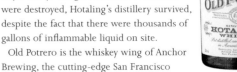

The great San Francisco earthquake of 1906 destroyed 28,000 buildings and claimed countless lives. Some religious leaders blamed the entire event on the city's wicked ways. Oddly, though a number of churches were destroyed, Hotaling's distillery survived, despite the fact that there were thousands of gallons of inflammable liquid on site.

Old Potrero is the whiskey wing of Anchor Brewing, the cutting-edge San Francisco brewery headed by brewing genius Fritz Maytag, and their intention is to re-create whiskey as it used to be. To do this they malt rye and use it as the only ingredient – a 100 per cent single malt rye. And this is, quite simply, incredible. The nose is spiky and pithy, with a touch of water kick-starting waves of aromatics. Taste-wise it has a peat-like intensity of earthy spices mixed with chocolate honeycomb followed by floral notes and then finishing off with some orange and lemon chews.

Old Potrero Single Malt Straight Rye Whiskey 45% ABV
www.anchorbrewing.com

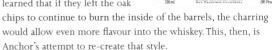

Over time whiskey-makers learned that if they left the oak chips to continue to burn the inside of the barrels, the charring would allow even more flavour into the whiskey. This, then, is Anchor's attempt to re-create that style.

It has an oily putty-ish nose, with some meaty almost kebab-like notes. On the palate it is like mixing Talisker with Jamaican fruit cake, a delightful mix of berry fruits in soft cake plus sweet pepper. It is delicate, too, with aromatic and floral notes. A total delight.

Pappy Van Winkle Family Reserve Rye 13-year-old 47.8% ABV
www.oldripvanwinkle.com

This is all old polished wood-panelled office in feel. It's as uncompromising as whiskey gets, with dark chocolate and espresso notes fighting against hickory, sharp pepper and orange fruit and plum. It is to other whiskeys what Them Crooked Vultures are to rock music: an edgy and challenging experience but ultimately a rewarding one.

Pikesville Supreme 40% ABV
www.heaven-hill.com

While we tend to think of Kentucky as the centre of American whiskey production it was not always that way. Tennessee clearly has a strong whiskey tradition, but so did Virginia, Pennsylvania, Indiana, Idaho and Maryland. Pikesville is named after the last rye to be made in Maryland and is meant to be based on that recipe. Even so, it has been made in Kentucky for 30 years and is part of the Heaven Hill empire. This is clean and zesty, with apple and pear sours, some rich candy chew and spice notes.

Rittenhouse 40% ABV
wwwheaven-hill.com

Rittenhouse's time seems to have come. Once one of the few brands keeping the rye style alive when everyone seemed to have turned their backs on it, Rittenhouse has not only survived but also started picking up the very highest international awards. What makes it particularly special for me is the fact that the three most available expressions of it are so different from each other. This is probably the poorest of the three, but that doesn't mean it is not a great whiskey. The 40% ABV means it works as a good entry-level rye, although it is quite spiky.

Rittenhouse 23-year-old 50% ABV
www.heaven-hill.com

This is a monster: a dusty, damp, oaky and musty room with a treasure chest packed with colour and flair. You have to work your way through the woody and spicy intensity to unlock the delights within, but boy is it worth it. Ancient by American whisky standards but undoubtedly a wonderful world-class whiskey.

Rittenhouse 100 proof
Bottled in Bond 50% ABV
www.heaven-hill.com

Arguably the best of the three bottlings on offer here, because fruit has a bigger say in the mix and when battering against the rye it makes for oral fireworks. This is complex because a fruit bowl of flavours make their case one by one. Impressive stuff.

Sazerac 6-year-old Rye 45% ABV
www.buffalotrace.com

Sazerac Rye's big brother is the weighty 18-year-old, which is part of Buffalo Trace's Antique Collection and a superstar. A bit like having Muhammad Ali for a big brother. But this is no wimpy kid or Sazerac Lite – the mouth-feel is big and assertive, and there is lots of spicy and oak. It is not particularly complex and far less challenging than many others in this category but that is actually no bad thing. Very well balanced, too.

Sazerac 18-year-old Rye 45% ABV
www.buffalo-trace.com

This is a linebacker in a skirt. One of the truly great American whiskeys, this would seem to be almost overwhelmingly muscular and brawny in terms of oak, spice and deep dark fruit. But it is also surprisingly feminine around the edges – almost floral and honeyed at the heart. The peppery notes are a delight, and weave in and out of the oak and fruit unpredictably – which means that every sip is an adventure in taste.

Templeton Rye 40% ABV
www.templetonrye.com

The makers of this are based in Chicago, but claim that this rye is made to the same recipe as one that a town in Iowa produced during Prohibition. Its owners claim that the rye the town produced was so good that it commanded premium prices on the black market and became the drink of choice of Al Capone himself. It was sold in speakeasies in Chicago, Des Moines and as far afield as San Francisco.

It's a good marketing pitch, but this version has only been available for four or five years and is a bit of a curio – well made and enjoyable, it is sweeter and less spicy than most ryes and has a distracting smoothness. Definitely worth seeking out because it stands apart from other ryes.

Thomas Handy Sazerac 63.8% ABV
www.buffalo-trace.com

The Sazerac was invented by Antoine Peychaud, who made it at his pharmacy in New Orleans' French Quarter. Originally it was made with brandy, absinthe and a secret mix of bitters. It became popular and was copied across coffee shops in the city. But its whiskey link came courtesy of Thomas H Handy, who bought the Sazerac Coffeehouse and added rye whiskey instead of brandy.

He would have been proud of this. It is big, bold and has more up and downs than a baby in a bouncer. There are boiled candy fruits and jagged ryes battling against each other, oak and alcohol punching in and out then traces of nutmeg, tarragon, chilli and mint.

Wild Turkey Russell's Reserve Rye 45% ABV
www.wildturkeybourbon.com

Six years old but surprisingly set at a slightly lower strength than the favoured 101, this is nevertheless another giant. There is some unexpected honey, nuttiness and mint in the mix, some distinctive woodiness and lots and lots of spice.

Wild Turkey Rye 50.5% ABV
www.wildturkeybourbon.com

This the most bourbon-like rye on the market but is no worse for that. The trademark rye pepper is all present and correct but a wave of vanilla, liquorice and aniseed and some orange fruits make this rye easy and palatable.

Bottled at Jimmy Russell's preferred 101 proof, there is enough weight and richness to make this worth seeking out.

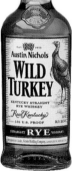

Wheat whiskey

Wheat whiskey is made in the same way as bourbon but the wheat content must account for at least 51 per cent of the grist. Wheat is not a particularly common ingredient in bourbon, but it was what Bill Samuels Snr used to give Maker's Mark its softer, more female-friendly personality. Wheat whiskeys are also rare, but Heaven Hill has had significant success with Bernheim and some of the new generation of micro-distillers are turning to the style, most notably Dry Fly. The style is softer and sweeter than bourbon, more in keeping with a pure grain whisky.

Bernheim 45% ABV
www.heaven-hill.com

For many years, Heaven Hill stood apart from the other distillers in Kentucky as the lone producer of both wheat and corn whiskeys. Now, though, as the United States wakes up to the potential of different whiskey styles, a new wave of both styles is upon us.

Wheat whiskey is notoriously difficult to make. The grain is more delicate and requires delicate handling. But as this bottling shows, the results can be remarkably impressive. This is the American drinking equivalent of wrapping yourself in a soft down duvet, a melt-in-the-mouth orange and lemon sorbet with a vanilla overcoat and honey and spice in the finale.

Dry Fly Wheat Whiskey 40% ABV
www.dryflydistilling.com

I have not tasted this, but it is included for three reasons: 1) because wheat whiskeys are so rare that any release in the category is a news story. 2) because in early 2010 this beat Bernheim in an Internet-based awards event, suggesting the company behind it means business; and 3) because it seems that this is a 100 per cent malted wheat whiskey, making it pretty special. Dry Fly also produces other spirits using only local ingredients and is based in Spokane, Washington. By all accounts this is not easy to find at all, but is well worth the effort.

Corn whiskey

Corn whiskey breaks all the rules when it comes to American whiskey production. It must include more than 80 per cent corn, does not require ageing, and if it is matured, the barrels must be either virgin oak or used – they cannot be new and charred or toasted as with bourbon production. This is the style of whiskey most normally associated with moonshine – and the marketeers do not shy away from this fact when they are considering such things as packaging and bottle labelling.

Moonshine was produced on homemade stills and barely matured in casks and the whole idea of drinking it young is part of the experience. That is at least partly due to the fact that corn makes for good sweet whiskey, like an alcoholic corn on the cob. If a drink genre ever reflected its culture it is this one – it is no-frills hillbilly whiskey and damn proud of its history and heritage.

Dixie Dew ??% ABV
www.heaven-hill.com

NASCAR racing is one of the biggest commercial draws in the United States and it has its roots firmly entwined with the days of whiskey-running. Cars would be converted to maximize storage space for moonshine and the engines would be customised to ensure that if the law did try and catch up with the whiskey-makers they could out-motor them and race to cross a state line where legal jurisdiction changed. Cue the long-running US television series *The Dukes of Hazzard*.

Dixie Dew has a rough-gut youthfulness about it, some sweet liqueur notes and entertaining corn notes – corn on the cob in vodka perhaps. An acquired taste and a basic one.

Georgia Moon 50% ABV
www.heaven-hill.com

The amateurish label, the jug-style packaging and the proud boast that maturation only took days should pre-warn you that this is going to be a cross-country motorbike ride, as rough around the edges as drinking whiskey gets. This is almost winey and vegetal, everything about it is short and sweet, and it is about as subtle as bare-knuckle boxing. Nonetheless, it feels and tastes pretty authentic.

Hudson New York Corn 46% ABV
www.tuthilltown.com

New York Corn is smooth and sweet, and while lacking some of the bite and aggression of most Kentucky bourbon, is a pretty good entry-level whiskey. The smart packaging has ensured a smooth passage for the whiskeys into some of New York's cooler bars, and Tuthilltown can be credited with helping to change the attitudes of many urban drinkers towards the bourbon category.

JW Corn 50% ABV
www.heaven-hill.com

Searching for rare corn whiskeys should be declared a sport. This seems to have just about fallen off the map, but does turn up very occasionally. Older bottlings of it exist that contain eight-year-old whiskey originally distilled in Indiana. More recently it has been bottled as a four-year-old and the younger version is sweet and much fruitier than Georgia Moon and with less oily corn notes. Almost certainly it is produced by Heaven Hill. The JW refers to James Walsh & Co.

Mellow Corn 50% ABV
www.heaven-hill.com

If Georgia Moon comes across as a good impression of moonshine, this is at the other end of the spectrum. It is a soft, sweet and full-corn whiskey with rounded and smooth edges, a gentle landing and green apples and treacle toffee on the palate. This is easy-drinking whiskey and tastes significantly softer than most bourbons.

Other American whiskeys

Contrary to popular belief bourbon doesn't have to be made in Kentucky, and nor is it the only style of whiskey made in America. For many years now a small number of distilleries have operated in other parts of the country making malt whiskey. Now a new generation of micro-distillers are experimenting with wood types, grains, special finishes, ground-breaking blends and hybrid products that mix production techniques from both single-malt whisky and bourbon production. It is all reminiscent of what happened in the States with beer a few years back, albeit slower and smaller. It would be impossible to cover them all here – some are producing on the tiniest of scales or intermittently, but this is a dynamic and exciting category all the same.

Early Times 40% ABV
www.brown-forman.com

Another whiskey that is bending the distilling rules, Early Times is produced at Brown-Forman's Louisville distillery and disqualifies itself from being called bourbon because some of the spirit is matured in used barrels. The result is perfectly acceptable – a light, sweet vanilla ice cream with maplewood syrup and crushed nuts.

Catdaddy 40% ABV
www.catdaddymoonshine.com

Piedmont Distillers is based in Madison, North Carolina, and this is a triple-distilled flavoured moonshine. It is made by New Yorker Joseph Michalek who came to North Carolina and spotted an opportunity to reproduce the taste of some of the great illegal moonshine that was available at public events in the state. He won't say what spices and fruits are added to the mix, but technically this is somewhere between whiskey and flavoured vodka.

A sister product that I have not come across, is called Junior Johnson's Midnight Moon, named after a famous moonshiner, and is described as 'smoother than vodka, better than whiskey. Best shine ever.' Mmmm...

Edgefield Hogshead 46% ABV
www.mcmenamins.com

McMenamins is a hotel company in Oregon and prides itself on originality and authenticity. It has been brewing its own beer for 25 years now, making it an easy fore-runner of the recent micro-brewery insurgency, and it now has an impressive 24 breweries producing 200 new recipes a year. It makes its own wine, roasts its own coffee, and as of 12 years ago, started distilling. This big soppy monster of a whiskey is proof that someone knows what they are doing. It is a toffee-rich and full-fruited single malt with a unique character and an unsubtle, uncompromising mouth-feel. Some honeycomb and wood enter the mix, too.

Charbay Hop Flavored Whiskey 64% ABV
www.charbay.com

Not strictly a whiskey at all because hops are used in the mashbill, giving a distinctive hoppy and floral aspect to the taste. But this warrants inclusion because it is one of several examples that shows where American micro-distillers might head – effectively creating new whiskey-infused drinks categories and potentially setting the world of whisky on fire. This is made in St Helena, California, and is big, bold and impressive.

Kessler 40% ABV
www.jimbeam.com

This is an American blended whiskey, which means it is a mix of bourbon and un-aged or grain neutral spirit. As a style it has fallen from popularity but Kessler is one of the category's biggest labels. It is named after Julius Kessler who sold whiskey in the late 1800s and the whiskey's motto is 'smooth as silk.' It certainly lives up to its claims, though some liquorice, citrus and spice notes ensure that the experience here is far from bland.

McCarthy's Oregon Single Malt 47.5% ABV
www.clearcreekdistillery.com

If ever a distillery sounded like it was in Kentucky, it is this one. And if ever an American whiskey tasted less like bourbon, here it is.

This is a single malt that is a smoky monster, with engine oil, barbecued fish and a charriness on the nose. Taste-wise it is very sweet and rich in peat, but delightfully balanced by the grain. This is the drinking equivalent of American soccer – it appears to be very like the European game, but has been tweaked to give it a personality of its own.

Stranahan's Colorado Whiskey 47% ABV
www.stranhans.com

An unlikely alliance between a Colorado spirits connoisseur and a part-timer fireman who helped save his barn from burning down, Stranahan's is a single malt dressed in a Kentucky Colonel's finery. So you get candy stick, vanilla, honeycomb, leather polish, spice and oak, but the whole mix has a barley malt heart. A bit like drinking very old grain whisky matured in bourbon casks – arguably providing the best of both worlds.

Rogue Dead Guy 40% ABV
www.rogue.com

Oregon-based Rogue is part of the new wave of great American beer-makers and it makes some of the most exciting and tasty beers in the world, selling them in irreverent almost punk-like packaging. Dead Guy was released by the company some years back to mark the Mexican Day of the Dead, and its rich flavours are the result of four different malts. This whiskey is distilled from that beer and is every bit as quirky as the ale. There is a delicious spiciness as well as youthful fruitiness.

Triple Eight Notch 44.4% ABV
www.ciscobrewers.com

Triple Eight distillery is part of Sisco Brewers on Nantucket Island, Massachusetts. The company makes a range of spirits and was at the vanguard of the micro-distilling revolution when it was formed in 1997. The company's single-malt whiskey was created with the support of former Morrison Bowmore distilling consultant George McClements. The whisky is finished in ex-Merlot casks – potentially risky – but the result is impressive, with soft tinned fruits and vanilla in the mix. It's been given the name 'Notch' because it's not Scotch. Geddit?

St George 43% ABV
www.stgeorgespirits.com

Made in Almeda, California, this is a single malt that so impressed a couple of members of my whisky club they made a detour while on holiday in the United States just to visit the distillery. St George is made in very small quantities and each batch differs from the next but it is distilled from a smoky brown ale, due to the barley being heavily roasted. Some malt is dried over alder and beech. The spirit is matured for three to five years mainly in bourbon casks, but also in French oak and port casks. Sounds good? It is. It has been a while since I tasted this, but the batch we had was sweet, very fruity and quite complex with some cocoa, milk chocolate, toasted oak and a touch of mint at the finish.

Wasmund's Rappahannock Single Malt 48% ABV
www.copperfox.biz

The Copper Fox distillery sits beneath the Blue Ridge Mountains of Virginia and distiller Rick Wasmund is on a mission. He learned his trade by spending some time working at Bowmore but came back to America with a burning desire to use all he had learned but to take it to a new place. So some of the malt here is dried over apple and cherrywood and it shows in the end product. Wasmund's is made barrel by barrel so there will be some variety in taste. But expect to pick up some oak and smoke and some unusual yellow fruit notes. Bizarrely, this is exported to Liechtenstein in Europe, which, as described elsewhere in this book, has just started bottling its own whisky.

THE WORLD'S BEST WHISKIES

CANADA

Canada

Several years ago the late whisky and beer writer Michael Jackson was invited to Canada to visit a distillery, so he extended an American trip and headed north.

But when he arrived at the Canadian border he was refused entry and quizzed about his reasons for entering the country.

'I'm a journalist and I want to write about a whisky distillery in Canada,' he announced.

Not good enough, he was told, to justify giving him an entry visa.

'Canada has journalists of its own,' he was told. 'Why would we let a foreign journalist come and do a job that a Canadian could do?'

Perhaps because an unbiased international whisky writer stating that Canada had great whisky to discover would have more authority in

overseas whisky circles than if one of your own sang its praises, Michael pointed out.

In the end the Canadian authorities relented, but the story goes some way to explaining Canada's disjointed relationship with the rest of the world of whisky. To be fair, it has less to do with Canadian whisky and more to do with the over-officious and outdated protective nature of the country's authorities. Even so, Canadian whisky does not attempt to sell itself in the same way as Irish whiskey or bourbon does.

Or at least not in Europe, anyway. With Scotland dominating the world of whisky today, and Ireland providing it with much of its historical context, there is an assumption that other whisky markets should kow-tow to the 'old' markets. Not Canada. It has a proud whisky tradition of its own and knows which side its bread is buttered on – and that side is known as the United States.

Canadian whisky still sells by the ocean-load in the United States and much of it is owned by international companies with large US interests. Beyond some key brands such as Canadian Club and Crown Royal, there is simply not that much of an incentive for Canadian brands to seek out markets elsewhere.

The American connection has helped define Canada's whisky. Although Canada is associated with rye, whiskies from the country are nothing like the fierce, spicy and flavoursome American ryes that are exciting whisky enthusiasts across the world.

ONTARIO

● VANCOUVER

QUEBEC ●

CANADIAN DISTILLERY PROFILE

TORONTO ●

GRIMSBY ● 1

1 Kittling Ridge

Canada's whiskies have been lighter in style, easy-drinking, easy-mixing whiskies made through a complex process of combining many different whiskies, which are produced using an array of grains. Most Canadian whisky is blended, although there are a few grains and a notable exception at Glen Breton in Nova Scotia where, unsurprisingly, the local folk look to Scotland's single-malt whisky for inspiration. The distillery achieved international fame (or notoriety depending on your point of view) when the Scotch Whisky Association went to war with it and, in the eyes of many, made an ass of itself in the process.

There are other reasons why Canada stands alone. Its liquor sales are controlled by the state, and its whisky-making industry, once characterised by hundreds of small distilleries, has in recent years been the story of drinks giants such as Schenley, Seagram and Hiram Walker. Some Canadian brands are owned by Kentucky bourbon producers, and some even include bourbon in their recipe due to a somewhat bizarre law that permits a fraction of a Canadian blend to be made up with another liquid, which can often include fruit juice or foreign whiskey.

So it should come as no surprise that some parts of the Canadian whisky industry have an identity crisis and other bits appear complacent, satisfied and smug.

The final part of the picture, however, is made up by the small number of innovators and trend setters within the country. Unfortunately, for many of us they are too small to make too much of a mark internationally, but they provide enough evidence that Canada as a whisky market is not finished quite yet. It just needs to get better at opening its doors to the world and telling us its story.

Single malt

Glenora Distllery is in Nova Scotia, and unsurprisingly folks, they are proud of their links with Scotland. So when they decided to make malt whisky they imported Scottish barley Glen Breton and turned to Scotland for their stills.

They have been producing whisky on and off for 20 years now but it has been a bumpy journey. Lack of funds threatened to unseat them and they also attracted the ire of the Scotch Whisky Association, which made few friends with its heavy-handed approach to the distillery. Thankfully, despite this, the whisky is still flowing.

Glen Breton 10-year-old 43% ABV

The nose here is slightly doughy and oily, with a trace of orange and some honeyed sweetness. Taste-wise there is toffee and fruit and a gentle wave of prickly peat. Comparisons with Scottish single malt are inevitable. This is slightly lower down the soccer league, more of a Hibs or Hearts than a Rangers or Celtic.

ABOVE The Cabot Trail winds its way along the Gulf of St Lawrence at Cape Breton.

Blends

The dominant style of Canadian whisky is a combination of several different whisky styles, including a number of different rye recipes, often from the same distillery and mainly produced in column stills. Sometimes Kentucky bourbon is used in the mix.

Alberta Premium
40% ABV

A complex and challenging whisky with orange and lemon, and vanilla on the nose, and a chewy toffee and rich fruit heart. It is nicely balanced, perfectly palatable and is subtle and nuanced.

Alberta Springs 10-year-old 40% ABV

If you have a sweet tooth then this is for you. It is a rye-dominated whisky and a perfect starting point to understand how different the Canadian version is to the American one. This is about vanilla and caramel, with some pepper in the mix.

Canadian Club 6-year-old 40% ABV

This may well be the brand that caused the St Valentine's Day massacre, as it was shipped in huge quantities by Al Capone down the lakes from Canada and into America during Prohibition. Undoubtedly the brand was established as a big player at that time and it has maintained its position as one of the world's best-known whiskies. The whiskies are mixed after distillation and before maturation, and there are a number of expressions available.

This is oily and spirity with a fruity base. It is stereotyping the whisky I know, but this really does show its best and truest colours when mixed. Neat it's like chewing on olives.

Canadian Club Classic
40% ABV

Vanilla, yellow fruits, and honey on the nose, raisin, berries, overripe banana and vanilla ice cream on the palate and a icing sugar and cinnamon spice to top it all off. This is a real treat.

Canadian Club Reserve 10-year-old 40% ABV

Arguably the best expression in the Canadian Club range. Here the oiliness works alongside green fruits and some white wine flavours, there is some wood and spice in the mix, and considerably more body than you might expect.

Canadian Mist 40% ABV

An oddball whisky from an oddball distillery that has achieved big sales in the United States. It is made using corn and malted barley, then transported to Kentucky where it is mixed with a proportion of Kentucky rye. And for what exactly? A whisky that whispers, an innocuous, mild, sweet and fruity nothingness. Like any winner of *The X Factor* (with the exception of Leona Lewis); pleasant enough but easily forgotten.

Crown Royal 40% ABV

Now part of the Diageo empire, this whisky was originally created by legendary drinks boss Sam Bronfman when he was head of Seagram, and it has a long and illustrious history. It is a thoroughbred blend too, flowing with juicy grains, rich and delightful fruit and some stunning peppery notes. Unlike some of its national rivals it is not over-sweet either.

Crown Royal Special Reserve 40% ABV

It is hard to remain focused on the job in hand sometimes, and the mind wanders, especially when you are faced with some pretty ordinary whiskies that hand-on-heart you know will not make the cut.

Before getting to this, for instance, I had three samples that will remain nameless, and while tasting them I found myself wondering what odds I'd get on Eddie Izzard becoming Britain's first transvestite prime minister. If you are reading this and wondering who on earth I am talking about, then that would suggest pretty good odds. If you are thinking he is just an oddball comedian and would never get elected as a politician, you're probably right.

But my reasonings are these: he is very intelligent, much loved, has a social conscience and is debating standing as a Labour candidate in the future. He is an Internationalist and respectful of other cultures. I once took a French girl to see him on stage and such is the nature of his comedy that she spent the entire performance asking me to explain his jokes, so that being there was a waste of time for both of us. Weeks later she rang to say she went to see him again in Paris and he did the whole performance in French. And in 2010 he pulled off the almost-impossible feat of running 43 marathons in 51 days and raised more than £1 million for SportsAid – a quite awesome achievement made all the more so by the fact that he is chubby and he has bad feet from wearing high heels. This makes him a British national treasure.

Yep, definite long-term prime minister potential I'd say. But perhaps I am just delirious after too much bad Canadian whisky. Thank goodness we are back on track with this one, then – lots of fresh tropical fruits, traces of spice and rich, oily rye. Quite possibly my favourite Canadian whisky.

Forty Creek Barrel Select 40% ABV

The nose does not do this whisky any favours. It is young and spirity and not great, to be honest. Thankfully the taste picks up the pace, with an intriguing layered attack. On the surface it is as flat as a summer pond, underneath there are some grungier, meatier notes among the fruit.

Forty Creek Double Barrel Reserve 40% ABV

Soft, fruity and candied, with strawberry and sweet lime present early on, then a mix of fruits, some spice, and some oil from the grain as this complex whisky opens up.

It is like going on the latest ride at the theme park, one that is like nothing that has gone before. But whether you will like the experience or not is another matter. All credit to Kittling Ridge for daring to be different, though.

Forty Creek Port Wood Reserve
45% ABV

Bold winey nose that is almost liqueur-like. The mouth-feel is rich and oily and you can taste a battle between the Canadian rye and the port and fruit influences. It is almost chewy in its intensity and opens new doors for whisky from this part of the world.

Seagram's 83 40% ABV

The number refers to 1883, the year the company was founded. This is a classic Canadian blend, with a sharp grainy core, some lemon notes and a rich and smooth taste that provides the perfect platform for mixers.

Wiser's Deluxe 40% ABV

One of the fruitiest whiskies to come out of Canada and one of the most pleasant: the oil-paint nose that characterises a lot of Canadian whisky is a turn-off, but the soft grains, the honeycomb heart and some attractive vanilla and oak alongside the rich fruits all work in this whisky's favour.

KITTLING RIDGE ESTATES WINES & SPIRITS

297 South Service Road, Grimsby, Ontario, Canada L3M 1Y6
www.kittlingridge.com

In some parts of the world making innovative and exciting whiskies is akin to climbing a mountain without a map – and you have got to be a bit crazy to do it.

Take the case of John Hall, the man behind the Forty Creek whiskies produced by Kittling Ridge in Canada.

The Canadians will hate it being said, but Canadian whisky has stagnated and has failed to keep up with the pace of progress in other parts of the world. Canadian whisky is still a player – it sells more than Scottish, Irish and American whisky put together in North America – but its whiskies are owned by big companies and unlike virtually every whisky-making country, Canada has few innovators or exciting and dynamic new whiskies. In the nineteenth century Canada had more than 200 independent whisky-makers. Now there are hardly any.

John Hall, though, is proving that Canada can produce whisky of the highest standard, and since 1992 when he set up his distillery, he has been doing it by tearing up the rule book and experimenting with tastes and flavours. A winemaker by trade, he came to whisky-making with no baggage.

'I am a first generation whisky-maker so I have no restrictions as to how I paint my canvas,' he said. 'I have often thought that if I was a 12th-generation whisky-maker it would be a really boring job having to make whisky exactly the way it had been made for 12 generations. I am not bound by tradition, I am inspired by it.'

He started by throwing away the test book that explained how he needed to put the mashbill together and then turned to the way the spirit was distilled.

'I followed my intuition,' he explains. 'After all, I didn't make wine by mixing all the varieties together. At breakfast time I don't mix my cereals together. Corn doesn't taste like barley and rye doesn't taste like corn, so why would you mix them together at the start of the process? So I treated each of my grains the same way as a noble grape variety, trying to bring the best taste characteristics of each varietal grain.

'This meant I would make my whiskies as single grains bringing out the fruitiness and spiciness of the rye, the nuttiness of the barley and the heartiness of the corn. Each of these grains has unique taste characteristics and to me it was important to define them and bring them out as singular whiskies.

'In Canada all whiskies are column-distilled. It wasn't like that in the 1800s. Back then, whisky-makers used copper pot stills but whisky-makers moved to column stills because it was cost effective. I use copper stills because they capture not just the alcohol but the flavour.'

Hall has also taken a radically unusual approach to maturation and barrel selection, too, and has even gone as far as to make his own sherry to fill casks that would later be used to hold whisky.

'The first thing I learned as a whisky-maker was that I needed more patience and passion,' says Hall. 'As a wine-maker I could have a wine out on the market within a couple of years. As a whisky-maker I would have to wait 10 years. If you are truly passionate then the tedious preparation of the barrels must be done. It's very time-consuming but it has to be done.'

Hall's approach has resulted in a range of whiskies that taste like nothing else on earth and are taking Canadian whiskies into new and exciting areas. He has not abandoned his country's whisky traditions and his whiskies are distinctly Canadian, but they are rich with new and exciting flavours. His efforts have been recognised across the world, and all the signs are that there is plenty more to come. He is climbing up the mountain when everyone else seems to be getting off it because the conditions are so bleak.

'I am very humbled to be acknowledged by the industry, by fellow whisky-makers, customers and whisky writers,' he says. 'These accolades have reinforced my quest to continue to follow my dream. And I hope that my passion for creating hand-crafted Canadian whisky will encourage many others to follow.'

KEY WHISKIES

Forty Creek Barrel Select 40% ABV
Forty Creek Double Barrel Reserve 40% ABV
Forty Creek Port Wood Reserve 45% ABV

ABOVE TOP The Kittling Ridge Distillery in Grimsby, Ontario was founded in 1992.

ABOVE John Hall, founder of Kittling Ridge, inspects one of his new, highly regarded Canadian whiskies.

LEFT The distillery's distinctive copper column stills.

THE WORLD'S BEST WHISKIES

IRELAND

Ireland

Until the spring of 2007 Ireland's whiskey industry was like a big old dusty museum. You could visit a whiskey distillery in the Irish Republic alright – you were just not able to experience whiskey being made.

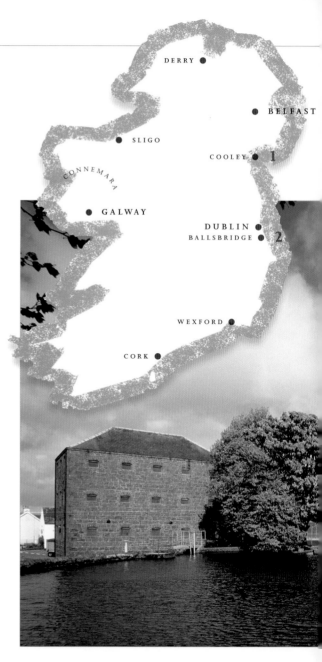

There is plenty for the whiskey tourist to do. The Jameson visitor centre is plush and stylish – but free of the aroma of fermentation and distillation. There is the stunning old distillery at Midleton, where you can all but hear the laughter of the workers, but today it is a mass of open space and disused distilling equipment. And most depressing of all is Tullamore, a distillery in a rural backwater where you can walk around the museum exhibits then sit by the canal that once took the casks away to the ports and off to the rest of the world, and now sits idle, its banks over-growing and the midges dancing in the summer sun. There are ghosts to be found everywhere.

Until spring 2007 you could have added Locke's Museum at Kilbeggan to the list of ghost distilleries. That was until owners Cooley fired up one of the old stills and started distilling there once more. In 2010 the company bottled its first whiskey at the site.

Ireland does produce whiskey, of course. It is just that certainly in the south, whiskey is produced where people are not permitted to visit. The only two large fully operational distilleries are Irish Distillers' huge and impressive Midleton plant at Cork, which towers over the old distillery and is probably the most advanced distillery in Europe, and Cooley, which occupies the site of an old industrial alcohol plant and is hidden away on Ireland's east coast.

Cooley is looking at the possibility of allowing visitors there, too, but for the time being it means that Ireland does not celebrate its whiskey in the same way that Scotland, America, Japan and Canada do.

'It is true,' says Cooley's managing director Jack Teeling. 'Ireland's still got plenty of pubs, but no distilleries to visit.'

The good news, however, is that Ireland does have whiskey – very good whiskey. And with Jameson opening the door for Ireland in more and more markets, Diageo giving some much-deserved support to Bushmills, a single-malt distillery in the north, and Cooley playing the role of maverick by shaking up the industry and giving drinkers a diverse and unusual range of whiskeys to choose between, Irish whiskey is in pretty good shape. Ignore all the blarney about how Ireland has the oldest whiskey, and how none of it is peated and all of Scotland's is, and how it is all triple-distilled and none of Scotland's is. The repetition of such inaccuracies sounds like a nation clutching at straws.

Instead get yourself a glass of something special – an older Bushmills, a rare Midleton, a vintage Jameson, a peated Connemara or a stunning Tyrconnell perhaps – and enjoy Irish whiskey for what it is: first-class spirit perfected over generations, and still as relevant as ever.

ABOVE Bushmills is Ireland's oldest whiskey distillery, located just a few miles away from the spectacular Giant's Causeway. It is now owned by the drinks giant Diageo.

RIGHT Noel Sweeney, master distiller at Cooley distillery near Derry in Northern Ireland, noses a sampling next to the still.

Irish single malt whiskey

Until the launch of Cooley a few years ago, Irish single malt whiskey had become something of a novelty, a tradition kept alive at Bushmills, North of Belfast. But Ireland once had scores of distilleries, many of them making whiskey using only malted barley. Cooley has resurrected some of the lost names and given Irish single-malt whiskey a new lease of life through award-winning single malts such as Connemara and Tyrconnell. Cooley has also started emulating some of the diversity found in Scotland by introducing peated whiskies as well as whiskies finished in a range of cask types.

Bushmills 10-year-old 40% ABV

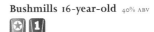

This is summer fruits in a glass, with orange, yellow and green fruit wrapped up with honey in the nose, while sweet grape, summer fruits and red apples appear on the palate before dark cocoa and pepper arrive to give the whiskey some shape. A definitive Irish whiskey.

Bushmills 16-year-old 40% ABV

The extra few years in the cask give this expression an extra weightiness, with oak and spice adding an extra dimension to the malt. Beautifully crafted, and elegant on the palate.

Connemara 40% ABV

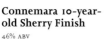

Gentle smoke, twiggy and dry leaves, then a heady mix of apple, fresh barley, green fruits and just enough smoke to keep it all interesting. The peat and savoury notes get stronger and more noticeable towards the end.

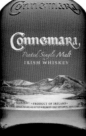

Connemara 10-year-old Sherry Finish

46% ABV

A strange journey indeed this. Early on this is like cooking a cob of corn on an open fire – you get rootsy embers and musty flavour but then, on the palate, peat and plum grapple with each other and sherried notes march through the middle. But the peat wins out. Extraordinary.

Connemara 12-year-old 46% ABV

This is a wicked mix – a bit like Run DMC guesting on an Aerosmith single or Lemmy, lead singer of heavy rock band Motorhead appearing with Cheryl Cole – not quite what you might expect but it has the potential to be quite wonderful. This is soft, rounded and gently smoked, but with gooseberries, oak and unripe green fruits dominating before a strong and spicy conclusion.

Connemara Cask Strength 60% ABV

Here you will find an aroma of Hornby train set, oily burnt dust on the nose with some polished wood notes. The palate is quite sublime: tinned soft fruits, wood fire and some sweet milk chocolate and cocoa. Smoke stays in the conclusion.

Locke's 8-year-old 40% ABV

This tastes young, with fresh cereal and some lemon and orange notes on the nose, while later on some sour lemon and lime, cutting chilli pepper and a degree of astringency appear.

The Tyrconnell 40% ABV

Anybody who tells you that Irish whiskey cannot offer variety should line up a Locke's, a Connemara and this. It is all sherbet fruits and Starburst candy on the nose, some apple and pear, orange and mandarin on the palate, and some oak. Refreshing, summery and full of flavour.

The Tyrconnell 15-year-old Single Cask 957/92 46% ABV

Lemon, bitter orange and melon on the nose here, while the palate is rich with demerara sugar, sweet fruits, some wood and spice and nutty almonds. The finish is pleasant and medium-sweet.

The Tyrconnell 15-year-old Single Cask 1850/52 46% ABV

Sweet melon, yellow fruits, vanilla and clean grain on the nose, a dash of chewy spearmint, then toffee apple. Late on you will encounter other green fruits with a bit of pepper at the finish.

The Tyrconnell 10-year-old Madeira Finish 46% ABV

This is an extraordinary, world-class whiskey by anybody's standards. The nose is a wonderful mix of fresh exotic fruits with sweet lime, fruity and sherbety. It tastes like tinned fruits covered in jelly and it just goes on and on, with fruity ice cream on tinned pears dominating the finish.

The Tyrconnell 10-year-old Port Finish 46% ABV

Here is another one that reaches for the stars but just falls a tad short of the Madeira Finish. This has some rum-and-raisin notes and richness that are due to the port.

The Tyrconnell 10-year-old Sherry Finish 46% ABV

Dusty lemon-polished wooden office notes on the nose, then sherry fruits, red and blackberries and some wood. Pleasant and balanced but just a tad directionless given this brand name's very high quality standards.

The Wild Geese Single Malt 43% ABV

If you have ever been around a brewery or better still, a cider-maker's, you will know the unusual aroma that is a mix of yeast, malt and slightly stale ale. It is not unpleasant, just unusual, and you get it on this whiskey, at least initially. Then toffee takes over and there are some fresh apple notes. The taste is actually quite meek after the intro, but perfectly pleasant, with apple and pear and some spice.

Irish blended whiskey

Irish blended whiskey is the signature whiskey style from Ireland but it is a different drink entirely from the blends produced by Scotland. In Ireland a blend is a mix of pot still whiskey and grain whiskey, and unlike Scotland, the various whiskeys are blended before going into the cask for maturation. Irish blends were traditionally regional, so that in Dublin it was Guinness and Paddy, in Cork and the southwest, Murphys and Powers. The two main distilleries in the south, the mighty and massive Midleton, and the smaller but flexible Cooley, are complex in that they produce grain and malt whiskies and then blend them all under the same roof, using different combinations of pot still and column-still whiskeys to make different brands.

Bushmills Black Bush 40% ABV

Black Bush is an old and iconic whiskey – a fine example of what the country is capable of when it comes to full-bodied blended Irish whiskey. There is a mountain of fresh fruits in the taste, but juicy sultanas and a clutch of savoury and sweet spices ensure that this twists and turns in a delightful manner from start to finish.

Bushmills Original 40% ABV

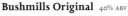

If Bushmills is a prize-fighter of a whiskey, this is the street equivalent, a bare-knuckle bruiser trained at Ryan's gym and as rough and ready as you would expect. You can almost see the tattoos. That said, the grain at the core is vintage Ireland, and it is good value for money. File with Powers and Paddy in the 'unreconstituted' section of the whiskey library...

COOLEY DISTILLERY

Riverstown, Cooley, Co. Louth
www.cooleywhiskey.com

Until a few years ago Ireland's whiskey industry found itself floundering on the margins, increasingly becoming a bit player with a couple of solid brands.

No longer. While it would be exaggerating to say that Irish whiskey has undergone a revolution in the last decade, it has certainly been transformed; and although still relatively small, it is more dynamic than it has been for many a year.

There are three reasons for the turnaround: the success of Jameson on the world stage, and with it the desire by Irish distillers to launch expressions of the brand into the premium whisky category; the new life given to Bushmills since it was sold to Diageo and came out of the shadow of Jameson; and most of all, the arrival of Cooley to provide Irish whiskey with a much-needed shot in the arm.

Cooley is the brainchild of John Teeling, a somewhat larger-than-life figure who has made his money in mining, including for gold and diamonds. The day-to-day running of the business has now been placed in the hands of his two sons, Jack and Stephen.

The company's importance to the Irish whiskey story cannot be over-estimated. Its arrival just about doubled the number of whiskeys on offer to the customer and has provided real choice. For a while virtually all Irish whiskey from south of the border was made at Irish distillers' Midleton plant – from Jamesons to Paddy's, Powers and Redbreast through to whiskeys such as Green Spot and Tullamore Dew.

Worse still, you had to travel north of Belfast to see a working whiskey man. Midleton does not allow tourists and the only places you could visit – Tullamore, Locke's and the Old Jameson distilleries in Dublin and Midleton, are museums. Or, in the case of Locke's, were, because Cooley has been bringing the distillery at Kilbeggan back to life.

'It's true enough that Ireland has always had more than its fair share of pubs but no distilleries to visit,' says company managing director Jack Teeling. 'It makes it hard for the whiskey enthusiast to share the experience as they can in Scotland and America. It's something we have been very aware of and have tried to do something about.'

With a determination bordering on craziness Cooley set about trying to produce whiskey at Locke's. No easy task

because while the equipment there was beautifully preserved it was, quite literally, from another era. But in 2007 the company started distilling on the site and in 2010 bottled their first whiskey from it.

Cooley has brought a fresh impetus to Irish whiskey. The peated but fruity Connemara is a reminder that peat did play a role in Irish whiskey's past, and is a bottled poke in the eye to all the Irish tour guides who claim Irish whiskey never uses peat while all Scottish malts do. Tyrconnell is world-class premium whiskey by any standards, and Greenore is a quality grain whiskey, demonstrating another aspect to the nation's distilling past.

Cooley has battled hard to survive and prosper through difficult times, but now armed with a clutch of awards for its brands and a solid portfolio that is becoming better known by the month, the future is looking bright.

'Perhaps we need to inject some of the fun back into Irish whiskey,' says Teeling.

'Jameson has kept the door open for Irish whiskey and is finding new markets. We have some great whiskeys for those who want to explore further.

'But other countries are offering a whiskey experience which we need to match, and it is within the Irish character to do it well. If we get that right Irish whiskey can prosper. It's win-win for everyone.'

Indeed it is – and with the three Irish rivals competing with each other but working for Irish whiskey the comeback is set to continue. That's good news for all of us.

ABOVE Cooley is helping to bring some of Ireland's more neglected and dilapidated whiskey museums back to life.

RIGHT This may be a case of smoke and mirrors, but the Kilbeggan distillery is at last enjoying a new lease of life under Cooley.

KEY WHISKEYS

Connemara 40% ABV
Connemara 10-year-old Sherry Finish 46% ABV
Connemara 12-year-old 46% ABV
Connemara Cask Strength 60% ABV
Greenore 15-year-old 43% ABV
Kilbeggan 40% ABV
Kilbeggan 15-year-old 40% ABV
Locke's 40% ABV
The Tyrconnell 40% ABV
The Tyrconnell 15-year-old Single Cask 957/92 46% ABV
The Tyrconnell 15-year-old Single Cask 1850/52 46% ABV
The Tyrconnell 10-year-old Madeira Finish 46% ABV
The Tyrconnell 10-year-old Sherry Finish 46% ABV
The Tyrconnell 10-year-old Port Finish 46% ABV

Jameson 40% ABV

This is a world trailblazer right now, single-handedly burning a path for Ireland into new and exciting territories as the world once more realises that Ireland can produce world-class whiskey. This may be a standard and ubiquitous whiskey but do not let familiarity breed contempt – it is a beauty. All the rounded fruit content is there and present, but there are some luscious red berry notes from the sherry, some oiliness from the pot still whiskey, and some spices and oak. This is the work of distillers at the very peak of their craft – and a total delight.

Jameson 12-year-old Special Reserve 40% ABV

The years in wood give this a richer and fuller sherry content than the standard bottling, there is more pepper and spice, and a noticeable and delightful toasted oak content.

Jameson 18-year-old Gold Reserve 40% ABV

For many years Jameson employed a man named John Ryan as a brand ambassador. His sophisticated and cultured accent gave little indication of his Irish roots but he loves his country and knows its history and culture inside out – including its fractious relationship with Britain. His approach to promoting Irish whiskey to journalists was simple – don't force it on them, or try to market it. Just give them a wonderful Irish experience that happens to include whiskey and they will naturally fall in love with it. Some years ago we were put up at a hotel near Cork where it was required to wear suit and tie for dinner. The entertainment was the sort of plastic Paddy didddl-ie-do stuff and John Ryan was so appalled by it that he decided to take us to a 'real' pub in Cork. Before he went in he told us that we should leave when he told us to.

So we walked through the door in suits and ties and the pub fell silent and a group of leather-jacketed youths just stared at us. It turns out that we had gone into a staunchly Republican pub.

Ryan orders a bottle of Jameson,.produces an acoustic guitar and heads off to a back room where he proceeds to regale us with IRA and Republican

songs. He offers the bottle round the bar and within minutes the regulars have joined our table for a whiskey and some rousing versions of songs about freeing Ireland and beating the Brits.

John Ryan insists on ordering another bottle and then challenges we English to sing a song. There is only one volunteer, and all he can muster was a weak version of 'Ilkley Moor Bah't 'at' to general amusement among our hosts. Then after some more IRA songs Ryan announces we are leaving. The locals insist their new Brit friends stay, but Ryan is adamant. So to loud applause, pats on backs and shakes of hand we leave. That is whiskey for you.

Another wonderful example of aged Jameson, with the fruity green fruit flavours mingling with oak, spice and some quite delicious sweet honeycomb. Some red berries are in there, too, and it is all held together by the rich oiliness provided by the pot still whiskey. Outstanding.

Jameson Rarest Vintage Reserve 46% ABV

Nobody can throw a party quite like the Irish, and when they launched this most special of Irish whiskeys, Irish Distillers brought journalists from around the world for a hoolie and a half. They put us up in a new hotel near Cork that was so big it took 20 minutes to walk to your room. This made the round trip 40 minutes: and that is my excuse for taking the decision in the early hours to ensure I did not miss an early morning plane departure by sleeping in the bar. The party included an exclusive concert by the amazing Sinead O'Connor who not only performed a surprisingly hit-friendly set, but sat on my table. Watching her sing 'Nothing Compares 2U' in a small venue while drinking this whiskey is up there with my best memories.

The whiskey is stupendous, made with the finest and very old whiskeys and with a price tag to match. But it is the fruitiest, tastiest, oiliest, spiciest and fullest Irish whiskey you will ever taste. Best of all, its strength has been boosted from 40% to 46%, giving it muscle power to compete with the top whiskies of Scotland, Japan and the United States.

Kilbeggan 40% ABV

A value-for-money whiskey that puts up quite a showing. There are cereal notes and some fresh barley, but plenty of green fruit and the odd hint of lemon at the finish.

Kilbeggan 15-year-old 40% ABV

The man behind Cooley, which makes this whiskey, is not a natural whiskey-maker – he made his money in, among other things, diamond, gold, copper mining, and bizarrely, mining zinc in Limerick, Ireland. He is just a little crazy and opened Cooley in 1987 because he thought it would be fun. One of his crazier ideas was to get Kilbeggan up and running again, but in 2007 he did just that. Kilbeggan sits on the main route from Dublin to the west coast, and when the economy was booming, Friday nights through the region was

one long traffic jam as affluent Dubliners headed off to their boats. So imagine their outrage when they found the road blocked by a pot still. Cooley brought traffic to a standstill for hours as they tried to put new stills in place. But whiskey is being produced again at the site. If it matures as well as this has, it will be worth waiting for. This has cereal, honey and rich oak notes as well as the trademark fruit.

Locke's 40% ABV

If you have a sweet tooth then this should be right up your street. It is a solid, chunky, honey monster of a whiskey, with a pleasant and balanced mix of malt and grain.

Midleton Very Rare 40% ABV 2008 BOTTLING

Midleton is the name of the big Irish Distillers'-owned distillery near Cork and this is a small-quantity annual release so it will vary from batch to batch. On the whole, though, the standard is pretty good. This one starts off with soft fluffy apples and then is taken over by a sharp razor-edged wave of oak and spice, suggesting that some very old whiskeys are in the mix, and concludes with a honeyed oiliness. Great stuff.

Paddy 40% ABV

This is included here because Paddy is in the memory banks, a throwback to a different, quieter, more naive Ireland, when every village had at least one pub that looked like someone's living room and where you were made to feel completely at home, whoever you were. Every one of those pubs had an old boy nursing a pint of stout and a whiskey chaser, studying the racing form. Give him the chance and he would tell you amazing stories from his past and offer sound advice. Paddy was that old boy. I am sure that pubs like this still exist in Ireland but

there have been huge changes over the last 30 years. As a brand this is going nowhere and it is an acquired taste – but it is a taste of history, an everyday blend with some pleasant pot still-induced moments, a straight ahead maltiness mostly, and then a twist of pepper to finish.

Powers 12-year-old 40% ABV

A blend dominated by rich mouth-filling oily, grainy, pulsating pot-still whiskey and another traditional, classic Irish whiskey. This time, though, this is relevant in the way that a big old Triumph Bonneville bike is relevant, powered on the twin engines of hard solid grain and the pot still whiskey. Big rich fluffy green fruit and a sharp and incisive wave of spice.

Powers Gold Label 40% ABV

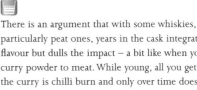

There is an argument that with some whiskies, particularly peat ones, years in the cask integrates the flavour but dulls the impact – a bit like when you add curry powder to meat. While young, all you get from the curry is chilli burn and only over time does the spice become integrated and balanced. Thing is, if you like a big chilli hit, younger is best. This is what has happened here. It is much mellower, smoother and rounded than the original version, so that the oily pot-still and pepper spice is more balanced and pleasant but nowhere the near roller-coaster ride. Better than standard Powers? Debatable. I'm a raw chilli man myself.

IRISH DISTILLERS

Simmonscourt House, Simmonscourt Road, Ballsbridge, Dublin 4
www.irishdistillers.de

There is no doubt that this is a golden age for Irish whiskey.

If you take Irish Distillers' three wise men – master distillers Barry Crockett, Billy Leighton and David Quinn, include retired maestro Brendan Monks, maverick whiskey-maker Barry Walsh, Cooley supremo Noel Sweeney and Bushmills' gifted Colum Egan, then we are truly looking at the whiskey world's Magnificent Seven.

Ireland's whiskey world is small but perfectly formed, and it is starting to gain accolades on the international stage once more. Without doubt a great part of this is down to the dedicated and focused efforts of Irish Distillers.

It is unusual to find three master distillers at one distillery of course, but then Midleton, the futuristic and somewhat enigmatic super-distillery that produces Jameson, Redbreast, Midleton, Powers, Green Spot and Paddy, is no ordinary distillery. The very nature of Irish whiskey demands that it needs to be treated in a special way.

'We simply cannot make blended whiskey the way that the Scots do because we do not have the portfolio of whiskies here from which to work,' says Crockett. 'We have to create different styles of whiskey within the one distillery, but we're reaping the rewards from investing in the finest wood back in the 1980s and with trying different things during the distillation process.'

In recent years Irish Distillers has been faced by some real

Green Spot 40% ABV
Jameson 40% ABV
Jameson 12-year-old Special Reserve 40% ABV
Jameson 18-year-old Gold Reserve 40% ABV
Jameson Rarest Vintage Reserve 46% ABV
Midleton Very Rare 40% ABV
Paddy 40% ABV
Powers 40% ABV
Powers Gold Label 40% ABV
Redbreast 12-year-old 40% ABV
Redbreast 15-year-old 46% ABV

competition after decades of having events pretty much all its own way. But it must be commended for the way it has not only stayed ahead of the pack, but it has excelled, opening up new markets for Irish whiskey and playing a crucial and fundamental role in establishing a premium for the category. It has done so by creating higher strength, older and rare whiskeys that are just as good as the very best Scottish output. Jameson has been the battering ram to knock down doors and the brand has helped the whole Irish category, providing the platform for Cooley to thrive. That is why, though, Jameson cannot get complacent, says Crockett.

'We think we are doing well and we are, but then we hear other companies say we are providing them with a way in for their brands. We must make sure that we do the same thing with our other whiskeys.'

It is a very good point. If there has been a criticism of Irish Distillers in recent years it is that it has not paid as much attention to other whiskeys in its stable, such as the wonderful pot-still whiskey Redbreast, as it might have done. That is set to change, with plans by the company to put some proper investment behind the rest of the portfolio, including the Redbreast and Powers brands.

The skill will be to bring on such whiskeys while maintaining the growth of Jameson. That is going to happen predicts

Billy Leighton. 'We are operating close to full capacity now and we are ploughing additional money in to building new warehouses,' he says. 'But we need to expand significantly by adding more pot stills, and new brewing facilities. Plans are in place. No one is quite sure how big the expansion is going to be, but we might be looking at building up the distillery and doubling the production capacity within 10 years.'

That is exciting, positive news and further proof that Irish whiskey is well and truly back from the brink. A golden era indeed – and with so many distillers performing at the top of their game, it can only get better.

FAR LEFT The old distillery manager's accommodation at the Midleton distillery.

ABOVE The impressive waterwheel at the old Jameson distillery, now a popular tourist attraction.

LEFT The smart and stylish Jameson range – putting Irish whiskey back in the front line of the top distillers.

Tullamore Dew 10 years old 40% ABV

Pretty mainstream Jameson-like blend, with apple and pear fruits, some nice grain and pot-still notes, plus polite levels of oak and spice. It is not going to set the world on fire but is perfectly drinkable and well put together.

The Wild Geese Fourth Centennial 43% ABV

And just to make the point about 400 years of hurt, this is a special bottling that is light, honeyed and rounded. It is slight and delicate, a tad fey, but if you look carefully, all the classic Irish whiskey traits are here – fruit, vanilla, oily grain and malt all make a showing.

The Wild Geese Rare Irish 43% ABV

The Wild Geese refers to the huge number of people who have left Ireland over the last four centuries and built Irish communities in all parts of the world. The whiskey is a relatively recent addition to the Irish offering and has been effectively designed to service what is perceived to be a demand for premium whiskey. It is made at Cooley for an independent company, and although the brand does not have much in the way of provenance, it is extremely well made. There is a great interplay between grain and malt, some fierce shard-like spicy notes and some hints of honey, lime and oak.

Irish pot still whiskey

You would think it does exactly what it says on the tin – or more accurately, copper – but you would be wrong. Indeed it sounds like a bad joke: when is a pot still whiskey not a pot still whiskey? When it is made just in a pot still.

If ever there was a territory that needs to sort out its definitions, it is Ireland – and thankfully that is exactly what it is doing. The problem comes from the fact that there are some who have claimed that if an Irish whiskey is distilled in a pot still it's a pot still whiskey. This is not only wrong, but hugely damaging to the Irish whiskey category. After all, that would mean that all Scottish single malt is pot still whisky.

Pot still whiskey is a style unique to Ireland, and contains a mix of malted barley and another grain, often unmalted barley, in the initial grist. This is then mashed, fermented and distilled in a pot still and makes for a rich, oily whiskey.

Green Spot 40% ABV

A few years ago *Whisky Magazine* had an event called Best of the Best. Every two years they would take their best scoring whiskies from the tastings pages, divide them into flights – Irish, Scottish blends, bourbons etc. – and tour them round the world, to Tokyo, Bardstown Kentucky, Dublin, Edinburgh and London, where representatives of the industry would taste them and score them, awarding one in each category an award and one overall winner the title of Best of the Best.

Judges were asked to give them a minimum of five out of 10 and to be generous with their marks, as these were already high-scoring whiskies. Judges could also write comments.

In Kentucky the Islay single-malt category had them flummoxed. One by one the score sheets came back with every whisky scored five, and the comment 'peaty' or 'smoky'. In Scotland they didn't get bourbon, but being Scotland they ignored the scoring advice and gave them between zero and two, with the supporting comments 'crap' and 's**t'.

There are two reasons for mentioning this. One, because the tasting in Dublin was held at the wonderful old shop of Mitchell & Son, who own this brand. And two, time and again this whiskey would score well at Best of the Best, seemingly able to appease the palates of both flummoxed Kentuckians and grouchy Scotsmen.

Not surprisingly, this is arguably the cleanest, sharpest, fruitiest whiskey known to man – on one level bursting with youthful exuberance and with a sweet heart, and on another, a complex whiskey with oily pot still traits, some white pepper spice and a trace of liquorice, menthol and cocoa.

Oh, and in case you are wondering, the Irish judges did not 'get' peaty whisky or, surprisingly, bourbon.

Redbreast 12-year-old   40% ABV

Redbreast is another classic Irish whiskey, a marvellous example of rich, full and tasty pot still whiskey, with the grains and oils coating the mouth and refusing to let up. The spices dance across the mouth, sherry bobs in and out, the oily pot still whiskey bursts out for a solo spot from time to time, liquorice and coffee have cameos and on it goes. Have you seen Take That's *Circus* tour? This is the whiskey equivalent – so much going on you have to try it all again. Awesome.

Redbreast 15-year-old   46% ABV

A limited edition and a rarity for Ireland – a whiskey weighing in at 46% ABV and with a solid 15 years behind it. The nose has a grungey, tough sulphury note to it at first, but this is merely a bit of macho posturing and a statement of intent. Give it a couple of minutes and it goes, like early morning mist, giving way to warming sunlight. The nose is fresh, clean, floral and fruity all at once, but the magic lies in the taste. Crisp red apples, underripe pears, some citrus notes and pepper form the centre of the taste and then something wipes everything to the side to leave a long fruity and spicy finale. This would be a contender for a top 20 place in any definitive list of the world's best whiskies, let alone the top 750.

Grain whiskey

As is the case in Scotland, the term 'grain whiskey' in Ireland tends to refer to whiskey that is made with a grain other than malted barley, and in Ireland it is also taken to be a category distinct from pot still whiskey. There are plenty of people who believe that this style of whisky has great potential and is under-rated.

Some Scottish companies are actively promoting grain as a style. Irish and Scottish grain whisky are very similar and although Ireland doesn't produce much of it, Greenore has picked up awards around the world and is a leading player in the category.

Grain whiskey is most often produced in a continuous still as opposed to a copper pot still. Quality casks play a major role in the development of good grain whiskey and Greenore has achieved its success by double-distilling then maturing its grain whiskey in bourbon casks for at least eight years.

Greenore 15-year-old   43% ABV

Elegant, rich, sweet and chewy, this is proof if ever you wanted it that grain on its own can still make for a significant and impactful whiskey. This won the award for World's Best Grain in the 2010 World Whisky Awards and no wonder. This style of whiskey will never have great depths but there is an interesting interplay between sugar and spice, a great sweet grain core and some woody notes to stop it all becoming too cloying at the end.

THE WORLD'S BEST WHISKIES

JAPAN

Japan

I have long held the view that as we move to a more homogenised and globalised world there will be a counter-reaction by consumers. We are already growing sick of travelling halfway round the world to a remote tribal village in darkest Peru only to find Carlsberg, Guinness and Bacardi on sale in the ramshackle bar.

Increasingly we will seek out products with a serious heritage and a traceabale provenance, drinks with a proper story to tell and a unique way of telling it. All this is very good news indeed for single-malt whisky, which has provenance and heritage by the bucket load.

But woe betide any drinks company that dresses its brands in the clothing of heritage and provenance. When the public discover they are looking at a Top Man suit and not an Armani one, they will be uncompromising in their rejection of it. All those claiming to distill whiskey in Bardstown, Kentucky, but are not part of Heaven Hill or Tom Moore, please take note. American owners of Canadian brands containing small amounts of American bourbon should pay heed. And Ireland needs to watch itself too.

But most of all, Japan's two biggest whisky-making companies Nikka and Suntory need to get their act together. There is a strong argument that Japanese whisky has already been held back in some countries by its questionable approach to making blended whisky, which has often included a significant proportion of Scottish whisky. In the future, as people take a greater interest in what they are drinking and where it comes from, they will take a dim view of hybrid brands with no meaningful story to tell.

Japan's problem in this area is created by the fact that the country has relatively few distilleries and a work culture that pretty much rejects the concept of co-operating with rival companies. The best blends contain a large number of different whiskies and in Scotland producers pool their resources to everyone's benefit.

They do not do that in Japan, so they only have two options: to create a number of different styles of whisky in each distillery, or to buy in whisky from other countries. Both options are in play.

Thankfully no such problem exists with the country's single malts, and it seems that the word about how good the country's malts are is well and truly out. For some years now whisky writers have written glowingly about them, and they have scooped a clutch of major awards. But growth has been relatively slow, partially because supply has been patchy.

All that, though, is changing. When the Whisky Shop opened a branch in Norwich, England four years ago it requested large stocks of Japanese whisky and was told that there was little of it anywhere across the 15-shop estate, and no demand for what there was. So it gathered in all that was available and sold the lot within the first month – Norwich is in the far east (of England) after all. Now the Suntory brands are not only available across the whole group but they are selling well – even in the Scottish outlets.

I know it is a terrible pun, but you could sum up the situation for whisky from Japan in the phrase 'the land of the rising Suntory'. The company dominates the country's whisky export market, though Nikka has some excellent whisky too, and although it is operating from a small base, the Number One Drinks Company (also in Norwich – what a place) is bringing Japanese whisky from smaller distilleries to the attention of whisky enthusiasts.

Traditionally, Japanese whiskies have emulated the single malts of Scotland and are closer in style to them than the whiskeys of Ireland, America and Canada. But in recent years they have increasingly developed their own style and character, and many have distinctive mushroomy/fungal notes. It sounds odd and may require a taste re-calibration, but it adds distinctive and attractive characteristics to the whisky in the same way that the savoury and arguably discordant flavours contribute to the overall taste of olives or blue cheese.

Most importantly for Japan, its whiskies are growing in popularity and people are buying in to their provenance, history and heritage. As drinkers continue to explore further afield, it all augurs well for Eastern whisky.

NAGASAKI ●

ABVOE AND ABOVE RIGHT
The gleaming stills at Suntory and Ichiro.

Japanese single malt whisky

The Japanese have done with single malt what they have done with cars – taken the model, stripped it down, worked out how to make it and rebuilt it, not only matching much of the competition in the process, but surpassing it. Japan does not pretend it looked any further than Scotland for its whisky inspiration, its two biggest companies Suntory and Nikka were both effectively set up by an individual who learned his trade in the Highlands. Japan has been making malt whisky for a long time now but widespread critical acclaim and a clutch of awards suggests it has now passed Canada up the league table and is giving Ireland a run for its money as whisky's third most important market.

Fuji Gotemba 15-year-old 43% ABV

A strange nose that is part dry shredded wheat, part doughball. The taste is sweet and clean, with honey on vanilla ice cream and escalating mouth-feel before a wave of sweet spices and some oaky notes arrive late on.

Hakushu 10-year-old 40% ABV

Sometimes you taste a whisky and you taste a colour. A lot of Japanese whiskies are russet or autumnal brown. This one, though, is spring-like and green, with a wonderful crispness to it. Imagine pear crumble and custard followed by toffee apples. The palate has some earthiness underneath and is like a Scottish Bladnoch or an Irish Connemara.

Hakushu 12-year-old

43% ABV

This has a very unusual and complex nose, with freshly cut leaves, clean and chewy barley, some citrusy notes and a touch of peat. The peat is noticeable on the palate but is not dominant. Among the fruits are some pleasant liquorice notes. All in all a little gem.

YOICHI
SAPPORO

3

N

MIYAGIKYO

J A P A N

CHICHIBU

1

TOKYO

KYOTO

OSAKA

JAPANESE DISTILLERY PROFILES

Hakushu 18-year-old 43% ABV

In terms of the contribution from the cask, the tide was in with the 15-year-old. Indeed, for many this whisky will be a step too far. Right from the first aromas – big polished church pews, sawdust and some smoke, you can tell what is coming and it does. But before that, it is like the sun making a brief appearance on a cloudy day – as bright apple and pear flavours and some enticing and tantalising sherbety notes shine through for a while. Then the big, dark, brooding, oaky clouds roll over again and by the finish the astringency is mouth-puckering

Hakushu 1989 60% ABV

A big grouchy bullfrog of a whisky, that gives little away on the nose but is uncompromising in its concentrated sherry attack on the palate. It comes into its own when water is added, however. Rich stewed plums, toasted oak, lemon and grapefruit and some incense-like fragrance all contribute to a big, bold but complex whisky.

Hakushu 25-year-old 43% ABV

After the oaky intensity of the 18-year-old, you approach the 25-year-old with something that borders on trepidation. I can't think of one single example of a 25-year-old that is better than its 18-year-old younger brother – and that includes Highland Park. This, though doesn't even try to compete and swims off in a different direction

Hanyu Single Cask 1991 57.3% ABV

By Japanese standards this has a surprisingly delicate and floral flavour, with sweet toffee and citrus notes on the nose and a big mouth-feel, with intense fruits, spices working their way through, and some menthol and liquorice notes. The finish is quite long, sweet and spicy.

Hanyu 1988 55.6% ABV

If you've ever heard Deep Purple performing 'Highway Star' on the band's live masterpiece *Made In Japan* you'll have a good idea of what to expect from this whisky. No messing around, everything turned up to 11 and bang! we're off...This is the full-aged sherry shooting gallery, with wave after wave of power chord marmalade up front, a wicked solo from dark cocoa, and a pulsating spice and oak rhythm section. Altogether now: 'Ooh, it's a killing machine, it's got everything.'

Hokuto 12-year-old 40% ABV

This is the whisky equivalent to one of those disturbing television thrillers that you can't quite decide if you're enjoying watching or not, but can't bring yourself to turn it off. A curious and unusual whisky with stewed fruits, oak and some dusty wood shavings on the nose, rose petal water and sherbet on the palate, a stewed prune heart, with pepper and oak late on. The finish is long and spicy.

Ichiro Malt Eight of Hearts 56.8% ABV

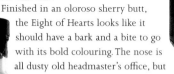

Finished in an oloroso sherry butt, the Eight of Hearts looks like it should have a bark and a bite to go with its bold colouring. The nose is all dusty old headmaster's office, but the taste is surprisingly fresh and jolly, with pepper, ginger, nutmeg and cinnamon all making an appearance and some juicy currants in the finale.

Ichiro Malt Five of Spades 60.5% ABV

Very sherried trifle, with strawberry flan and vanilla custard on the nose and a bold, nutty, sherry-rich taste with some oaky and peppery notes on the palate. A traditional, tweed-jacketed sort of a malt.

Karuizawa 17-year-old 59.5% ABV

Stewed apples filled with mincemeat on the nose, with some nuttiness and dry sherry notes. But it is a complex and evolving nose, and after a while it becomes zesty and sherbety. The whisky has a big full flavour, but is nonetheless surprisingly gentle and rounded, with a nice balance, the right amount of oak and spice, plus lots of soft fruits, almost like a cordial. The finish is long and warming.

Karuizawa 1985 Single Cask 60% ABV

A big rich autumn woodland of a nose, with musty mushroom, rich prune fruits and oak. Nothing quite prepares you, however, for the intense and fruity taste of this big whisky, with plum, prune juice and intense red fruits and oak. With water, added sherry comes to the fore. The finish is rich and sherried – Japan's answer to Scotland's *A'Bunnadh* for sure.

Karuizawa 1986 Single Cask 60.7% ABV

At first this whisky is shaped by damp rootsy fungal notes, with celery and truffles. With time some lemon and grapefruit notes appear and the refreshing citrus notes extend to the palate, which flip-flops and is altogether a lot less grungey than the nose suggested. It has a big, rich mouth-feel with orange barley in the mix, while the finish is chewy, with barley notes

Karuizawa 1976 32-year-old Single Cask 63% ABV

Slow to open out but when it does there is an almost lemony quality to it, but there are also redcurrant, raspberry and raisins in the mix. The taste is thick and concentrated, with blackcurrant to the fore but also some menthol, overripe melon and exquisite wafting smokiness. But just when you expect everything to freefall into an astringent and sharp conclusion, a puffy pillow suddenly appears and you are left with an exquisite soft and rounded conclusion.

Karuizawa 1971 Cask 6878 64.2% ABV

This is to whisky what the Australian rock band Wolfmother is to music – a monster-sized roaring 'amps up to 11' throwback to another era but still very contemporary and relevant. This is a serious burnt fruit-and-nut case, all served up with Christmas cake and wrapped up in oak. Want a malt to relax with at the end of a hard day? Don't go for this one. This is for surfers – some of the time you go with the flow, at others you have to battle the currents and rips, and all the time it's a white knuckle ride. Just like listening to Wolfmother. And if you've got a rock-and-roll heart then both band and whisky will have you head-banging and leave you exhausted and contented by the end.

Karuizawa 1967 42-year-old Single Cask 58% ABV

Same age as my wife at the time of tasting, and while nowhere near as beautiful or elegant, it's nearly as spritely and wearing quite well all the same. In fact there's a youthful zestiness about the nose, with grapefruit marmalade and clean sweet fruit. The taste is very much an all-or-nothing one. If you can get past the astringent oaky barricade at the entranceway there's much to recommend this, with rich orange and grapefruit and even some nuttiness.

Miyagikyo 10-year-old 45% ABV

This doesn't start very well, with a dull score draw of a nose, but it kicks into life when you taste it, with an intense dual between sweet fresh fruit and savoury spices. The fruit just about wins it.

ICHIRO'S MALT

Hanyu Distillery, Chichibu, Japan
www.one-drinks.com/hanyu.php

In a country where the whisky industry is so totally dominated by
two companies, Ichiro is a rarity – an independent and free-spirited
whisky-maker, taking an individual approach to the industry.

KEY WHISKIES

Ichiro's Malt Eight of Hearts 56.8% ABV
Ichiro's Malt Five of Spades 60.5% ABV

ABOVE The purpose-built distillery at Chichibu was completed at
the end of October 2007 and has been busy ever since.

That does not mean he is new to the alcohol business, however – far from it. His family has been making *sake* in Chichibu since 1625, and his grandfather, who represented the 19th generation of the family in the drinks business, built the Hanyu distillery in 1941.

When his family's business ran into problems at the start of the new millennium, Ichiro saw it as his duty to pick up the baton and run with it.

'We sold the business, including the Hanyu distillery, at that time,' he says. 'But the new owner was only interested in quick business and had no desire to continue maturing whisky. I rescued the last 400 casks from the distillery before they were re-distilled. Whisky is in my blood.'

Having made the step into the whisky business, Ichiro set about doing things a little bit differently. He has been bottling his whisky stocks in small batches with each one bearing a playing card on its label. A gimmick? Not at all, he says.

'When I visited bars in Japan I was struck by how difficult it is to remember the years and the numbers of single casks on the bottles,' he says. 'I wanted to find something distinctive which would look good on the back of the bar but would also be easier to remember. That's when the card series came to me. There will be 53 releases in total, so I will finish off the series with the joker.'

Selling existing stocks of whisky is one thing, making it is another. But Ichiro is going down that route, too. He has built a new distillery at Chichibu and the first fruits of his labours, young malt spirit, has been released to critical acclaim. Among the standard ex-sherry and ex-bourbon casks are some made with Japanese oak, and Japanese barley is also being used.

'Ultimately I want our whisky to be uniquely Japanese,' he says. 'Chichibu Distillery is very

small and I want the whisky to be handmade. I would like all my experience and that of my ancestors, to be appreciated in each bottle from Chichibu. I have carefully studied every aspect of the whisky-making process at first hand. As well as working at Hanyu I have distilled spirit at Karuizawa and at BenRiach, and I want this to show.'

Chichibu is producing three different types of spirit – a non-peated medium-bodied one, a non-peated heavy one, and a heavily peated one. Ichiro is excited about the arrival of his first whisky but is already looking forward to producing 10-year-old, 20-year-old and 30-year-olds.

'The intention is to release six casks from Chichibu annually, three for the domestic market and three for export,' he says. 'It's a small operation but when I travel and see many people enjoying whisky it fills me with hope. I see young people enjoying whisky and I am pleased that Japanese whisky is being recognised. It makes me optimistic about the future.'

ABOVE LEFT New casks used in the distilling process are made from American oak and Japanese Mizunara oak.

ABVOE RIGHT Reused casks are also integral to whisky production at Ichiro and include American, Japanese, French and Spanish oak examples.

LEFT The Ichiro's Malt collection is a series of bottlings based on a complete pack of playing cards.

Miyagikyo 12-year-old 45% ABV

Gooseberry, rhubarb and cocoa on the nose, then the softest and sweetest of starts when you taste it. Don't be fooled, though, because pretty quickly a razor-blade wave of sharp spiciness arrives and takes you through to a peppery conclusion.

Miyagikyo 15-year-old

45% ABV

The aromas here are of Christmas cake, raisins and sultanas and sweet spices, while the taste is mouth-coating, with plummy fruits, raisins and a pleasant malty core.

Miyagikyo Single Cask 1989 61% ABV

Nikka's Miyagikyo is at once enigmatic and disconcerting. Just when you think you have got it sussed, it throws up a curveball, as with this one. You expect sweet, easy-going fruity whiskies; what you get is a big, chubby unbalanced but utterly intriguing and exciting whisky. A very pleasant surprise.

Nikka Single Cask 1991 58% ABV

A light and breezy whisky, this has candy, vanilla, banana and toffee on the nose, and a taste of sweet fruit soda, and blackcurrant Starburst. The finish is clean and sweet with a touch of spice.

Yamazaki 10-year-old 40% ABV

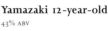

Lots and lots going on here, and surprisingly complex for what is effectively the distillery's standard flag-bearer, with sweet spice and fluffy apples on the nose, and fresh sweet lemon, melon and apple in the taste. Very clean and fresh, an easy-drinking delight.

Yamazaki 12-year-old

43% ABV

Starts off with aromas of polished wood and pine then opens out with summer fruits on the nose. The whisky marches into the mouth and occupies it. The word that springs to mind here is luscious – this is as juicy as whisky gets, as if someone has made a redcurrant, raspberry, blueberry and blackcurrant smoothie and mixed it with alcohol. The fruity finish is long and very warming.

Yamazaki 18-year-old 43% ABV

I tasted this while staying at Center Parcs and it seemed totally appropriate, because the aroma is like damp leaves and an early morning stroll in the forest. There are also some juicy raisin notes on the nose. The palate is astounding – lots of sherry and wood, dark chocolate and rum and raisin. Lurking under the surface are some meaty, grungey notes, probably from sulphur, but this only adds to the fun and festivities of this whisky and it's effectively a defiant two-finger salute to anyone who deducts marks from all sulphur-tinged whisky as a matter of principle. There are a few thoroughbred whiskies in this Japanese section, and more than one from this distillery. This, though, is arguably the pick of the bunch.

Yamazaki 1984 48% ABV

This whisky has an almost liqueur-like quality, with sweet barley and orange fruits on the nose, and with water, lemon and grapefruit. The taste is big, full and unusual but quite

THE YAMAZAKI SINGLE MALT WHISKY DISTILLED IN 1984

appealing, with menthol, orange and cherry-flavoured cough lozenges. The finish is long and sweet with some medicinal notes – daringly different.

Yamazaki 25-year-old 43% ABV

Like a dusty old polished office – stately and imposing at the same time, with full rich sherry, raisins and berries and some dustiness and mustiness and a trace of mushroom. The taste is rich and mouth-filling, with plum chutney and orange rind. The finish is long and fruity, with a nice balance of oak and spice.

Yamazaki 1993 62% ABV

Ha! Just as you are getting to grips with this wonderful distillery and you are well and truly focused on your target, they go and move the goal posts. Completely. All the way to Islay in fact. This has barbecued fish, white pepper and smoke on the nose and a taste that bobbles about like a rowing boat in a swell, with oil, peat and fishy boathouse notes on the one hand and buttercups, sweet lemon and hickory on the other. The peat holds out longest and dominates the finish.

THE CASK of YAMAZAKI 1993 HEAVILY PEATED MALT

Yamazaki 1979 Mizunara Oak 55% ABV

Mizunara oak usually imparts a strong spiciness to whisky and that is definitely the case here. There is also a strong woodiness to it – and not much else. Certainly there is little in the way of balance. Not for everyone then, but if you enjoy hot chilli sauce and charcoal-grilled steak, it is worth a punt.

Yoichi 10-year-old 43% ABV

We live in safe times. Nobody dare have an opinion on anything for fear of losing their job or being reprimanded. Which is why the live album *White Stripes* released in 2010 is so important – it sounds like it might fall apart at any moment but never does, making for a thrilling ride. This is the whisky equivalent – the sherry, toffee, peat and vanilla should not work together at all, but they just about do.

Yoichi 12-year-old 45% ABV

Another intriguing mix of sherry and peat, though the sherry is by far the senior partner, with dried fruits and sultanas very much to the fore. There are also some vanilla and candy flavours here, too, and a rich sweetness, making for an outstanding, complex malt.

Yoichi 15-year-old 45% ABV

This is an absolutely fantastic whisky if you can't resist peaty smoky whiskies with a rich chewy fruit heart – and I can't. This is an extremely difficult distilling trick to pull off and only a handful of whiskies manage it. But Yoichi excels in this area, and would give any whisky of this type a run for its money. What makes this such a sublime experience is the way that the sherry and smoke are battering rams, but once they have gained access, there are all sorts of flavour nuances to savour – like dipping an orange in a pepper pot, with lots of citrus.

Yoichi 20-year-old 52% ABV

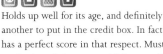

Holds up well for its age, and definitely another to put in the credit box. In fact Yoichi has a perfect score in that respect. Musty but captivating all the same, with burnt toffee and raisin, nut cluster and treacle on the nose. The taste is soft and rounded, with peanuts and honey, and paprika towards the finish.

SUNTORY

5-2-1 Yamazaki, Shimamoto-cho, Mishima-gun, Osaka
www.theyamazaki.jp
www.suntory.com

When Suntory's Dr Koichi Inatomi speaks about his company and the whiskies it makes, he does so with pride.

ABOVE The Suntory distillery, built in 1923, sits in the vale of Yamazaki and was the first malt-whisky distillery in Japan.

LEFT On the outskirts of Kyoto, where the climate is highly humid and the water pure, the enviroment is perfectly suited to the successful maturation of whisky.

ABOVE RIGHT Copper stills are used to create a superior Suntory. The distillery process is similar to that of Scotland.

Dr Inatomi is something of a whisky legend. He's responsible for creating some of Suntory's finest whiskies, including the Hibiki range. Hibiki 21-year-old was awarded the title of world's best blended whisky in the prestigious 2010 World Whisky Awards.

Now retired but still a brand ambassador for Suntory's Yamazaki and Hakushu single malts and its Hibiki blends, he is the perfect spokesman for a company that has not only put Japanese whisky on the map but has established it as a major and growing force in world whisky.

'These are very good days for Japanese whisky,' he says when we meet in Glasgow, Scotch whisky's heartland. 'You can now find Suntory whiskies in whisky shops around the world and even in Scotland. It has made huge progress.'

Meeting in Glagow is no coincidence. Dr Inamoto is based here and in the Glasgow suburb of Springburn you'll find the headquarters of Morrison Bowmore, owners of Auchentoshan, Bowmore and Glen Garioch distilleries and a company now owned by Suntory – a sign of just how big the company is.

Japanese whisky might be relatively new in many international markets but it has a history stretching back to the 1920s and Suntory goes back even further than that.

'The company was formed by Shinjiro Torii as a wine-importing business,' explains Dr Inamoto. 'The name is taken from Torii and the symbol of the sun, which is very important to Japanese culture'. Then in 1907 he launched a sweet wine called Akadama and it became very successful. The company still makes it. It provided the money to allow him to build Japan's first whisky distillery, Yamazaki.'

To help him make fine quality whisky Shinjiro Torii turned to Masataka Taketsuru, who had spent some years in Scotland perfecting the techniques of distilling whisky. The rest, as they say, is history. Today Suntory has two distilleries, producing very different malt whiskies – Yamazaki between Kyoto and Osaka, from where both Yamazaki and the Hibiki blends emanate; and Hakushu, a giant and complex distillery that produces the Hakushu range.

Suntory's whiskies were hugely successful in Japan and remain very popular with, in particular, older Japanese drinkers. But one of the whisky world's greatest ironies is that while the rest of the world has caught on to the high quality of Japanese malt, younger Japanese drinkers have fallen in love with Scottish single malt.

'But this is often the way,' says Dr Inamoto. 'Younger drinkers in the bars of Glasgow don't often drink Scottish single malt. But one of the jobs we have to do is win over the next generation.'

In the meantime Suntory is putting time and effort in to bringing its whiskies to new territories. The huge critical acclaim they have had from whisky experts across the world is ensuring that they are getting a fair hearing, and along with other Japanese whiskies they're now regularly picking up top international awards.

'It does make me very proud,' says Inamoto. 'I have seen Suntory whiskies go from nowhere to the very top of the whisky world. These are very exciting times indeed for our Japanese whiskies.'

Japanese blends

Japan has a long and proud tradition of making quality blended whisky, even though it has had to face considerable hurdles to do so. It makes blends in pretty much the same way as the Scottish whisky industry does – by taking a number of matured malts and mixing them with grain whisky before bottling. This is a bigger ask than it is in Scotland because there simply aren't the number of different malts to choose between. As a result Japanese whisky producers have developed complex distilleries where several yeasts and recipes are used to create a range of different malts under one roof. Certainly the country is now producing world-class blends. Like other Japanese whiskies the country's blends are not shy when it comes to big, rich and full flavours.

Hibiki 12-year-old 43% ABV

On the nose there is plum liqueur and exotic fruits. The taste is extremely gentle and sweet, with zesty fruit and lots of vanilla. It's a refreshing summery blend and very drinkable. Some spices give the overall experience some depth.

Hibiki 21-year-old 43% ABV

This was chosen as the world's best blended whisky in the 2010 World Whisky Awards, and it's not hard to see why. The flavours here are all bold, precise and irresistible. Orange marmalade and Christmas cake are on the nose, while the palate includes glace cherry, raisins and currants, all perfectly balanced and in tune.

Hibiki 17-year-old 43% ABV

Unripe banana, red berries and vanilla on the nose, and the green bananas extend to the palate at first. This is a big whisky and it coats the mouth, with other fruits arriving, some oak and spices having a say, and a degree of stringency towards the end. Big, full and rounded – very nice indeed.

Nikka Rare Old Super 45% ABV

This is a brave whisky. There is no age statement but it claims to be old and rare and it is veritably buzzing with aged oaky whisky. The nose is beguiling but it's little more than a curtain-raiser for the taste – it bursts with rich grain, big peat, sharp spice flavours. It says on the bottle that it's a smooth whisky – claptrap. This is a feisty, prickly wee beastie, with few blunt edges. A truly delightful blend that is up there with the very best in its unusual category.

Japanese vatted/blended malts

As with Scotland this category refers to whiskies made up just of malt whisky with no added grain. There are a limited number of them in Japan, most of them from Nikka, although in 2008 the country passed a landmark when a blended malt was released containing malts from rival companies. Traditionally, rival companies have tended not to cooperate with each other. The whisky in question picked up several awards but is no longer available. No matter. Without exception these mixed malt whiskies are complex, challenging and worth trying.

Nikka Pure Malt 12-year-old 40% ABV

If you are of the view that there is little point in mixing malts then you ought to try this, because it is definitely greater than the sum of its parts. The nose is all sweet fudge and soft toffee, but the taste is altogether different, with bitter dark chocolate, some chilli spice and an interesting peppery finish.

Nikka Pure Malt 17-year-old 43% ABV

By Japanese standards this is a surprisingly neutral whisky. You would never guess it was 17 years old, for a starter, with little coming from the cask. Instead it is sweet, smooth and pleasant. I was going to say it's a bit like listening to Coldplay, but it is not that bad, and the peatiness in the tail is a treat.

Nikka Pure Malt 21-year-old 43% ABV

The distinctive Japanese earthy mushroom is present and correct on the nose, while the taste reveals a masterclass in whisky making. There is rich juicy fruit, over a delicious peaty base, enough oak to give proceedings shape, and some bitterness for balance. The whole shooting match is soft and rounded. All in all, this is a cracker of a whisky.

Nikka Pure Black 43% ABV

This has an intense and savoury nose with autumn forest, horse chestnut, damp leaves and dark treacle. The palate is complex and evolving, with cherry throat lozenges, some earthy peatiness, soft orange fruits, tinned peach and mango, and some spice. After such a wave of flavours the finish is relatively slight, with some fruit and traces of spice.

Nikka Pure Red

43% ABV

This flip-flops from an initial burst of luxurious cocoa-rich dark chocolate and exotic fruits over an oaky base into something you might find in a delicatessen. Imagine one of those very expensive hand-made chocolates presented in a little polished wooden box, then pickle it with olives and German sausage meat. It doesn't sound great I know, but when you take the plunge, it provides a tangy taste sensation.

Nikka Pure White 43% ABV

Not quite sure about this colour coding but I do know a good peaty whisky when I taste one and this is a belter – lots of rich oil, grilled trout and intense peat all wrapped up in a sugar-and-spice blanket, with a saltiness that any Islay distiller would be proud of. All the controls are set to high for this one and if peat and smoke rock your boat, it is not to be missed.

NIKKA

Hokkaido Yoichigun Yoichimachi Kurokawacho 7–6
www.nikka.com

What is the difference between the rock band Status Quo and the Japanese whisky company Nikka? Status Quo have been rockin' all over the world for years, Nikka is just about to.

Or at least that's how Nikka's Naofumi Kamiguchi light-heartedly puts it when he talks confidently about the future for his company's whiskies.

'Yes, we're going to be rocking all over the world,' he says. 'The sales of Nikka outside Japan are now starting. The first reaction is superb, we're confident it can spread further in the future.'

He has every reason to be confident. The growth in interest in Japanese whisky in recent years has been phenomenal, the number of whiskies finding their way to all parts of the world is growing apace and most importantly of all, the quality is mind-blowingly high. Tasting Japanese whisky for this project was one of the true highlights – and no other country can boast such a consistent and uniformly high standard across the board. Every whisky tasted has been included and there were no duds. Remarkable.

Nikka is Japan's second biggest whisky maker and is dwarfed by Suntory. But it was founded in 1934 by Masataka Taketsuru, the same man who brought whisky-making skills to Suntory 10 years before. Taketsuru learned his trade in Scotland and had a vision for Japanese whisky. He set up the country's first distillery in 1924 but 10 years later found what he considered an even more perfect site for a distillery. To build Yoichi on Hokkaido he had to set up his own business, and so the

company that was to become Nikka was formed. A second distillery Miyagikyo was built in 1969.

Although widely accepted and increasingly praised by the whisky-loving community, Japanese whisky is still relatively small but growing rapidly. But Naofumi Kamiguchi believes that Japan has the quality of whisky to continue growing in to the future.

'Over three years the sales of Nikka have exploded in France,' he says. 'The whisky's reputation is growing across Europe and the sales are coming, and the next step is America and Asia. Our friend Suntory is investing aggressively in its expansion and in that sense Nikka is the follower. But we're proud of the quality of our whisky and we think it is unique. We think, for instance, that our distinctive coal-fired distillation at Yoichi is helping us to make the best whisky in the world.'

ABOVE The Nikka Miyagikyo distillery.

RIGHT The Nikka Yoichi distillery.

Although modelled on the whiskies of Scotland what's exciting whisky enthusiasts the most about Japan is the way that its malts continue to evolve and are heading off in their own direction. Japanese whiskies are designed to be consumed with food and with that comes a distinctly Japanese way of drinking. Mizuwari-style means adding ice and water to dilute the whisky as a long drink and may become increasingly popular as understanding of Japanese whisky grows.

One thing's for sure – we're going to hear a lot more about Japanese whisky, and the malts from Nikka will certainly be in the front-line.

'Our main issue is making sure younger people drink whisky,'

says Naofumi. 'We have to recruit a new generation for the future, but we can do that. Certainly we are keeping up the high tradition of whisky making while never forgetting the need for innovation and improvement.'

No doubt about it, Nikka's on a roll. Maybe it's time to get the air guitar out.

EUROPE

Europe

You would expect countries with a tradition of making alcohol from grain to make whisky, and ones in which the grape is the main source for alcohol beverages to have little interest in it.

This is not the case at all. Outside the traditional whisky territories of Ireland and Scotland, there is no long whisky-making tradition in Europe. You would expect beer-making countries such as Germany, Belgium and the Netherlands to have distilled their products into whisky. Instead they traditionally made either jenever or distilled fruits for fruit liqueurs.

There has been an explosion in distilleries making whisky across Europe in recent years, however, and some of it is very good indeed. Most of it is based on a pot still production system but much of it is made on small and unusually shaped stills, and some of it tastes radically different to Scottish single malt. A proportion of it, though, is outstanding and there are at least five distilleries that are making a case for promotion to the whisky world's premier league.

3 VALBO ●

SWEDEN

ENGLAND

WALES

4 PENDERYN ● **5** ROUDHAM ●

NETHERLANDS

GERMANY

BELGIUM

1 GRÂCE HOLLOGNE ●

2 EGGOLSHEIM ●

LIECHENSTEIN

AUSTRIA

FRANCE

SWITZERLAND

CORSICA

SPAIN

TOP RIGHT A distillery tour at Blaue Maus in Germany.

MIDDLE RIGHT Rolling out the barrel at the Whisky Castle in Switzerland.

BOTTOM RIGHT Sweden's Mackmyra Distillery is making world-class whisky from its base in Valbo.

EUROPE DISTILLERY PROFILES

BELGIUM

The Belgian Owl 2/2009 46% ABV
www.belgianwhisky.com

Single malt

A tad too young and under-developed this, but with enough to recommend it nevertheless. The nose is sweet and toffee-ish. The taste is zesty and sherbety with some liquorice notes. The finish is spicy, with citrus fruits and green fruits emerging from the sweetness.

The Belgian Owl 10/2009 46% ABV
www.belgianwhisky.com

Single malt

This is between three and four years old and vanilla has joined the toffee on the nose. But it is the flavour that impresses – pear dessert mixed with apple crumble. The finish is short and dies away quickly but that just makes it more-ish. Proof that this distillery knows what it's doing.

The Belgian Owl 10/2009 74.2% ABV
www.belgianwhisky.com

Single malt

Nearly four years old, this is a monster cask-strength whisky but with trademark sweet pears and apples, vanilla, marzipan and some spices. A potential award-winner this.

THE NETHERLANDS

Dutch Rye 5-year-old 40% ABV
www.zuidam-distillers.com

Rye whisky

Not as assertive as its US cousins, but the rye is distinctive and the whisky very well made. It includes 100 per cent pot still rye, not the easiest grist to work with. A spicy and prickly nose with some raspberry, plus hickory and spearmint flavours, and some vanilla candy.

Millstone 7-year-old 40% ABV
www.zuidam-distillers.com

Single malt

The Dutch angle to this malt is that the malted barley is ground by machinery powered by a traditional Dutch windmill. Merely a gimmick? Not necessarily. The process is slower than commercial mills but as a result little heat is generated so there is no scalding of the grain. Over in America Maker's Mark would back this approach because it does a similar thing, arguing that scorched grain has a bitterness to it. Certainly this is a beautifully balanced whisky, with a soft floral, blackcurrant and honey core and some vanilla and coconut – one more wonderful discovery made while researching this book.

Millstone 8-year-old French Oak
40% ABV BOTTLED NOVEMBER 2009
www.zuidam-distillers.com

Single malt

The distillery says that the warm and dry conditions in which this whisky is matured accounts for its rapid maturation and a large annual evaporation of 4–5%. This might explain the malt's aggressive nose and its pine-like characteristics. But so might the fact that at least some new oak is used – French oak in particular is capable of giving whisky a spiciness. There is plenty going on here and the finished malt steers its way, in an excellent manner, through a myriad of interesting flavours.

Millstone 8-year-old American Oak
40% ABV
www.zuidam-distillers.com

Single malt

This is quite lovely, a big, creamy vanilla- and honey-dominated whisky with some delicious creamy coconut notes. There are distinctive bourbony, candy and leather notes and then late on it gets winey. It is strange and complex, but utterly beguiling.

FRANCE

Armorik 40% ABV
www.distillerie-warenghem.com

Single malt

This is French whisky's version of its national Rugby Union team – it looks ugly and brutal on first appearances but is in actual fact a delightful mix of ruggedness and beauty. There are lots of spices in this, but some sweeter notes, too.

Breizh 42% ABV
www.distillerie-warenghem.com

Blend

This is a Breton blend made up of 50 per cent grain and 50 per cent malt. It tastes sweet and delicious, with lychee and sweet pear.

Eddu Gold 43% ABV
www.distillerie.fr

Buckwheat spirit

This really walks the line. Buckwheat might be called *Blé Noir* in French (and Eddu in Breton) but it isn't a grain, it's a pulse and so you have to question whether we have whisky at all. But Brittany is a fascinating whisky-producing region and this is no slouch. There are fluffy apples and overripe pears in both nose and palate, some slushy melon comes into play and the whole ball game is sealed off with a spicy finish. A very pleasant experience.

Eddu Silver 40% ABV
www.distillerie.fr

Buckwheat spirit

There is nothing subtle about this whisky but that is no bad thing. It is rich in fruit and honey, the oak and spices slap you round the mouth a bit, and the finish is pleasant and intense.

Eddu Grey Rock
40 % ABV
www.distillerie.fr

Blend

Surprisingly assertive and grungey for a blend, with plenty of fruit but a coastal tang and some smoke. The appley notes mixed with the earthiness give this whisky a distinctly different and attractive character all its own. Impressive.

Glann An Mor 46% ABV
www.glannarmor.com

Single malt

There are many things to get excited about at this distillery in Brittany, not least its judicious use of casks and the way that even its young whiskies are balanced and complete. There are grassy, hay-like notes on the nose here, and the salt-and-pepper flavours are not totally in balance with the fruit but the beautiful big apple and pear flavours and gorgeous rich oak suggest that this distillery is well on the way to producing some whisky classics.

THE BELGIAN OWL DISTILLERY

Rue Sainte Anne 94, 4460 Grâce Hollogne, Belgium
www.belgianwhisky.com

It is easy to get confused about Etienne Bouillion's whisky-making operation. He might know exactly what he is doing when it comes to malt, but the naming of his distillery is something else.

For a while it went under the name Pure, until someone advised him that 'pure' was likely to be a no-go area for European malt whisky. Then some confused his whisky with his fruit liqueur business Lambicool.

So let's get this straight. This wonderful, charming, haphazard and utterly unique distillery in and around Liège is called The Belgian Owl. And it makes great sweet, apple- and pear-flavoured malt whisky that even in its youngest versions was clearly of the highest quality.

I say in and around Liege because the production process for whisky here has been carried out at three sites. Barley was grown at a farm in the rolling Belgian countryside before being sent away to be malted. It was then fermented at the farm before being transported by tanker to Etienne's distillery where it was distilled in portable French brandy stills. And from there it was transported to the suburbs of Liege to the sort of industrial and garish-lit storage warehouses where you expect to find cardboard boxes, not whisky casks. Such are the warm and dry conditions in the warehouse that the alcoholic strength increases quite dramatically during maturation.

It was clearly not the most ideal or efficient way of making whisky, but bizarrely it worked. Note the past tense, though. Finance-allowing, the whole operation is to move to the farm. It is a move fraught with potential problems. While in theory the new distillery setting will enhance the whisky, you change your production techniques at your peril.

Only time will tell but what is without doubt is that Bouillion is a whisky maker of the highest order and he has had the good sense to take what distilling knowledge he has and to seek out the very best source of information for malt whisky production in the form on Bruichladdich's maestro-distiller Jim McEwan.

The whisky is well packaged, too, and at last Bouillion has got the name right.

ABOVE The local and unique barley from which the Belgian Owl single malt is made.

OPPOSITE FAR RIGHT The entrance to the farm courtyard where the Belgian Owl is based, complete with pagoda.

OPPOSITE ABOVE RIGHT Whisky-maker Etienne Bouillion.

RIGHT The Belgian Owl whisky range.

The Belgian Owl 2/2009 46% ABV
The Belgian Owl 10/2009 46% ABV
The Belgian Owl 10/2009 74.2% ABV

Guillon No 1 46% ABV
www.whiskyguillon.com

Single malt

Guillon brings a touch of France to the whisky party by maturing its malts in wine casks. This has the potential to topple into the disaster zone but in this case it never does and this whisky is a revelation. There are rich, sweet orange and citrus notes at play, sponge and malt in the centre and swirling, whirling red fruits late on, with a touch of earthiness in there too. A complex and impressive whisky.

Meyer's Alsacien 40% ABV
www.distillerie-meyer.fr

Single malt

The nose is rustic and youthful and on the palate there is soft barley, and the most delicate of fruits. No real assertiveness but this is very pleasant. Just when you think it's going to sneak away quietly, a very late burst of spice provides a finale.

Uberach 42.3% ABV
www.distillerie-bertrand.com

Single malt

If you don't like sulphur notes in your whisky, look away now. Uberach is from Alsace and is from a distillery specialising in fruit liqueurs and brandy but if you're expecting a clean, sweet fruity whisky, think again. There is a gritty industrial side to this that divides drinkers. I suspect, though, they know exactly what they're doing here. Germany is just around the corner and this sort of thing goes down well with the German palate. It works for me, too, in the same way as the new wave of lively Glendronachs work.

CORSICA

P&M Pure Whisky 42% ABV
www.brasseriepietra.com

Hybrid whisky

Certainly not pure and arguably not a whisky, this has a delicious and totally original taste. P&M is made from a beer containing chestnuts as well as grain, so this strictly isn't whisky. But there are attractive liqueur-like flavours, soft fruit notes and toasty cereal.

P&M Blend Superieur 40% ABV
www.brasseriepietra.com

Blend

A bold-flavoured blend with lashings of citrus and yellow fruits and a soft mouth-coating but with a gentle palate.

SPAIN

DYC 50th Anniversary 40% ABV
www.dyc.es

Single malt

Released in 2009 to mark the 50th anniversary of the distillery's opening, this single malt is lighter and safer than the cask-strength version. It has a clean and crisp, green fruit taste, a nice balance between spicy and sweet notes, from bourbon casks, then heather and grass.

DYC Pure Malt 40% ABV
www.dyc.es

Blended/vatted malt

DYC is owned by Beam Global and is a malt and grain distillery, blending plant, packaging store and electricity power station all in one. This whisky includes Spanish and Scottish malt, including Laphroaig, but is smoother and softer.

GERMANY

Austrasier Single Cask Grain 40% ABV
www.fleischmann-whisky.de

Single grain

This is a delight – unlike any whisky I've ever tasted. With fudge and liquorice on the nose, the palate is soft, gentle and honey-combed, with some spices that stay firmly in the background. Bourbon, candy, vanilla and hickory also appear.

Blaue Maus 40% ABV
www.fleischmann-whisky.de

Single malt

There is some off-putting linseed oil on the nose, but get past this and you will discover the most gentle honeyed and fudge-like taste, then finally a significant, but not harsh, level of spice.

Blaue Maus 1983–2008 40% ABV
www.fleischmann-whisky.de

Single malt

There are some quite delicate flowery notes on the nose here, with Parma violets and blueberries. The taste is like bourbon liqueur with intense candy, honey, nutmeg, liquorice and pepper. A big, beguiling whisky.

Blaue Maus Fasstarke 58.9% ABV
www.fleischmann-whisky.de

Single malt

Treat this one carefully, it is capable of biting. The nose is oily and pruney, the taste liqueur-like, with intense fruits and a fierce, un-Fleischmann-like wave of pepper. But it is a pleasant experience, with a malty heart.

Grüner Hund 40% ABV
www.fleischmann-whisky.de

Single malt

This has soft fudge and honey on the nose, with polished wood and beeswax making an appearance. The taste is liquid honey – soft and rounded, beautifully put together and delivered on a palate of very delicate and gentle spice.

Grüner Hund Fasstarke 51% ABV
www.fleischmann-whisky.de

Single malt

The most bizarre whisky in the whole Fleischmann stable, this has lots and lots going on. On the nose there are pistachio nuts, and rich fruit liqueur notes. This takes you out of your comfort zone but ultimately rewards you with a smörgåsbord palate of Camp coffee, burnt treacle and a wave of spice.

Old Fahr 40% ABV
www.fleischmann-whisky.de

Single malt

Nougat and roasted nuts on the nose with some fresh wood polish, then chocolate-chip nut ice cream, fresh liquid honey and traces of cherry. Another gossamer-like whisky experience from the mighty Fleischmann whisky empire.

BLAUE MAUS DISTILLERY

Bamberger Strasse 2, 91330 Eggolsheim, Germany
www.fleischmann-whisky.de

**I know a German whisky writer who is
extremely well respected in the industry.
He is a Keeper of the Quaich, a recognition by
the Scottish industry of the contribution he
has made to the promotion and celebration of
Scottish whisky. He is a good man.**

But he refuses – point blank – to accept that any good
whisky will ever be made in central Europe, and particularly
in a German-speaking country.

'If they were meant to have produced whisky they would
have done it centuries ago,' he rages. 'Germans are meant
to make beer and fruit liqueurs. They simply cannot
make whisky.'

I like my friend, but he is wrong. We have
discussed holding events where we each
present the arguments for and against
Europe to an audience while tasting
some of the whiskies from Belgium,
France, Austria, Germany and
Switzerland.

I have always been confident that
I could win these debates on any
territory, including in Scotland. But
now I know without doubt I would
win. I could even do it by using whisky
samples from just one German distillery:
Blaue Maus.

There aren't many European distilleries
outside Scotland and Ireland that can boast that it
has a 25-year-old malt, but Germany's Blaue Maus is a pretty
special distillery altogether.

Let's start with the name. It means Blue Mouse, and it's
not the only wacky whisky name being produced by the
company. Other whiskies include Grüner Hund (Green Dog)
and Schwarzer Pirat (Black Pirate). Then there's the whisky
itself. Let's get something straight – this isn't Scottish single-
malt whisky and isn't trying to be, and nor is it bourbon or
Irish whiskey – but that doesn't mean they cannot be great.

And Blaue Maus does make great whisky. Adjust your
taste buds, throw away your prejudices and approach these
whiskies as if they were a brand-new drinks category all of
their own, and you may find yourself enjoying a rollercoaster
ride. Taste is subjective of course, but if you find the right
wavelength then this is malt nectar – honeyed,
toffee, milk chocolate delights, each one of
the range (and there are more than 10 of
them) a soft and subtle delight.

Blaue Maus distillery was set up
by Robert Fleischmann in 1980 on
the same site as the original family
grocery and tobacco business in
Eggolsheim to make brandy. In
1983 it made its first whisky. The
distillery says that the first attempts
were poor, but Fleischmann
took the view that practice made
perfect. Interestingly a 25-year-old
malt released in 2008 is very good, so
either the early efforts weren't so bad or
maturation has worked wonders.

Since then the distillery has blossomed,
developing a maritime theme reflected in its Spinnaker
whiskies. It started selling whisky commercially in 1996 and
has expanded its range, which now also includes Austrasier
and Old Fahr.

Now run by Robert's son and daughter-in-law Thomas and
Petra, it bottles single-cask whiskies under a range of names.
Every one of my samples was a total treat. Not just great
German whisky but great whisky full stop. Now, Bernard,
my old German friend – put that in your pipe and smoke it.

TOP AND ABOVE The Fleischmann family has been making whisky
in Eggolsheim, Germany for 25 years.

RIGHT The Blaue Maus distillery has gone from strength to
strength and now runs popular distillery tours.

Schwarzer Pirat 40% ABV
www.fleischmann-whisky.de

Single malt

Some oddball nutty and fruit notes on the nose, then fruit cake, jam sponge and a dusty oaky and spicy ending. Not the normal distillery fayre – but none the worse for that all the same.

Slyrs Bavarian single malt 43% ABV
www.slyrs.de

Single malt

Both beautifully packaged and beautifully made, with sweet pear and apple, honey and toffee strutting along merrily and being buffeted by the warmest oak and milk chocolate notes. There's an attractive bitter-sweet thing going on here, too. World-class whisky by any standards.

Spinnaker 40% ABV
www.fleischmann-whisky.de

Single malt

I am not sure it is possible to get malt whisky any softer and rounded than this – not in a dull way. It's more like eating alcoholic Crunchie bars. Even by this distillery's remarkable soft honeycomb standards this is the oral equivalent of falling onto a down feather bed.

Spinnaker Fasstarke 48.2% ABV
www.fleischmann-whisky.de

Single malt

Not the greatest of noses – too much like oil paints. But the taste is intriguing, a strange mix of bourbon and malt with ginger liqueur and a touch of schnapps to add body. Chewy and chunky, too. An altogether very impressive-tasting whisky.

Spinnaker 20-year-old 40% ABV
www.fleischmann-whisky.de

Single malt

Another oily, not too distinctive nose, and yet another Fleischmann whisky which redeems itself on the palate, starting with trademark demerara sugar and honey, some chewy barley and a late wave of spices. Some oak as well, but nothing too abrasive. Excellent.

AUSTRIA

Reisetbauer 7-year-old 50% ABV
www.reisetbauer.at

Single malt

One of Austria's oldest distillers, Reisetbauer double distills its spirit in pot stills and matures it in Austrian wine oak casks. The distillery makes fruit liqueurs and traces of fruit in the cask find their way into the final whisky. This has been matured for 12 years and bottled at high strength, and is rounded and cerealy with some toasted oak and nutty notes.

Reisetbauer 12-year-old 50% ABV
www.reisetbauer.at

Single malt

The nose on this is a nightmare, stodgy and oily with linseed and paint – a typically off-European nose. The palate is altogether better – I guess we are not in Kentucky any more, but reset the taste buds and there is plenty to enjoy, including some cereal and straw notes, and what is the oral equivalent of intense church incense.

SWITZERLAND

Santis Edition Dreifaltigkeit
52% ABV
www.santismalt.ch

Single malt

The whisky equivalent of one
of those big European smoked
cheeses. This is like barbecuing
peppered trout over charcoal
embers. There is some oiliness to
this but it is robust, well balanced
and thoroughly enjoyable. Brauerei
Locher in Switzerland mostly
produces beer but this is another
most pleasant new discovery made
during the course of this book.

Santis Swiss Highlander 40% ABV
www.santismalt.ch

Single malt

Matured in beer oak casks, this has a soft and
easy straw nose. On the palate it is gentle
and honeyed vanilla ice cream and
soft fruit, then some peppery spice
appears later on. It is clean and
sweet, elegant and sophisticated
– and very refreshing.

Swissky 40% ABV
www.swissky.ch

Single malt

A clean and crisp nose here, with a sweet and
barley-drenched
palate. This is as refreshing and refined as the chill Alpine air, with a
weighty malty core.

Whisky Castle
Doublewood 43% ABV
www.whisky-castle.com

Single malt

Not for the faint-hearted, this is big-
boy whisky, but very different and
intriguing, too. The savoury flavours
are bold and aggressive but there is a
distinctive corn-on-the cob taste and
texture, with a buttery oiliness that
coats the mouth.

Whisky Castle Smoke Barley
43% ABV
www.whisky-castle.com

Single malt

This is my personal breaking point:
the only alcoholic concoction I can
think of to present the palate with
a bigger challenge would be olive-
flavoured tequila. Lots going on here
– cereal, rootsy vegetable, oiliness – but
overall it's a whisky for S&M fans.

Zurcher Single Lakeland 42% ABV
www.lakeland-whisky.ch

Single malt

Zurcher is a brewery relatively new to whisky-making, but all the
signs from this are that it is learning the game very fast indeed. This
is matured in sherry casks and is surprisingly complex for a malt
that is just three years old. Lots of spice, some smoke, some vanilla
and sweet honey make for a satisfying and enjoyable whisky.

LIECHENSTEIN

Telsington 42% ABV
www.telsington.com

Single malt

Liechtenstein's two biggest exports are apparently false teeth and sausage skins. It may well be that whisky will be up there before too long, too. This bottle looks different to anything else on the market, coming as it does in a wooden wrap-around that makes it look like an over-sized giraffe in a coffin. The nose doesn't give much away but this is a traffic-light of a whisky on the palate – it starts off with a distinctly Germanic/Swiss resinous and winey start, it changes to a softer, malty sweet centre and finally it mutates again so it's all go, into a spicy, salty and dark chocolate-tinged conclusion. This is triple-distilled and matured in Pinot Noir casks and tastes like nothing else in the whisky world. Great fun and the last whisky I tasted for this book. I'm happy with that.

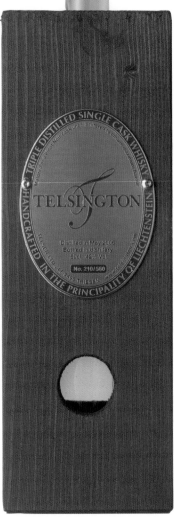

SWEDEN

Mackmyra Preludium: 05 48.4% ABV
www.mackmyra.se

Single malt

Mackmyra has done its growing up in public, launching some of its earlier releases under the name 'Privus' and some under the name 'Preludium' to make it clear that the distillery recognised that the whiskies were not the finished article. Some of the earlier releases showed great potential but were difficult, the fruit squeezed out by saltiness, by earthy peat and by a wave of spices running riot. Not the best release from the distillery but the first to truly announce that here we have a major player. An oily malt but sweet, with chocolate, vanilla and sweet citrus fruits.

Mackmyra Preludium: 06 50.5% ABV
www.mackmyra.se

Single malt

E-i-e-i-e-i-o up the whisky league we go… We have take-off. This is complex and immense, with sweet lemon, melon, and pear all dressed smartly and proudly representing fruit, oak, salt and pepper providing the deli counter, and cereal and barley showing off the whisky's agricultural roots. Sweetness abounds but there is enough growling smokiness to keep everything interesting.

Mackmyra The First Release 46.1% ABV
www.mackmyra.se

Single malt

The public dress rehearsals are over but compared to the older bottlings it is as if they have turned the serious drama we have watched so far into a musical. At first it is sweet with some orange liqueur-like notes, then sweet medicinal notes arrive plus tangerine and eventually it is rounded off with earthy spice. An unmitigated joy.

Mackmyra Special: 01 51.6% ABV

www.mackmyra.se

Single malt

Rich in fruit, and a delightful journey down a clean and sweet pear and lychee pathway. It has a big mouth-coating and concentrated flavour, some almond notes, icing sugar and pepper to finish.

Mackmyra Special: 03

50.6% ABV
www.mackmyra.se

Single malt

A tangy taste sensation, with salt and pepper turned up high, but the melon and citrus notes battle gallantly, and the barley at the core of the malt is solid. This is big, oily and with a chunky and weighty level of peat, but it is an utterly pleasant and rewarding malt-whisky drinking experience. Superb.

UK: ENGLAND

St George's Chapter 6 46% ABV

www.englishwhisky.co.uk

Single malt

Respected Scottish whisky-maker Iain Henderson was charged with producing England's first new malt spirit for more than 100 years and he did an outstanding job. The distillery bottled the spirit at various stages of its development but the real excitement came at the very end of 2009, when English whisky was launched. It is, of course, young and immature, but maturation is faster in the east of England than it is in Scotland and even at three years there are a few feisty, cerealy notes and while not complex, this fruity whisky has all the signs of a major malt in the making.

UK: WALES

Penderyn 46% ABV

www.welsh-whisky.co.uk

Single malt

Penderyn's owners set out to make a unique-tasting malt whisky and they have succeeded. Each batch of Penderyn varies but there are some consistent threads. There is a sweet almost liqueur-like sweet wine flavour to this that is probably the result of the high proportion of Madeira casks used in maturation. There is plenty of sweet raisins and some spice, but no peat or oak at all.

Penderyn Peated 46% ABV

www.welsh-whisky.co.uk

Single malt

A very small amount of Penderyn has peat in it. The story goes that this expression was discovered by accident, when some casks sent to Penderyn from Scotland were not peat-free as ordered. In other words, the peatiness comes from the wood and not from the barley. The plus here is that the peat adds more depth. The downside is that grizzly peat and sweet grape are not the best match.

Penderyn Sherrywood 46% ABV

www.welsh-whisky.co.uk

Single malt

This is the whisky equivalent of removing your elegant throwing quarterback from the game, and replacing him with a running quarterback. Not better or worse—just a different way of playing. The Madeira influence is much reduced, and a grittier, spicier alternative appears in its place. The busier, more fruity, and nutty characteristics are closer to a single malt.

MACKMYRA DISTILLERY

Bruksgatan 4, 818 32 Valbo, Sweden
www.mackmyra.com

**Trust the Swedish to give the world its most
democratic whisky distillery, and while we are
about it, one of its most unusual.**

ABOVE Mackmyra distillery is making unique malt whisky with a
distinctive Swedish flair.

LEFT Charring the casks – Swedish oak is very different from other
European or American woods.

FAR RIGHT Mackmyra uses an old mine to store some of its
maturing spirit, 150 feet below the surface.

Mackmyra was set up by a group of friends who had hired a chalet for a skiing holiday. Each was asked to bring a bottle of something to furnish the bar, and each brought a bottle of Scotch. Which got them to thinking, several whiskies later, why Sweden had not got its own distillery and whether they might provide one.

As with most late-night whisky-fuelled ideas, this one went to bed when most of the party did. But two of the group got up next day and continued dreaming the dream. Now Mackmyra is a dynamic and thriving business with some of the most attractive whiskies outside the traditional regions.

So how did the dream become reality? The distillery's marketing manager Lars Lindberger takes up the story.

'This was at the time of the dot.com boom so no serious investor was going to look at this project,' he says. 'So the group agreed to give up their next holiday or a new car and put the money into distilling one batch of whisky to see how it went. If it worked they could try making some more, if not, well they would each have some Swedish whisky of their own.'

Then someone hit upon the idea of advertising the project on the internet and offering shares in the project and a right to have a say in how the whisky was made in return for a small amount of investment. They struck a chord with the Swedish public, attracting scores of investors and establishing a bond that has meant that queues form at the state-owned liquor store every time Mackmyra releases a new whisky.

And the whisky is distinctively Swedish. The barley is Swedish, Swedish oak is used where possible and a unique peat that is salty from years under the Baltic sea, has helped contribute to a distinctive flavour. Juniper twigs, used as a smoking agent in traditional Swedish cooking, have been used for drying malt.

Early malts from the distillery were something of a struggle, but they have improved by the year and have hit their stride and have been consistently good for a while now. Should you want to, you can buy your own quarter cask and choose from several sites where you'd like to mature it.

Whisky of the people, by the people for the people – or something like that. It is very Swedish, very eccentric and very good. What more could you ask for?

KEY WHISKIES

Mackmyra The First Release 46.1% ABV
Mackmyra Preludium 5 48.4% ABV
Mackmyra Preludium 6 50.5% ABV
Mackmyra Special No 1 51.6% ABV
Mackmyra Special No 3 50.6% ABV

ST GEORGE'S DISTILLERY

The English Whisky Company, Harling Road, Roudham, Norfolk NR16 2QW
www.englishwhisky.co.uk

PENDERYN DISTILLERY

The Welsh Whisky Company, Penderyn CF44 9JW, Wales
www.welsh-whisky.co.uk

In whisky terms we have a United Kingdom once more – for the first time for well over 100 years England has joined Scotland, Wales and Northern Ireland as a whisky-producing nation.

Scotland has, of course, produced malt whisky consistently for nigh on 1000 years, and in Northern Ireland, Bushmills can lay claim to be the world's oldest licensed distillery, having registered to produce malt whisky in 1608, though amusingly, and some would say typically of the Irish, the media was invited to a 400-year anniversary party in early 2009. All that time to plan...

So Scotland and Ireland have the form, but Wales and England are not without a little bit of previous form of their own either.

England made whisky more than 100 years ago, but it was mainly for export to Scotland to go into blends and it struggled to compete with the distillation of gin. The English, history shows, have always enjoyed getting drunk and had little time for any notion of waiting for spirit to mature in casks and preferred to drink it straight off the still, its unsavoury flavours made more palatable by aromatics. Thus gin was born and with it, the infamous drinking palaces of London.

English whisky distilleries were therefore victims of economics. The last one to close was in Stratford, East London, and is under the Olympic stadium.

Welsh whisky was also well established way back, too, but its demise was as a direct result of the Temperance movement, which considered alcohol as an evil curse and sought to banish it from their communities. Stories abound that distillery workers worked at night, leaving their houses under the cover of darkness so that their neighbours didn't know what they did. Eventually, though, they were driven off, and many emigrated, which was good news for US whiskey – among the descendants of Welsh immigrants to the US were the parents of Evan Williams and Jack Daniel.

There was a feeble attempt to re-establish Welsh whisky a few years ago but it ended in criminal proceedings. The company involved basically bought up cheap Scotch, added a load of spices bought from local supermarkets, and called it Welsh whisky. Visit Penderyn today and ask them about the rugby balls full of 'Welsh' whisky...

Penderyn though, is the real McTaffy. It's not just a genuine attempt to put a distinct and original Welsh whisky on the map, but a successful one, too. The distillation process takes place on an innovative still unique to the company, and its unusual method of maturing its spirit in Madeira casks, Buffalo Trace bourbon casks and used Scottish casks – mainly unpeated but there is a small-scale smoky Penderyn created by old Islay casks if you look for it.

So popular has Penderyn become that every batch created has to be bottled, and there is now only a small amount of stock maturing for the future.

While the Welsh are heading off on a route all of their own, the English have played it safer.

St George's Distillery in Norfolk, England, is modelled on a Scottish malt distillery, complete with a pagoda roof. It bought its stills from north of the border and employed whisky-making legend Iain Henderson as its first distiller, the malt equivalent of non premier-league Norwich City football club signing David Beckham.

I happen to live on the distillery's doorstep so have been able to monitor its progress closely since the distillery started producing spirit in late 2006. Now a young whisky in both peaty and non-peaty form, it's maturing far faster than Scottish malt does, and it's very well made indeed. Drinking it is like watching a teenage rugby player make his debut for a senior team. You can see the talent is all there and you'd bet that there's a star in the making, but there's some bulking to be done, some refining is in order.

The signs are all good though. And a United Kingdom of whisky looks on course for a long and prosperous future.

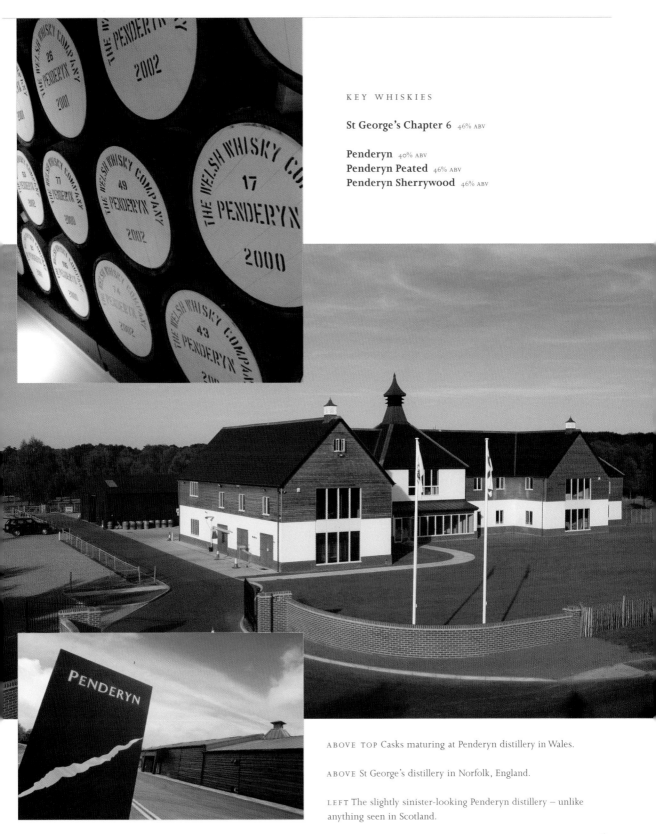

St George's Chapter 6 46% ABV

Penderyn 40% ABV
Penderyn Peated 46% ABV
Penderyn Sherrywood 46% ABV

ABOVE TOP Casks maturing at Penderyn distillery in Wales.

ABOVE St George's distillery in Norfolk, England.

LEFT The slightly sinister-looking Penderyn distillery – unlike anything seen in Scotland.

REST OF
THE WORLD

Rest of the world

Given how long it takes to make and mature great whisky, changes to whisky's natural world order have been remarkably swift in recent years.

For decades whisky was pretty much the domain of just four territories – Scotland, Ireland, America and Canada. Other countries – most notably India and Japan – made whisky but it was mainly for consumption in local home markets.

While Japan has made whisky since the early part of the twentieth century it remained, to a great extent, a world secret. But boy, how that's changing.

As recently as the beginning of the new millennium whisky writers started to get excited about the innovative whiskies coming out of Japan and soon after that, the whiskies began winning awards.

Now Japan has not only been elevated into the whisky world's premier league but it has arguably moved above Canada and Ireland into third place as the most productive and exciting whisky maker on the planet. Japan's success may have played a crucial role in encouraging other countries to step up their efforts to make good whisky and sell it beyond their own national boundaries. Some countries are natural candidates – Australia and New Zealand, for instance, have big expatriate communities from Ireland and Scotland for instance. But whisky is starting to emerge from all sorts of other interesting places, too. Taiwan, already a major consumer of whisky, has now got a distillery that suggests

it could easily follow Japan onto the world stage. India has a world-class whisky producer in Amrut and its 2009 releases were among the world's very best.

What makes the rest of the world intriguing is that the producers operate outside any clearly defined view of what whisky is. The definition of what whisky and single-malt whisky are in Europe, for instance, is defined under European law. American whiskey categories are defined in American law. So what's that got to do with someone in Wellington or Delhi? 'Whiskies' exist that are made with molasses and not grain, for instance. There are plenty of so-called whiskies that have never met copper or oak and are effectively coloured vodkas.

Under European law malt spirit must be matured for three years before it can be called whisky. Three years in, a new oak cask will result in a spoiled, wood-dominated drink. But what if you live in a hot, humid country where maturation is faster, and the rules don't stop you using new oak for, say, 18 months? There are grounds for experimentation here, new flavours to explore and exciting new 'whiskies' to create.

AUSTRALIA

Bakery Hill Classic 46% ABV
www.bakeryhilldistillery.com.au

Single malt

You might assume that Bakery Hill distillery is named after David and Lynne Baker, who run it, but it isn't. The label of the whisky features a miner's pick and shovel and the name comes from the name of a hill where a miners' rebellion started in 1854. For years there had been growing unrest among miners who were denied the right to vote, had to pay for costly equipment and licences, and were forced to use some of their paltry income to buy a small piece of land from which they could keep any gold or valuable stones they found, but invariably yielded nothing. About 10,000 miners gathered at Bakery Hill, and after a few days' stand off between the miners and the authorities the miners set up the Eureka Stockade. The uprising was suppressed brutally three weeks later, with scores of miners killed and many others fleeing to die lonely deaths in the wilderness. But the rebellion was a watershed because it prompted political reform and the granting of rights to the workers, excluding Aborigines.

This is further proof that the Australians are coming – the fruit and barley are perfectly balanced, there are some nice milk-chocolate notes, and the overall taste is pleasant and fruity, with apples and marzipan in the mix.

Bakery Hill Classic Cask Strength Malt 60.1% ABV
www.bakeryhilldistillery.com.au

Single malt

'Born Sandy Devotional' by Australian band the Triffids is one of the finest albums ever made. Released in the 1980s when Australian sporting prowess meant that Australia was soaked in its own cockiness, the album revealed a more sensitive side to the country, and hinted at its insecurities and fears. It captures perfectly a sense of desolation in Australia's vastness. I listened to it again while tasting whiskies from Bakery Hill, and the combination is perfect. Like that album. this whisky is about nuance and detail, almost the opposite of the brash experience you may associate with Down Under. There are some strong citrus notes, clean, fresh apple and pear and a layer of sweet vanilla. Songwriting genius David McComb died from heroin poisoning following a car crash just before his 37th birthday. This one is for him.

Bakery Hill Cask Strength Peated Malt 60% ABV
www.bakeryhilldistillery.com.au

Single malt

This is a chunky, chewy and classy malt that displays a concentrated mix of lemon and bitter orange and dusty smoky peat. Hickory and liquorice are at the whisky's core but then it just melts away with the softest of peaty endings – extremely impressive.

Bakery Hill Double Wood
46% ABV
www.bakeryhilldistillery.com.au

Single malt

A mix of bourbon and French oak wine casks make for a busy and playful malt, with vanilla and coconut mixing with Christmas cake and stewed fruits. It is as rich and unpredictable as Richard Branson, but utterly captivating.

Bakery Hill Peated Malt
46% ABV
www.bakeryhilldistillery.com.au

Single malt

Surprisingly refined, with a soft and sweet vanilla dominated core and gentle smoke notes. A touch of pepper and wood are in the mix but nothing too heavy.

Lark Distillery Single Malt
43% ABV
www.larkdistillery.com.au

Single malt

A sure sign that things are moving swiftly forwards for this wonderful distillery can be seen from the fact that these days Bill Lark's daughter Kristy is now in charge of distilling. You can't see the joins because after some over-young malt in the past, the whisky has continued to move forwards. This is crisp and clean, like the Tasmanian air. Fresh green fruits and cocoa are held together by mouth-coating oils.

Lark Single Malt Cask Strength 58% ABV
www.larkdistillery.com.au

Single malt

Melbourne band Wedding Parties Anything were described as the Australian Pogues and one of their best tracks is 'A Tale They Won't Believe', based on a true story from Robert Hughes' excellent history of Australia, *The Fatal Shore*.

It tells of how a group of convicts escaped from prison in Tasmania when Australia was a penal colony in the hope of finding a boat and sailing back to England. When one prisoner was caught some time later he told how the desperate men had eaten first a prisoner who had died and then the weaker members of the group until finally there was just him left. The authorities didn't believe him, deciding he was using the story to cover up the other prisoners' escape. He was returned to prison only to escape again with one other man. And the authorities started to believe his original story when they recaptured him again – with body parts of his fellow escapee in his pockets...

A few years ago I was good friends with a Tasmanian girl who spoke so affectionately about her homeland that you couldn't help but want to visit. Throw in some stunning scenery and garish history and the island becomes utterly irresistible. After hearing this song the desire became even stronger. The distillery is yet further reason for a trip Down-Under one day as is its top-quality malt whisky. Get past its distinctive linseedy oiliness and you get a big fruity treat, with apples, pears, some chocolate and pepper. A corker.

Lark Distiller's Selection 46% ABV
www.larkdistillery.com.au

Single malt

Talk to anyone involved with the Australian whisky industry and they'll talk about boutique whiskies and how small-still producers are giving the Scots a run for their money because most of Scotland is sacrificing quality for quantity. It's not as black and white as all that, but undoubtedly the small distillers from Germany, Belgium, the Netherlands, France and Australia that are getting it right have all brought some small-still qualities to their whisky.

This is a case in point. There are some chunky oily notes, some rustic notes, and some sharp and crisp green fruit notes. Very good indeed.

Limeburners Barrel M27 43% ABV
www.distillery.com.au

Single malt

If there were a special award for most improved whisky, this would win it hands down. Just 12 months before this version was bottled Limeburners was a mighty challenge, bottled far too young and with a vicious and unpleasant linseed oil and eucalyptus mix. This is by no means perfect but it's come on leaps and bounds and it suggests without a shadow of a doubt that Australia has another superstar in the making, Some of the linseed notes are still there, but now they're joined on the nose by some pineapple, melon and treacle notes. It's still very young on the palate – the distillery was only set up in 2007 but the fruit's getting greater and when the wood and some depth kicks in, well...

Sullivan's Cove 40% ABV
www.tasmaniadistillery.com

Single malt

Sullivan's Cove has played a pioneering role in the story of Australian whisky, and was one of the first to get its malts into the European market. The distillery is one of several on Tasmania. Like so many distilleries across the world, however, its earlier efforts were immature, unbalanced and unpleasant. The distillery doesn't get it right the whole time even now, but nevertheless it has come forward in leaps and bounds. This standard bottling is a pleasant, easy-drinking and unchallenging with some oiliness and rich fruit.

Sullivan's Cove 6-year-old 60% ABV
www.tasmaniadistillery.com

Single malt

We've already given the award for the most improved whisky to Limeburners, but Sullivan's Cove should get a mention in Dispatches. While some of its whiskies have been hit-and-miss in the past, this one is a delight, with vanilla, chocolate and big dollops of sweet fruit.

Sullivan's Cove Cask Strength Bourbon Cask 60% ABV

www.tasmaniadistillery.com

Single malt

If you are wondering what sort of country produces whisky like this, then take a listen to 'So Much Water so Close to Home' by Paul Kelly. Based on a Raymond Carver short story, it tells of a group of friends who go away on a fishing trip. Once there, after a long trek, they discover the body of a young woman in the water. They debate going back to report the find but have looked forward to their trip so decide not to. This whisky is perfect for such a grim scenario: big and gutsy, with plenty of oak, hooney and spice battling against the barley.

Sullivan's Cove Double Cask 40% ABV

www.tasmaniadistillery.com

Single malt

This is a mix of malts from both bourbon and port casks and it makes for a weird combination, though not unpleasant. The chocolate and honey are still there, but winey intense berry fruits join the mix for an unusual finish.

NEW ZEALAND

Mackenzie Blended Malt 40% ABV

www.hokonuiwhiskey.com

Blend

Surprisingly feisty this: prickly and spicy, with strong rich savoury notes on both the nose and palate. There's some honey and sweet vanilla in here, but the overall experience is more challenging than you might expect. Not entirely sure what this is – it is described as a blended malt but there is talk on the website about a mix of malt and grain. That is the new labelling for you – at best a mess, at worse a bunch of old baubles.

Milford 10 Year Old 43% ABV

www.milfordwhisky.co.nz

Single malt

It is possible that New Zealand has one of the biggest small-time private distilling industries in the world, but when it comes to commercial and official stills, well, they are rarer than the weta, a scary-looking beastie unique to Aotearoa.

But New Zealand has a significant Scottish population and ought to have a whisky industry, and the hope is that it's on the way back. The owners of this whisky are set to start production at a new distillery in the South Island and there is a growing interest in producing malt elsewhere in the country.

This, though, is an oddball.

Milford 15-year-old 43% ABV

www.milfordwhisky.co.nz

Single malt

Good golly, talk about curve balls. For a starter, you struggle to find any great influence from the cask after 15 years, which suggests the wood has not been top rate – and yet it works. It is softer, more rounded and more palatable than the 10-year-old, so age has worn down the edges in some ways. And then just when it seems to be wondering off harmlessly, it heads off in to a sharper, more citrusy direction.

Milford 1989 19-year-old 43% ABV

www.milfordwhisky.co.nz

Single malt

That we can still taste and enjoy whisky of this quality is down to Warren Preston, a man with a passion for whisky and a man on a mission. He has set up a little whisky world around his business in New Zealand's South Island, and this particular whisky is proof that the country can offer something genuinely special to the world of malt. This lovely whisky tastes salty but there's more zesty and youthful fruit than any of the younger expressions. Simply delightful.

LARK DISTILLERY

14 Davey St, Hobart, Tasmania TAS 7000, Australia
www.larkdistillery.com.au

If you fancy a wager from time to time, then how about a punt on Australian whisky to be as accepted by 2025 as its wines are now?

Crazy? Not if you're old enough to remember back to the 1970s, when the concept of Aussie wine was an international joke. Now look at it.

The progress of its whisky industry in the first 10 years of the 21st century have been nothing short of remarkable, and already some of its malts are good enough to be picking up international awards. Others are young and wayward like a teenage Shane Warne, cricketer extraordinaire, but you just know once they get their line and length right, they are going to be at the top of their game for years. Australians seem to excel at whatever they turn their hands to, and whisky's proving to be no exception. I am a big fan.

There are two distinct sides to Australian whisky. One is the concentrated whisky region emerging in Tasmania, which is Australia's answer to Islay, and the other is a scattering of distilleries on the mainland. But wherever you look for whisky in Australia, you will come across Bill Lark.

Bill Lark is the Che Guevara of whisky. He does not look much like a revolutionary but behind the Santa-like white beard and affable personality is a shrewd planner and a canny businessman, and he's leading an Australian uprising in the world of whisky.

He runs the Lark distillery with his wife and daughter in the pretty port of Hobart. Lark, along with Sullivan's Cove nearby, is the most established distillery in the Antipodes. But there are several others at varying stages of development

and most of them have had help from Bill Lark. It seems that with every passing year new projects are coming on line, and Lark is refreshingly enthusiastic about them all.

'It's all great news for Tasmania and our attempts to establish it as the whisky state of Australia,' he says. 'The latest project is by a farmer called Peter Bignall, who has constructed a 500-litre copper pot still to produce Tasmanian rye whisky. He grows rye grain on his farm at Kempton in Tasmania. This will be the only rye whisky in Australia, and he is going to brew the wash himself.'

'I have also been having discussions with another chap who has bought property in southern Tasmania near Port Arthur with a view to establishing a small distillery to produce malt whisky and other fruit spirits. His point of difference will be that he will use a Holstein still, rather like most of the craft distilleries in the USA.'

Lark has also set up a distillery school for would-be distillers covering everything from how to make whisky to legislation. Interested parties have attended from across Australia and New Zealand. And Lark offers visitors the Ultimate Whisky Experience tour.

'It includes a day trip to our peat bog in the central Highlands, where they are treated to a Tasmanian trout, whisky-cured and smoked over a peat fire,' says Lark.

'Mind you, that's only if they dig enough peat to bring back to the distillery for peat smoking the malt for the next day's production. It's a full hands-on experience lightened by trips to gourmet wine luncheons and haggis-whisky dinners.'

Exciting times for Tasmania, then, but Lark hasn't forgotten he has a core business to run of his own. He has succeeded in establishing a distribution deal for Europe through Maison du Whisky in France, is exporting into Asia through Singapore, has some distribution in America, and Lark products are now available throughout Australia.

'Yes, it's heads down, bums up for all at Lark just keeping up with production and looking after the many new visitors being attracted to whisky in Tasmania,' says Lark in typically Australian fashion. 'It just seems to get busier and busier.'

Outstanding Australian whisky? Maybe you won't get such good odds. Bookies rarely give money away on dead certs.

LEFT Lark's first copper still was sourced at an antiques auction.

LEFT BELOW Tasmania's peat bogs and pure soft water are perfect for creating world-class whisky.

KEY WHISKIES

Lark Distiller's Selection 46% ABV
Lark Distillery Single Malt 43% ABV
Lark Single Malt Cask Strength 58% ABV

LEFT Bill Lark, founder of the Hobart-based Lark Distillery – one of Australia's leading spirits distilleries.

Milford 20-year-old 43% ABV
www.milfordwhisky.co.nz

Single malt

Bizarrely this one is the fruitiest of the entire batch, with some oak and spice. If you had told me this was 12 years old I would have accepted it, but twenty years? Really?

That said, it is a match for some very good 12-year-old Speyside malts and the fruitiness of it is really very attractive indeed.

INDIA

Amrut Single Malt 40% ABV
www.amrutdistilleries.com

Single malt

Amrut has come on an amazing journey. From the early days when it turned heads at Whisky Live London, to distribution through a number of British curry houses, the company has built up a reputation for high-quality whisky. This is where it started – a balanced malt with clean barley, toffee and vanilla at its centre, plus hints of oak and spice to finish.

Amrut Cask Strength 61.9% ABV
www.amrutdistilleries.com

Single malt

An intense, outstanding roller-coaster ride of a malt. There is lemon and citrus on the nose and an intense bitter-sweet battle going on in the taste. Astringency from the casks gives an added depth, then there are some honeyed, dusty spice notes and a sweet, rich barley core.

Amrut Fusion 50% ABV
www.amrutdistilleries.com

Single malt

In a moment of exuberance and no doubt after an extra glass of this whisky as a reward for a long tasting session, I wrote in my notes 'is this the most exciting distillery in the world at the moment?' I don't think this holds up to scrutiny in the cold light of day, but you get the point. I defy anyone to go from Two Continents to Fusion and not conclude that Amrut is competing in the upper echelons of the premier league, with its intense, wonderful fruit notes, lashings of oak, smoke, and dark chocolate.

Amrut Peated 40% ABV
www.amrutdistilleries.com

Single malt

This is an intriguingly different take on the normal peated whisky model, with youthful barley and fruit holding their own well in the mix, but the smoky component gives the whisky a smoked-fish flavour. The elements of smoke drift in and out, making for a strange but captivating drinking experience, giving this whisky an identity all of its own.

Amrut Peated Cask Strength 61.9% ABV
www.amrutdistilleries.com

Single malt

There have been some wonderfully defining moments at Whisky Live London over the years but some of the best have been when a company from outside the recognised whisky-making world has not only dared to set up shop among the finest Scottish, Irish and American distillers, but has flourished in the company. A few years back there was a genuine buzz around the show when this whisky was unveiled. Not surprising: it's a gem, with peppered smoked fish dancing around the fruit and barley. It seems to have found a niche of its own while maintaining enough recognisable flavours to win over hardened Scotch fans. Very classy indeed.

Amrut Two Continents 46% ABV
www.amrutdistilleries.com

Single malt

This is extremely hard to find because when the word got out about how good it was, it flew off the shelf. It is an intense flavour experience – with an almost Ardmore-like savoury peatiness and then the most attractive rounded and balanced fruitiness to it. It gets its name from the fact that it is matured in India and then Europe. If you've any lingering doubts about the world-class quality of this distillery this will well and truly banish them. Wonderful.

SOUTH AFRICA

Bains 43% ABV
www.distell.co.za

Single grain

This is produced at the James Sedgwick distillery in Wellington, South Africa, and is a captivating and somewhat feisty number for a grain whisky. Indeed, it starts off aggressively, with a distinctive sharp and fiery bite before softening up into a soft and honeyed tipple with an apricot heart and the gentlest of spices. Grain can be too sweet and soft for my palate, but this is a robust and intriguing dram.

Three Ships 5-year-old 43% ABV
www.distell.co.za

Blend

The company website says that this is a blend of Scottish and South African whiskies. The result is perfectly acceptable and pleasant. Certainly there is enough flavour, particularly from some sherry casks, and a distinctive oakiness to hold the attention. The real winner, though, is the peat that gives the whisky a smoky base to hang off.

Three Ships Bourbon Cask Finish 43% ABV
www.distell.co.za

Blended whisky

This is the latest and best release from the Distell company. Blended from South African malt and grain, then returned to bourbon casks for a further period of maturation, it has the sort of honey and vanilla heart that you get from real ice cream-van ice cream.

TAIWAN

Kavalan Solist Cask Strength ex-Bourbon Cask 57.3% ABV
www.kavalanwhisky.com

Single malt

As surprises go, this is as big as it gets. Each year judges for the World Whisky Awards are sent samples marked only with a country of origin and an alcoholic strength. In the 2010 awards samples judges were offered four samples from this distillery – and two of them were quite excellent. One of them even reached the final stage of judging.

From a large distillery, the King Car, with ambitious plans and a world-renowned whisky expert Dr Jim Swan as a consultant, this whisky has a rich creamy flavour with sweet exotic fruits and sugary spices. Truly delectable.

Kavalan Solist Cask Strength Sherry Cask
57.3% ABV
www.kavalanwhisky.com

Single malt

If the bourbon sample was all bright summer and sunlight, this is all winter and night-time, with a huge blast of sherry, some distinctive winey notes, and a mix of toasted raisins and dates that suggests several years of ageing. Maybe there is a clue to the whisky's youthfulness in the fact that all the flavours are upfront and there is no great depth, but the deep flavours and remarkable spicy undernotes, make for a very enjoyable ride.

AMRUT DISTILLERIES LTD

Kambipura, Bangalore-560074, India
www.amrutdistilleries.com

**It would not be quite right to describe Amrut
whisky as an overnight success – the distillery
that produces it was founded in 1948 and it has
been making whisky since 1980.**

But the reputation of the company's malt has been increasing
at a rate in recent years and now there are plenty of people
who will argue that the whisky from here is not only good,
but is among the finest in the world. Taste the 2009 bottling
Fusion – if you can find it because since it started earning
plaudits it's been in very great demand indeed – and you'll
discover an exceptionally fine, luxurious and complete malt.
And when you add Amrut's Two Continents to the equation
it's pretty clear that something very special is emerging.

Amrut is based in Bangalore and primarily uses Punjabi
barley. But for Fusion it mixed Indian barley with some
Scottish barley, and distilled it in Bangalore. So good was
the whisky that the first batch sold out in weeks and a
second batch sold out on pre-order before it even reached
international markets – not bad going for a distillery that had
to overcome some natural prejudices.

'It was not easy for us to begin with,' says the company's
international sales manager Ashok Chokalingam, 'mainly
because we're not a traditional whisky country and some of
India's whiskies are not noted for their quality, though to be
fair that is to do with pricing and consumer behaviour. I find
equally poor-quality whiskies in Britain, too.

'But now consumers are starting to believe that we can
produce good quality single malts and therefore the trend
will grow for sure.'

Amrut always intended to establish a malt whisky that
was distinctive and different to those from Scotland, and
from the earliest days when the brand was targeted mainly
at curry houses, the identity of the whiskies has got stronger
and stronger. In particular, two cask-strength whiskies – a
peated and a non-peated one – launched in the early part of
the millennium – had whisky experts enthusing about the
superior quality.

'We never had any intention to copy anyone else or adopt a
particular style of whisky that was being produced anywhere
else,' says Ashok. 'We wanted to produce something
different, and you get that with the liquorice taste our whisky
has. There are a few elements which contribute to Amrut
having a distinctive style – the strength at which we distill
at, for instance, the flavour of our home-grown barley, and

LEFT Much care is taken over the labellling and presentation of Amrut's fine collection of single malts.

LEFT BELOW Amrut is named after a golden pot containing the elixir of life from Indian mythology.

BELOW The Amrut distillery, founded in 1948, is based in Bangalore in the state of Karnataka

KEY WHISKIES

Amrut Cask Strength 61.9% ABV
Amrut Fusion 50% ABV
Amrut Peated 40% ABV
Amrut Peated Cask Strength 61.9% ABV
Amrut Single Malt 40% ABV
Amrut Two Continents 46% ABV

perhaps most importantly, the pace at which the whisky matures in the cask.'

Not everybody's convinced – root around the internet for long enough and you will find people who just won't accept that single-malt whisky can come from anywhere apart from Scotland, let alone India. But frankly they are wrong, and the pure quality of the whisky on offer from this distillery means such people are becoming a dwindling minority. Ashok's aware of the nay-sayers, but you suspect he couldn't care less about them.

'We're cautious about where we send our whiskies for review and we will not send samples to some organisations which are just acting for some specific territory,' he says.

'But a lot of the serious whisky writers have been very positive, as have the likes of the Malt Maniacs. And most importantly it doesn't matter about reviews as long as whisky drinkers acknowledge the quality they find here. And that is most certainly the case.'

It most certainly is. Amrut is one of the most exciting distilleries on the planet.

Independent bottlers

Wander in to a whisky shop and you will find on the shelves a whole range of bottles that are listed not only by distillery name.

These bottlings are ranged under banners such as Connoisseurs' Choice, Old Malt Cask or The Vintage Collection, and contain malts of different ages and from different distilleries. Many of the bottles are limited in number, and contain whisky from just one cask. When they're gone, they are gone forever, but there will always be new ones on the way. This is an evolving, dynamic end of the whisky market that really excites enthusiasts.

The bottles are marketed by companies known as independent bottlers. They buy up stocks of surplus malt, often a single cask or a handful of casks, and bottle them. Some independents are fastidious about what they do, and go in search of quality whisky, bottling only what they consider to be of the highest standard. Others buy whatever ingredients they can get their hands on via the Internet and bottle them, without asking too many questions.

So the world of the independent bottler is a hit-and-miss affair, and the bottlers tend to enjoy a love-hate relationship with the rest of the whisky industry. Producers do not particularly like them because they have no control over the quality of the malt that is being bottled under their name – a single cask may taste significantly different to an official distillery bottling, and might well be considered by the producer as only of good-enough qulality for inclusion in a blend, and not good enough to be bottled in its own right.

Some companies go out of their way to ensure that their whiskies do not end up being bottled by independents. Glenmorangie, for instance, adds a small amount of malt from another distillery to its casks so that they cannot be sold on, as either Glenmorangie or as single malt. Some bottlers in the past have reached an agreement whereby they do not mention the distillery from where the malt is sourced, instead they use labelling such as 'Speyside's finest' – although this now falls outside the laws governing bottle labels. And you can always tell when the world of whisky is thriving and malt is in short supply, because the whisky producers start referring to the independents as 'parasites'.

Truth be told, though, the independent sector plays an important and necessary role in the world of whisky. It provides a demand for excess malt when there is a glut, and it plays a crucial role in fuelling the passion of whisky fans, who are constantly in search of something new and exciting, and who would quickly get bored and frustrated if restricted only to proprietary bottlings.

What is more, the great independent bottlers have histories as long, or longer, than many of the whisky producers, and have access to some of the world's rarest and most cherished malts. They employ the finest warehousemen and seek the very best wood to ensure that they are producing the very best whisky, so you may have every chance of finding your dream malt. You may equally, however, pay a considerable amount of money for a malt which is just not that good.

So two pieces of advice then: seek out as much information about your independent purchase as you can, and if you can taste it before purchasing, do so. If you do find your dream dram, buy as much of it as you can afford. Chances are it will not be around for long.

Here is a list of some, but by no means all, of the top independent specialists in Scottish malts, with a couple of recommendations from each.

LEFT The Connoisseurs' Choice collection, bottled by Gordon & MacPhail, is highly collectable.

Adelphi

Based in Argyll, Adelphi specialises in single cask and cask-strength single-malt whisky.

Choice:

Breath Of the Isles 1993

Glen Garioch 1990, 19-year-old

Berry Bros & Rudd

London-based wine merchant that sells an excellent range of whisky and is the custodian of Glenrothes.

Choice:

Berry's Own Selection 1989 Mortlach
Berry's Own 1989 Girvan Grain

Blackadder

Placing a particular emphasis on Sweden, Blackadder specialises in single-cask whisky bottled at cask strength. Whiskies from this bottler tend to get snapped up very quickly indeed.

Choice:

Blackadder Raw Cask
Blackadder Smoking Islay

Cadenhead

Scotland's oldest independent bottler, with more than 260 years' experience under its belt.

Choice:

Authentic Collection Aberfeldy 1996 13-year-old
Ardmore 1997 11-year-old

Dewar Rattray

Dewar Rattray has been selling whisky for more than 200 years and specialises now in unusual and exclusive malts.

Choice:

Cask Collection
Glencadam 1990
Glenallachie 1990

Douglas Laing

Glasgow-based company Douglas Laing is now run by brothers Stewart and Fred, and has access to a broad range of exciting whisky. It specialises in bottling whisky of an unusual age and its labels include Old Malt Cask and Provenance. The company has shown an admirable degree of creativity in recent years, mixing malts from different distilleries to create new whiskies.

Choice:

Big Peat (four Islay malts including Port Ellen)
Double Barrel (combinations including **Glenrothes** and **Ardbeg**, **Highland Park** and **Bowmore**, **Laphroaig** and **Macallan**, and **Caol Ila** and **Braeval**).

Duncan Taylor

Based in Huntly in Speyside, Duncan Taylor has a spacious treasure-laden grotto of a shop in the town and consistently bottles great whisky. Some of its aged grain whisky is particularly wonderful.

Choice:

Rare Auld Caperdonich 37-year-old
Peerless Glenlivet 40-year-old

Glenkeir

The independent bottling arm of the Whisky Shop chain, that has 15 outlets across England and Scotland. The range includes a number of whiskies available from the cask in the company's shops, and a number of limited-edition bottlings at cask strength. Many are available for sampling before purchasing at the shops.

Choice:

Springbank 17-year-old
Glenfarclas 40-year-old

Gordon & MacPhail

One of the longest and most established independent companies, Gordon & MacPhail owns Benromach distillery and has a wonderful shop in Elgin in the heart of Speyside. Its independent labels include Connoisseurs' Choice. In 2010 it revealed just how rare and special malt owned by independents can be, when it bottled the world's oldest whisky, a 70-year-old Mortlach.

Ian MacLeod

Owners of Glengoyne Distillery and with some outstanding blends and blended/vatted malts.

Choice:

Smokehead – a peated independent bottling of Caol Ila.
Six Isles – containing malt from six different Scottish islands.

Scotch Malt Whisky Society

A membership club that bottles cask-strength whisky and has won a reputation for high quality. Traditionally it has not named the distillery from which the malt comes. Instead it refers to the distillery by number and provides a clue in its taste descriptions.

Choice:

Lots of great whisky here, but favourites include **Tamdhu**, **Rosebank** and **St Magdalen** bottlings.

Signatory

The independent company owned by Andrew Symington, who also owns Edradour Distillery.

Choice:

Laphroaig 1990 17-year-old

Whisky festivals & events

You can talk and write about whisky all you like, but the only proper way to experience it is of course to drink it. So how can you go about trying a number of different whiskies without taking out a mortgage?

The most obvious way is to go and visit a distillery or two. Whisky tourism is big business these days and many distilleries now offer a visitor experience. Others will show you around if you ring in advance. The pick of them in the main whisky markets are listed on these pages.

There are also a number of whisky festivals and tasting events held across the world. Events come and go, but there are now a number of well-established shows, some of which tour large cities each year. The key ones are listed here.

FESTIVALS

Kentucky Bourbon Festival
www.kybourbonfestival.com

Normally held in the third week of September in and around Bardstown Kentucky, this is a week of events celebrating bourbon. It includes a cigar and bourbon evening, events at individual distilleries, and the prestigious black tie gala on the final Saturday night.

Feis Iie
www.theislayfestival.co.uk

The Islay festival is a celebration of music and whisky held on the island over the second May bank holiday weekend. Events are held at all eight distilleries and on Jura.

Spirit of Speyside Whisky Festival
www.spiritofspeyside.com

An annual celebration of the distilleries of Speyside. This takes place over the first bank holiday weekend at the end of April/beginning of May.

Autumn Speyside Whisky Festival
www.dufftown.co.uk

Normally held late September and based in and around Dufftown.

Whisky Live
www.whiskylive.com

Whisky Live events are organised by *Whisky Magazine* in England and they are now held all over the world. The events vary from territory to territory but in essence they offer whisky drinkers the chance to try different whiskies, to meet the people who made them and to learn more about their whiskies by attending masterclasses. The events attract some of the industry's biggest names.

The principle destinations are:

New Delhi, India	January
Tokyo, Japan	February
Brussels, Belgium	February
London, England	March
New York, USA	April
Shanghai, China	May
Taipei, Taiwan	May
Glasgow, Scotland	September
Paris, France	September
Sydney, Australia	September
Los Angeles, USA	October
Fort Lauderdale, USA	October
Toronto, Canada	October
Barcelona, Spain	October
Leiden, Netherlands	November
Cape Town, South Africa	November
Johannesburg, South Africa	November

Whiskyfest
www.maltadvocate.com/docs/whiskyfest

Organised by top American whisky magazine *Malt Advocate*, WhiskyFest is a whisky show held in three American cities and features more than 200 whiskies, gourmet buffets and seminars by distillery managers and master blenders.

The events are held in:

Chicago	April
San Francisco	October
New York	November

Whisky Luxe
www.whiskylive.com/luxe

Whisky Luxe is a new event introduced by *Whisky Magazine* and is a niche show that puts premium whisky alongside some of the world's most prestigious luxury brands. Tickets are extremely limited and guests are pampered with luxury travel to the event and treated to the finest cuisine. Events tend to be held in the finest hotels and other exhibitors have included Canali, Versace, Ducati, and Remy Cointreau.

Events lined up include:

New Delhi, India .... *January*
Shanghai, China.. *May*
Singapore.. *May*
Madrid, Spain .... *May*
Taipei, Taiwan .... *August*
Moscow, Russia .... *September*
Sydney, Australia.................................... *September*
Glasgow, Scotland .... *September*
Paris, France .... *September*
Barcelona, Spain .... *October*
Los Angeles, USA .... *October*
Toronto, Canada .... *October*
Fort Lauderdale, USA .... *October*
Cape Town, South Africa ....*November*
Johannesburg, South Africa......................*November*
Leiden, Netherlands..................................*November*

Other whisky shows include:

The Whisky Show
www.thewhiskyshow.com

First launched in 2009 at the Guildhall in London, the Whisky Show is a luxury whisky tasting event focused on premium whisky brands and aimed at the connoisseur. Held late October.

Whisky Fringe
www.royalmilewhiskies.com

Held around the time of the Edinburgh Festival in late August/early September, this is organised by Royal Mile Whiskies and features more than 200 different whiskies.

Whiskies of the World Expo
www.whiskiesoftheworld.com

Held annually each March in San Francisco, this show features whisky, bourbon and a range of other artisanal and craft spirit products.

Whisky Fair Limburg, Germany
www.festival.whiskyfair.com

Held each April this has grown in to one of the world's most popular whisky events and attracts thousands of visitors.

Whisky Show Budapest
www.whiskytumbler.tumblr.com

Hungary's first whisky event was launched in April 2010.

Toronto Annual Whisky Gala
www.spiritoftoronto.ca

Held in April, this is a well-established and highly respected whisky event and includes live jazz, gourmet catering, cocktail bar and tutored tastings.

Whisky directory

MAGAZINES

Whisky Magazine
A UK-based magazine published eight times a year. Its website hosts a forum and the magazine is also published in French and Japanese.
www.whiskymag.com

Malt Advocate
American-based quarterly magazine that also hosts an Internet forum and the very informative 'What does John know?' feature.
www.maltadvocate.com

Whiskeria
Published by The Whisky Shop in the United Kingdom and edited by the book's author, this magazine is aimed at entry-level whisky enthusiasts and has a circulation of 30,000. Also published in digital form.
www.whiskyshop.com

Unfiltered
Magazine of the Scotch Malt Whisky Society
– see Whisky Experiences

BOOKS

Michael Jackson's Malt Whisky Companion
fully updated by Dominic Roskrow, Gavin Smith and Will Meyers 2010
The sixth edition of the world's best-selling whisky book has 550 new tasting notes and new chapters on Japanese, world and vatted/blended malt whiskies.

The Whisky Bible
by Jim Murray
Frank, funny, direct, and occasionally offensive, notes to hundreds of world whiskies from the industry's answer to Jerry Sadowitz. Updated annually.

The Malt Year Book
edited by Ingvar Ronde
Updated every year with new features written by the whisky world's leading writers, this is an essential annual purchase. The author has contributed to it for four years and provides tasting notes for each new edition.

WHISKY EXPERIENCES

Distillery Visits
Distilleries across the world offer tours to varying degrees. Many have dedicated visitor centres and offer a range of tours from novice to a lengthy and involved VIP version. Some do not have visitor facilities as such, but will be happy to show people around if the visit is planned in advance. Check on individual websites for whether visitors are allowed, and for opening times.

The Scotch Whisky Heritage Centre
The SWHC is situated on the Royal Mile in Edinburgh and is the perfect gateway in to the world of whisky, offering guided tours and an introduction to whisky as well as information.
www.whisky-heritage.co.uk

CLUBS AND ORGANISATIONS

The Scotch Malt Whisky Society
Members can buy exclusive cask-strength whisky, receive the excellent magazine and can take guests to the Society's properties in Leith Edinburgh, Queen Street Edinburgh, and London. The Society also holds regional tastings.
www.smws.co.uk

The Whisky Tasting Club
On-line club offering members the chance to taste special whiskies from around the world and then comment on them at the club site. The club also aims to be a one-stop shop for whisky fans with blogs, forums, latest whisky news and opinion.
www.thewhiskytastingclub.co.uk

There are lots of websites and blogs and they continue to grow by the day. Here are a few that I enjoy.

Dr Whisky
Dr Feelgood! Likeable and laid back.
www.drwhisky.blogspot.com

The Whisky Exchange Blog
Live arm of the Whisky Exchange in London.
www.blog.thewhiskyexchange.com

The Whisky Grotto
No frills and not fancy, but comprehensive and worth checking out.
www.whiskygrotto.com

The Scotblog
American Kevin Erskine's site is the one that everyone else has to match up to. Excellent.
www.inebrio.com/thescotchbog

Whiskyfun
My type of site. A bit rock and roll, a bit kooky and undoubtedly written with authority by Malt Maniac Serge Valentin.
www.whiskyfun.com

Caskstrength.net
One of the better up-and-coming sites. Pitched perfectly.
www.caskstrength.net

Edinburgh Whisky Blog
Written by 20-something year-old students – and done extremely well. Nice and irreverent.
www.edinburghwhiskyblog.com

What Does John Know
The boss! Malt Advocate's publisher John Hansell brings his considerable expertise to this blog. Essential reading.
www.whatdoesjohnknow.com

Nonjatta
Independent and intense Japanese-facing site.
www.nonjatta.blogspot.com

The Malt Madness Blog
Another awesome mix of frighteningly knowledgeable information and delightful zaniness, this time from Malt Maniacs mainman Johannes van den Heuvel.
www.maltmadness.com

Whisky index

The whisky index is organised by whisky name, then distillery owner and country of origin.

Index

Figures in italics refer to captions.

Acknowledgements

AUTHOR'S ACKNOWLEDGEMENTS

Although this isn't my first book project, it's very much a culmination of the last 20 years as a drinks journalist and nine specialising in whisky. There have been many shared drinks, many great moments and lots of happy times. Perhaps unsurprisingly, therefore, there are far too many for me to remember and I couldn't start to thank all the people who have played some part in getting me to this point. However, some deserve a special mention for services beyond the call of duty.

Let's start with this book. A huge thank you to my amazing editor Jo Copestick, who not only offered me the chance to write it, but pretty much gave me free licence to do with it what I wanted. Or at least, allowed me to think she did. Jo reined in my wilder editorial indulgences (really!) while steering the good ship whisky book through all sorts of obstacles during what have been the three most intensive writing months of my life. If any of this is any good, then it's down to her composure and good sense.

A special thank you to the 'Burt Bacharach' of book design, Robin Rout. Time and time again I sent him works in progress and he sent me rich, sophisticated and beautifully produced completed gems; to Jacqui Small, for backing me from the offset, offering advice as necessary, but trusting me by leaving me to it; and to the rest of the Jacqui Small team, especially Kika 'rottweiler' Sroka Miller, who went in search of pictures from across the world and, amazingly, found them. Respect. Perhaps my biggest thanks of all should go to Marcin Miller, who started all this off by taking me on as editor of *Whisky Magazine* and who has been a friend and co-conspirator ever since. And a big thanks to Rubyna Sheikh, who works in Marcin's office, makes miracles happen, and has consistently supported me over the years.

I'd also like to thank Damian Riley-Smith and Rob Allanson of *Whisky Magazine*, for giving me access to Whisky Mag's whisky cellars, and to John Hansell and Lew Bryson at *Malt Advocate* for being thoroughly good guys. A massive thanks to Ian Bankier, for being a friend and sounding board as well as a business partner, and to all the team at The Whisky Shop, but particularly Chris Rodden in Norwich and Peter Semple and Catherine Service in head office, for constant support.

A special thank you to Dave Broom for being a friend and mentor ever since we first debated *Uncut's* Albums of the Year over a dram or two back in the day, and to Jim Murray, whisky writer extraordinaire. I made it a point of principle that I didn't refer to other whisky books when I wrote this. But I'd be a liar if I didn't acknowledge two – *Murray's Whisky Bible*, which I carry everywhere, and his book on American bourbon, rye and Tennessee whiskey. I hope my American section updates and does justice to the work Jim has done in the past. And while on the subject of America, a big thank you to Susan Dallas and all at the Louisville Convention and Visitors' Bureau for all the wonderful support and hours of driving round ol' Kentucky.

I'd like to thank the Norwich VIP Whisky Club massive, who have been listening to this book for the last three years – Derek, Susie, Mark, Mary, Peter, Andrew, Sue and Geoffrey. Also thanks go to my new business partners in the Norwich Whisky Tasting Club, Pat, Tony and Michelle.

I'd like to thank my mum, who started me on my whisky journey many, many years ago by letting me have a taste of her peated whisky when I was very small; my little brother Ben and his family who have provided a home to me on many occasions over the years.

And most of all, my long-suffering wife Sally, who is my very own Flaming Heart, and my children: Jules and Louie, my wee men who are just realising how weird it is to have a dad who drinks for a living, and adorable Maddie, who keeps it all real.

I'd like to thank Dr Oetker for his whole grain peach yoghurts – and grapefruit juice manufacturers everywhere. Also my sporting heroes who have given me hundreds of good and bad moments to reach for the whisky bottle over the years – Leicester City, the mighty All Blacks and the Dallas Cowboys.

Finally to those 'missing in action' – my father, a good man who I think of every day and who taught me that strong doesn't mean tough or physical; Peter, the best friend I ever had or ever will have; and Lewis, wherever or whoever he is now: I wouldn't have got in to drinks journalism let alone whisky writing without him.

And I'd like to thank every one of my distillery friends across the world for so generously sharing their world with me; anyone anywhere who enjoys a whisky; and the scores of enthusiasts everywhere who make the world of whisky such a dynamic one.

This has been, without doubt, the best experience of my life and I never want it to end. If you're ever in Norwich, pop in to The Whisky Shop in Swan Lane, the Rumsey Wells in St Andrews Street, or Franks Bar in Bedford Street and ask for me. I'd be delighted to make your acquaintance.

PUBLISHER'S ACKNOWLEDGEMENTS

The publisher would also like to thank the following people who helped in the production of this book:

Pat Roberts of malts.com; Tim Forbes of The Whisky Exchange; Marcin Miller and Rubyna Sheik of No. 1 Drinks Company and Ann McMichael.

Chris MacLean of The Whisky Shop and Michael Hopert of Royal Mile Whisky for the loan of whisky and glasses for photography; Riedel for the loan of glassware for photography; Patricia Michelson of La Fromagerie for the loan of cheese boards and knives; Stewart McCarroll for the loan of two oak quaiches for photography.

For cocktail recipes: Esther Medina Cuesta of Bureau Club; Stuart Hudson of Viajante; Nidal Ramini of Brown-Forman Spirits, Alistair Malcolm of Lab, Soho, London; Vamsi Putta of Salt Whisky Lounge and Dining Room.

PICTURE CREDITS

The publisher wishes to thank the many distilleries from around the world that kindly provided images of their whiskies and distillery facilities that are reproduced here.

Special photography by Simon Murrell:
Cover image; pages 1-33, 36-51, 162-163, 204-205, 212-213, 226-227, 244-245, 264-265, 286-288.

All other images are credited to their respective distilleries excluding the following:
Page 34 food shots malts.com; **35 food shots** malts.com; **60 Arran** The Whisky Exchange; **70 Blair Athol** The Whisky Exchange; **85 Glen Elgin 16 Year** The Whisky Exchange; **92 Glen Garioch 15 Year** The Whisky Exchange; **94 middle** Louise McGilviary – fotolia.com; **103 background** Brian Stewart-Coxon – fotolia.com; **104 Hazelburn 8 Year** The Whisky Exchange; **111 Laphroaig 30 Year** The Whisky Exchange; **112** C. Spreiter; **113** C.Spreiter; **114 Longmorn 17 Year** The Whisky Exchange; **117 Miltonduff 15 Year** The Whisky Exchange; **118 background** Louise McGilviary – fotolia.com; **123 Spring Bank Vintage 1997** The Whisky Exchange; **129 Tamdhu, Tamdhu 25 Year** The Whisky Exchange; **146 Te Bheag** The Whisky Exchange; **188 top, bottom** Ann McMichael **middle** Melissa Farlow/Getty Images; **192 top** Ann McMichael; **193 portrait** Ann McMichael; **202 Charbay Hop Flavoured** Mitch Rice; **207 bottom** istockphoto.com/Pgiam; **250 top** Thierry Mariot; **251 top left, bottom right** Thierry Mariot; **268 all Bakery Hill** Andrew Ashton.